Civil Rights Childhood

Picturing Liberation in African American Photobooks

Katharine Capshaw

UNIVERSITY OF MINNESOTA PRESS

MINNEAPOLIS • LONDON

An earlier version of chapter 5 was published as "Remembering the Civil Rights Movement in Photographic Texts for Children," in *Representing Children in Chinese and American Children's Literature*, ed. Claudia Nelson and Rebecca Morris (Farnham, UK: Ashgate Publishing, 2014); copyright 2014.

Permission to quote from *Poems by Kali* granted by Kali Henry; copyright 1970 by Kali Henry.

Published by the University of Minnesota Press
111 Third Avenue South, Suite 290
Minneapolis, MN 55401–2520
http://www.upress.umn.edu

LIBRARY OF CONGRESS CATALOGING-IN-PUBLICATION DATA
Capshaw, Katharine.
Civil rights childhood : picturing liberation in African American photobooks /
Katharine Capshaw.
Includes bibliographical references and index.
ISBN 978-0-8166-9404-4 (hc : alkaline paper)
ISBN 978-0-8166-9405-1 (pb: alkaline paper)
1. African Americans—Civil rights—History—20th century. 2. Civil rights movements—United States—History—20th century. 3. Social justice—United States—History—20th century. 4. African American children—Social conditions—20th century. 5. African American children—Pictorial works. 6. Picture books—Social aspects—United States—History—20th century. 7. Photography—Social aspects—United States—History—20th century. 8. Art and social action—United States—History—20th century. 9. African American arts—Influence—History—20th century. 10. United States—Race relations—History—20th century. I. Title.
E185.615.C315 2014
323.1196'073009045-dc23   2014027722

Printed in the United States of America on acid-free paper

The University of Minnesota is an equal-opportunity educator and employer.

20 19 18 17 16 15 14   10 9 8 7 6 5 4 3 2 1

For Steve, Liam, and Finola

CONTENTS

INTRODUCTION

Toward the end of Langston Hughes and Milton Meltzer's *A Pictorial History of the Negro in America* (1956), within a section titled "Trouble in the Deep South," a small photograph of a smiling boy appears (Figure I.1). African American readers of Hughes and Meltzer's text would recognize the face of this boy even without the caption, which reads, "Emmett Till, fourteen, whose vacation ended at the bottom of a river 'to teach him a lesson.'"[1] Identifying Till initially with youth and leisure, the caption plummets readers into the horror of the event and the hatefulness of the murderers' motivation. Early in the morning of Sunday, August 28, 1955, Till was taken from the house of his uncle by Roy Bryant and J. W. Milam, two white men who believed that Till had insulted Bryant's wife. The boy's mutilated body was found three days later in the Tallahatchie River. The child's mother, Mamie Till, refused to have his body buried in Mississippi, insisting that Till be brought back to Chicago, where an open-casket viewing from September 3 until September 8 enabled thousands of people to witness the atrocity. That circle of witnesses widened extensively when photographs of Till in his casket appeared in *Jet* magazine and the *Chicago Defender*, among other publications.[2] Thulani Davis explains the effect of such witnessing: "As a six-year-old, I found Till's battered face in *Jet* magazine. Most white Americans were completely unaware that simply seeing that photograph was a trauma for thousands of African-Americans."[3]

The photograph of Till's mutilated body in black newspapers and magazines was typically coupled with that of the smiling child dressed in a shirt and tie, the one that appears also in Hughes and Meltzer's text.[4] Black children during the civil rights movement were thus aware of two images of Till: one that evoked respectability, youth, and serenity, and another that demonstrated a frightening possibility for black childhood within a racist society. Echoing each other, the two images were tied together in public awareness. This is, perhaps, an effect of the form of photography itself, as John Berger suggests: "The only

Figure I.1. Widely circulated photograph of Emmett Till, often coupled with lynching images in newspapers and magazines. Copyright by Corbis Corporation.

decision [a photographer] can take is as regards the moment he chooses to isolate. Yet this apparent limitation gives the photograph its unique power. *What it shows invokes what is not shown.* One can look at any photograph to appreciate the truth of this."[5] In fact, understanding the devastation of Till's death would be impossible without visual construction of his integrity. In turn, the image of a desecrated Till signaled for readers a possible future for any child of color in the United States, returning them to a consideration of their similarities to the happy boy in the shirt and tie. If each image of Till remains haunted by the other, together they make clear the dialectic of life and death, of past and present, implicit in the form of photography. Remembering Till permits us to understand the reverberation of images against each other and against the social context, allowing us to recognize that no moment in black childhood framed by a photograph can ever exist alone, and that photographs of the past can touch and affect the present.

Joyce Ladner, the prominent sociologist, educator, and former Student Nonviolent Coordinating Committee (SNCC) member, explains the threat immanent in the death image of Till: " 'All of us remembered the photograph of Emmett Till's face, lying in the coffin. . . . Every one of my SNCC friends . . . recall[ed] that photograph. [It] galvanized a generation as a symbol—that was our symbol—that if they did it to him, they could do it to us.' "[6] Within the African American civil rights movement, photographs of children held immense political power. Many of the movement's most familiar images represent the threat of racism to childhood: in photographs, we witness the Little Rock Nine entering Central High School in 1957, thronged by angry crowds; we see young people attacked by police dogs and fire hoses during the 1963 Birmingham "Children's Crusade"; we see dozens of girls imprisoned in Birmingham after protests.[7] The most affecting images emerging from the midcentury campaign were of children not only threatened by racist violence but destroyed by it. Just as the circulation of images of Till in the black media helped inspire a generation of activists, images of the four little girls who perished in the bombing of the Sixteenth Street Baptist Church in 1963 drew national attention to the Southern Christian Leadership Conference's efforts in the South and helped change national opinion about the legitimacy of the movement. Photographic coverage of the Children's Crusade helped turn the tide of national sympathies and ignited support for the Civil Rights Act of 1964.[8] Picturing childhood became a powerful instrument of civil rights activism, because children carry an important aura of human value and potential, and threats to the young made the stakes of the movement palpable to individuals and to the nation. Undoubtedly, images of children under siege had generative effects for the civil rights campaign.

Images of Emmett Till mobilized a generation of activists, but there were other photographic articulations of black childhood available to child readers during the civil rights era. Across the 1940s, '50s, '60s, and early '70s, photographic books by black authors engaged the subject of youth, including texts by Ellen Tarry, Langston Hughes, Toni Morrison, and June Jordan. Very often those photobooks considered, explicitly or implicitly, the possibility of child political agency. Whether responding to photographic tropes of child martyrdom or creating a space for psychological freedom, photobooks took the prospect of child activism seriously. *Civil Rights Childhood: Picturing Liberation in African American Photobooks* considers civil rights as a point of genesis for visualizations of youth citizenship, arguing that the movement authorized a wide range of approaches to representation.

Beginning with fiction and nonfiction books that address school desegregation, housing reform, and social-integration efforts, *Civil Rights Childhood* looks at the particular place of the photographic book to articulating a demand for change. Because the Cold War era generated the possibility for civil rights reform even as it delimited acceptable civil rights discourse,[9] the photographic book for the young in the 1940s and 1950s became an ideal space for staging visual arguments about the need for social transformation. These early photographic books are trickster texts: they speak very little about the project of reform; instead, they offer provocative photographs that evoke concepts like school integration or present children's narratives that mask the reformative intent of the book. Civil rights photographic books for adults during the 1960s, like Lorraine Hansberry's *The Movement: Documentary of a Struggle for Equality* (1964) and Richard Avedon's *Nothing Personal* (1964), have been explored by critics like Sara Blair who sensitively argue for the photograph as a fundamental aesthetic commitment for black writers.[10] In terms of the 1960s, *Civil Rights Childhood* recovers a children's book produced in 1965 by activists associated with SNCC and other groups. *Today*, published by the Child Development Group of Mississippi, uses the form of the photographic book as a means to inspire children's psychological freedom and to articulate a new conceptual vision of bookmaking as a form of liberation.

Civil Rights Childhood next moves across the second half of the twentieth century, focusing on children's photobooks of the Black Arts Movement in the early 1970s that respond to the disappointments of civil rights efforts and play with documentary photography in order to make an argument about the signal position of childhood to nationalist articulation. The book concludes by considering the ideological malleability of the civil rights movement in the modern moment. The best modern photographic books ask the reader to consider unfinished the project of civil rights, and revisit iconic photographs in order to reveal their inability to tell the whole story of the movement. Emmett Till, along with the four little girls of Birmingham, shadows many 1970s and contemporary photographic books, allowing writers to consider notions of power and civic accomplishment in the face of the losses of the movement for young people. *Civil Rights Childhood* is not a book of photographic theory; it explores the role of photobooks in representing civil rights and children's activist possibilities. The project expands the visual archive by examining texts that have been overlooked in scholarship. It enriches our knowledge about the range of movement representation of children, adding images of childhood joy, resilience, confusion, and ambiguity to the visual lexicon of the socially engaged child. In addition to revising our knowledge about representation, *Civil Rights Childhood* considers the photographic book as a form particularly suited to arguing for children's continued civic engagement. This is a book about the way children's photographic books work: how they stage ideas about the present and the past and how they play against the strictures of the static image in order to make an argument about the continuance of social action.

Civil Rights Childhood claims various kinds of photographic books as participants in the conversation about children's political possibilities. The project looks at fictional texts that draw on traditions of the illustrated picture book in order to construct a reader's engagement with the visual landscape. The project also examines books of history and biography, including photographic compendiums like Hughes and Meltzer's *Pictorial History of the Negro*, the text that includes the opening image of Till. The project also looks at books that had a significant child readership but were not ostensibly aimed at children, like Toni Morrison's *The Black Book* (1974)[11] and Hughes and Roy DeCarava's *The Sweet Flypaper of Life* (1955). Photographic books are intrinsically social, and books like these were read in "family" settings in which children asked questions about the images and sequences. The photobook as a form springs from various generic sources—the art book, coffee-table book, illustrated children's picture book, magazine photostory, middlebrow history book, documentary photographic book, newspaper coverage—and, as such, it assumes a range of expressions. This multiplicity makes it challenging to theorize generally about the shape and tendency of its word/image interactions, particularly because the quality of narration differs from book to book: some use captions and blocked text, as in the case of *Pictorial History*'s Emmett Till illustration, whereas others are books of poetry, like Carole Boston Weatherford's *Birmingham, 1963* (2007), and still others take experimental verbal forms, such as June Jordan's *Dry Victories* (1972). Instead of striving for a totalizing formulation of visual/verbal exchange in photobooks, *Civil Rights Childhood* reads the relationship between word and image through the lens of each book's formal, historical, and cultural context. For the purposes of this study, the "photobook" refers to a book with a child readership that sequences images and attaches that sequence to a narrative, whether fictional or nonfictional. This capacious definition reflects the range of the genre and enables the study to consider why the photographic book, in a variety of incarnations, has been a consistent site of engagement with the civil rights movement.

The form of the children's photobook does generate evocative possibilities for civil rights representation. First, the photobook is essentially metatextual and draws attention to itself as a constructed object. A reader opening a photobook faces a collision of word and image quite different from that of the illustrated picture book, in that photographs connect to an outside, rather than an imagined, world. In addition, the photograph, in other manifestations, is its own material object, one the reader has likely encountered in life, whether at home with family pictures or in newspapers and magazines. When placed into a book with a narrative, whether that narrative describes history or offers a fictional story, the photograph evokes a material thing and thus spurs consideration of the book's own constructed nature. The stitches and seams of a photographic book become apparent, because a reader can assume that someone had to write the words, that someone had to take or arrange the images, and that the images reflect experience outside the book. Writers, photographers, archivists, and editors all have a hand in making a photobook, and the disparity between word and image draws attention to the book as created object. Sometimes the book is singularly created, as in the case of photographer John Shearer's *I Wish I Had an Afro* (1970), and sometimes it is created through multiple sources, but it is always present to the reader as a constructed narrative.

Second, because photobooks typically represent visually some dimension of a world outside the book, they aim to convey something about that outside world to a reader. The pressure in a photobook for the young thus falls on communication (rather than immersion in another world), probably because of the photograph's nonfiction association, though the children's photobook is often fictional. A photobook implicitly tells a reader not only that a person (or persons) made this book for him or her, took the photos, selected which would appear, arranged the photos on the page, and wrote a narrative, but also that the point of all of this effort is to tell the reader something about the world. Unlike illustrated books that sometimes ask the reader to become absorbed in the universe that the author and illustrator have created—a place that often exists nowhere else but within the pages of the book—a photobook asks the reader to look at the form and to think about both the makers' hands and the world outside the book.

The best photobooks about civil rights use the form's metatextual status in order to permit the child to recognize that meaning is constructed, that knowledge and history are, to use June Jordan's words, "the business of choose and show,"[12] and that the reader can actively make sense of how the ideas in the book connect to experience outside the book. This is the reason a children's photobook about civil rights can both reflect and provoke, both envision movement experience and aim to shape a response to the events of the book. Although concerned with expanding the archive of representation, *Civil Rights Childhood* is particularly invested in the way the photobook places demands on the young people reading it. Very often, the metatextuality of the photobook puts pressure on readers to intervene in the world or to alter their ideas about themselves and their possibilities. Not only do these photobooks represent black childhood in a new way, but they very often reflect on the process of representation (and the photobook as a form facilitates that reflection) and then ask children to take part in interpreting and engaging the world around them. A nonfiction book might require a more critical engagement with narrative by yoking photographs to different verbal forms: for instance, in Ruby Bridges's *Through My Eyes* (1999), photographs bear captions, text blocks from John Steinbeck, Robert Jay-Green, and Robert Coles offer commentary, and reports from the *New York Times, Good Housekeeping*, the *New Orleans Times-Picayune*, and other periodicals interrupt Ruby's own story. The narrative multiplicity fragments our attention, producing Ruby as a conspicuous site of interpretation, a character one must assemble from various sources of information (she mourns such fragmentation in her personal narration but uses it strategically to destabilize the reader's expectation of a familiar and easy civil rights hero story).

With multiple sources and forms of information, photobooks often require a thoughtful and critical reader, one immersed in the process of piecing together the narrative rather than one submerged or lost in story. Books about civil rights often ask readers to extend the critical processes engendered by reading a photobook—the process of piecing together meaning from sites of information and the awareness through the book's metatextual form that knowledge is constructed—into the world. In considering the photobooks, *Civil Rights Childhood* does not stage an instrumentalist reading, does not argue that these books actually caused social change. With the exception of *Pictorial History*, which inspired Joseph McNeil and others to stage the historic 1960 Greensboro, North Carolina, Woolworth-counter sit-ins, the photobooks themselves are not players in the history of civil rights. They may call for intervention, but *Civil Rights Childhood* is more concerned with how the books stage that call through word and image than with their material effects.

My approach to the metatextual photobook follows Joe Sutliff Sanders's observations about generic differences between word/image forms. In discussing illustrated picture books and comics, he argues that formal qualities of texts should be discerned by attending to the *"different reading situations* that [forms] anticipate."[13] For Sanders, the illustrated picture book differs from comics, because it involves another mediator of meaning who interprets words that, in turn, limit images; that mediator, the adult "chaperone" of the picture book, not only frames the reading for the child but frames it in a way that confirms adult investment in the picture book as a site of nostalgia. In photobooks, the reading situation often requires a chaperone, especially if the reader is preliterate, but calls more insistently on the adult (regardless of the reader's age) for explanation and discussion, because images in the book reference historical events or the outside world, contexts that may not be addressed fully in the text's language or about which the child may have questions. This "reading situation" permits not only performance of the text as it stands but also further discussion of the images offered in the book and the opportunity for the adult chaperone to connect those events to experiences in the child's family history or life. The reading situation is social, prompting collaboration and connection that can serve the book's imperative to bring critical practice into the world. The photobook shape also often facilitates community building: historical compendiums like *The Black Book* are large and do not fit easily on a bookshelf; *Pictorial History*, as both a coffee-table book and an alternate history, was laid out on tables for family and community conversation; books of the Black Arts Movement were smaller, able to fit into a back pocket for a reader to carry easily and pass around to others. And some texts took both forms: June Jordan's *Dry Victories* (1972) was published in both pocket size and a larger, decorative version. These books were meant to be shared, their images prompting discussion between child and adult, and, as Sanders reminds us, such a reading situation helped determine the qualities and tendencies of the content. Photobooks enable adults to share stories about the past and present, expanding the chaperoning of the book beyond the words on the page; as social objects binding child to family, history, and public event, photobooks have a stake in building connections between adults and children.

That adults are invested in children's reading, in terms of both form and content, is a cornerstone precept to understanding children's literature, as Perry Nodelman's book *The Hidden Adult* argues in depth and complexity. Both Sanders and Nathalie op de Beeck explain that the children's illustrated picture book is a fundamental form for the adult embrace of nostalgia.[14] Nostalgia—a frame through which writers construct children and through which adults select books for young readers—seems perfectly fitted to the experience of an adult reading an illustrated picture book to a child. According to op de Beeck, "Every picture book is a ready-made antique, because its significance encompasses past, present, and future."[15] The children's photo-picture book, then, would also seem to be an ideal site for a nostalgic representation of childhood, particularly because photographs themselves have been understood wistfully. Susan Sontag's meditation on the photograph encapsulates one traditional critical perspective on the image: "Photography is an elegiac art, a twilight art. Most subjects photographed are, just by virtue of being photographed, touched with pathos. . . . All photographs are *memento mori*. To take a photograph is to participate in another person's (or thing's) mortality, vulnerability, mutability. Precisely by slicing out this moment and freezing it, all photographs testify to time's relentless melt."[16] Photographs, for Sontag, Roland Barthes in *Camera Lucida*, Eduardo Cadava on Walter Benjamin, and others, bring time's passing into relief and nostalgically memorialize the ephemeral. They point backward toward a moment that has been lost. It would seem, then, that photographic picture books for children might bear a double burden of the nostalgic, and in cases of books outside those examined in *Civil Rights Childhood* they very well may.

But nostalgia does not fuel the photobooks in this study. Even the best contemporary photo texts that look back at the civil rights movement, those addressed in the last chapter, refuse the comfort of nostalgia for an insistence on the unfinished status of civil rights efforts. How do these photo texts avoid the double burden of nostalgic photograph and children's book? Op de Beeck's explanation of the roots of picture-book nostalgia is helpful: "[T]he purveyors of these texts tend to represent a dominant Anglo- or European American middle class with specific anxieties around leisure, labor, citizenship, and immigration," for nostalgic books offer "insight into early twentieth-century tastes, hopes, and fears constellated around cherished, even sacred notions of childhood and U.S. citizenship."[17] The texts examined in *Civil Rights Childhood* spring from African American cultural and visual contexts; when they conspicuously adopt ideals about childhood innocence, they do so strategically to make an argument about the need for social change in order to preserve the tenuous, if not impossible, state of black-child innocence. There is little nostalgia for a better moment in time or an earlier version of black childhood, except in books like Walter Dean Myers's *One More River to Cross* (1995), which includes images of happy families from history. Myers, though, employs those images in order to make a case for the ongoing commitment of African American families to social action, not to express a longing for something that is lost. Yoking historic images with contemporary photographs enables Myers to argue for the continuance of an ideal in the present. The children's civil rights photobook pushes forward by focusing on the child as a site of cultural instantiation and insisting that narratives should spur new stories and active response.

Further, this type of photobook plays against traditional constructions of time in photography. As Sara Blair discusses in *Harlem Crossroads: Black Writers and the Photograph in the Twentieth Century*, the mid-twentieth century witnessed a shift in populist uses of the camera. She explains that "the very lability and promiscuity of the modern camera endowed its images with multiple, simultaneous lives: as a form of evidence, a mode of sensation, a call to arms, a considered aesthetic artifact."[18] African American children's writers, sensitive to the enlarged uses of and possibilities emerging from the democratization of photography and the multiplication of images across venues, discovered that drawing from the immediacy of newspaper and magazine photographs granted urgency to the concepts articulated in their books. This is to say not that photobooks "cover" events per se but that often they lift documentary and newspaper images out of their original contexts and reframe them in new settings that make an argument about time; particularly, many argue for the need to act in the present either by drawing correspondences between events across time or by amassing historical photos in order to make a case for the pressure of history on unfulfilled concepts of justice and equality. These books play with documentary photography in order to make the past present and insistent.

If these children's photobooks do interact with the idea of the image itself evoking a past moment in time, they frequently flip that temporal logic by focusing on the child's protean, unfinished body. The culmination of an idea attaches to the inevitability of the child's growth. The photobook on civil rights thus frequently pushes a reader forward in time through images of children in motion, freezing their bodies in photographs in order to draw attention to the thrust of historical event and the certainty of change. These children's photo-books often frame images as incarnating possibility rather than stasis, future life rather than death. Although the child's body in motion, which is common in social-justice images, is not part of a recognized photographic aesthetic, it does emerge from technological changes and shifts in the subjects of journalistic attention. The "so-called Leica revolution"[19] of the late 1930s led to the domi-nance of quick-shutter, portable, compact cameras that could record through sequential images bodies in motion and that were, of course, invaluable in docu-menting moments of crisis, like the social protests of the 1960s and 1970s and the Vietnam War. On-the-scene photography of activist settings, like marches, protests, and riots, as well as coverage of wartime, contributed to the emer-gence of the child in motion as a trope figuring social change in some of the texts within this study. Further, these books are not single photographs that ask for immersion alone, but narratives that unfold over time, over the course of reading the story. A narrative pushes forward, and, for a child readership of a text with nonfiction resonances, that narrative often wishes to nudge the child toward a different perspective on the world. Images of children's bodies in flux tilt meaning forward rather than backward, just as the narrative moves through time to a conclusion.

In framing the terms of "civil rights" as an ongoing effort, the project is indebted to scholars like Jacquelyn Dowd Hall, whose formulation of the "long civil rights movement" has helped reshape the sites scholars examine and the critical lenses they employ.[20] Like Hall's work, *Civil Rights Childhood* resists truncating the movement from the *Brown v. Board of Education* decision of 1954 to the Civil Rights Act of 1964 and the Voting Rights Act of 1965, seeing in-stead the emergence of arguments for social, political, and economic equality extending from the late 1930s through the Cold War era and into the liberation efforts of the late 1960s and 1970s. *Civil Rights Childhood* pays particular atten-tion to the strictures placed on civil rights discourse after World War II, for instance, and examines dimensions of Black Arts Movement creativity that con-nect expressly with the failures of the early 1960s. Deborah Willis, whose work has been deeply influential on this project, explains that "[i]n reading African-American photographs in particular, the context of production, reception, and recollection needs to be specified and analyzed."[21] With Willis in mind, the project examines the contexts that contribute to eruptions of photobook productivity. Those eruptions are often connected to moments in the civil rights struggle that engage backlash against black familial structures. Politicized domesticity after World War II provided the opportunity for artists to articulate a commitment to what was termed the "American creed" of faith in democracy and egalitarianism, while at the same time arguing visually for continued pursuit of such unachieved values. The Freedom School effort of 1964 made apparent to some activists the need for the family to be involved in liberation, which then inspired a photobook as a path for psychological freedom. The defamations of the 1965 Moynihan Report, with its infamous charge that the black family expresses a "tangle of pathology," incensed black artists, and the report is one of many factors influencing the upsurge of the children's photobook as an expression of integrity during the Black Arts Movement. And in the mid-1990s, with state attacks on "welfare queens" and urban youth, along with an embrace of amity rather than legislative intervention as a means to racial goodwill, renewed attention to civil rights as an ideologically malleable moment led to an influx of photobooks on Martin Luther King Jr., Rosa Parks, and other heroes of the movement, with varied results.[22] Photobooks take up both the efforts of the long civil rights movement and the defamations of black familial structures in white culture. In addition to exploring uses of form, then, *Civil Rights Childhood* investigates the reception of the photobook in order to determine its cultural resonances.

The photographs in this study spring from various image traditions, including documentary photographic books, magazine publications, journalistic coverage, SNCC and civil rights activist photography, black photo groups, conduct books, and domestic photography. *Civil Rights Childhood* places texts within particular traditions in order to understand how the shape of the children's book, and the pressures of the historical moment, inflect the expression of those traditions. For instance, in chapter 1, which positions the photobook within cultural demands for silence about injustice, different perspectives on the photograph inform the texts' approaches: Jane Dabney Shackelford's *My Happy Days* (1944) takes *Life* magazine as its avowed inspiration, Alexander Alland works from ideals of multiculturalism drawn from Louis Adamic to frame Ellen Tarry's *My Dog Rinty* (1946), and Roy DeCarava resists the social documentary in Hughes and DeCarava's *The Sweet Flypaper of Life*. Similarly, in chapter 4, a Black Arts Movement aesthetic of "black light" informs images in Kali Grosvenor's *Poems by Kali* (1970), and John Shearer, a protégé of Gordon Parks, defies the strictures of the journalistic exposé in *I Wish I Had an Afro*.

The project thus places each book within its particular photographic lineage. However, what looms large in the background of all of the books in this study is the documentary photo tradition,[23] one that has often aimed to frame minority subjects through a lens inflected by the sociological. As William Stott, Paula Rabinowitz, and others have detailed, the documentary tradition placed certain expectations on the relationship between photographed subject and viewer. Documentary photography represented "experience in such a way as to render it vivid, 'human,' and—most often—poignant to the audience,"[24] viewers who would be moved by the implied authenticity of the people in the image. The seeming ingenuity of the traditional subjects of documentary photography also aimed to promote an affective response from a sophisticated viewer. As Stott maintains, "The poor, the primitive, and the young are the natural heroes of photography; all others have learned too much disguise."[25] The children's photobook plays with and against these constructions, sometimes framing middle-class narratives as the "truth" of black American life in order to counter documentary images of poverty, sometimes invoking childhood ingenuity in service to uncovering the truths of prejudice and oppression, and sometimes reveling in the features of black childhood as a site of political agency rather than of documentary confinement. While playing with the "truth-value" of the photograph, all of the books in the study claim the power to frame that truth as a counterpoint to visual and sociological denigration of black subjects. And yet the books in this study evoke, in some ways, the moral energy of that 1930s documentary tradition. Rabinowitz suggests that documentary photography "is meant to instruct through evidence; it poses truth as a moral imperative."[26] The children's photobooks thus reflect loosely a documentary ethos by telling stories of the people in order to engender a response. But frequently that response would be overtly political and would rely on a sense of parity and identification between the child reader and the photographed subjects. Instead of offering the abject to a sophisticated viewer, these books assemble alternate visual versions of blackness in order to reshape the "truth" of black history and identity for a young audience.

The emergence of a black children's photobook tradition dovetails with the progressive-education movement of the 1930s and 1940s. In emphasizing lived experience and the development of emotional complexity and morality, progressive educators had much in common with the documentary approach. In fact, the children's photographic book was a form adopted by the Bank Street School of Education community, by those proponents of the "here and now" aesthetic, and by other photographic experimentalists in the 1930s and 1940s. Lucy Sprague Mitchell published several books illustrated with photographs, including *Skyscraper* (1933) and *Manhattan: Now and Long Ago* (1934).[27] Margaret Wise Brown published *They All Saw It* (1944), *The Sleepy Little Lion* (1947), *O, Said the Squirrel* (1950), and *The Duck* (1953), all illustrated by animal photographer Ylla (Camilla Koffler). One of the most famous photographic picture books of the 1930s, Lewis Hine's *Men at Work* (1932), had adolescents as its intended audience, and Mitchell replicated some of Hine's famous images in her *Skyscraper*. Edward J. Steichen, with his daughter Mary Steichen Martin, issued *The First Picture Book: Everyday Things for Babies* (1930) and *The Second Picture Book* (1931), texts that op de Beeck reads persuasively as embracing upper-class values. White religious progressive Mabel Garrett Wagner published a photographic book of a black child's migration from Arkansas to San Francisco, *Billy Bates* (1946). One can understand why the photographic mode appealed to revolutionaries in children's picture-book making, as it enabled them to concretize the world surrounding the child reader, an individual often figured as urban with an interest in animals, buildings, and machinery. For writers like Ellen Tarry, as we will see, the "here and now" afforded by photography enabled expanded, alternate articulations of urban experience and civil rights demands. Remembering the shaping influence of documentary photography, the project explores writers' engagement with the possibilities and limitations of "truth" and moral imperative.

Behind this project stands the work of critics on the black image, such as Deborah Willis and Blair, who "call for alternative frames—particularly visual contexts—in which to understand black cultural production."[28] The project is deeply indebted to the work of Shawn Michelle Smith, whose discussion of the relationship of baby pictures to eugenicist programs, as well as her study of the confluence of the familial and sociological in W. E. B. Du Bois's 1900 American Negro exhibit at the Paris Exposition, offers a model for *Civil Rights Childhood* of interpreting photographs through intersecting aesthetic and historical vectors.[29] Certainly the large body of work on lynching photography demonstrates the necessity of pursuing photography's implication within contexts of systemic racism, and this project has been enhanced by consideration of the way lynching images can be mobilized within black communities.[30] One subject frequently discussed among scholars of the photograph is the daguerreotype representation of antebellum black women with their white child charges, familiarly known as the "mammy" image.[31] Laura Wexler notes the absence of black childhood from antebellum images of black mothers, seeing the white child as signifying the absence of the "nursemaid's own baby, who remains invisible."[32] Wexler calls this phenomenon a visual erasure, and one might consider the way in which black childhood has been almost completely absent as a subject of inquiry in text/image criticism.[33] Anne Higonnet explains that, for professional photographers and art historians of white childhood, the child as subject inhabits a marginalized space: "Consigned to forms of art treated as minor, relegated to artists refused access to prestigious careers, childhood was made to look charmingly innocent—and also trivial, passive, and exploitable."[34] As Higonnet observes, critics have often dismissed the child subject as inconsequential and have regarded the photographer's attention as an extension of her gender role. *Civil Rights Childhood* responds to the erasure and dismissal of childhood, particularly black childhood, as a topic of photographic study.

Recent exciting criticism on civil rights photography has transformed the way we envision the freedom struggle in the 1950s, 1960s, and 1970s,[35] moving discussion away from considering images as indexical and toward aesthetic and political analyses.[36] In particular, Erina Duganne's groundbreaking *The Self in Black and White: Race and Subjectivity in Postwar American Photography* and Leigh Raiford's influential *Imprisoned in a Luminous Glare: Photography and the African American Freedom Struggle* have enabled *Civil Rights Childhood* fundamentally by offering nuanced histories of photographic groups and approaches, as well as sensitive readings of particular images and consideration of the traffic of images across cultural and publication contexts. Leslie G. Kelen's edited collection *This Light of Ours: Activist Photographers of the Civil Rights Movement* has profoundly altered our awareness of the role of individual community members (and photographers) in grassroots social action. Margo Natalie Crawford's essays on visuality, aesthetics, and the Black Arts Movement have helped shape *Civil Rights Childhood*'s approach to the openness of photo texts. In enabling a new understanding of child agency in relationship to the civil rights era, Rebecca De Schweinitz's *If We Could Change the World: Young People and America's Long Struggle for Racial Equality* has been formative, as have Julia Mickenberg's comprehensive study of progressive children's literature, *Learning from the Left: Children's Literature, the Cold War, and Radical Politics in the United States;* Michelle H. Martin's exceptional *Brown Gold: Milestones of African American Picture Books, 1845–2002;* and Robin Bernstein's transformative work on black childhood, *Racial Innocence: Performing American Childhood and Race from Slavery to Civil Rights.*

Much of black photographic scholarship has concentrated on the overtly horrific, as in lynching photography, or covertly brutal, as in the racialized photographic practice of the nineteenth century and the sociological damage of Farm Security Administration (FSA) interpretations of black life. *Civil Rights*

Childhood redirects attention to the pleasure involved in image making and bookmaking, a dimension nearly absent in estimations of the role of photography in black culture. By taking children's texts as its subject, the project reflects on the sense of enjoyment and power underlying reconceptualizations of black identity. Especially appropriate to the project is bell hooks's observation that "[p]roducing images with the camera allowed black folks to combine image making in resistance struggle with a pleasurable experience. Taking pictures was fun!"[37] Taking pictures *is* serious fun, as is storytelling, and they share an ability to reshape and respond to constructions of black culture. *Civil Rights Childhood* keeps in the forefront the notion of pleasure in art and in storytelling, the joy that comes from shaping visual narratives and discovering through reading a path of resistance and site of power.

Chapter 1 of this project, titled "Friendship, Sympathy, Social Change," begins in the 1940s with books by Jane Dabney Shackelford and Ellen Tarry, and extends into the 1950s with *The Sweet Flypaper of Life*, by Langston Hughes and Roy DeCarava. The democratic ideology of World War II impelled fresh expectations for school integration and new perspectives on image making. Given the era's insistence on racial amity as an expression of egalitarian accomplishment, photobooks from this moment seek an affective connection through the exchange of viewer with photographed subject. Chapter 1 focuses on fictional books, exploring their trickster behavior within a context of narrowly acceptable civil rights discourse: these books layer meanings in image and story, insisting on social reform without triggering a backlash that might accuse a book of complaining too much. Chapter 2, "Pictures and Nonfiction: Conduct and Coffee Tables," also acknowledges that Cold War texts tread lightly when articulating the need for social change. As in chapter 1, these nonfictional texts stage a form of innocence—here impartiality—as a means to push for reform. Louis B. Reynolds, the black Seventh-Day Adventist author of *Little Journeys into Storyland* (1947–48), and Hughes and Meltzer in *Pictorial History* grapple with the activist possibilities of narrating history. Reynolds is invested in visual tropes of black conduct material and uses photographs to link model historical figures to present-day children. Reynolds reenergizes the conduct tradition by proclaiming that the black child can be spirited as well as obedient, joyous as well as pious. For Hughes and Meltzer, a stance of objectivity emerges by suturing image to historical subject, but *Pictorial History* also employs language *within* images in order to make urgent the need for progress: images thus unfold across the narrative, but embedded language insists that photographs serve conspicuously the imperative of the text. Nonfiction books like those of Reynolds and Hughes and Meltzer use the configuration, accumulation, and teleology of sequenced images to demand reader action.

Chapter 3 places the children's photobook at the heart of the civil rights movement. "*Today*: Framing Freedom in Mississippi" examines a book produced by the Child Development Group of Mississippi, an effort of the newly created Head Start program that was staffed by black community members and civil rights workers from SNCC and other groups. This beautiful little creation, *Today*, expands conceptually the possibilities of the photobook. *Today* offers a new model for the photobook as a vehicle of psychological liberation through an ongoing process of play with representation and bookmaking. Activism originates in a transformation of mind, *Today* declares, the freedom to see oneself anew and to take control of the terms of representation. Chapter 4, "The Black Arts Movement: Childhood as Liberatory Process," extends from *Today* the concept of the photobook as a vehicle for continuing engagement with ideas. During the late 1960s and early 1970s, photobooks articulated the Black Arts Movement's central representation of childhood as an icon of both the black nation and that nation in generative process of development. The photobook became a site of psychological liberation encouraging readers to reconstitute identity and create social change. All of the texts examined in chapter 4 engage the losses of the civil rights movement and grapple with the question of power in the face of tangible devastation; as in *Today*, agency in *Poems by Kali*, *I Wish I Had an Afro*, and *Dry Victories* takes the form of freedom in action, an ongoing process of reflection and critique in the material world. The final chapter, "Blurring the Childhood Image: Representations of the Civil Rights Narrative," examines the politically protean representation of the movement from the 1990s to the current day. Drawing from Leigh Raiford and Renee C. Romano's argument about the "consensus memory" of the civil rights movement,[38] the chapter argues that the best photobooks question or complicate iconic figures from the movement, such as Martin Luther King Jr., Ruby Bridges, and the four little girls of Birmingham. Myers's *One More River to Cross*, Morrison's *Remember: The Journey to School Integration* (2004), Bridges's *Through My Eyes*, and Weatherford's *Birmingham, 1963* all acknowledge the pressure for consensus and closure in framing civil rights. But the books that are most successful aesthetically and politically use the metatextual form of the photobook to insist that social progress is unfinished business, that readers can shape a response to historical representation, and that young people should be active interpreters of images and ideas.

Photographers and writers use the photobook to intervene in representations of civil rights that ignore child involvement or emphasize child passivity.

Examining an overlooked archive of photobooks, *Civil Rights Childhood* makes plain the stakes of writing about the movement for young people. On the contested terrain of civil rights, photobooks declare that children have a role to play. These photographic books reshape movement representation but also stage their own kind of interventionist action in arguing that child readers can fashion knowledge about history, reinvent themselves and their sense of possibility, and work for justice in the world. Emmett Till may haunt photographs for black children, but the photobooks in *Civil Rights Childhood* mobilize alternate possibilities for the child as a social agent.

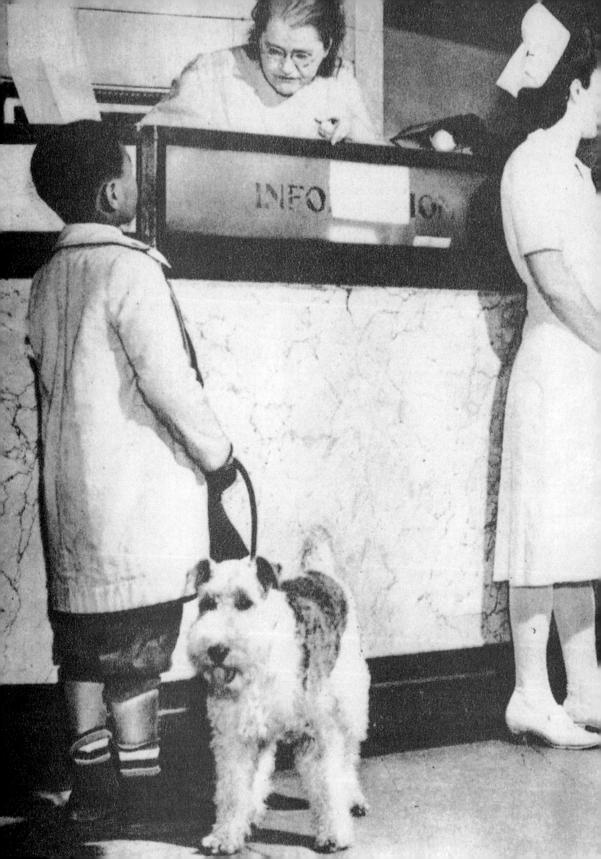

1

Friendship, Sympathy, Social Change

> "O, buy it for me, Mother, please!" . . . "I know him! He's a *good* guy.
> I talked to him when he came over to our school to practice for the
> music festival." . . . He opened [the book] to Rex's photograph and said,
> "Here he is. Look at him, Mother, look at him! He's *almost* white!"
>   —Jane Dabney Shackelford, "Book Signing"

At a 1945 book signing, a nine-year-old white boy pleads with his mother
to purchase a photographic picture book depicting an African American family. The boy wants the book because it contains pictures of a child he actually knows in life, his friend Rex. Both the black boy in the book and the white boy outside the book live in the same town, Terre Haute, Indiana, the home of Jane Dabney Shackelford, the author. The white boy insists that his mother recognize a relationship that crosses racial lines, one that would seem aberrant to the adult but that emerges from the boy's lived experience. He pleads for his mother to see the features of his own life as well as that of Rex, his friend, a *"good guy."* The boy respects Rex, and they have a relationship that the parent would see as transgressive. When the mother refuses to look at the life of her child, refuses to respect that her son has connected with a black child, the boy again pleads for recognition of his friendship, using terms that would register within a prejudiced adult culture: "Look at him, Mother, look at him! He's *almost* white!" The mother will acknowledge Rex only if the child's racial categorization retreats. Rex becomes visible, and the relationship between her son and Rex material, only when the mother can see him through the lens of whiteness.

Photography's attachment to apparent truth telling propelled new interest in picture books for the young during the 1940s and 1950s. Photographs bear particular weight in representing black childhood midcentury, for they enable visual engagement across barriers of race and age; black authors began advocating for social change through yoking the supposedly innocent technology of the camera with the supposedly innocent child subject. The construction of childhood in photographs bears traces of authenticity and could be employed by black writers to convince a readership of "true" commonalities across racial lines. Authors employed such equivalences in order to argue, subtly, for political change.

Visual representation of childhood thus took on a new political investment for civil rights advocates, both adults and young people. On the one hand, photographic texts demonstrate adult investment in fighting prejudice and advocating for integration: adults composed, published, marketed, purchased, and reviewed these texts. On the other hand, photographic picture books at midcentury also demonstrate a distinctive child investment in representing black lives and in supporting school-integration and housing-reform efforts. As opposed to books that are illustrated, photographic books represent actual children rather than fictional children. Although we cannot know the child subject's level of awareness or engagement with the ideology surrounding the text, the book becomes a site where the child subject can look back at the adult photographer, can interact with the perspective that shapes and interprets his or her experience, and can engage in a moment of visual connection with an audience.[1] As Roland Barthes argues in *Camera Lucida*, "The photograph is literally an emanation of the referent. From a real body, which was there, proceed radiations which ultimately touch me, who am here. . . . A sort of umbilical cord links the body of the photographed thing to my gaze: light, though impalpable, is here a carnal medium, a skin I share with anyone who has been photographed."[2] Photographic books are distinctive, then, in their demand that a reader (adult or child, white or black) *see* black childhood, in tandem with and even at times aside from the interpretation cast by the authors and photographers. Although that vision might be slanted, as in the case of the mother who can see a black child only as nearly white, these early children's photobooks offer a first step toward visual exchange between subject and audience. They are distinctive because an actual child peers out of the photograph. "Look at him, Mother! Look at him!" takes on enormous cultural power, as we can imagine Rex, if only in a photograph, looking back into the eyes of the racist mother in a rare visual meeting point. Midcentury photographic picture books were the first opportunity for widely circulated, politically embedded representations of black children that could reach adult and child across racial lines. The photobook offers a space—framed by the viewpoints of photographer, writer, child subject, and audience—for first articulations of an interracial connection that, the authors believed, could produce social change.

Jane Dabney Shackelford's *My Happy Days* (1944), Ellen Tarry's *My Dog*

Rinty (1946), and Langston Hughes and Roy DeCarava's *The Sweet Flypaper of Life* (1955) play with the form of the photobook in order to stage civil rights work. Each text dismantles assumptions of black familial degradation, contesting portraits from sociological documentary tradition that emphasized black-child victimhood in the face of poverty and racial bias. An examination of Shackelford's book enables us to understand the larger cultural milieu for all three texts, for each emerged during a post–World War II emphasis on politicized domesticity. Attention to *My Dog Rinty* allows a broader understanding of the publishing context for children's books midcentury and the way in which the children's photobook engages and recasts the documentary photographic tradition. Finally, considering Hughes and DeCarava's photobook in light of the earlier children's texts allows us to think of the landmark work in new ways. Children's publications informed *Sweet Flypaper*'s representation of the black family, as it drew from this new genre of black-child photobooks and allowed Hughes to continue his literary commitment to children as readers. Like the earlier books, *Sweet Flypaper* responded to the context of efforts at school integration; whereas the climate of the 1940s precluded overt criticism of the systemic causes for social and educational inequities in Tarry's and Shackelford's texts, by the mid-1950s Hughes and DeCarava could use *Sweet Flypaper* to present such a structural critique by juxtaposing the pleasurable domestic space against the distressed landscape of Harlem. *Sweet Flypaper* appeared during Hughes's deepest investment in children's literature, as he turned to children's texts in response to the McCarthy-era attacks on his supposed communism. *Sweet Flypaper* was read in family settings and attracted preliterate visual readers as well as those young people emerging into literacy. All three texts demonstrate the commitment to social change through photographs of black children, and each responds to the particular pressures of an era demanding conformist patriotism and politicized domesticity.

The decade between *My Happy Days* and *The Sweet Flypaper of Life* was marked by innovations in illustrated-picture-book creativity. Margaret Wise Brown's fertile imagination produced *Little Fur Family* (1946), *The Important Book* (1949), and her masterpiece, *Goodnight Moon* (1947), among many others. Theodor Seuss Geisel, "Dr. Seuss," published *If I Ran the Zoo* (1950) and his popular follow-up to *Horton Hatches the Egg* (1940), *Horton Hears a Who!* (1954). In the mid-1940s, writers from the Bank Street School of Education, including Lucy Sprague Mitchell, became involved with Golden Books, which issued color picture books for only twenty-five cents apiece. These were exciting times for children's illustrated books; yet few mainstream texts contained images of

African American children (and, extremely rarely, the stories of such children), and when they did, the images were frequently stereotypical or subservient.[3] At the same time, librarians and educators recognized in nonfiction a means by which American democratic ideals could be articulated though books about African American history. Bette Banner Preer of the Boston Public Library wrote in "Guidance in Democratic Living through Juvenile Fiction" (1948) that "noteworthy contributions by the Negro to American civilization" had begun to draw interest from publishers and authors, both black and white;[4] Arna Bontemps's 1948 Newbery Honor book, *Story of the Negro*, can be seen as part of this trend in envisioning black accomplishment as part of the story of American identity and evidence of America's democratic principles. But illustrated picture books were nearly silent on the black experience.

Given that illustrated children's books of the period rarely depicted African American characters, one might consider the absence of black picture books as reason enough to connect the mid-1940s photobooks to Hughes and DeCarava's *Sweet Flypaper of Life*. But acknowledging the difference in genre (as Shackelford's and Tarry's books were expressly children's texts, whereas Hughes and DeCarava's became family reading) and the gap in time between Hughes and De-Carava and the earlier texts, I consciously position *Sweet Flypaper* within the landscape of children's publishing and photobook traditions. As one of the most important writers of the century, Hughes might be considered exceptional, a singular innovator. However, his energies dovetail with tendencies in the earlier children's books, and understanding the predecessors enables an enriched appreciation of the subtle experimental accomplishment of *Sweet Flypaper*. Hughes certainly could sustain his own chapter in this project, especially given that *A Pictorial History of the Negro in America* (1956), the subject of chapter 2, appeared within the same cultural moment as *Sweet Flypaper*. But by placing Hughes alongside lesser-known (and less radical) contemporaries, I hope to articulate Hughes's interaction with the era's aesthetic and political currents. I also wish to work against the "hero" approach to historical memory, a methodology that would extract extraordinary individuals in order to demonstrate their singularity. Instead of isolating Hughes, the study places him within a conversation about youth, civil rights, and photography.

PHOTOBOOKS AND THE POLITICS OF FRIENDSHIP

Black children's photobooks emerged during a period of intense discussion about the place of African Americans in national identity. In the wake of World War II, international attention turned toward the failure of democratic ideals in

America under segregation. The government began to embrace new representations of race in the United States in order to stake a claim to global leadership. As Mary Dudziak documents in *Cold War Civil Rights*, United States ascendancy after World War II was predicated on the exhibition of democratic values at home.[5] National redress of the so-called Negro problem thus became a site of governmental concern; the nation's commitment to a galvanizing embrace of personal liberties and egalitarian ideals was documented in government-issued propaganda and visual representations, such as in pamphlets, posters, and photographs issued by the Office of War Information (OWI) in the early 1940s. This popular construction of race relations, termed racial liberalism, constructed racism as a form of personal bias rather than an effect of institutional economic and political disparities and injustices. As Jodi Melamed argues perceptively, racial liberalism as an official state antiracism disavowed critique that centered on material or economic conditions. Rather, race problems became constructed through psychology, through a problematic white attitude that blocked African American access to values assumed to be stable and unitary in American culture: if not barred by white attitude, black Americans inevitably embrace property, patriotism, and national cohesion, the logic of racial liberalism argued.[6]

Gunnar Myrdal's *An American Dilemma: The Negro Problem and Modern Democracy* (1944) was the landmark articulation of racial liberalism. Sponsored by the Carnegie Foundation, *American Dilemma* argued that blacks and whites live in ignorance of each other and the values they share, and that the problem of inequality arises from white ignorance of the similarity of black Americans to themselves. Myrdal asserted that all Americans share an American creed consisting of the belief in equality and liberty, however abstract, and that if white hearts were changed, then the problem of racism would disappear. Personal contacts with each other, Myrdal proposed, and greater information about the values of each other would help eradicate racism. Eradication of black oppression offered the United States an opportunity to demonstrate the practice of its egalitarian ideals, the best site to establish global ascendance: "America saving itself becomes savior of the world," Myrdal proclaimed.[7]

Friendship, then, was what was needed between the races. As a result, mutual understanding became one dominant articulation of representation within racial liberalism. American culture imagined social change taking place through getting to know particular African American individuals (a phenomenon also referred to as "human relations" in this era). Trenchant critique of social history or economic conditions was not endorsed as a path to the improvement of race relations, nor was racism considered a federal issue. Melamed explains that literature became a main vehicle for sharing knowledge and building imagined relationships, for within literary studies the race novel, born of the institutionalization of race studies within sociological and philanthropic contexts, permitted white readers to hear the "real stories" of black experience. Many race novels focused on what racial liberalists would describe as the damaged psychology of black America. Characters became damaged by contact with whites who themselves had been distorted by racism. Literature became a vehicle by which white readers could recognize the damage that prejudice inflicts and could connect with the shared values of egalitarianism and patriotism across racial lines. A politics of identification dominated many race-liberal representations, and literature became an evidentiary mode through which whites could see themselves in black America. Of course, such a construction severely delimited the possibilities of black critique, rendering a version of whiteness normative and excluding systematic evaluations of racism based on class or on Afrocentric perspectives. The ideal of friendship, of amity based on a politics of sameness, structured much race-liberal writing in the 1940s, including children's photobooks. The two poles within race-liberal publications—one of a damaged black psyche and the other of black American success—brought with them the imperative that white readers recognize these versions of black life and sympathize with them.

One can see how the boy's cry "Look at him[!] . . . He's *almost* white!" might have played within such a climate. In fact, the mode of a children's photobook placed intensified pressures on the race-liberal ideology. First, photographic texts in the 1940s intersected with the institutionalization of race studies, particularly given the dominance of sociological study in discussions of race.[8] Photographic texts, those issued by the OWI or published by mainstream race-novel presses like Viking, participated in the race-liberal agenda of literature as "information retrieval,"[9] relying conspicuously on the theoretical truth-value of the image. Further, the supposed innocence of children's texts, coupled with the supposedly innocent gaze of the camera, served to naturalize race-liberal values like patriotism, consumerism, and equal opportunity.[10] Children's photobooks in the 1940s, then, emerged from a milieu that valued naturalized constructions of interracial identification, friendship, and sameness. For these texts, transformation of white attitude toward black Americans was predicated on the appeal of childhood, particularly in domestic spaces with middle-class parents. How could one turn down the appeal to friendship extended by an ingenuous child in a smiling close-up photo? And if that close-up focused on a happy, patriotic, materially and psychologically successful child, would not that friendship change the heart of a white reader?

Certainly, black-authored photobooks from the 1940s play in the terrain of racial liberalism. Jane Shackelford's *My Happy Days* is perhaps the most prominent adherent to the pattern of patriotism and consumerist success. It would be difficult to imagine children's photobooks of this moment not engaging the official antiracism, particularly if authors wanted success and school circulation, as did Shackelford. Further, the texts are enmeshed in photographic traditions that dovetail with the institutionalization of race studies, especially through documentary photography, as well as with popular-magazine photo traditions that instantiated black-national patriotism and economic success through the metonymic black family. But although children's books conspicuously aim to eliminate prejudice through friendship, as well as to demonstrate the success of American ideals through black family life, race texts like the ones examined in this chapter also resist the dominance of racial liberalism in subtle but palpable ways. They push toward civil rights intervention by playing on the surface the game of racial liberalism while at the same time employing images and narration that render open-ended questions of structural and economic injustice. In other words, the black American success story is not a closed narrative in these children's texts. The books exist within a web of cultural and national articulations of black visual identity, and they draw on various energies in order to depict a domestic space that reverberates both in support of racial liberalism's theory of racial inclusivity in an American creed and also in refutation of its resolute accomplishment. For Hughes and DeCarava, *Sweet Flypaper of Life* even takes issue with the terms of racial liberalism, particularly in its appropriation of the domestic space for a national agenda. Although the warm, joyous domestic space might be read by white audiences as evidencing the success of American norms in black life, in all three of the texts examined here, there is a sense that the reinvention of the domestic visually has radical potential for a black audience. Race-liberal texts have often been read with Myrdal in mind; undoubtedly, children's photobooks conveyed predictable ideals to a white readership. Although critics have acknowledged the narrowing of radical potential for critique in race-liberal articulations, subtle undercurrents of dissatisfaction and of civil rights demands still course through texts written by black authors and offered to black and white audiences. These are trickster texts, books that play the game of amity expected by an interracial audience but that insist in visual undercurrents on the unfinished status of black citizenship.

MY HAPPY DAYS: THE AFRICAN AMERICAN
DEMOCRATIC HOME SPACE

Jane Dabney Shackelford's 1945 photographic picture book *My Happy Days* documents the life of an African American family through the eyes of Rex, the eight-year-old son. Shackelford, a middle-class African American woman who served as a teacher in Terre Haute, Indiana, schools for forty-three years, published her photobook through Carter G. Woodson's Associated Publishers, one of the few African American publishing houses of the early and mid-twentieth century. As a fictionalized account of suburban life, *My Happy Days* contains images of Shackelford's sister's family; Rex Manuel Sr. was a police radio patrolman in Terre Haute, his wife, Mary, a housewife and mother to their two children. Despite the inflection of the family's last name, there is no evidence that the family was Latino as well as African American,[11] although Shackelford renames the family Nelson in the photobook, perhaps to erase any ethnic associations. The narrative of *My Happy Days* might appear to a twenty-first-century reader to be quite ordinary: Rex lives in a middle-class house, plays games with his five-year-old sister, goes fishing with his father, attends a nicely appointed school, visits the doctor, and enjoys the community library and art gallery. There is no plot tension. There are no conflicts between adults and children, or even among children. And yet, within the context of race relations during World War II, *My Happy Days* offers a far-reaching political statement about the success of democratic ideals and the shape of economic prosperity in the United States. Shackelford's text answers charges by the international community about American racism, intervening in debates about the role of democracy on the home front. Her text addresses the particular moment in which American ethical commitments to equality, democracy, and social freedom were questioned; in fact, the book confirms United States government propaganda about the successful practice of democratic ideals, embracing official antiracism. At the same time, however, the book speaks to the African American community about the need for social change, particularly in relation to school integration. *My Happy Days* speaks on two registers: of black economic and social success to a mainstream white audience, and of the need for school integration to African American and leftist white audiences. Whereas to a modern reader, Shackelford's text seems an innocuous rendering of a family's daily life, in the book's day its meaning was anything but prosaic. By representing a domestic life that intersects both with international demands during World War II for evidence of racial justice and with black desire for social change, *My*

Happy Days offers an intricate argument about the political significance of the black family to definitions of American identity. In large part, this investigation is a kind of treasure hunt: in order to understand the significance of what might seem to a twenty-first-century reader to be an unchallenging and uncomplicated book, we must look to political and cultural context, as well as to reviews of the text. An understanding of *My Happy Days* relies on context, because the book deliberately eschews direct articulation of its politics.

American engagement in World War II was founded on a commitment to worldwide democracy and to antifascism, even as the nation facilitated segregation and racial inequality at home. The United States thus found itself embarrassed internationally at the dynamics of domestic race relations, particularly in the South, and the persistent social and economic injustices endured by African Americans. Dudziak charts the political implications of the contradiction between ideals and practice apparent to the international community, explaining that racism at home appeared as "a blot" on the record of America,[12] and a variety of governmental efforts emerged in order to insist on the success of relationships between black and white individuals and communities, including the United States War Department's documentary film *The Negro Soldier* (1944), directed by Frank Capra. The OWI offered a photographic series on interracial work sites, and, as Nicholas Natanson explains, "[w]ith the establishment of an aggressive Negro Press Section within the OWI (headed by the black editor Theodore Poston, and including the ambitious young black photographer Roger Smith), with the release of two glossy OWI Domestic Branch pamphlets, 'Negroes and the War' and 'Manpower: One-Tenth of a Nation,' images of black strength and interracial cooperation gained added circulation."[13] *My Happy Days* appeared within this context, and although it does not technically offer interracial images, as I will explain in what follows, it joins the trend of documenting American ideological victory by promoting African American social and economic success. It participates in the dominant American propagandistic inclination by eliminating any overt description of racial prejudice or conflict.

Official Antiracism: Patriotism and the Family

First and foremost, the book contains straightforward assertions of patriotism and of American commitment to democracy at home (Figure 1.1). Alongside an image of Rex holding the flag while five of his classmates pledge allegiance, the text reads, "I think I am very fortunate because I live in the United States of America. The children in our country have so many freedoms to enjoy."[14] On

Figure 1.1. Rex and his classmates pledge to the flag outside their school.
From Jane Dabney Shackelford, *My Happy Days* (Washington, D.C.:
The Associated Publishers, Inc., 1944). Photograph by Cecil Vinson.
Reprinted with permission of the Association for the Study of African American
Life & History, http://www.asalh.org/.

the topic of education, Shackelford then sidesteps a discussion of school integration by asserting, "We have free schools for all. Every one in our country has an opportunity to get an education" (116). Shackelford does not conspicuously address the topic of school integration but rather focuses on a more general discussion of the black child's investment in definitions of the nation: "I am proud to be a citizen of the United States of America, and I love to hold my country's flag while the children say: 'I pledge allegiance . . .'" (116). The larger picture of black citizenship comes to the surface rather than the particulars of social injustices; this broadening strategy extends to the photograph, which is taken outside in the yard of the school rather than in a classroom. The children's national identity is not bounded by the walls of the classroom but extends out into the community and the nation. This general attestation to citizenship allows Shackelford to enjoy the benefits of participating in propagandistic media; the children assert their patriotism, define themselves through national loyalty, and demonstrate (in the photograph) that their citizenship is unbounded by debates about the classroom. Remembering the call that starts this chapter, "Look at him[!] . . . He's *almost* white!," we can understand Rex the leader as assuming a patriotic position associated with whiteness.

In effect, the era's insistent propagandistic tendencies limited the possibilities for civil rights intervention. Speaking explicitly of racial injustice would appear subversive and traitorous. Dudziak's analysis of public discourse (in newspaper accounts and individual testimony) addresses also the predicament faced by writers like Shackelford; Dudziak explains that "to criticize the nation before an international audience and to air the nation's dirty laundry overseas was to reinforce the negative impact of American racism on the nation's standing as a world leader. It was seen, then, as a great breach of loyalty."[15] Such demands led during the Cold War to "a narrowing of acceptable civil rights discourse," as writers and activists faced pressure to avoid speaking out against the nation.[16] Of course, not all activists were silent in the 1940s, but the cultural milieu placed writers like Shackelford under that expectation. Placing the black family on the center stage was a courageous move, one that cannily drew on the energies of American propagandistic nationalism and the relationship of the family to the nation in the white mainstream media. Shackelford naturalizes the black family, enabling it to represent both the success of democratic ideals at home and, as we will see, the need for America to effect social change.

By spotlighting the family, Shackelford speaks the language of mainstream democratic national ideals. White American culture had a deep investment in the 1940s, and even more intensely during the 1950s, in the domestic space as a concretization of American political and economic safety. Elaine Tyler May's landmark study of the midcentury family describes the phenomenon: "Americans turned to the family as a bastion of safety in an insecure world, while experts, leaders and politicians promoted codes of conduct and enacted public policies that would bolster the American home. Like their leaders, most Americans agreed that family stability appeared to be the best bulwark against the dangers of the cold war."[17] Shackelford uses similar language in describing the political significance of her book; in a preface, "A Message to Parents," she concludes, "I hope it will establish a pattern that will be followed in many homes, because we all realize that strengthening family life is a bulwark of democracy." In this phrasing we see that, in spite of the documentary, evidentiary pretext of the book, its recording of "the activities of a real family, a family in which all participate, have a feeling of belonging, and enjoy the democratic way of life," in fact Shackelford stresses that the family is *not* typical but is an exceptional "pattern" that will enable child readers, and their parents, to learn democratic behavior at home. The democratic accomplishment of the United States depends, for Shackelford, on following the model of family and community relations presented in the text. Here is where we see a subtle nudge toward social change, an acknowledgment that her text does not represent a social equality already accomplished but is an ideal to which the nation should aspire. This nudge coheres with the official antiracist stance: the nation's democratic identity should take shape at home.

Because Shackelford's overall strategy draws on the dominant cultural mode of representing American success through the success of the family, it takes on activist implications by placing a black family at the heart of national identity. In particular, Shackelford's book intervenes in the idealization of suburbia as the incarnation of American democratic success.[18] Actual black exclusion from suburbia was covert, as May describes, since bank lending policies at both local and federal levels prevented black families from purchasing homes, and as a result areas like Levittown, New York, became synonymous with segregation. But even as exclusion was predominant, official discourse assured Americans of the ascendance of democratic ideals.[19] Shackelford's book, then, does not contravene the mainstream propaganda on housing equality. Instead, it contravenes lived experience by placing a black family happily in the heart of suburbia. It speaks through its images of the success of the middle-class black community and its embodiment of "American" values.

My Happy Days demonstrates American democratic ideals by describing the family's production of a suburban home from the ground up. Together the family gazes at the plans that an architect has drawn up for their new house. The image emphasizes the physical and emotional closeness of the family as they crowd together to review the plans, which are, of course, the first stage in making the idea of a black suburban home materialize. Shackelford's description of the image pushes the idea of democracy into new territory; as she mentions learning about democracy at home in her note to parents, the language here puts equality into practice. Rex explains: "When Dad built our new home last year, all of us had a share in planning it" (10). Each family member names a space he or she would like to create: a sewing room, fireplace, and "many closets" for mother; a playroom and sandbox for daughter; and "a room of my own . . . and a place in the basement to make things" for son Rex (10). Each room, of course, reflects Shackelford's awareness of the social implications of space: "many closets" signify the mother's consumerist accomplishment, just as the sewing room suggests an investment in the homespun, play defines early childhood, and command over personal space and creation marks the well-developing male child. The larger suburban community is not pictured; instead of meeting neighbors or imagining the family's arrival in the new home, Shackelford turns attention away from social relations. The family's activities at home are insular and middle-class: the daughter plays with dolls and dollhouses, the mother creates scrapbooks, Rex builds a birdhouse, and together the family plants trees in the yard.[20] Although Shackelford's discussion is framed by conservative tendencies—the erasure of social relations in building the new home and the traditional gender politics of the family's hobbies and activities—she pushes into new ground by offering an image of black suburbia and by emphasizing that democracy in practice includes the voices of children, even if they are arbitrated by Dad.

Domesticity and the Press

In order to understand the way in which Shackelford spoke the language of the mainstream, we might briefly consider two factors: the role of her publisher, Carter G. Woodson; and the influence of *Life* magazine on the text's strategy. As the "father of black history," Woodson is often identified with the founding of Negro History Week, the Association for the Study of Negro Life and History, and the *Journal of Negro History*. He produced the *Negro History Bulletin* for schoolteachers from 1937 until his death, in 1950. In short, with Woodson's legacy in mind, one might expect that *My Happy Days* would bear a more overtly race-radical import because of its imprint. But, like Woodson's publication of poetry for children in the 1930s,[21] Shackelford's photographic picture book implicitly argues for another version of Woodson, one that suggests his investment in the success of the contemporary black family as a template for a democratic America and in a desire for a mainstream, interracial reading public. Woodson may be remembered as a visionary black historian—despite Myrdal's critique in *American Dilemma* of Woodson's work as race propaganda with "[e]xcellent historical research" but "definite distortion in the emphasis and perspective given the facts."[22] Given Woodson's publication of *My Happy Days*, we see the groundbreaking black historian toward the end of his life valorizing African American domesticity in terms that would register with a white as well as a black audience.[23] This is an alternate version of Woodson, one in tune with the currents in popular antiracism.[24]

Suburbia as signifier of American democratic accomplishment became prominent in non–African American photographic representations, as is demonstrated by the popularity of *Life* magazine.[25] *Life* is the clearest progenitor of *My Happy Days*, as is apparent even in a cursory reading of the book, and becomes conspicuous in the image of Rex reading the November 29, 1943, issue (Figure 1.2). On the cover of the issue is General Ira Eaker, deputy commander of the U.S. Army Air Forces, and Rex's interest in the issue signifies his investment in the war effort and its resistance to fascism and authoritarianism. Aside from war coverage, *Life* was deeply concerned with associating domesticity with American citizenship, as Wendy Kozol argues.[26] Shackelford also draws on particular representational strategies employed by *Life* in order to stabilize her version of race relations, one that intersects with nationalistic propaganda and also calls implicitly for social change. *Life* frequently employed a metonymic strategy, using a typical family or individual to stand in for national values. But very few average or typical African Americans were subjects of *Life*'s attention, and as a result black "ordinary" people were rarely valorized or made representational. Instead, *Life* transformed exceptional individuals into the metonymic, arguing that the prized qualities of black celebrities or public figures were, in fact, expressive American features, particularly if those figures were good fathers and mothers.[27] Through the domestic, *Life* transformed celebrity African Americans into "normal" parents who represented the ideals shared by Americans, both black and white. In *My Happy Days*, a similar process takes place, for certainly the Manuel family is exceptional, given their ability to design and build a suburban home and live without racial conflict. Their accomplishment is normalized through the text's invocation of *Life* magazine and Shackelford's insistence that the "real family" on the page exists in life.[28] They are the pattern for American democratic ideals.[29]

Figure 1.2. Rex at home, reading *Life* magazine, with a cover image of General Ira Eaker, deputy commander of the U.S. Army Air Forces. From Jane Dabney Shackelford, *My Happy Days* (Washington, D.C.: The Associated Publishers, Inc., 1944). Photograph by Cecil Vinson. Reprinted with permission of the Association for the Study of African American Life & History, http://www.asalh.org/.

Normalizing the exceptional is a phenomenon that dovetails with the dominant perspective on race relations during the 1940s in the United States, the race liberalism that insisted prejudice was a matter of attitude rather than of structural inequities. Photographic picture books like *My Happy Days* thus served as sites of "human relations," as friendship spaces in which a white reader could engage a specific, idealized (exceptional but normalized) black family, which also stands in for a valuable and viable black middle class, which in turn signifies the values and health of the nation. A reader can meet the black family, can recognize its representational function as evoking black America and investing black America in citizenship; and transformation in race relations and "human understanding" would result.

Undoubtedly, *My Happy Days* speaks to a white readership on this register. Its depiction of Rex and his family touches on very little in terms of race. In fact, aside from the fact that Rex's school is named after Carter G. Woodson and he plays at Booker T. Washington Park, race surfaces only when Rex creates a school project on Washington and later asserts, "I am reading more stories about great Negroes. Learning about my race also helps me to grow in self-respect" (114). Rex never makes an issue of race or interracial relations. The book thus becomes a site of contact between a white readership and the idealized American family, which happens to be black. "Look at him, Mother, look at him! He's *almost* white!" constitutes the social signification of the Manuel family. Interracial understanding could result from such a contact, Shackelford suggests, and white communities could be reassured of the lack of a need for systemic economic and social transformation.

Shackelford's Activist Text: Companionate Family and Antiauthoritarianism

A conservative overlay thus increases market appeal and places the book within *Life* magazine's legible visual discourse about American identity and values. But the friendship orthodoxy is only one way in which *My Happy Days* speaks;[30] the book evokes changing perspectives on the relationship of childhood to social progress and addresses African American audiences and white progressives in visual codes that demand advancements in social and educational integration. In an era of patriotic conformity and what May calls a time of "domestic containment,"[31] the book must tread lightly in order to argue for social change, must speak in ways that would register with progressives but fly under the radar of traditionalists.

A primary component that leads to an appreciation of the progressive underpinnings of *My Happy Days* is its investment in reinventing social dynamics through childhood. In this era of intense interest in the home space, its stability an imagined reassurance against political chaos, psychologists and social scientists became convinced of the importance of child rearing to a democratic society. As Diana Selig explains in *Americans All: The Cultural Gifts Movement*, educators and theorists no longer considered prejudice in the same terms: "Rather than describing prejudice as the result of ignorance, as they had done in the 1920s, researchers now came to see it as a psychological problem that originated in interpersonal relations dating back to early childhood. In this new formulation, the solution lay in the reform of family life and personality devel-opment."[32] Prejudice began to be imagined as a psychological disorder, with its source in childhood tensions, disturbances, and conflicts. John Dollard's 1939 *Frustration and Aggression* led the way toward understanding the influence of home spaces, and Theodor Adorno's *The Authoritarian Personality* (1950) and Bruno Bettelheim and Morris Janowitz's *Dynamics of Prejudice* (1950) both con-tributed to a new understanding of the psychological sources of racism and to the emphasis on childhood as the time to facilitate healthy racial attitudes. Selig refers to Adorno's landmark study: "Bigots were not bigots because they lacked full information, but rather because of deep-seated psychological disorders, for prejudice was 'the defense system of an insecure ego.'"[33] To be clear, this phe-nomenon is connected to the official antiracist emphasis on human relations, because for both, racism is connected to psychology, but progressive thinkers figured prejudice as disorder rather than misunderstanding and urged transfor-mation of child rearing as a response.

Reformation of the home seemed paramount to progressives who aimed to eliminate prejudice against minorities. Rather than offer information in school settings about the particular histories or accomplishments of minority cultures, some progressive reformers wished to shape a new antiauthoritarian family life. Researchers like Samuel H. Flowerman of the American Jewish Committee sought to discover the sources of bias by talking with children; Flowerman is quoted in the *New York Times* on his 1946 studies: "Perhaps armed with the knowledge of a cause, we may come closer to a cure."[34] Some theorists, like Bettelheim and Janowitz, suggested that transformation of the home should come through greater parental affection, because "intolerance toward minority groups was associated with the recall of lack of parental love and harsh disci-pline."[35] Flowerman's essay on "the authoritarian man" places the burden of reform on the home—"We must reach parents so that they can learn the im-portance of affection and equality in the home"—and Flowerman sees the tide turning toward egalitarian households—"[M]odern parents are less ashamed of loving their children."[36] Parental love and egalitarian family structures were po-litical efforts to eliminate prejudice. In this light, Shackelford's relentless insis-tence on the happiness of Rex's household and on the parity between adults and children seems a deliberate attempt to model reform of race relations. Through happiness and an egalitarian household, Shackelford sets forth her best effort toward eliminating prejudice. White readers meeting the black family might grow in "human understanding," but Shackelford's intent is more incisive; the book aims to form the child's psychology through modifying adult behavior in the home space. An egalitarian household would lead to the elimination of all impulse toward prejudice.

Shackelford's "A Message to Parents" emphasizes that in this idealized home, "the parents are companions to their children, daily enriching their lives by giving them a background of fine appreciations of art, music, literature, and outstanding achievements." What emerges from examining the photographs is a strong sense of the adults as friends, as peers, to the children. I have argued elsewhere that Shackelford infantilizes the parents,[37] and I think the text enacts a claustrophobic vision of family life, in which the parents and children share the same interests and investments. But such a companionate family was a function of the progressive milieu and the attempt at reform of authoritarian households. The photographs take pains to place the adults visually in the sphere of childhood, as in the image accompanying "Making Scrapbooks," in which the mother does her work at the children's table, or the drawing that accompanies "Keeping My Body Clean" (Figure 1.3). In the latter, the image behind Rex appears crudely drawn, and one might assume that the child has scribbled in the bath. Instead, Rex tells us that "I like to look at the pictures Dad drew on our bathroom wall" (58). The father has been in the place of the child, literally, and has left an image for the child's enjoyment. The drawing, further, points to another companionate image; because the drawing depicts a fish in the reeds, the reader is reminded of the passage "Dad and I Go Fishing." The photograph accompanying that moment further equalizes the pair, because it places the father as visually the same size as the son. Together they enjoy a laugh as they catch only an old shoe instead of a fish, as Shackelford links fishing to play rather than sustenance.

In aiming to develop generous, affectionate, liberal parents, Shackelford's book enacts an antiauthoritarian model of the family, one that demonstrates the "happy" family atmosphere necessary to produce children without prejudice. This is a fundamentally progressive stance on relationships between adults and children. We can further place Shackelford's work within a liberal tradition by examining Rex's attitude toward the world around him. Although some of the images in the book seem innocuous at first glance, they are weighted with the ideology of the leftist tradition in children's literature, particularly as it approached race and social change. In tracing the influence of the leftist 1930s on children's literature in the 1940s, Julia Mickenberg identifies science as a suggestive metaphor for commitment to change and open-mindedness: "Articles in education journals in the 1930s and 1940s often spoke of the relationship between science and democracy and the social implications of science. Many

Figure 1.3. Rex bathes under the drawing created by his father.
From Jane Dabney Shackelford, *My Happy Days* (Washington, D.C.:
The Associated Publishers, Inc., 1944). Photograph by Cecil Vinson.
Reprinted with permission of the Association for the Study of African American
Life & History, http://www.asalh.org/.

of these articles argued that science study should teach children a questioning
attitude toward all received authority, teach them to test all of their hypotheses
and to see their limitations, and teach them to see the social and ethical implications of science."[38] Mickenberg interviewed many children's-book editors and
advocates from the left, including Betty Bacon, who was the juvenile editor at
McBride, who started a line of juvenile books at International Publishers, and
who reviewed children's books for *New Masses*. Bacon imagined science books as
transmitting a Marxist perspective without offering any overt discussion of politics; through science, children "would understand that they live in a dynamic
world where there is a lot of change going on. And it is important for children
to understand change. The more we look upon change, the more we encourage
it to take place. And encouraging it to take place is often a danger to the status
quo."[39] In children's books of the era, often descriptions of cell development,

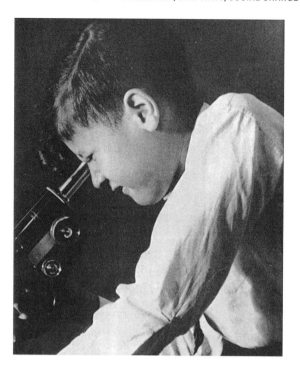

Figure 1.4. Rex peers into the microscope at his school. From Jane Dabney Shackelford, *My Happy Days* (Washington, D.C.: The Associated Publishers, Inc., 1944). Photograph by Cecil Vinson.
Reprinted with the permission of the Association for the Study of African American Life & History, http://www.asalh.org/.

evolution, and chemical transformations were politicized statements of the inevitability of change.

Within *My Happy Days*, Rex adopts a progressive scientific perspective through technology and inquiry. In the section entitled "My Microscope," Rex peers into his equipment, looking for a closer perspective on the world around him (Figure 1.4). The photograph pictures Rex actively seeking knowledge; we see his face only in profile, his squinted eye suggesting that he focuses his attention keenly on the material he scrutinizes. The text reads, "My microscope shows objects many times their natural size. I can see many things which I can not see at all with the naked eye. I have learned many interesting new facts about familiar objects all around me. With my dictionary, my microscope, and my thinking cap, my world grows larger every day" (44). In fact, to depict a black child peering through a microscope was revolutionary in and of itself, as it positioned black childhood as active, thoughtful, intelligent, and modern. The depiction of Rex and his microscope coheres with constructions of childhood within science texts produced by, for instance, Young World, an arm of the Communist Party's International Publishers, and other leftist venues that sought to demonstrate through children's literature a commitment to logical inquiry and looking beyond the surface of things.[40] Shackelford herself was not a political radical; her book, however, draws on the energies of leftist children's publishing in its depiction of a child who questions and analyzes his environment.

As part of the book's antiauthoritarian subtext, Rex demonstrates his autonomy and authority when evaluating his surroundings. In a passage titled "Answering My Own Questions," Rex explains, "When I was a very little boy, I depended upon my parents to answer all of my questions for me. Whenever I saw something new I would ask, 'What is it? Where did it come from? How did it work?' Now I try to answer my own questions because I am older. I find some of the answers by looking very carefully at everything I see" (42). Demonstrating an antiauthoritarian stance toward information and influence, Rex moves from an acceptance of his parents' knowledge to building his own perceptions by scrutinizing "everything I see." His hobbies also cohere with the nonfiction genre of how-to books about building things, popular within progressive children's literature as a generative response to the destructive effects of war.[41] Rex combines the left's emphasis on thinking for oneself with a desire to create: "My favorite hobby is making things. . . . Last Christmas Dad bought me an erector set with an electric motor. Now I have fun building my own cars and running them with electric power. Some day I want to visit an automobile plant to see how cars are made" (14).[42] Rex wishes to look at the world around him closely, to examine received knowledge, to make discoveries and create. *My Happy Days* encodes its alignment to the leftist social movements through its depiction of the companionate family and its commitment to scientific inquiry as the basis of knowledge. Rex's words might not explicitly connote the need for social progress, but, read in the context of the progressive field of children's literature in the 1940s, Rex appears the ideal antiauthoritarian progressive child: he believes in change, and he believes in himself.

A Photographic Argument for Integration

The most transparent political statement encoded by the text is its visual endorsement of integration. As I argue elsewhere,[43] Rex's skin tone is strikingly fair, and he is often set side by side with darker children, and often in classroom settings. Images like the one attached to the "Working in Groups" chapter is typical of the book's approach. Rex sits next to a darker child and, with his hands on the material, appears to lead her through an activity (Figure 1.5). The language emphasizes the egalitarian import of the image: "Miss Hodge lets us work in groups to find the answers. First we choose our leader. We choose leaders who are good workers. They are kind and thoughtful boys and girls who get along with every one" (76). The ability to "get along" with a variety of people signals a prointegrationist meaning to this classroom moment. Similarly, Rex leads his classmates through "a make-believe radio program" and plays marbles with his darker classmates. It is telling that these images appear in school settings, for whereas the representation of suburbia avoids social configuration by emphasizing the family's insularity, at school Rex is consistently set in visual juxtaposition to his friends and is always positioned as a leader. He represents

Figure 1.5. Rex helps a classmate with schoolwork. From Jane Dabney Shackelford, *My Happy Days* (Washington, D.C.: The Associated Publishers, Inc., 1944). Photograph by Cecil Vinson. Reprinted with the permission of the Association for the Study of African American Life & History, http://www.asalh.org/.

integration in action; as his real-life friend shouted to his mother, "He's *almost* white!" Of course, this configuration might also speak to white progressives of the need to prioritize white integration activism, a figuration that may appear problematic to a twenty-first-century reader.

Shackelford sets her most conspicuous prointegrationist image within the classroom and in doing so connects her integrationist goals with the democratic ideology of World War II. In the chapter entitled "Helping Others," Rex finishes a booklet of his best work ahead of his classmates and is asked to help those who are less speedy. The image depicts Rex leaning over a darker classmate's desk, assisting the friend with his work. Behind his left shoulder appears the American flag (Figure 1.6). Not only is the whiter boy the classroom leader in this image, but also the physical positioning of Rex with his classmate echoes precisely the war-effort poster immediately to Rex's right. And if the invocation of democratic ideals were not enough to emphasize the need for school integration, what is figured on the poster underlines the text's ideology: entitled "United We Win," the 1943 poster is an Office of War Information image by Alexander Liberman, of an integrated aircraft factory. The integrated factory workers stand under the American flag, as do Rex and his classmate. Shackelford could not be more clear about her text's purposes. Although she invokes the legitimizing genre of *Life* magazine to nationalize Rex and his family, her motivation is not simply general "human understanding" of a typical suburban black family in order to demonstrate U.S. democratic success; she uses the images to direct the reader's attention to the viability, justice, and patriotic imperative of school integration, an open question yet a fundamental need in terms of black citizenship.

There are other gestures toward the larger political landscape of civil rights within *My Happy Days*. Within a discussion of music at school, most of the activities appear fairly mainstream; schoolchildren play the Victrola and listen to

Figure 1.6. Rex assists a peer, with a 1943 War Information Office integration poster behind him. From Jane Dabney Shackelford, *My Happy Days* (Washington, D.C.: The Associated Publishers, Inc., 1944). Photograph by Cecil Vinson. Reprinted with the permission of the Association for the Study of African American Life & History, http://www.asalh.org/.

NBC's program for classrooms, the "Music Appreciation Hour," which was led by conductor Walter Damrosh and featured classical music.[44] But within this description appears a nod to the larger social context: "When we have a rest period, we enjoy hearing Marian Anderson sing 'Ave Maria'" (84). This line refers to the April 9, 1939, recording of Anderson's landmark performance on the steps of the Lincoln Memorial, which was arranged by President Roosevelt, Eleanor Roosevelt, and Walter White of the NAACP as a result of Anderson's exclusion from a Daughters of the American Revolution concert at Constitution Hall. Anderson's Lincoln Memorial performance to seventy-five thousand people, and to an audience numbering in the millions on the radio, became a watershed moment in civil rights efforts at refuting segregation. What comes next in *My Happy Days* is an obvious nod to the antifascist leftist movement of the early 1940s: "On our patriotic programs we listen to Paul Robeson sing 'Ballad for Americans.' When we first played this record, we wondered who Paul Robeson represented. We thought he would tell who he was every time the people on the record asked, 'Who are you?' but he did not. We waited until the end of the record to hear him say 'American!' We were proud to be Americans too" (84). Michael Denning refers to "Ballad for Americans," written by John La Touche and Earl Robinson and performed by Robeson at a pro-Russia rally in 1939, as the Popular Front's "anthem," one that speaks to an inclusive American identity that reaches across race, ethnicity, religion, and class.[45] Shackelford's invocation of the "Ballad for Americans" enables Rex to proclaim his national identity and that of his classmates, as well as to align himself and the text with Popular Front cultural production.[46] The brief discussion of Robeson's song is as direct as Shackelford can be in announcing the progressive politics of her text. As was mentioned earlier, the dominant mode of civil rights discourse was upbeat and resisted calling out directly America's failures or limitations. To criticize segregation overtly smacked of disloyalty during wartime. But Shackelford uses photographs to speak when language cannot. The photos of Rex interacting with his classmates call directly on the reader to understand the political import of her argument. Interestingly, her reluctance to speak about civil rights adheres to the approach of many leftist children's books that feature black characters, as well as her evoking the behavior of some black public figures in integrated settings. For instance, Mickenberg cites Jerrold and Lorraine Beim's book *Two Is a Team*, published the same year as *My Happy Days*, as the first interracial picture book: "Although the illustrations make it very clear, nothing in the text indicates that one of the two friends is white and one is black. Throughout the story, the two boys play together and learn that everything works out better when they cooperate."[47] In Langston Hughes's *The First Book of Negroes* (1952), a black child, Terry, goes to a Louis Armstrong concert with a white boy, David, but no mention of the interracial depiction appears in the language. Depictions of black public figures in interracial settings sometimes emphasized the lack of discussion of racial politics as a form of triumph: if the figure did not mention race, he or she was a credit to interracial dynamics. Mary White Ovington wrote in the *Crisis* in 1937 of scientist George Washington Carver's lecture tour to white colleges: "Without saying a word on the subject of race, Professor Carver is the best propagandist for the doctrine of good fellowship that the Interracial Commission knows."[48] If silence on the subject of race was a form of cultural power, then the photographs in *My Happy Days* spoke of the need for integration without saying a word.

Reviews and Intertextuality as Suggestive of Cultural Significance
The text may be silent, but reviewers took note of the political imperatives of the book, commenting in terms of its resonance both with official antiracism and with progressive antisegregation efforts. Responding to the overt race-liberal message, reviews of the text focus on the color-blind "American" identity of Rex and the contentment of his companionate family.[49] *Survey Graphic* offered the book a three-page spread in February 1945, reproducing several of the images of Rex with his friends at school, including one that depicts Dad as a "pal." Phyllis A. Whitney of the *Chicago Sun Book Week* asserted, "They are the happy days of any American child. In fact, I doubt if a better portrait has ever been presented of our healthy everyday American life." Whitney connected the book's depiction of a black family to the war effort, explaining that the elements of Rex's life are "the things we are fighting for now across the world." She then evoked the international embarrassment that results from racism at home: "Three quarters of the people of the earth are not 'white.' . . . [W]hen we speak of Democracy and the Four Freedoms these people look to our treatment of the American Negro to see how much we really mean our words."[50] The review that particularly emphasizes the photographs as silently speaking about social change was W. E. Garrison's in the *Christian Century:*

> Among the books making for the demolition of the walls of prejudice between Negroes and whites, this is one of the most effective that has come to my attention—and it does not say a word about the subject. Neither the word "prejudice" nor any synonym for it occurs in the book, and the word "Negro" is used only once. The question of Negro life and of

the Negro's place in the American scene is lifted out of the area of controversy and is approached from such an angle that, since argument for
the Negro's rights is avoided, counter-argument is obviously irrelevant.[51]

The review praises Shackelford for excluding incendiary terms like "'social
equality,' jimcrow cars, racial segregation in schools and churches" that would
immediately generate "heat" from white readers. Instead, according to Garrison, the text succeeds in advancing these causes by stating nothing in words and
allowing the photographs to demonstrate affinity in democratic values and material affluence between whites and blacks. Another review that reads the text
as advocating integration came from Mrs. Paul (Eslanda) Robeson, who wrote
in the *Hartford Courant*, "The fact that Rex Nelson is a Negro is incidental, as I
believe it should be. However, it may occur to some alert white folks that they
are missing a great deal when they segregate themselves from the Nelsons and
the many Negro families like them!"[52] Reviews do not mention the fair color
of Rex's skin, nor do they register the text's leftist elements; but they do understand the book as advancing the cause of school integration, and in this those
leftist elements are certainly contributive. This quiet book about the life of a
black American family resonated with reviewers across the country in large part
because it was articulated in the codes of verbal silence and visual articulation
that were palatable during a moment of profound cultural tension.

Shackelford is also conspicuously interventionist in the field of photographic
representation, because she saw her text as a response to Stella Gentry Sharpe
and Charles Farrell's photobook for children *Tobe* (1939).[53] Although she ad-
mired the production value of *Tobe*, she wished to represent black suburbia and
to dislodge photographic representations from their depiction of black children
performing agrarian work. Aside from Shackelford's resistance to agrarian identity, however, the books intersect ideologically and reveal a shared investment in
using photography for antiprejudice work. Sharpe, a white educator from North
Carolina, collaborated with Farrell, a white photographer, to produce a book
that, in part, was written to show the affinities between rural workers across
races, as Sharpe indicates in a biographical statement included in Farrell's papers: "It is not an unusual family. They do not have a hard life, and they always
have enough of everything to live healthy normal country lives. The games that
Tobe and his brothers play are just the sort of games that all country children,
both white and colored, play in this part of the South. Tobe's mother does the
same things that every farmer's wife does. I do the same things myself."[54] Such
an equalizing impulse, one that equates black and white, anticipates Shackel-

ford's depiction of a "typical" American home and makes evident the impulse toward friendship through commonalities in photobooks. The origins of *Tobe*, according to Farrell, point to a guiding desire to use children's photobooks to refute racist stereotypes, a feature that further links Shackelford to Sharpe. Farrell explains in his papers that a black child asked Sharpe to write a book that rejected stereotypes: "Tobe was a six year old colored boy who lived on the farm of Mrs. Stella Gentry Sharpe. One day he asked Mrs. Sharpe why all his books were about little white children. He said he would like to read about nice little colored children who didn't talk like Hambone. Mrs. Sharpe thought this a good idea."[55] The characters in *Tobe* do not speak in the vernacular, and the book does not draw on pickaninny stereotypes but represents farm labor straightforwardly, if ideally, much as Shackelford idealizes black suburbia. In fact, *Tobe*'s upbeat depiction of labor and photographs of a modern school building drew disapproval from the National Child Labor Committee, which criticized the book in its magazine *The American Child* and wrote directly to Farrell with statistics about child labor in the South and school attendance. African American publications like *Opportunity* magazine embraced the southern idealization: "*Tobe* is without reservation the finest juvenile book on Negro life in America yet to come off the press. It is made so by the sympathetic, intelligent treatment accorded the subject matter by the author and by the meticulous care and painstaking accuracy with which Charles Farrell posed and photographed the pictures to illustrate it."[56] One might also see *Tobe* as participating in the milieu of the Farm Security Administration representations of African Americans, because it connects with Jack Delano's series of photographs on the life of Boyd Jones, a black rural child worker. Natanson describes the Jones series:

> Delano's presentation of black well-being, for all its shortcomings, avoided some of the most demeaning typecasting. It was a bright, able, generally dignified Boyd, more than an entertaining Boyd, who took center stage here, as would be the case with the many Boyd equivalents rendered by Gordon Parks for the OWI. The assumption, implicit in the Jones series, that blacks formed part of the nation's rural backbone was not without its progressive implications in 1941: strength deserved cultivation, in economic terms and perhaps beyond. Still, these implications remained distant.[57]

These early photobooks of black-child culture convey further intertextual echoes. Farrell's papers suggest that *Tobe* was in fact a reaction against *Flop-*

Eared Hound (1938), a photographic book for children by Ellis Credle and her husband, Charles de Kay Townsend, a photographer with the National Gallery of Art. Credle's book first caught the attention of *Tobe*'s editor at the University of North Carolina Press, William T. Couch, because its photographs were taken in North Carolina and it was published by Oxford University Press. But Credle's book includes objectionable stereotypes drawn from pickaninny images in popular culture, and Couch had established a reputation for publishing socially progressive texts. William Stott notes that Couch had already issued a number of important photographic books for adults: "The University of North Carolina Press published a series of books on rural life—Charles M. Wilson's *Backwoods America* (1934), and Muriel Sheppard's *Cabins in the Laurel* (1935), for example—with superb, and unaccountably forgotten, photographs by Bayard Wootten."[58] In fact, prominent journalist Gerald W. Johnson wrote to Farrell about the open-mindedness of the University of North Carolina Press, concluding that *Tobe* "is one of the subtlest arguments about race prejudice I know."[59] From the OWI, to Credle, to Sharpe, to Shackelford, we hear intertextual reverberations, as each photographer and writer shape and reshape the meaning and uses of black childhood.

Shackelford herself saw her picture book functioning in tandem with *Tobe* as a means of recouping the black family and resisting stereotypical representations of black childhood. Her papers reflect the influence of Langston Hughes's 1932 essay "Books and the Negro Child" in the *Children's Library Yearbook*, in which he explains that "[f]aced too often by the segregation and the scorn of the surrounding white world, America's Negro children are in pressing need of books that will give them back their own souls. They do not know the beauty they possess."[60] Shackelford includes this passage several times in her papers, commenting at one point, "I am trying to write books that will supply that need. 'My Happy Days' like 'Tobe' has splendid photographs of real Negro children *doing what other children do.*"[61] Moreover, Shackelford was resolutely in charge of the photographs taken by Cecil Vinson, a white principal of the Cruft School in Terre Haute. At one point, Vinson suggested taking photographs of "two little *unkempt* colored boys" because " 'people will feel sorry for them and do for them' "; Shackelford replied, "I did not want people to feel sorry for them, I wanted people to *respect* them."[62] Shackelford's text shares much ideologically with that of Sharpe: both are intertextual responses to earlier photographic books, and both idealize a black family in order to intervene in race relations and in representations of black childhood.[63] Shackelford's insistence on respect for black childhood, both in her papers and in the text, links her to efforts at material change in school integration.

Rex Manuel Jr., the actual child pictured in Vinson's photographs, suffered greatly for the way in which his appearance unsettled racial lines. According to Shackelford's papers, Rex as a teenager signed up for swimming classes at the YMCA in Terre Haute. After taking classes for a week, he appeared at the pool, and the instructor would not let him enter, saying, "'I'm sorry, Rex, I hate to tell you this, but we didn't know you were colored. Some of the parents found out and they objected. They said they wouldn't let their boys go in if you were allowed in the pool. It isn't the boys, Rex. They're crazy about you. I want you to know that.'" A few weeks later, on July 15, 1948, Rex went swimming in a gravel pit and drowned. Shackelford recounts her sister's response: "'O, Jane, that YMCA has killed my son, and they call themselves Christians." Writing late in her life, Shackelford concludes her discussion by noting that Rex's death happened *"before* the Civil Rights Movement,"[64] noting the difficult racial climate faced by young African American people, a period when candid antiprejudice work was difficult to carry out. Shackelford's book trusts in the power of the photograph, the image yoking the supposed innocence of technology with the innocent before the lens in an attempt to dispel racial prejudice. The first image in the book is perhaps the most poignant in considering the impact of the book, its context, and the fate of black children like Rex under prejudice (Figure 1.7). This close-up of the child's open and smiling face suggests a naive trust in the interaction between reader and subject. The language focuses on meeting Rex, as though he were stepping out of the photograph to shake a reader's hand: "My name is Rex Nelson. I am eight years old. I live in a city. I go to Carter Woodson School. All my days are happy days. Let me tell you why" (2). To represent an innocent black child is an act of resistance in and of itself: it permits resistance to racist systems of power that malign and distort blackness through caricature; it enables resistance to the exclusion of black childhood from the terrain of childhood innocence;[65] and it allows black adults and children a renewed faith in the power of childhood to remake social relations. Rex's straightforward gaze emerging from the picture book connotes the era's fundamental hopefulness about

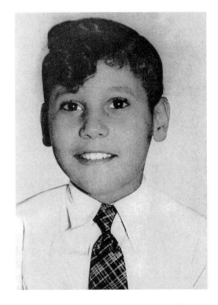

Figure 1.7. An opening image of Rex, dressed up. From Jane Dabney Shackelford, *My Happy Days* (Washington, D.C.: The Associated Publishers, Inc., 1944). Photograph by Cecil Vinson. Reprinted with the permission of the Association for the Study of African American Life & History, http://www.asalh.org/.

the possibility of transformed social relations in the wake of the democratic ideology of World War II. A late image of Rex in *My Happy Days* places him in the cockpit of a small plane as it soars high above Terre Haute. Rex's father's friend, a pilot, has let Rex sit at the controls, and the text reads, "I watched the altimeter as we rose higher and higher. When we were one thousand feet high I looked down. What a sight it was!" After they land, Rex repeats a phrase his father had said earlier: "'[Y]ou haven't really seen this old world until you see it from an airplane'" (106). The text draws to a close with this image of modernity and vision enabled by distance, a distance one might read metaphorically as representing the distance between the "happy days" depicted in the photobook and the lived experience of the child Rex. As Rex takes flight, he embodies the text's sense of hopefulness and possibility. Soaring high above the town, Rex is a black child without limits.

MY DOG RINTY: PROGRESSIVE EDUCATION, CHILDREN'S PUBLISHING, AND THE DOCUMENTARY PHOTOGRAPHIC TRADITION

Understanding *My Happy Days* relies on the contexts of culture, politics, and reception. With those elements in mind, my reading of Ellen Tarry's *My Dog Rinty* (1946), published two years after *My Happy Days*, turns to midcentury children's education and publishing as lenses for understanding Tarry's political intent. Tarry's experience as the Bank Street School of Education's first Negro Scholarship recipient and her relationship with May Massee and Alexander Alland through Viking Press combined to produce Tarry's landmark story of African American childhood in Harlem.[66] Her first two picture books, *Janie Belle* (1940), which was illustrated by Myrtle Shelton, and *Hezekiah Horton* (1942), which was illustrated by the prominent African American cartoonist Oliver Harrington, each concentrated on relationships between black children and white adults in New York City. Neither book is without its limitations—*Janie Belle* idealizes an adoption by a white nurse of a black child who was left in a trash can, and *Hezekiah Horton* depicts a black child's desire to drive a white man's car—but they both apparently were drawn from Tarry's experience in an interracial social community.[67] With the publication of *Janie Belle*, Tarry became the first African American picture-book author.[68] Her most significant children's text is *My Dog Rinty*, the photographic picture book that allowed Tarry to give substance to her ideas about urban black culture: the material and spiritual beauty of Harlem's families and larger community is Tarry's main concern. Whereas *My Happy Days* refocused attention on an insular family within suburbia, *Rinty* reaches outward into the streets and public spaces of Harlem, allowing Tarry to take the reader on a visual tour of Harlem's landmark sites. Like Shackelford's account, Tarry's book has a palpable social discourse; but instead of supporting school integration, the book advocates for housing reform in urban sites and, in doing so, interacts with a documentary photographic tradition that spotlighted the decrepit kitchenettes and slums inhabited by urban families. Tarry's work thus gathers and restyles ideas from the major cultural forces of progressive education, mainstream children's publishing, and documentary photography. In terms of photography, if *My Happy Days* takes *Life* magazine as its originary influence, *My Dog Rinty* responds overtly to the urban documentary photographic tradition.

The fictional impulse within a photographic book might seem peculiar, but in fact Tarry and Alland extend the approach of many documentary books from the 1930s. In the most celebrated photobooks for adults, like James Agee and Walker Evans's *Let Us Now Praise Famous Men* (1941) and Erskine Caldwell and Margaret Bourke-White's *You Have Seen Their Faces* (1937), the subjectivity of the observer becomes paramount, whether that be in the way Caldwell imagines the voice of the people in Bourke-White's photographs or in Agee's long ruminations that sometimes appear disconnected from Evans's images. An element of fictionalization, then, goes hand in hand with the supposed truth telling of the photographs. *My Dog Rinty* takes this dimension further in fully fictionalizing the story; although the title might suggest that the story purports to be a first-person account, as in *My Happy Days* (which is also fictionalized—there was no Carter Woodson School in Terre Haute, for instance), the narration of *Rinty* is entirely in third person, though the naive close-up of the boy subject, David, demands—as in Shackelford—that the reader engage with the innocent child subject (Figure 1.8). There is an intimacy that comes through a visual connection with the child, one that evokes the race-liberal insistence on friendship as a means to social progress; in Tarry's case,

Figure 1.8. David sits with his arm around Rinty, the dog. From Ellen Tarry and Marie Hall Ets, *My Dog Rinty* (New York: The Viking Press, Inc., 1946). Illustrations by Alexander and Alexandra Alland. Reprinted by permission of SSL/Sterling Lord Literistic, Inc. Copyright by Ellen Tarry and Marie Hall Ets.

empathy for David extends into the fictional rendering of his life in Harlem. The neighborhood becomes as much a character as the child, and friendship with David extends into a friendship with Harlem.

Ellen Tarry, Progressive Education, and Viking Press

Studying at the Bank Street College of Education from 1937 to 1939, Tarry developed friendships with educator Lucy Sprague Mitchell and Margaret Wise Brown, author of landmark picture books like *Goodnight Moon* and *The Runaway Bunny*. Tarry became the first Negro Scholarship recipient at Bank Street after her friend Claude McKay turned down an offer from children's librarian Augusta Baker, who had contacts at the school. What Tarry found at Bank Street surprised her: "Since I was a product of public, state, and convent schools, I was bewildered by my first contacts with progressive education. The children in both schools at Bank Street [the Harriet Johnson Nursery School and the Little Red Schoolhouse] came from ultra-modern homes and their frankness, particularly that of the nursery school children, was in direct contrast to my mid-Victorian upbringing."[69] In an interview, Tarry confided that she was "appalled" that "these children just treated everyone like a companion."[70] In fact, the revolutions in psychological theory so influential to Shackelford's text—the antifascist movement that endorsed family love, equality, and companionship—have manifest connections with the progressive-education movement.[71]

The Bank Street School's emphasis on learning through lived experience and its nurturance of children's creativity and capability crystallized in Mitchell's famous aesthetic philosophy of the "here and now." In short, Mitchell emphasized the need for literature to address the lived experience and sensory impressions of young readers, and her school instituted a writing laboratory in which writers (like Tarry) could share their work with actual young people and could hear the stories created by the children in order to get a better sense of the young people's perspective and interests. Much has been written about the influence of the Bank Street School and the here-and-now philosophy on the trajectory of twentieth-century children's literature, as it shifted children's publishing away from the fantastic and toward books that connected with the world around children, like those that depicted machinery, building, household goods, and family-life experiences.[72] Importantly, the Bank Street philosophy was not divested from social concerns, as Mickenberg explains: "In Mitchell's view of things, 'social education' was one of the most important aspects of her teacher-training program. A teacher 'must care,' she said, 'both about children and the world. He must have convictions. He must have a definite approach to life situations which include what he wishes children to become and what he wishes the world to become.'"[73] A commitment to the legitimacy of the urban experience of children came to the fore, as Mitchell and her colleagues envisioned the city as a place where greater social equality could take place through an awareness of the variety of people and their relationships.

For Tarry, who soon embraced the liberating perspective of Bank Street, progressive education permitted her to consider the way in which children's literature could be linked to her own experience, the here-and-now of one young writer's life in Harlem. Tarry remained surprised (even when interviewed at age ninety-three) that readers did not appreciate her attempts to tell the truth about her experience of interracial friendships in urban settings. Speaking of *Janie Belle*, Tarry said it "ran into great difficulty because Southern readers said that it would be offensive to Southerners—this business of a white nurse adopting a black baby"; she further insisted that because the story spoke to her own fear as a child that she was actually adopted (she was a light-skinned child who did not resemble her father), the story was perfectly within the here-and-now perspective of "writing from your experience and the experience of children."[74] When she turned to photographic picture books, she found a milieu for assumed truth telling about childhood in the city that did not, apparently, cause problems among white audiences. Tarry saw *My Dog Rinty* as the first picture book to address black childhood in a city, and although she considered Stella Sharpe's *Tobe* positively—"A beautiful child, lovely illustrations, but it was not the urban scene"[75]—she explained to the *Baltimore Afro-American* the need for books about the black experience in cities: "So many children live in the city that it is essential to have a book on and about them."[76]

Tarry did not initiate the composition of *My Dog Rinty*. It emerged from the publishing structure of Viking Press and its powerful children's-book editor, May Massee. According to Tarry, the children's writer Marie Hall Ets, author of three books before *My Dog Rinty*, contacted Massee to ask whether Ets could collaborate with Tarry. According to Tarry, a letter arrived from Massee "telling me that she had another writer who had seen my work and was interested in a collaboration because there was a need for a book depicting the urban black child."[77] Together, in 1944, Ets and Tarry drew up an outline for the book, and they collaborated on its composition until the birth of Tarry's daughter, in November 1944, and into the spring of 1945. Initially, Tarry thought the book would be illustrated, but Massee made the choice to use photographs. Tarry explains Massee's rationale: "She said trends in illustration would change, but pictures would remain. So that was her idea. . . . She *insisted* on the photographs."[78]

Massee imagined the photographic genre as marketable and compelling, and Viking had a long track record in race novels and photobooks. The initial conception of *My Dog Rinty* thus appears to have been generated by Massee and Ets rather than Tarry, although Tarry seemed like an ideal partner, given her background at Bank Street and publication of interracial, urban illustrated picture books.

Once the photographic production began, however, the book went squarely into Tarry's hands, as she coordinated the images with the photographer, Alexander Alland, and persuaded African American individuals and businesses to participate. She first selected a family, originally from Haiti, whom she had met at the interracial Catholic Friendship House, where she volunteered.[79] When Tarry wished to have them photographed at their own house, Massee objected. Tarry explains: "She said we couldn't use their furniture because he [the father] was a French upholsterer and all the furniture was fancy. She said, 'We can't have that. Nobody would expect to see all that French furniture in Harlem.' "[80] As a result, Tarry used her own house, her own daughter as the baby in the photographs, and her friends, like Augusta Baker,[81] as figures in the photographs. As a result, the text as a combination of word and image reads as Tarry's creation rather than that of her coauthor, Ets, whose work for children had focused on animal stories and *The Story of a Baby* (1939), an illustrated explanation of childbirth. Once the editor selected the medium of photographs, as well as the urban setting, the book became Tarry's: "The story was written but we had to find a 'typical' family and get permission to take pictures. Though it was hard finding a family to fit our needs, getting permission to take pictures in homes, places of business, public service centers, and churches in Harlem was an enormous task. My people's understandable suspicion of the white man and anything connected with the white man's world created situations which would have defeated the purpose of the book if I had not presumed upon many friendships."[82] Just as Shackelford refused to permit her photographer to take images she did not approve, Tarry had control over the types of scenes captured on film; the preceding description, from Tarry's autobiography, says much about the hesitancy among African Americans to permit themselves to be represented by whites, reflecting the urban dweller's awareness of the way in which photographs have been used to exploit the urban poor.

Alexander Alland and Cultural Gifts

The photographer for *My Dog Rinty*, Alexander Alland, is best remembered today for rescuing from obscurity the photographs of urban documentarians

Jacob Riis, Jessie Tarbox Beals, and Robert Bracklow. Alland's work rediscovering Riis, the social-documentary photographer who published *How the Other Half Lives* (1890), included unearthing glass negatives by the photographer and producing a new exhibit of Riis's work in 1947, entitled "The Battle with the Slum, 1887–1897," at the Museum of the City of New York.[83] But in the early to mid-1940s, Alland was deeply invested in the work of the Common Council of American Unity, serving as the photography editor for its journal, *Common Ground*, from 1941 to 1944. During this period, Alland worked with Louis Adamic, the multiculturalist who supported recognition of America's ethnic diversity. According to Denning, "Adamic's vision was one of uplift and education: his 'nation of nations' project was a series of books on different ethnic and racial groups, a vast counterencyclopedia of America. *Common Ground* was invented as the voice of this 'diversity,' this 'multicultural America,' to use terms to which Adamic himself appealed."[84] As its photography editor, Alland published in *Common Ground* a variety of pictures of particular ethnic experiences; and in an interview about his experience as a Russian Jewish immigrant, Alland positioned himself as a photographic version of Adamic: "Louis Adamic, I don't know if you know the man, the famous author on the subject of ethnic groups, he's an author of many, many books which are known in the series Nation of Nations. So I began to do [in] pictures what he did in writing."[85]

Alland published two significant photographic books just before *My Dog Rinty*, and awareness of their position helps uncover the import of his collaboration with Tarry. The first of Alland's books was *American Counterpoint* (1943), which describes itself as a "family album" of America based on images of ethnic individuals and small groups.[86] Much like those in *Rinty* and *My Happy Days*, the photographs in *American Counterpoint* are captioned by fictional "testimony" of the subjects' experience as ethnic Americans. Alland sometimes uses first person, as in the first section, which includes an image of a contemporary Native American drinking tea and eating a doughnut: "Sure, I'm an American! . . . My people came here from Siberia maybe ten, maybe twenty-five thousand years ago. Sure, they were immigrants too! If you ask me, you're all pretty recent arrivals. I'm what you call an American Indian, but I'd rather be called just American, like the rest of you."[87] Most of the photographs in the text are captioned not with narrative, however, but with the particular name of the ethnicity represented, such as "Danish American" and "Portuguese American,"[88] and most of the images include some American iconography—a flag in the background or on a pin worn by an individual—as well as signifiers, through dress or activity, of a subject's ethnic heritage. The leftist signification of the book is apparent through images like the "Puerto Rican American," in which a family reads *PM Daily*.[89] Pearl Buck's introduction to *American Counterpoint* places young people at the center of the discourse around ethnicity and tolerance: "The teachers of youth would do well to guide youth's passionate need for conflict toward these [the prejudiced] who really threaten our country, not against those who are innocently born of darker color or of a certain blood."[90] Understanding Alland's perspective on race and American identity in *American Counterpoint* and his next major photographic book, *The Springfield Plan* (1945), is necessary in order to understand Harlem's signification within *My Dog Rinty*.

The Springfield Plan (1945) appeared from Viking Press, the publishing house that would issue *My Dog Rinty*, and was authored by James Waterman Wise. Describing the citywide effort in Springfield, Massachusetts, toward greater intercultural understanding, *The Springfield Plan* contains a range of images of civic and educational settings, many of which depict interracial subjects, like an integrated classroom and integrated government meetings. The Springfield effort seems in line with Adamic's ideas about the importance of ethnic immigrants to the democratic identity of the United States, given that the book includes much discussion of the need for respect for differing national, ethnic, and religious origins.[91] But in its perspective on education, *The Springfield Plan* resembles an earlier, influential model of interracial understanding: the "cultural gifts" movement. The "cultural gifts" movement in education began as a response to anti-immigrant nativism in the 1920s. As Selig explains, this movement envisioned immigrant-group identities as enhancing American national identity.[92] Cultural-gifts education programs often included school reports or performances based on supposedly characteristic qualities or social contributions of particular ethnicities; for instance, a class might enact a Japanese dance, or examine French artwork, or wear Mexican textiles. Within Wise and Alland's *The Springfield Plan*, the cultural-gifts model of education dominates, as the text explains that children in Springfield identify themselves through ethnicity and their curriculum is based around the gifts of their home cultures: "The varied national origins of the children becomes an introduction to the global derivation of the United States. These origins are traced and studied in terms of the major contributions which have been made by immigrants and their descendants from all countries."[93] The term *contributions* in this description echoes the language of the cultural-gifts movement and invokes the need to represent positively, if reductively, the identity of immigrant communities.

African Americans were included as one type of identity within the cultural-gifts movement, and in Alland's Adamic-influenced *American Counterpoint*, they are listed generally as "American Negro" several times,[94] although people of African descent are also identified as "Haitian American" and "Jewish American (Ethiopian Hebrew)."[95] Overall, the cultural-gifts movement did not become invested in the particular legal or political situation of African Americans, eliding issues of violence and injustice. Instead, it advanced the dominant perspective among whites toward developing interracial understanding, and that was through individual attitudinal change rather than systemic or legal transformations. Although Selig does see the cultural-gifts movement as a predecessor to the 1950s and 1960s civil rights movement,[96] in the late 1930s and early 1940s, the cultural-gifts movement resisted singling out black experience and instead placed African Americans alongside immigrant ethnic communities, focusing on national unity in diversity and on each group's cultural contributions to America.[97]

By 1946, the year of *My Dog Rinty*, the cultural-gifts movement had become passé in the face of totalitarianism and Nazi ethnocentrism, because educators feared that embracing particular non-U.S. national traits might dissolve American unity. But the cultural-gifts movement had already had a profound influence on children's literature before *Rinty*, as books began describing ethnic and racial identity as culturally rather than biologically determined.[98] Just as the cultural-gifts movement tended to diminish the particular legal and moral dimensions of African American experience by placing it side-by-side with a range of immigrant cultures, children's publishing focused on ethnicities and their origins through what Nathalie op de Beeck calls its "ethnographic gaze."[99] Cultural gifts may have been out of fashion by 1946, but children's publishing leading up to *Rinty* had been deeply invested in representing the ethnic, immigrant other in terms that emphasize cultural distinctiveness.

Alland and Tarry, then, came to Viking with particular progressive investments that corresponded with trends in education and publishing. Tarry's here-and-now commitment intersected with Alland's desire to demonstrate American inclusiveness and the cultural contributions of particular communities through photography. In many ways, May Massee was on the cutting edge in children's publishing by pursuing a book about an urban black child's experience; no wonder she "insisted" on the photographs and pulled Tarry into writing the book. At Viking, Massee had spearheaded the international multicultural movement in children's literature by publishing, in 1929, what she called "the first of the international picture books"[100] and issuing landmark texts like Marjorie Flack and Kurt Wiese's *The Story of Ping* (1933). In addition to Wise and Alland's *The Springfield Plan*, Viking published Richard Wright and Edwin Rosskam's

12 Million Black Voices (1941), a text that looms large in the background of *My Dog Rinty*. If Massee understood the way in which a photographic book would appeal to progressive educators and audiences, we could consider *Rinty* as interacting with the documentary tradition in order to refute the depiction of urban family life in Wright and Rosskam's book and to offer a new approach to advocating for housing reform.

The Federal Writers Project and the Legacy of Documentary Photobooks

Although there was a range of documentary images of the city in currency in the early 1940s—from the May 1940 *Look* spread (Michael Carter's "244,000 Native Sons"), which presented images from the Photo League's "Harlem Document"[101] to Aaron Siskind's "The Most Crowded Block"[102]—Wright and Rosskam's powerful *12 Million Black Voices* seems a salient precursor to Tarry and Alland's *My Dog Rinty*. Not only were they issued by the same press, but they also both addressed an urban landscape with potent images of family life. *12 Million Black Voices*, an analysis of the dispossession of the rural South and migrations to the urban North, employed Chicago coverage by the Farm Security Administration (FSA) and included images of decrepit kitchenettes and dilapidated tenements and factory houses, as well as the unsmiling families that inhabited them.[103] The connection between Wright and Tarry is genuine, for they worked together on the Federal Writers Project (FWP) in New York City in the mid-1930s, along with Roi Ottley, Claude McKay, Ralph Ellison, Henry Lee Moon, and Ted Poston. Together, Wright and Tarry and others created the copy on Harlem for a major FWP project, the "guidebooks" to New York: *New York Panorama* (1938) and *The WPA Guide to New York City* (1939). FWP guidebooks responded to New Deal stigmatization of Harlem as a ghetto by offering urban planning as the solution to overcrowding and housing shortages, as J. J. Butts explains, and "immersed these writers in the exploration and representation of urban space, a lesson that was remembered in their post-FWP literary work."[104] Along with Wright's photo text, McKay's *Harlem: Negro Metropolis* (1940) and Ottley's *New World A-Coming* (1943) explore urban spaces as indicators of national investment in black citizenship. As Butts reminds us, in guidebooks, "spaces are made to stand in as symbols of the health or decline of the nation."[105] Tarry and Wright, then, emerged from the same training ground, engaged similar urban landscapes, and employed documentary photography, but they argued for radically disparate visions of that landscape and its effect on black citizenship and national commitments.

For the purposes of depicting the black family, Wright and Rosskam altered at least one photograph in order to eliminate the agency of childhood. Nicholas Natanson explains that a portrait of a black mother and her children, taken from a series that originally included the father as well as the mother, became "an illustration for Wright's bemoaning of the broken family."[106] Further, in the original image, a girl was sticking her tongue out at the camera. Natanson argues, "It did not fit the desperate mood of *12 Million Black Voices*, but instead of simply using an alternative image, Rosskam did something worse. Careful retouching erased the girl's tongue, and the cleaned-up image became the illustration for Wright's thundering indictment: 'The kitchenette blights the personalities of our growing children, disorganizes them, blinds them to hope, creates problems whose effects can be traced in the characters of its child victims for years afterwards.'"[107] Although space precludes a close comparison of *Rinty* to *Black Voices*, one can imagine Wright and Rosskam's image of the victimized black family looming overhead. Rosskam's erasure of the feisty black child becomes particularly salient for understanding the impetus behind *Black Voices*'s representation of the black urban family: fatherless, crumbling, complacent, wretched, the family unit is destroyed by the urban blight that surrounds it.

Although Wright's vision may diverge profoundly from Tarry's, the FWP drew the two writers together and generated a sense of mutual admiration. According to Tarry's biography, Wright appeared at the FWP as a young, introverted person, and Tarry was asked by other writers to draw him out into conversation. She then brought him to the Bank Street School to discuss *Uncle Tom's Children*, his collection of short stories: "The thirteen-year-olds at the Little Red Schoolhouse were anxious to meet him and he went down with me one day and talked to them at length."[108] In an interview, Tarry suggested that Wright's connection with the children at Bank Street had much to do with his lack of pretentiousness: "[H]e was basically a—he had the simplicity of a child. There was something refreshing about him."[109] When Wright was criticized for Communist affiliation upon the publication of *Native Son*, Tarry wrote a passionate essay in the liberal Catholic magazine *Commonweal*, titled "Native Daughter," in which she "rejoice[s]" over his success and challenges her largely white readership, saying, "Without a doubt Mr. Wright is recording the harvest of hate that White America has, perhaps unwittingly, sown. Can you honestly blame him?"[110] Friends and coworkers on the FWP, Tarry and Wright turned their attention toward the city space, and although *My Dog Rinty* and *12 Million Black Voices* diverge substantially, both writers, trained through guidebook writing, examined urban spaces as indicators of cultural and national health. The differences may well be generic, as children's picture books in the 1940s required an upbeat outlook, as well as philosophical, given that Tarry's Catholicism and embrace of interracial collaboration fueled her fundamentally optimistic perspective on race and national identity.

Rinty's rebuttal to the vision of *Black Voices* rests on the former's depiction of an intact, attentive family within an urban space. The first image that greets us depicts the family at home, and all but one member of the family is involved in reading (Figure 1.9). Although this image contains elements that interact with the visual language of black poverty—the boy on the right's clothes are torn, and the child on the far left wears working overalls—the image clearly underlines the fact that the children are actively pursuing education. Further, the father dominates this picture: while he sits in his chair, his family flanks him in a half circle; he is clearly present, the center of the family.

Figure 1.9. David's family reads together in the evening. From Ellen Tarry and Marie Hall Ets, *My Dog Rinty* (New York: The Viking Press. Inc., 1946). Illustrations by Alexander and Alexandra Alland. Reprinted by permission of SSL/Sterling Lord Literistic, Inc. Copyright by Ellen Tarry and Marie Hall Ets.

In an image that comes soon after, the mother is pictured in a kitchen, visually interacting within the kitchenettes so crucial to the Wright and Rosskam text (Figure 1.10). Although the background of the kitchen seems worn down and the mother's hem is undone, the focus is on the element of the narrative the image depicts: David gives his mother a note from his teacher about his dog being a nuisance at school, a plot element that demonstrates the collaboration of home and school in the black child's life. We see that narrative pulls the reader away from lingering on the economic or material status of the subjects.[111] Like Shackelford, who lets the images suggest the unfinished process of child citizenship, Tarry here introduces the impoverished city space without pathologizing it.

On balance, other representations of domestic spaces within *Rinty* approach the idealistic. An image of a neighbor's house shows a mother bathing her baby

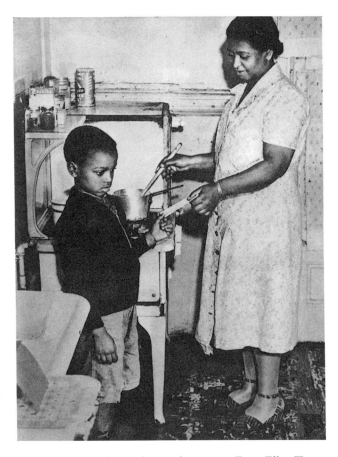

Figure 1.10. David gives his mother a note. From Ellen Tarry and Marie Hall Ets, *My Dog Rinty* (New York: The Viking Press, Inc., 1946). Illustrations by Alexander and Alexandra Alland. Reprinted by permission of SSL/Sterling Lord Literistic, Inc. Copyright by Ellen Tarry and Marie Hall Ets.

in front of frilly curtains while wearing a ladies' suit. In another image, at a friend's house, the boys wear neckties and play with an electric train on a beautiful rug. Sitting in an ornate chair next to a bookshelf, a girl wearing dainty shoes and a delicate headband cuddles a black doll (Figure 1.11). At dinnertime at David's house, the family gathers around a table set with a tablecloth and enjoy a dessert together. The chairs might not match, but the visual emphasis falls again on the dominant presence of the father in the home. His back turned to the camera, as though protecting his family by blocking the viewer from the

Figure 1.11. David visits friends, who play with train sets and African American dolls. From Ellen Tarry and Marie Hall Ets, *My Dog Rinty* (New York: The Viking Press, Inc., 1946). Illustrations by Alexander and Alexandra Alland. Reprinted by permission of SSL/Sterling Lord Literistic, Inc. Copyright by Ellen Tarry and Marie Hall Ets.

intimate space of the table, the father is the largest figure in the image. The intact, involved, committed family is at the heart of Tarry and Alland's portrait of urban life.

My Dog Rinty is a bifurcated book, its attention split between depicting the home space and offering images of buildings in Harlem. Rinty repeatedly gets free of David and runs through the streets of Harlem with the child on his tail. As a result, the reader is able to see images of the outer life of Harlem as well as the inner, a move that echoes Tarry's experience on the FWP guidebooks; in *Rinty*, Harlem becomes nearly a tourist site.[112] *Rinty*'s dualistic quality also attaches the book to that of Wright and Rosskam, who themselves spend much visual attention on a version of urban decay, focusing on empty lots, falling-down houses, and "the streets" that "claim our children,"[113] as well as to the work of

Hughes and DeCarava, as we will see. As David chases his dog around Harlem in *Rinty*, the reader visits visually the businesses and municipal establishments that characterize a flourishing middle-class community. David stops in a five-and-dime run by a well-dressed woman in pearls, passes by a tempting candy store, and visits the library to listen to story hour, which includes a photograph of the illustrious Augusta Baker. He visits Harlem Hospital, which appears to be an integrated work space, where a black man speaks authoritatively to a group that includes what could be read as a white nurse, while a racially ambiguous clerk works nearby (Figure 1.12).

David and his sister visit "Sugar Hill where the rich people live," and they gaze with admiration at the beautiful buildings while a man tells them, "[E]verybody knows 555. That's where Joe Louis lives when he is in town. It's that place up the street where the doctor is going in" (Figure 1.13).[114] The

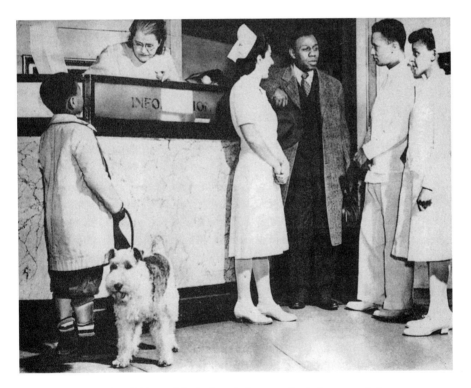

Figure 1.12. David and Rinty visit the hospital, a seemingly integrated site. From Ellen Tarry and Marie Hall Ets, *My Dog Rinty* (New York: The Viking Press, Inc., 1946). Illustrations by Alexander and Alexandra Alland. Reprinted by permission of SSL/Sterling Lord Literistic, Inc. Copyright by Ellen Tarry and Marie Hall Ets.

Figure 1.13. David and Rinty visit Sugar Hill, an affluent section of Harlem. From Ellen Tarry and Marie Hall Ets, *My Dog Rinty* (New York: The Viking Press, Inc., 1946). Illustrations by Alexander and Alexandra Alland. Reprinted by permission of SSL/Sterling Lord Literistic, Inc. Copyright by Ellen Tarry and Marie Hall Ets.

celebratory vision of Harlem recalls the stylish street portraits of James Van Der Zee, photographer during the Harlem Renaissance, who would take images of the black middle class proudly standing beside Cadillacs, donned in furs. Alland's visual portrait of Harlem culminates in a double-page spread of 125th Street (Figure 1.14). Automobiles race past a thriving business district dominated by the movie theater at its center, with well-dressed people strolling along the street. David and his dog are barely noticeable in the image, their bodies dwarfed by the large display windows and signs for the Palm Café, a prominent jazz club and site of radio broadcasts; the Harlem Opera House movie theater; and the Lido jewelry store. With this vision of Harlem in mind, it becomes apparent that Alland and Tarry wish to stage their own version of the cultural-gifts movement by focusing on the material and aesthetic accomplishments of

Harlem. In contrast to the degraded urban spaces in photobooks like that of Wright and Rosskam, Alland and Tarry offer the best of Harlem to the reader. Exteriors of buildings mark affluence and accomplishment rather than a totalizing dismissal of black urban potentiality. The "gift" of Harlem is a space where the middle class can flourish and families can stay intact and vital.

Remembering that Rosskam in *12 Million Black Voices* erases child agency, we can understand better Tarry's deliberate focus on the will and experience of an individual child. It is not as though documentary books refused connection between reader and subject. As William Stott explains, "[D]ocumentary treats the actual unimagined experience of individuals belonging to a group generally of low economic and social standing in the society (lower than the audience for whom the report is made) and treats this experience in such a way as to render it vivid, 'human,' and—most often—poignant to the audience."[115] Such sympathy often had a moral purpose and used emotional connection to work toward social change.[116] In no way does *Rinty* represent the down-and-out of Harlem, nor does it make any explicit pleas to the audience for change. Given that it is coming from the same era as *My Happy Days*, we are aware that speaking out about discrimination or intolerable living conditions (especially to a family audience)

Figure 1.14. David and Rinty walk down busy 125th Street in the heart of Harlem. From Ellen Tarry and Marie Hall Ets, *My Dog Rinty* (New York: The Viking Press, Inc., 1946). Illustrations by Alexander and Alexandra Alland. Reprinted by permission of SSL/Sterling Lord Literistic, Inc. Copyright by Ellen Tarry and Marie Hall Ets.

could be read as inflammatory or un-American. But *Rinty* draws on the moral ethos of the documentary tradition in leading the reader toward recognizing the need for reform. Like *My Happy Days*, *My Dog Rinty* relies on friendship and identification rather than sympathy in order to make its case.

Harlem and Housing Reform

By emphasizing the integrity of the black family and the success of the Harlem landscape, Tarry makes an implicit argument for the viability of black culture within the larger American context. This might seem peculiar, making a case for housing reform based on black success under segregation. However, the images of happy, flourishing children stake a claim of shared values and economic ideals, and the success of Harlem argues for the potential ease of integrating black and white economic and social spaces; for Tarry, like Shackelford, did not wish to depict black America as piteous. Instead, she emphasized its successes in the domestic sphere and, with the help of Alland's photographs, its Harlem landmarks, like Sugar Hill and 125th Street. Part of Harlem's distinctiveness in Tarry's picture book is a new housing project. David visits friends who live at "those nice new River Houses." The housing development offers room to play and sights to see: "At 151st Street the children ran first to the playgrounds and looked across the river at the Yankee Stadium. Then they played on the slides." The photograph shows well-dressed children peering both at the camera, as does the hip young man on the middle slide, and at the baseball stadium (Figure 1.15). The Harlem River Houses were built for African Americans in 1937 as a response to the 1935 Harlem riot. They were considered a major success at the time, especially in the face of entrenched segregation, and included a wading pool, health-care office, and child care.[117] As J. J. Butts has discovered, the Harlem River Houses were also a cause for excitement within the *WPA Guide to New York City* (1939), the guidebook to which Tarry and Wright contributed in their work at the FWP. In the guidebook, as in *Rinty*, the Harlem River Houses manifested the state's commitment to providing black citizens a healthy, organized, modern space as an articulation of national belonging. Of course, in life, the erection of housing projects like the Harlem River Houses facilitated a program of urban renewal that eliminated local communities and entrenched racial segregation.[118] But within the world of *Rinty*, it is emblematic of urban success (even if David cannot live there because "[n]o dogs are allowed").

In fact, Tarry's text emerged during a particularly stressful moment for black urban families seeking housing. After World War II, according to May, "Ninety-eight percent of American cities reported shortages of houses, and over

Figure 1.15. David and Rinty visit the Harlem River Houses. From Ellen Tarry and Marie Hall Ets, *My Dog Rinty* (New York: The Viking Press, Inc., 1946). Illustrations by Alexander and Alexandra Alland. Reprinted by permission of SSL/Sterling Lord Literistic, Inc. Copyright by Ellen Tarry and Marie Hall Ets.

90 percent reported shortages of apartments. By 1947, six million families were doubling up with relatives or friends. The housing industry gained tremendous momentum after the war in the face of these immediate needs."[119] Of course, African Americans were often excluded from new housing developments, both in the outer boroughs of New York and in the suburbs. Tarry herself faced housing pressure in New York as she was writing *Rinty*, pregnant and unable to find a place to live.[120] The image of the happy children at the housing project might, then, seem viable, if idealized, progress, or perhaps an articulation of what Butts calls "speculative futurology," in which the health of the project articulated the success of federal housing reform generally.[121]

Despite the mention of the Harlem River project, *Rinty* does not offer a celebratory stance on housing reform. It instead demands affordable, habitable housing through its major plot point: the dog repeatedly escapes and causes damage to businesses and apartments, because he seeks out vermin. For example, the neighbor Mrs. Moseley exclaims to David, "'Just look at this!' And there her beautiful apartment was filled with feathers and down. 'I went out and left him alone, and he chewed up my pillows. And another thing,' she said, 'he jumps on all my friends, and they don't like it. And look at the hole he has chewed in my carpet. He's forever trying to get underneath.'" David figures out that the dog, a "born ratter and mouser," has been digging at carpets and floors throughout Harlem, trying to catch rodents. Eventually, David decides to put Rinty to work catching mice, and he takes out an advertisement for their business in the *New York Age*; they prove to be such a success that they are dubbed "the Pied Pipers of Harlem" and appear on the cover of the newspaper. Harlem residents may have "beautiful" apartments like Mrs. Moseley, signifying their respectability and material success, but what is "underneath," within the structure, is corrupted. A mouse-infested Harlem does not fit with its upright residents, a reader might observe, and the text concludes with the voice of a landlord who vows to take action: "But best of all, the owner of a block of old buildings where the poor people live in Harlem said: 'David and Rinty have shown me that my old buildings are full of holes. I'm going to tear them down and build new ones. And the new ones will have a big yard in the center where children and dogs can play. . . . And I hope David and his family *and his dog* will be the first ones to move in.'" This is the first the reader has heard of "poor people" in Harlem, and by concluding here, Tarry reshapes reader assumptions about the impoverished, as David and his family seem to fall within that category, being invited to live in the new building (we may also have noticed the kitchenette and shabby clothes earlier). And although the landlord evokes real-world housing-reform strategies that bulldozed neighborhoods and displaced the poor, David's community in this narrative would not be ejected from the city but would be reincorporated. Of course, this revitalization has not yet happened, in contrast with the Harlem River example. The text insists that landlords—not the government, as in the case of Harlem River—must take responsibility for the conditions and costs of housing in Harlem. Tarry will not be verbally silent about her book's reform agenda, as is *My Happy Days*, perhaps because Shackelford's argument for school integration might be perceived as more radical.[122] Tarry states her reform goals directly—humane response from property owners, revitalized urban living spaces—and, probably because she did not position a black family, however respectable, within white suburbia, or picture what could read as black and white children playing and learning together, Tarry's book can state outright the desire for quality housing for the respectable residents of Harlem.[123] In many ways, Tarry makes a "race-radical" argument by asserting that the rat infestation is caused by landlord inattention.[124] The landlord character's responsiveness might diffuse the critique a bit, but for a children's picture book in the 1940s, even acknowledging rat infestation and landlord responsibility was quite daring.

This demand for housing reform takes an entirely different approach from that of a vitriolic visual exposé like *12 Million Black Voices*. Yet *Rinty* plays on the same terrain in arguing that urban living conditions require intervention and redemption. Tarry's vision of the black family and investment in respectability link Tarry to Shackelford, but Tarry and Alland relish the particular visual landmarks of Harlem, and in doing so offer a version of the black urban landscape that maintains its inhabitants' dignity. The attitudinal change toward African Americans sought by leftists in the 1940s and by proponents of the cultural-gifts movement that influenced Alland remains a goal of both Tarry's and Shackelford's texts. Tarry's book was read typically as part of the intercultural-understanding movement, as Constance Curtis of the *New York Amsterdam News* wrote (in terms that recall reviews of *My Happy Days*): "David, and his brothers and sisters, parents, teacher and friends, is so typically American that even the most prejudiced cannot question his brown skin. The thought of questioning won't occur to the youthful readers of the book—and another link in the chain of understanding will be forged."[125] For this reviewer, the photographic book for children became a site of transformative human contact and connection. That desire for human understanding, for friendship between the races, structures responses to Tarry. But in addition to confirming the tenets of racial liberalism, Tarry's work benefits by its investment in the Bank Street School aesthetic, in Alland's embrace of cultural distinctiveness, and in exposing the material and structural causes of urban housing troubles. *My Dog Rinty*'s celebratory images of Harlem oppose documentary narratives of black pathology, offering black and white readers the rewards of a here-and-now version of modern, successful African American life. In doing so, the book also reminds a reader of the inadequacies of Harlem housing and the practical failures of social justice in the United States.

THE SWEET FLYPAPER OF LIFE: HUGHES AND DECARAVA'S CHILDHOOD IN HARLEM

Langston Hughes and Roy DeCarava collaborated on what would become the most important midcentury photographic picture book about Harlem, *The Sweet*

Flypaper of Life (1955). For black writers, the years between 1946 (which saw the publication of *My Dog Rinty*) and 1955 bore palpable changes aesthetically and politically. In African American literature, attention to urban experience, which was so important to Wright's work and to Ann Petry's popular *The Street* (1946), continued, but approaches became more experimental. For instance, Gwendolyn Brooks's Pulitzer Prize–winning book of poems chronicling a girl's growth into adulthood, *Annie Allen* (1949), contains a section titled "The Anniad," an epic poem indebted to *The Aeneid*. The profound accomplishment of Ralph Ellison's *The Invisible Man* (1952), a National Book Award winner, indelibly attaches the experimental to the urban in a spectacular narrative of individual and cultural transformation. James Baldwin published his first novel, *Go Tell It on the Mountain* (1953), a city novel that eloquently incorporates biblical rhetoric in its depiction of religious disillusionment. In short, the decade between *Rinty* and *Flypaper* brought new ways of treating urban spaces and social critique, new approaches to narrative voice and structure.

Although this period prefaced the explosion of civil rights activity after the mid-1950s, landmark legal and social developments set the stage for the grassroots action that would come. The inspirational accomplishment of Jackie Robinson's April 15, 1947, debut with the Brooklyn Dodgers anticipated larger integration efforts, and Truman's Executive Order 9981, issued in 1948, required the end of discrimination in the armed forces. Military desegregation took place in the early 1950s, although, like school desegregation to come, it was not uniformly executed. In 1950, Ralph Bunche won the Nobel Peace Prize for his work on the 1949 Armistice Agreements in the Middle East, becoming the first nonwhite person to attain the award. A turning point for this period arrived on May 17, 1954, with the Supreme Court decision of *Brown v. Board of Education, Topeka, Kansas*, which was argued in 1952 and 1953. The *Brown* decision asserted that public school segregation violated the Fourteenth Amendment's clause on equal protection, and overturned the 1896 "separate but equal" decision of *Plessy v. Ferguson*. Alongside the public accomplishments of Jackie Robinson and Ralph Bunche, the *Brown* decision made legal efforts at civil rights change visible on the national stage.

Published the year after *Brown v. Board of Education*, *The Sweet Flypaper of Life* thus emerges in a different context than that of *My Happy Days* and *My Dog Rinty*: a decade's time had lessened the postwar cultural demand for idealized domesticity and had seen the emphasis on individual affective response in reshaping race relations develop into the *Brown* case, a legal battle based not on federal investment but on violation of the individual rights of the plaintiffs.[126]

The personal and emotional effects of racism were at the heart of that decision, as they were in the famous Kenneth and Mamie Clark doll experiments, which served as evidence for black psychological damage under segregation. In this context, photography of children remained an affective endeavor. Hughes and DeCarava developed their photographic book in order to render black childhood and the family with great affection and gentleness. Their aims aesthetically were interventionist in the same way as those of Shackelford and Tarry: all three texts dismantle assumptions of black familial degradation, contesting portraits from a sociological tradition that emphasized black-child victimhood in the face of poverty and racial bias. However, Hughes and DeCarava did not use images as a call to action, as did Shackelford on school integration and Tarry on housing reform. Instead, their portrait emphasizes the liminality of the child and the black community in the wake of the *Brown* decision. *Flypaper* offers a portrait that, like the earlier children's books, imagines the integrity and agency of childhood within the family and in the face of social change, but the aesthetic approach involves the sophistication and nuance of the more experimental adult texts of the period. Part of the difference between the earlier children's texts and *Flypaper* has to do with narration: Hughes and DeCarava present the ambivalences of the urban space through an adult narrator who describes children rather than through a child focalizer. The warm and playful voice of Mary, Hughes's narrator, speaks affectionately of the Harlem community, even with its limitations and disappointments, an approach that, as in Tarry's book, implicitly talks back to the thundering, righteous collective narration of Wright's *12 Million Black Voices*. But Hughes frames the city space neither through child ingenuity nor through indignation but through the perspective of a homey, tender, knowing adult.

Flypaper is typically linked not with childhood or children's literature but rather with its rebuttal of documentary photography. Critical assessments of the text concentrate on the tenderness of DeCarava's photographs and on his masterful use of light, shading, and composition.[127] Maren Stange usefully places *Flypaper* within the photobook tradition, explaining that "[t]o read *The Sweet Flypaper of Life* as a documentary is misguided on all counts,"[128] because its contestation of sociological assessments of urban black life marks *Flypaper* as a "conscious mock- and anti-documentary."[129] Sara Blair confirms that Hughes and DeCarava employed terms from documentary photography in order to challenge them, arguing that Hughes "sequenced and paced the text with an eye toward refuting several decades of sociological and documentary gospel on Harlem poverty, crime, and psychic disintegration. . . . The resulting photo-story, whose recreation of extended family life was so convincing as to obscure its own fictionality, was read by critics as a signal instance of the form it sought to overturn."[130] Assessments of *Flypaper* saw the family as the linchpin in Hughes and DeCarava's resistance to sociological documentary practice, and are quite useful in understanding the way the text values kinship networks and alternate family configurations. If one remembers the text's play with documentary antecedents, the position of the child within that family takes on particular weight; for if Rosskam and Wright in *12 Million Black Voices* can alter the urban child's response to poverty (and to image making) by erasing the child's tongue as it is stuck out at the camera, then we can understand *Flypaper*'s vision as a deliberate assertion of child agency rather than of passivity or victimhood.

Family Reading and Brown v. Board of Education

In order to discern the resonance of the photographs of children within *Flypaper*, we might consider the way in which the text appeals to a multiply constituted audience. Imagined by the authors as akin to a coffee-table book, the initial printing disappointed DeCarava even though he had been warned about its small size: "[S]omehow I still expected a big, glossy book with my photographs lavishly laid out."[131] Later editions were much larger in size, and the text was one of Hughes's most popular books, selling out the first run quickly; as his biographer Arnold Rampersad explains, "No book by Hughes was ever greeted so rhapsodically."[132] The audience for this text was not circumscribed by age. As a household book, *Flypaper* was family reading for many children, as was the case for photographer and critic Deborah Willis:

> Every week my older sister and I went to the public library on Lehigh Avenue to select a book to read for the week. That was a ritual we had performed since we started elementary school. I can still remember browsing the shelves, looking for an easy-reading book that I could finish in time to go to the Saturday matinee. On one occasion I stumbled upon *The Sweetflypaper of Life* and proudly brought it home. DeCarava's photographs left an indelible mark on my mind. Hughes was already a household name because of the books my father had in his bedroom, and, of course, during Negro History Week we always read his poetry.
>
> As I struggled through the book, I was excited to see the photographs: it was the first book I had ever seen with "colored" people in it—people that I recognized, people that reminded me of my own family.[133]

Considering *Flypaper* as family reading helps uncover its significance for a generation of children approaching the civil rights movement. Popular for its warm and affirming depictions of black parents and children, the book anticipates the paradigm shift that took hold in the 1960s with the "black is beautiful" sensibility. For Willis, it transformed her sense of herself as a visual artist: "For me a veil was lifted. I made it a point from that day in 1955 to continue to look for books that were about black people and to look at photographs that told or reflected our stories."[134]

For Hughes, *Flypaper* emerged during his own recommitment to children's literature as a genre. Although his first publications were in W. E. B. Du Bois and Jessie Redmon Fauset's children's magazine, *The Brownies' Book* (1920–1921), and he published a poetry collection, *The Dream Keeper* (1932), along with *Popo and Fifina: A Story of Haiti* (1932) with Arna Bontemps, before the 1950s Hughes had not published texts for children in many years. By the mid-1950s, Hughes's socialist associations in the 1930s and poems like "Goodbye Christ" (1932) had drawn the attention of Joe McCarthy. Hughes met in private sessions with McCarthy's Senate Permanent Subcommittee on Investigations, and on March 26, 1953, the writer was publicly questioned by Roy Cohn and McCarthy. Hughes disavowed his earlier Communist allegiances and pledged his belief in the American justice system. Hughes's cooperation with McCarthy, according to Rampersad, stemmed from fear of being prevented from publishing; the year before the McCarthy inquisition, Hughes found himself drawn again to children's literature. Hughes wrote to Ivan von Auw in 1952, "Where, whence, and how come all the juveniles for me all of a sudden I don't know!"[135] He published *The First Book of Negroes* (1952), *The First Book of Rhythms* (1954), and *The First Book of Jazz* (1955) for the Franklin Watts publishing house.

Further, Hughes was personally invested in children at the moment of *Flypaper*'s conception. He sought mentoring relationships with young writers like a Nigerian admirer, Chuba Nweke, who referred to Hughes as a father and to himself as "[y]our son."[136] Hughes developed a relationship in 1954 with his friend Arna Bontemps's son Paul, who visited Hughes in New York, as well as with Ellen Tarry's daughter, Elizabeth Tarry Patton. Also in 1954, Hughes started a children's garden outside his townhouse on 127th Street; a famous photograph of Hughes among child gardeners appeared in the *New York Times* on August 27 of that year. In early July, DeCarava had contacted Hughes to show him the photographs he had taken of Harlem for DeCarava's Guggenheim Fellowship. By July 17, 1954, with the children's garden under his window, Hughes had surrounded himself with DeCarava's photographs of Harlem and was working on his autobiography as well as a new children's book, *The First Book of the West Indies*. Hughes wrote on July 11, 1954, to Maxim Lieber, "I'm becoming a children's writer these days. [Books are becoming] simpler and simpler! And younger and younger!"[137] While initially, in October 1954, Hughes sought simply to get DeCarava's pictures published in book form, an act that cohered with Hughes's vision of himself as a father figure to younger artists, Richard Simon of Simon and Schuster suggested that Hughes write an accompanying narrative. *Flypaper*, then, emerged from the height of Hughes's personal and professional investment in childhood.

Julia Mickenberg and Jonathan Scott each observe that Hughes's turn to children's literature may have been influenced by his experience as a leftist who was repeatedly attacked by social conservatives. As Mickenberg suggests, such a turn to children's literature does not imply a retreat from social issues, because children's literature in the 1950s was a vital site for politicized publication; and as Scott notices, children's literature was considered by the right to be "no less 'red' than radical political organizations."[138] In fact, critics of *Flypaper* have been more concerned with the aesthetics of DeCarava's images and with the connection between the text and the documentary tradition than with the text's conspicuous political positioning.[139] Although this text is in no way a book with a specific goal, as are *My Happy Days* and *My Dog Rinty*, it nonetheless locates itself within the civil rights context of the mid-1950s. The book is a first-person fictionalized account of the life of Mary Bradley, a grandmother in Harlem who introduces to the reader the various members of her family and explains their relationships to each other. The text begins with the arrival of "the bicycle of the Lord bearing His messenger with a telegram for Sister Mary Bradley saying 'Come home.'"[140] Although Mary is sick, she refuses to pass on, explaining that she wants to witness the social change that will come with *Brown v. Board of Education*:

> "For one thing," said Sister Mary, "I want to stay here and see what this integration the Supreme Court has done decreed is going to be like."
>
> Since integration has been, ages without end, a permanently established custom in heaven, the messenger boy replied that her curiosity could be satisfied quite easily above. But Sister Mary said she wanted to find out how integration was going to work on *earth* first, particu-

larly in South Carolina which she was planning to visit once more before she died. So the messenger boy put his wire back in his pocket and
departed. (7)

The frame of civil rights is often ignored in scholarship on *Flypaper*, but it links
Hughes's text to the earlier expressly political photobooks of (and for) black
children. Myisha Priest, one of the few critics who sees *Flypaper* as a response
to the civil rights movement, calls *Flypaper* an "experimental children's text"[141]
and reads DeCarava's photos of children as a rejoinder to the widely circulated
images of Emmett Till's physical desecration: "The transformation of the text
of the body arises from the redeemed flesh of the children who populate the
story."[142] The first image greeting the reader is one that echoes the photobooks
of the 1940s, that of a child looking directly out of the page and into the reader's
eyes, but with an alteration, because this child is not idealized through materiality (not dressed up like Rex or David) and is decidedly not smiling. The pairing,
then, of Mary's desire to see the fruition of integration in the South and the unsmiling face of the child who looks seriously at the reader for a response makes
Flypaper conspicuously political in its orientation. Unlike the earlier books, this
text does not ask for social change in a particular direction. Instead, it appears
as a liminal document, one set in between the alteration on paper that *Brown*
articulates and the possibilities of social justice that remain unrealized. Like the
child on the first page, and like Mary Bradley herself, the text waits to see what
the sociopolitical moment will bring.

Photography, Politics, and Domesticity
Flypaper is also connected with *My Happy Days* and *My Dog Rinty* because it
interacts with photographic precedent by representing black domestic life with
tenderness and subtlety. Just as Shackelford places Rex and his family within
the landscape of *Life* magazine and Tarry situates Harlem within the visual
lexicon of cultural gifts in the wake of the documentary, Hughes also confounds
documentary tradition, as Stange and Blair have explained, by visualizing integrity in African American culture. Hughes wrote to Maria Leiper at Simon
and Schuster on January 4, 1955, that "[w]e've had so many books about how
bad life is, that it would seem to me to do no harm to have one along about *now*
affirming its value."[143] When Hughes writes of books reflecting "bad life," he
probably references the work of Chester Himes, Richard Wright, Ralph Ellison, and James Baldwin, artists about whom he felt deep ambivalence.[144] The

publishing company picked up on the general intonation of Hughes's language, rather than its literary barb, for the *New York Times* advertisement of November 27, 1955. Entitled "Good for the Heart," the advertisement promotes "[s]unlit moments in the life of New York's Harlem" to "warmhearted people," a phrasing that again emphasizes the affective connection between the sympathetic book-buying public and this version of the black family.

To some black critics of Hughes's era, the mid-1950s was an in-between moment, one that saw the legal end of segregation but bore few material changes in race relations. Arthur P. Davis asks in *Phylon* magazine in 1956, "But what about the literature of this interim between two worlds—between a world of dying segregation and one of a developing integration?"[145] Davis suggests that the protest tradition dominant in the 1940s had lost its steam with the positive change in national attitude toward integration, and that in this intervening time between segregation and the realization of civil rights, authors would produce "good-will" texts,[146] which would candy-coat black experience in the hopes of pleasing white audiences; Shackelford and Tarry might come to mind initially when considering Davis's projection. Davis imagines *Flypaper* as a harbinger of the second type of interregnum literature, that of the "internal life of Negroes": "With the pressure of segregation lightened, the Negro artist will find it easy to draw such pictures of his people. He will discover, what we all know in our objective moments, that there are many facets of Negro living—humorous, pathetic, and tragic—which are not directly touched by the outside world. Hughes' *Sweet Flypaper of Life* is, I believe, a forerunner of many more works of this type."[147] In configuring the mid-1950s as a liminal period, Davis turns to Hughes as an example of a new interest in the rich communal experience of African Americans, one that evidences a turn away from literature addressing racial protest or interracial conflict. But it would be unfair to suggest that Hughes's work was solely a work of "internal life." Like *My Dog Rinty*, *Flypaper* juxtaposes the inner world of the family with the outer world of Harlem's streets; and, as we have seen, representations of the family were, perforce, politicized. *Flypaper*'s positive domestic emphasis, its expression of Hughes's long-standing investment in racial pride, was necessarily political in the mid-1950s, when, in the wake of *Brown*, "the whispered promise of integration was lulling many members of the black middle class to sleep" and many African Americans embraced raceless texts as au courant.[148] Beauty was political for Hughes, and his emphasis on black cultural dignity—in his poetry, children's books, and *Flypaper*—connected pride with social progress. This was the poet who wrote of America, "They will see how beautiful I am and be ashamed." Despite the decades between "I, Too"

(1926) and *Flypaper*, Hughes never abandoned his belief in the political power of beauty. By attending yet again to the richness and attraction of black culture, to the "sweet flypaper" of black family and community, Hughes is actually not turning away from the moment of *Brown* in his photobook, even though there are very few white people in the book and there is no intimation of a desire for integration; he confronts it head-on as the catalyst for Mary's musing on the nature of her family.

One might be tempted to see, then, the text's representation of beauty as in line with the agenda of *My Happy Days* or, especially, *My Dog Rinty*, in its depiction of Harlem's family stability and material accomplishments. *Flypaper*, however, is not as invested in images that dress children up in suits and ties as they play on the playground or that place nuclear families around the dinner table. Instead, Hughes and DeCarava offer a variety of family-life experiences, from black fathers pushing baby carriages next to baseball fields, to beer parties in the basements of brownstones, to parents who sing and dance in the kitchen. A capaciousness characterizes the affirming images of family life in *Flypaper*. And although certainly the images of fathers with children dominate representations of the family and therefore intervene in the sociological account of paternal abandonment, Hughes and DeCarava refuse to limit their portrait of the family; they refuse to respond (as does *My Happy Days*) by presenting a black version of the white nuclear family. Although the family in *Flypaper* has many branches and a variety of configurations, love, not obligation or adherence to social norms, binds father to child.[149]

With this version of family attachment, the response to the question of integration becomes more nuanced. Certainly the beauty of the family aims to convince "warmhearted" readers of black cultural dignity and could, of course, promote the kind of intercultural connection achieved through photographs by both Shackelford and Tarry. But, in truth, Hughes's text invokes integration only to demonstrate that such debates are discrete from the urban black family, and instead marks the cultural moment as one of anticipation of social change rather than of its fruition. Mary wishes to see what integration brings in the South, in a rural landscape where, it seems, black families are segregated into spaces that lack the rewards of urban life. In Harlem, liveliness means human interaction, as Mary explains: "New York is not like back down South with not much happening outside. In Harlem something is happening all the time, people are going every which-a-way" (63). Mary's pointed comment on the subways in New York highlights the distinction of the integration debates, which appear divorced from the lived experience of New Yorkers: "It's lonesome at night. But at the rush hour—well, all it took was the Supreme Court to decide on mixed schools, but the rush hour in the subway mixes everybody—white, black, Gentile, and Jew—closer than you ever are to your relatives" (63). Mary's gentle humor allows the reader to see integration as physical proximity rather than intimacy; the cityscape has already accomplished physical integration, Mary suggests. The possibility of meaningful societal integration simply does not surface in the text, in large part because the book revels in black social spaces. The later images in the text of a picket line, for example, are quieted through humor. The picket line does not reveal the topic for the protest: we cannot read the signs on the strikers' backs. We can, however, read the jaunty smile on the faces of the first two walkers, and we are comforted by the fact that the police officer behind the line is African American rather than white. The intensity of the street orator who shouts "African for the Africans" and "Ethiopia shall stretch forth her hand" becomes defused by images of middle-aged women conservatively dressed; Hughes offers both front and back images of the women, as well as the punch line "And some joker in the crowd always says, 'And draw back a nub!'" (82–83).[150] Hughes and DeCarava's portrait of social action, including integration, emphasizes the safety and integrity of the black family and community.

Childhood and Liminality

In their depiction of childhood, Hughes and DeCarava place the black community in an intermediate position, anticipating the form of social change that will come through the child's development into adulthood. The text waits on youth. It should be said that the book contains fifty-five photographs that include child figures, a number that in and of itself suggests the dominance of childhood within the text. Mary's concern for her grandson Rodney, who has already fathered a child and has been turned out of his house by his parents, is the clearest example of the text's liminality. Mary's fear for Rodney's future structures the text, however loosely, because Mary repeatedly returns to Rodney as she meanders through a description of her family. But initially she refuses to go to heaven with the messenger because, as she says, "Lord, I'm so tangled up in living, I ain't got time to die" (7); what follows are three images of children for whom Mary cares, as well as an image of Rodney. Other images of movement are attached to childhood and youth, including motor vehicles. Mary suggests, "All the young ones nowadays is just crazy about cars" (18), and Hughes offers an image of a young boy in full stride, walking briskly as he admires cars on the street. Motion, futurity, and possibility mark many depictions of childhood in the text, arguing visibly for the inevitability of change.

The heart of the book focuses on Jerry and his wife, Melinda, the party in their kitchen, and their affection for their five children. In this central series of images, Hughes and DeCarava place childhood above the pleasure of the parents. Visually, the ascendance of childhood becomes apparent when Jerry wishes to leave the house after the party for one last drink at a bar. The text reads, "But usually about that time one of the babies wakes up, Jerry goes and gets it." In the image that follows, Jerry appears resigned to staying with the child, as he holds the baby close to his face but in front of and slightly above him, signifying the precedence of the child over adult desire for gratification. The images that follow show Jerry comforting the baby, with the text reading, "And [Jerry] brings it into the kitchen: And laughs and loves that child to sleep: And the next thing you know, both of them's done dozed off: And that is their Saturday night" (51–52). Other images in this series show a particularly lively and challenging group of children; in photographs they smile, laugh, cry, pout, pull on pipes, tease their siblings, disrupt dinner, and provoke their parents and the camera. The text reads, "And sometimes, old as I is, they tries even my impatience" (55). With this caption, the reader sees the child in an image seeking further engagement with the grandmother and with the reader; he leans toward the camera to dare the viewer into further engagement. A potent retort to the victimhood inscribed in urban documentary photographs of children, images in Hughes and DeCarava's text bring the demands of childhood into the space of adulthood, both within the narrative of the text and to the viewer in the child's visual challenge. This is also not the idealized face of friendship close-ups; there is no Rex or David inviting friendship. This child provokes, teases, infuriates, and beguiles both Mary and the reader.

Alternately, several images in Hughes's text reveal children refusing to engage the viewer, whether it is a child lost in reading while sitting in a window that frames him off from the street and from the interior of his house, or a child who "ain't going no place at all" (69). Lying at a crossroads created by sidewalk cracks, the child faces away from the camera and is lost in her own imaginative life as she creates sidewalk drawings. Whether confronting adults or immersing themselves in their imaginations, children in *Flypaper* seem to determine their own attitudes toward others and toward the outside world; Mary may dismiss a child as "going no place," but the child refuses adult access to her inner life and does lie at a crossroads. What is before *Flypaper*'s children is a politicized future.[151] Hughes and DeCarava emphasize the space between the stability of adult community in Harlem and the economic and social forces that would influence the children's prospects, a moment echoed by the in-between time just after the issue of the *Brown* decision but before the upheavals of the 1960s. Two of the most important images in *Flypaper* address the liminality of childhood and the place of Harlem in a moment of social flux. Accompanying the famous image of a young person dressed up and walking across an empty lot, titled "Graduation" by DeCarava when exhibited separately, the text reads, "But it's nice to see young folks all dressed up going somewhere—maybe to a party" (69). The disjuncture between the girl's beautiful dress and the trash-strewn lot has been noticed by critics who link this image to a documentary tradition of social critique.[152] Maren Stange explains that the image encapsulates a moment of transition and entrance into adulthood.[153] The text emphasizes the instability of the child's future; she goes "maybe to a party," or perhaps she will cross over the line in the middle of the image, from the light of childhood into a dark future, as Stange argues.[154] Hughes and DeCarava may hint at the darkness that awaits the child on the streets, but Hughes's narration interprets the image through the perspective of Mary, who, like the reader, is in the process of viewing the scene and decides that "it's nice to see" rather than a threat. The words and image tug against each other: Hughes's demand that the reader attend to the child rather than the streets, and DeCarava requires that we look at the larger picture of the child's potential future as she crosses the lot. A push-pull structures the reading experience of the page. We recognize the decay of the environment and yet acknowledge the possibility embodied in a childhood that, as we have seen in images of spirited young people, determines its own response to circumstance.

To return to the topic of attitude as agency, the other famous child image in *Flypaper* emphasizes the fortitude and inscrutability of childhood in the face of pain. A boy stands in front of a lamppost with his hands behind his back. The line of the post bisects visually the white family that walks behind the child, serving to extend the child's body, as it is connected visually to his head, fracturing representationally the illusion of nuclear familial bliss based in white popular culture. The boy's hands are behind his back as though he were strung up on the pole like a criminal. Hughes and DeCarava give us, first, this wide view of the child, one that interacts with white expectations about the lack of black-family integrity, and the narration confirms that from a distance the child's identity is wrapped up in abandonment: "Rodney's child growed up like that little boy down the street, sad." But although Hughes and DeCarava do not deny that this is one version of the wide view of the abandoned child, they will not leave the reader with an image of the forsaken black child juxtaposed with the nuclear white family. They then offer a close-up of the boy, with the ambiguous caption "He don't never smile" (28). A viewer might seek the child's face for discernment of his attitude toward his situation, looking to ground an interpretation of the child's lack of warmth. Is he too wounded to smile? Does he refuse to smile as an act of defiance? What a viewer finds is that the child's eyes are shaded, his face taking on the abstract features of an African mask. Like the children who turn inward toward the imagination, this child will not offer an easy, accessible response for a reader. He protects himself from the intrusive gaze of the viewer and, in doing so, refuses to be a spectacle of victim-hood or pity.[155] Instead, there are ambivalence, pain, and enigma. Uncertainty overlays the image, an instability of interpretation that echoes the photo of the girl walking, perhaps, to a party. But the instability marks the liminal potential of childhood within the text, for the future is much less comforting and sure for these Harlem children than for their parents. What becomes apparent is the value of youth to the adults, those who hoist children onto their shoulders, monitor their schooling, support them financially, and seek the best for the children's future. The children in *Flypaper* offer an active emotional response to their families and environments. Whether that response is confrontational or obstructionist, assertive or reticent, children will act and will articulate them-selves as they choose in the face of social flux. Inscrutability and ambivalence, as much as sassiness and irreverence, articulate Hughes and DeCarava's principle: young people have the power to determine their attitude toward an inchoate future, and to determine a reader's access to that attitude. These children are not always an open book, but they are moving toward the future.

In fact, the final image of the text places the adult in the conventional posi-tion of a receptive, exposed, approachable child, especially if one reads *Flypaper* in light of children's photographic texts. In *My Happy Days* and *My Dog Rinty*, a smiling, ingenuous face greets the reader, and the texts naturalize their political arguments by invoking childhood innocence. At the end of *Flypaper*, the smiling face of the narrator is revealed, and it is that of Mary, the grandmother, who concludes the text with what sounds like an introduction: "Here I am" (96). The affective bond between a first-person narrator and the reader attaches to the grandmother rather than to the children in the text. Young people in *Flypaper* are in motion and in flux, inhabiting that liminal space between the home and dangers of urban futurity; the text offers us access only to the past, through this image of Mary. Sonia Weiner sees Mary as a trickster figure, with her nar-ration a mask over the variety of meanings in DeCarava's images, who points readers toward the mammy stereotype in order to deflect white attention from the subversiveness of the images. As we read with Weiner's argument in mind, the revelation of this visually masked figure at the end of the text (she hasn't been pictured before) refashions the supposedly ingenuous child close-up. As a trickster, now Mary echoes the child figure of the photobook tradition, one who seems to offer himself or herself in plain sight—as do Rex and David—but whose story speaks on multiple registers, in layered meanings. (We can understand the child close-up in those earlier texts as a kind of mask as well, one that extends friendship overtly while the texts argue for an unfinished civil rights process.)

Remembering the moment of 1955, when the black community waited to see what *Brown* would produce, allows us to recognize the deliberate indeterminacy of Hughes and DeCarava's work. *Flypaper* holds its breath when it comes to childhood. These children face an urban landscape that could destroy them, yet the authors insist on the resilience of youth and the ability of children to offer (or refuse) a viewer access to their reactions. Such agency suggests the possibility of survival. As Arthur P. Davis explained in early 1956,

> [O]ne must always keep in mind the paradox involved. We do not have actual integration anywhere. We have surface integration and token integration in many areas, but the everyday pattern of life for the overwhelming majority of Negroes is unchanged, and probably will be for the next two or three decades. But we do have—and this is of the utmost importance—we do have the spiritual climate which will eventually bring about complete integration. The Negro artist recognizes and acknowledges that climate; he accepts it on good faith; and he is resolved to work with it at all costs.[156]

Children embody Davis's "spiritual climate" in *The Sweet Flypaper of Life*, their liminality and indeterminacy echoing the political moment of the mid-1950s.

Like the boy with a face like a mask, children's photobooks in the 1940s and 1950s withhold and evade. Shackelford's book plays the game of racial liberalism, all the while arguing through images for the viability of school integration and antiauthoritarian ideals. Tarry presents an overlay of a boy-and-his-dog story to a book that offers one of the most beautiful and poignant visual portraits ever published of the Harlem community, both inside the home and outside of it. The book points backward toward the celebratory Harlem Renaissance street photography of James Van Der Zee and forward toward the proclamation of black cultural pride in the Black Arts Movement. But even its celebration of Harlem is a kind of layering, for underneath we find Tarry's plea for habitable and accessible housing for Harlem residents. These books cannily employ the ideological and aesthetic terms available to them, speaking through photographs and fiction the language of friendship, because straightforward confrontation of oppression would appear dangerous or impudent. For Hughes and DeCarava, masking and withholding culminate in the visual revelation of Mary, who takes the place of the ingenuous child, while the young people in the text stand on the cusp of the civil rights movement, armed with beauty, family, and emotional fortitude.

2

Pictures and Nonfiction

Conduct and Coffee Tables

Perhaps we have an invincible resistance to believing in the past, in History, except in the form of myth. The Photograph, for the first time, puts an end to this resistance: henceforth the past is as certain as the present, what we see on paper is as certain as what we touch. It is the advent of the Photograph—and not, as has been said, of the cinema—which divides the history of the world.

—Roland Barthes, *Camera Lucida*

The history of black liberation movements in the United States could be characterized as a struggle over images as much as it has also been a struggle for rights, for equal access.

—bell hooks, *Art on My Mind*

For Roland Barthes in the first epigraph to this chapter, photographs incarnate history, become material evidence of events that one can grasp with one's hands and hold on to as proof of the past. Although we recognize that all images are manipulated, subjective, selected versions of a viewer's perspective on a subject, there remains an ineffable attraction to the idea of the photo as truth, as documentation of moments that have faded into the past, and as evidence of a history that no longer exists in materiality. African American writers at midcentury were drawn to the idea that "what we see on paper is as certain as what we touch,"[1] and they used photographs to claim permanence to histories that had been quashed or erased by racist American mainstream culture. As Susan Sontag reminds us, "People robbed of their past seem to make the most fervent picture takers, at home and abroad";[2] communities that lack a recognized, public version of their history are especially drawn to the photograph as a means of documentation and as a weapon in the effort to articulate and concretize history. In the second epigraph to this chapter, bell hooks connects photography and civil rights explicitly as she makes transparent the intersection between social justice and power over image making. At midcentury, photographs held this material, evidentiary appeal for a nascent civil rights movement, one that in the 1940s and 1950s was deeply invested in the participation of black Americans in national categories of value, such as patriotism and military participation, and in demands for full rights under citizenship. Photographs enabled writers to demonstrate both the congruities between black history and American values, and the nation's failure to extinguish racial violence and to extend civil rights to its black citizens. Photographs offered black history that sense of certainty Barthes described, enabling African Americans to intervene in the public narrative of nationhood.

We find that engagement with history through the photograph in two non-fiction books of the midcentury by African American authors, Louis B. Reynolds's *Little Journeys into Storyland* (1947–48)[3] and Langston Hughes and Milton Meltzer's *A Pictorial History of the Negro in America* (1956). In many ways, the two books appear quite distinct: Reynolds's text was published for an audience of Seventh-Day Adventist children and combines brief biographical sketches of historical figures with conduct material; Hughes and Meltzer's text, a compendium of historical documents and more than one thousand images (including a few hundred photographs) gathered by Meltzer and narrated by Hughes, was issued for a national, interracial audience. Reynolds's text had a relatively limited audience and circulation, given that the book expressly addressed Seventh-Day Adventists, whereas Hughes's text became one of his best-selling titles. Reynolds's highly moralistic and restrictive narrative approach reflects the work of a single religious figure, whereas Hughes's far-reaching and inclusive ethos draws together written and visual accounts from a variety of sources. These books are drastically different, to be sure.

Yet the two texts share a fundamental interest in linking historical narrative with photographs in order to inspire social activism in the reader. For both books, the child reader was paramount to the texts' reformist imperatives. Reynolds explicitly acknowledges the child readership and its obligation to remake social relations, whereas Hughes intended that his book reach across populations of age and race in order to propel reform. Photographs became a primary agent in connecting versions of history to the current moment, for the concretization of historical event and biography enabled the authors to make real the linkage between historical social conditions and the modern reader. Acknowledging the profound differences in tone and strategy between the books, I intentionally consider them together in order to explore the way in which black writers play with the photograph at midcentury. This inventiveness becomes especially potent in the terrain of history, as both Reynolds and Hughes repurpose and reframe documentary images, pulling photographs out of their original context of use and deploying them as counternarratives to African American historical exclusion. For instance, Reynolds and Hughes both repurpose documentary and governmental photography: Reynolds uses Office of War Information images by Gordon Parks to argue for integration, for instance, and Hughes and Meltzer draw in a range of familiar photographs—of Jim Crow signs, of famous Americans, and more—to redress historical elision through juxtaposition and layering. These two disparate texts both forge new meanings from the visual fragments of the past. Setting them into dialogue with each other is purposeful, a means for consideration of playfully resistant black photographic and editorial practice at midcentury. As in chapter 1, which yoked Hughes to less prominent writers, in discussing nonfiction I similarly wish to bring the luminary into conversation with a contemporary who employed a related methodology. *Pictorial History* was a profoundly influential and successful book; examining it alongside a less major text enables an understanding of the milieu out of which Hughes worked, and a recognition that other writers—those forgotten or published by nonmainstream outlets—provocatively improvised historical meaning through photographic images.

It would be quite difficult to offer a comprehensive reading of these rich texts, though certainly they offer much opportunity for understanding youth historiography. By emphasizing instead the function of the photograph within a civil rights context, the texts' exercise of particular motifs in black visual culture comes into relief. In particular, Reynolds engages a tradition of the photograph within the black-conduct books, for he reimagines the role of the visual in teaching conduct by offering not uplift portraiture but rather images of joyful, vigorous, active young people. Hughes and Meltzer extend a tradition of documentation found in black newspapers, pageants, and histories that links the word to the image; in response to that tradition, Hughes and Meltzer offer photographs that explicitly invoke and involve language. A page in *Pictorial History* might include headlines ripped from a newspaper, images of signs above segregated water fountains, and portraits attached to quotations, all of which tie explicitly the image to the word in order to make visible the imperative for social action. According to Arnold Rampersad, Hughes's publisher was aware of the implications of visualizing black history: Robert Simon of Crown, which issued *Pictorial History*, saw the book as a progressive publishing opportunity, saying of other publishing houses, "They just don't know what is happening in this country."[4] By concretizing history through the photograph and by playing with visual tropes, *Little Journeys* and *Pictorial History* bring their young reader-ship into contact with a living history, one that uses images to engage temporal-ity in order to inspire a reader's social activism.

Part of the appeal of the photograph in children's histories at this moment recalls the political uses of the photograph within picture books of the 1940s and 1950s, as chapter 1 detailed. Just as the images in those fictional books fore-grounded the need for school integration and housing reform, ideas that might have been unspeakable within a Cold War context, in the histories the photo-graphs function similarly to make explicit, evidentiarily, the necessity for social action. One could suggest that by placing the imperative for social action within a history book, the authors were, on one level, covert in their intentionality, suggesting that the books addressed the historical alone rather than the present moment. This strategy might appear to be a kind of masking, as in the fictional texts in chapter 1, except that here innocence of social implication takes form as historical objectivity. But both Hughes and Meltzer believed in historical conti-nuity as a means of justifying social change. Their nonfiction book is not silent on civil rights, letting the photographs alone speak, as in the case of Shackelford and, to a large degree, Reynolds in *Little Journeys*. However silent the 1940s history and conduct book might be in language, Reynolds, Hughes, and Melt-zer use photographs to emphasize an active, reformist response to history, and render that imperative through a stance of objectivity.

NONFICTION AND EARLY CIVIL RIGHTS

The climate of American culture after World War II rendered nonfiction an ideological battleground, especially in pedagogy for young people, as claims about the "truth" about American history and identity were pursued by writers on the right as well as on the left. Whereas authors like Shackelford and Tarry took up silence on race issues as a response to their repressive cultural climate, expectations for putting a best face on American history took hold in educational publishing in the 1940s. In fact, the classroom became a site of articulation of a conformist nationalist ideology. Julia Mickenberg explains that American his-tory as a subject of school study began to take shape after World War II as a part of a large-scale effort at "citizenship education," involving teachers' oaths and book banning as well as curriculum scrutiny: she explains that "studying history became a lesson in patriotism, an attempt to validate the Cold War status quo."[5] But American historical figures had also been of deep interest to the left during the 1930s, as writers offered histories of the workers' movement to young people as well as stories of proletarian heroes like Abraham Lincoln,

Davy Crockett, and Daniel Boone, among others. By the early 1950s, leftist-authored children's biographies of figures such as Emma Lazarus, Ben Franklin, and Franklin Delano Roosevelt reached a large popular audience. Despite the pressure from the right on classroom curriculum, trade publishing enabled writers with progressive social agendas to intervene in definitions of American identity, and many of those writers, who were largely white, used African American historical figures in order to insist on the need for implementation of democratic values. Beginning in 1945, texts with African American characters began to appear more frequently,[6] and they often encouraged independent thought and social critique as a civic obligation. Certainly Hughes's history fits into Mickenberg's paradigm, and its status as a trade book, one with an inclusive, or amorphous, sense of audience, would not immediately draw the scrutiny that would meet an American history book within classroom settings. Further, Hughes's book aimed to trigger passionate civic response, and in this way is of a piece with leftist children's histories of the moment. Of course, both Reynolds and Hughes used their texts to intervene in the narrative of American history, a narrative granted the weight of "truth" by virtue of its status as nonfiction. As if it were not enough to recognize that history is informed by subjective shaping of events, children's biography participates especially in the fictional, as it offers ample space for writers to invent conversations and play with historical events. Reynolds's book takes such energetic liberties, all with the idea that the truth of a subject can extend beyond the limits of historical accuracy. In this way, children's historians use the generic expectation for truth in nonfiction as a means to convince the reader of a version of history influenced by ideology and social desire. Naturally, this is one reason for history's attractiveness to proponents on the right as well as on the left. Adding to the conversation about truth and fiction within children's history, Hughes and Reynolds draw in the photograph to tell the story, for just as history attaches in the mind to truth, so does the image. When photographic "truth" meets historical "truth," the argument for social change becomes doubly weighted.

LOUIS B. REYNOLDS, THE SEVENTH-DAY ADVENTIST CHURCH, AND THE JOY OF CHILDHOOD

Little Journeys into Storyland (1947) draws together historical biography, conduct material, and photographs in order to assert a vision of black childhood that is lively and playful as well as intensely moral. At times the text pulls against itself, offering, in language, narratives of children who disobey parents and suffer as a result (one child is hit by a train and dies), alongside images of joyous children cuddling their pet dogs and cats. It is a striking book, one that draws on the currents outlined in chapter 1 regarding acceptable articulations of civil rights, as well as on the theological energies of the black Seventh-Day Adventist (SDA) community. Its distinguishing feature, however, is its glorious photographs, many of which were taken from the Library of Congress's collection of images produced by the Office of War Information (OWI). As a result, the images originate with such photographic luminaries as Gordon Parks, the first African American photographer for *Life* magazine; and Marjory Collins, John Collier Jr., and Jack Delano, all of whom began with Roy Stryker at the Farm Security Administration (FSA) photography unit. Additional photographs within *Little Journeys* were drawn from press syndicates like Monkmeyer, Acme Newspictures, and International News, as well as from the collections of SDA photographers like S. M. Harlan and A. R. Simons and from unattributed SDA sources. The origins of the photographs within *Little Journeys* are various, and it is not my intention in this chapter to reflect on the original intimation of an image from, for instance, an OWI photographer or a news service. Such work could be exciting, but is not my primary concern in studying Reynolds's book. This chapter, instead, reads the images within the context of Reynolds's intervention in a civil rights discourse that required circumspection and, remembering the climate of appropriate civil rights discourse in chapter 1, a level of repression. Further, the politics of the Seventh-Day Adventist Church required intensified caution, as we will discover, in discerning the role of African Americans in the church community.

Louis B. Reynolds, the first African American editor of the *Message* magazine,[7] is listed on the title page of *Little Journeys into Storyland* along with Charles L. Paddock, a prominent white SDA author. Paddock, who published in 1938 *Gems from Storyland*,[8] was associated with *Little Journeys* as a white authenticating name rather than having contributed to the authorship of the volume.[9] For that reason, I refer to the text as Reynolds's alone. Reynolds may have needed to foreground white approval of his effort, given the difficult political situation of black Seventh-Day Adventists during the 1940s. As Benjamin J. Baker explains, the church had increased its African American population but was unwilling to permit black political power within the church: "The black membership was growing steadily (8,000 in 1930 and 20,000 in 1944), but the Adventist Church was not so progressive, especially on the issue of race. Probably the greatest indictment against the white membership of this church during this time was that they shared views similar to those of other non-Adventist whites on the race question."[10] All facilities of the church—including individual churches, cafeterias, and schools—were segregated, and blacks were excluded from Adventist hospitals. This situation became particularly pointed and upsetting to the black Adventist community when, in 1943, an African American Adventist woman from New York, Lucille Byard, sought treatment at the Washington Sanitarium, an Adventist hospital in Takoma Park, Maryland; when staff members objected to admitting Byard, she was transferred to Freedman's Hospital (today Howard University Hospital), where she died.[11] Her death, from pneumonia, was attributed to the segregationist practices of the Adventist hospital. This death, along with an earlier uproar from white Adventists about a Harlem pastor's desire for autonomy, caused much dissatisfaction among black Adventists about their place within the church.[12] Reynolds's own history of the black Adventist community, *We Have Tomorrow* (1984), discusses its experience of prejudice and discontent, as well as the decision, spearheaded by a group of black Adventists in 1944, to form separate regional conferences for African American members.[13] In this separate structure, black Adventists took leadership positions governing their own communities and representing their needs to the church at large. Regional conferences remain in place today. Although the decision to form a separate conference was not without controversy, Reynolds himself sought parity between the black and white conferences, explaining in his 1984 history, "If all Seventh-day Adventists could rise to the level of loving passionately not only their academies, colleges, medical institutions, and their missions installations, as they do, but also the rich and varied configuration of people—brown, black, and white—who dwell therein, with the untold possibilities for achievement that lie in such association, they not only would solve their greatest problem but also would be prepared with gallantry and courage to face the difficult circumstances of the future." Black Adventists, Reynolds explains, transcend discrimination psychologically, because "they believe in love—which is to say, as they have love—they do not have fear."[14] If Reynolds was still arguing against prejudice within the church as late as 1983 (he wrote the history just before he died), how much more pressing an issue it must have been in 1947, just three years after regional conferences were created within the larger church. Reynolds's use of a white coauthor strategically positioned him as one who sought collaboration and participation with the larger church and who worked to gain that church's recognition of the black viewpoint and voice. It is difficult to discern Reynolds's position on integration (whether within or outside the church) in his publications of the mid-1940s. Reynolds's editorials in the *Message* typically suggest that conflicts between people will end when individuals turn to Jesus: "Then the era of universal peace and brotherhood will commence."[15] Such reluctance to discuss race relations conspicuously is typical of the repressive cultural climate, and the turn to religion as a mode of equality does not surprise, given Reynolds's background and audience.[16]

In considering the images within *Little Journeys into Storyland*, then, we can reflect on Reynolds's position within a church that was deeply divided racially. As a spokesperson for the black Adventist community, Reynolds had the opportunity to provide a perspective on race relations that would bring forth greater understanding between the constituencies. His viewpoint on the separate black conference is unclear. He was not necessarily arguing for integration of the conferences, because segregation permitted black Adventists a degree of agency and self-governance; but, according to his daughter, Dawn, Reynolds was a supporter of the civil rights movement and social integration. Additionally, Reynolds's daughter describes her father as an accomplished watercolor painter who had studied with Aaron Douglas, the Harlem Renaissance artist, probably when Douglas led the art department at Fisk University in the 1940s.[17] In truth, Reynolds could have used his own art to illustrate the book. He decided on photographs, according to Dawn, because he wanted to make concrete and "real" both the idea "that black children were not caricature" and the traces of black accomplishment. *Little Journeys* documents Reynolds's desire for the black Adventists to have a voice in civil rights efforts through historical biography and conduct literature coupled with photography, a form Reynolds associated with the persuasive power of the real. By targeting black children rather than a white SDA structure, the book makes a case for social change by insisting on the possibilities of young people and on their receptiveness to photographs that record tangible black accomplishment.

Framing Prejudice in Little Journeys: Verbal Evasion and Visual Engagement

Like Shackelford, who speaks generally about democratic ideals, Reynolds in *Little Journeys* focuses in abstract terms on the troubles and trials borne by his readership. He asks in a passage on farming, "Who doesn't have disappointments? Who hasn't built castles in the air and then has seen them torn down? Who hasn't dreamed dreams which never came true? Who doesn't have troubles now and then?"[18] He speaks of prejudice metaphorically, as similar to the disquieting noises a car makes: "There are so many things to irritate us today. Life is tense and strenuous. We are so highly geared and drive so rapidly that we don't go far until the squeaks appear—little things which may not be serious but which get on our nerves. They annoy and trouble us" (155). He discusses discrimination obliquely, if at all, as when drawing readers in with provocative chapter titles like "Is Prejudice Robbing You?" (217). He discusses folkways rather than racism: he describes the refusal to eat lettuce and tomatoes because of superstition, and criticizes those who mistakenly consider night air to be harmful. "You have your ideas, and you are entitled to them. Some of them may be right, and it is possible some of them may be wrong," Reynolds concludes, but he advises, "[D]on't condemn until you have listened to the evidence and weighed it carefully" (221). One could reflect on Mickenberg's argument that many progressive writers encouraged children to become active thinkers, to use "questioning and experimentation" (204) in a quest for truth. Perhaps this is Reynolds's overall goal, and the bait and switch of offering a chapter title that evokes the topic of prejudice's harm but then discussing tomatoes appears strategic, given the tense relationship between black and white SDA members in terms of social integration.

In fact, the book resembles linguistically Shackelford and Tarry even more closely when we consider the editing of one section that predated the publication of the book. A biographical chapter on John Donovan Moore, an African American organist, was originally published anonymously in 1940 as "A Negro Mother's Sacrifice" in the *Church Officers' Gazette*, a white Adventist publication. At a time when the emphasis on intercultural education was at an apex, the 1940 description of Moore emphasizes his race and his accomplishment in the segregated South: "Finally, after many years of faithful and efficient service, his state recognized his ability; for he, a Negro, was asked to play at the dedication of the organ at the State College of South Carolina." Reynolds's version in 1947 does not mention Moore's race, either in introducing the character, as does the 1940 version, or in the description of his accomplishment, which reads, "They asked him to play at the dedication of the organ at the State College" (178). The text mentions that Moore trained Roland Hayes's accompanist, but that is the closest the text comes to indicating Moore's background.

Like Shackelford, Reynolds permits images to speak when language might be incendiary. Children's texts of the 1940s that seek explanations for natural and social phenomena participated in the zeitgeist of leftism among children's authors; when Reynolds turns to social practices, he spends a chapter on the "why and how" of American material and cultural life, answering questions like "Why are wedding rings worn on the third finger?" (85), "Why do people wear black or dress in mourning when some loved one dies?" (86), and "Do you know how that little bow got on the side of men's hats?" (88). The questions and the answers are devoid of engagement with racial, social, or economic progressivism, but the mere fact of questioning the background of social practices could be understood as empowering. The most courageous moment in the chapter, however, appears visually (Figure 2.1). Reynolds includes an International News Service photograph of General Benjamin O. Davis shaking hands with a young man in uniform. The image is captioned "Why do we always shake hands with our right hand?" (85), a topic the chapter discusses. There is no identifying information accompanying the image: no mention of the subject in the photo,

Why do we always shake hands with our right hand?

Figure 2.1. Benjamin O. Davis shakes hands with an enlisted man. From Louis B. Reynolds and Charles L. Paddock, *Little Journeys into Storyland: Stories That Will Live and Lift* (Nashville: Southern Publishing Association, 1947).

no mention that Davis was the first African American general officer in the military, and no discussion of his promotion (just seven years before the book's publication) rendering him the first black general in the United States Army. Instead, we see Davis out of uniform, decorated only by a ribbon, gazing serenely at the camera. This is a double-voiced image, one that is silent in language, by referencing handshakes alone, and silent visually to a white audience, by the lack of decoration for Davis's military accomplishments. But the inclusion of the image suggests Davis's prominence as a figure in African American households. They would recognize his face even without his identifying military decorations.[19] The young man's identity might be more oblique. On the one hand, because his race is unclear visually and thus the photograph cannot be read definitively as an interracial brotherhood image but rather as a generic figure of an enlisted man, the handshake becomes emblematic not only of Davis's acceptance by the military establishment but also of his ability to command enlisted men like the one in the photograph. On the other hand, readers of the *Message* may have recognized the image, as it appeared in the January–February 1941 issue. The young man is Benjamin Jr., and the occasion of the picture is his graduation from West Point in 1936.[20] If readers did recognize Benjamin Jr., the familial investment in American patriotic and democratic identity would come into relief. With the caption as a kind of cover, Reynolds offers an image that would speak potently to a black Adventist audience in the mid-1940s about black leaders as equals and as patriots, integrating white systems of power.

Reynolds obliquely criticizes the prejudice of the church in a chapter entitled "Positive Proof," which includes an image of an African American minister at the pulpit, originally issued by the U.S. Army Air Corps. The caption of the image reads, "This is what our old world needs today—more lay members, and preachers, too, who really live their creeds" (166). Plainly asserting the integrity and prominence of African American preachers, like the one in the image, Reynolds concludes that "[i]f the standards as given us by the Master were lived by every professing Christian today, this would be a much better world in which to live" (168). This statement is as close as Reynolds comes in language to engaging the racial politics of the Seventh-Day Adventist Church in the 1940s, a period in which actions seen as undermining the church hierarchy could result in expulsion from the church, as was the case with the Harlem minister who was barred in the early 1940s. In the rest of Reynolds's book, the photographs permit a reader to consider the need for social equality through images of prominent African Americans, like General Davis, as well as photographs that push a reader to consider social change.

Little Journeys does not always refuse to identify the historical figures in the images it assembles. The book contains chapters on George Washington Carver, Marian Anderson, Mary McLeod Bethune, Booker T. Washington, and others, along with photographs of the subjects. However, the text does not describe its subjects in terms of race relations but rather speaks in a kind of code about humble origins, handicaps, and burdens. In describing some of the most racially fraught moments in the subjects' lives, Reynolds elides explication by emphasizing the subjects' national recognition. For example, in narrating Carver's 1921 testimony on supporting a peanut tariff before the House of Representatives, Reynolds reinvents the hostility he faced (among other attacks, Representative John Tilson famously asked whether Carver "wanted a watermelon to go along with" peanuts) by making the attacks about age rather than race: "As Dr. Carver proceeded to open up his box containing his exhibits before the men of the House of Representatives, someone rudely shouted, 'Hurry up, old man!'" Reynolds follows this with the idea that "[t]he congressmen were deeply interested" in Carver's speech (11). Similarly, the chapter on Marian Anderson describes only Anderson's childhood desire for a violin: "Her determination to get it was much like the enthusiasm with which she has pursued her musical career until her songs are loved and heard the world over" (21). Reynolds offers no mention of the Daughters of the American Revolution refusal in 1939 to permit Anderson to sing at Constitution Hall, nor of Eleanor Roosevelt's and Walter White's support of Anderson's Easter performance on the steps of the Lincoln Memorial. Only in the chapter on Ralph Bunche, "From 'Pig Boy' to Peacemaker," published in a 1948 edition, does Reynolds make explicit the accomplishment of an African American under segregation: "[H]e was the first Negro to hold a 'desk job' in [the State] department," Reynolds explains, adding, "For the monumental achievement in settling the Palestine dispute, Dr. Bunche is now known the world over" (71–72). Reynolds then describes Bunche's grandmother's words, which Bunche himself used in several speeches, the most prominent of which were "Nothing Is Impossible for the Negro" (1949) and "What America Means to Me" (1950): "'Your color,' she counseled, 'has nothing to do with your worth. You are potentially as good as anyone. How good you may prove to be will have no relation to your color, but with what is in your heart and head. The right to be treated as an equal by all other men is man's birthright. Never permit anyone to treat you otherwise. Who, indeed, is a better American, a better protector of the American heritage, than he who demands the fullest measure of respect for those cardinal principles on which our society is reared?'" (72).[21] Reynolds is most assertive in this passage in demanding respect for black Americans; he places these words in the voice of a grandmother rather than that of Reynolds himself or of Bunche, although Bunche did in fact speak those words when giving speeches. Reynolds thus offers his most militant version of racial dignity in language through the voice of "a tiny woman of vibrant spirit and strong conviction" (72), a move that recalls Mary, the grandmother in Hughes's *Sweet Flypaper of Life*, who is able to articulate and embrace the complexity of Harlem's community. Reynolds speaks most bravely through a grandmother, a gesture that emphasizes the 1940s need to cloak public civil rights articulations in some mollifying element. Nowhere else in the volume does Reynolds refer in language to the national struggle for civil rights.

Patterns for Progress: Lincoln and Interracial Friendship

Reynolds instead employs the staple progressive icon of social change, Abraham Lincoln,[22] invoking a history of social transformation in order to push his audience toward action. Mickenberg explains that "[l]eft-authored children's books published in the postwar period rewrote popular myths and historical narratives—and celebrated 'people's heroes' like Lincoln—in order to emphasize a version of the past that predicted a more egalitarian future."[23] Reynolds's chapter on Lincoln emphasizes his kindness to children, mothers, soldiers, and animals, arguing that "[s]ome think it is a sign of weakness to be kind, but it is really a mark of greatness. Few men have had more troubles and perplexities than did Lincoln, yet few men are more sympathetic and considerate" (23). The slip into present tense in this passage suggests Reynolds's attempt to link Lincoln's approach to social difference through benevolence (although Reynolds includes not one mention of enslavement or of African Americans in this chapter), with an approach to civil rights in the mid-twentieth century that employs Christian love as a means to overcoming prejudice.

The images Reynolds includes are much more assertive. In a picture by Marjory Collins of the OWI office, two young African Americans stand before the Lincoln Memorial and appear to be talking with each other (Figure 2.2). One figure peers up at Lincoln while the other gestures as if in midsentence. Lincoln is elevated, hovering over the conversation as a static representation of racial progress and idealism. What intimates action in this image is the conversation between the two figures below; the response to Lincoln's memory is social engagement, the image suggests, a dialogue within the race that reflects on the legacy of the president and on emancipation, bringing the ideal of social change into the current moment. The caption, which is not repeated in the text

The great Lincoln is loved and honored by people of all nations because he was the champion of the poor and needy when their cause was just.

Figure 2.2. Two young people talk together under the Lincoln Memorial in Washington, D.C. From Louis B. Reynolds and Charles L. Paddock, *Little Journeys into Storyland: Stories That Will Live and Lift* (Nashville: Southern Publishing Association, 1947).

of the chapter, emphasizes this legacy and points toward civil rights activity: "The great Lincoln is loved and honored by people of all nations because he was the champion of the poor and needy when their cause was just" (22). The cause of the modern moment, the image suggests, is a movement in progress and in conversation, and is sanctioned by the memory of Lincoln.

A second image of Lincoln, published originally by Acme Newspapers,

In Jim's heart there was a sense of real joy, a feeling of victory, a happiness from having been man enough to be honest.

Figure 2.3. A student sits below a portrait of Lincoln. From Louis B. Reynolds and Charles L. Paddock, *Little Journeys into Storyland: Stories That Will Live and Lift* (Nashville: Southern Publishing Association, 1947).

accompanies a chapter on honesty that immediately follows the biographical chapter on Lincoln. In the narrative about honesty, a boy, Jim, refuses to cheat on a test. The image of Lincoln appears as a framed photograph hanging on a wall above the head of an African American student at a desk (Figure 2.3). The framing of Lincoln makes clear his status as an icon for black youth: with several layers of frames and matting emphasizing the significance of the image,

Lincoln's picture is valorized figuratively, rendering him a representative of the ideals that motivate young black America. Most of the photograph is taken up with the young man's body, his lanky legs and right arm outstretched along the edge of the desk evoking the image that appeared just before this one, of the seated Lincoln of the Lincoln Memorial. The young man thus becomes a new version of Lincoln, one posed facing forward, looking out toward the right side of the frame into the future. Further identifying the young man with the president, his head intersects the frame of the Lincoln image, breaking the boundaries between the mind of the young person and the space of the idealized Lincoln. The discussion of honesty in the text, of course, makes young Jim walk in the footsteps of "honest Abe," as the picture suggests that the model of Lincoln takes new shape in the body and vision of young African America.

Unlike the image of General Davis, whom children as well as adults would be able to identify, this young-Lincoln image contains a subject who might be recognizable only to parents—and perhaps then only to progressive parents—reading *Little Journeys* along with children. The young Lincoln is Angelo Herndon, the black Communist who in 1932 led an interracial labor protest. He was imprisoned and convicted of violating a Reconstruction-era law against insurrection; the U.S. Supreme Court eventually overturned the conviction. His name was often linked with the Scottsboro Boys in the 1930s, and he became "a national figurehead for both cases."[24] Like many of the images in *Little Journeys*, Herndon's was originally included in the *Message*, alongside an unattributed essay titled "Lincoln, the Emancipator," in 1939, which speculates about which elements of Lincoln's history occupied the mind of Herndon. That essay concludes of Lincoln, "We have suggested that he brought liberty to two races, for he had as much to teach his own as the colored race about true liberty. Soul liberty is not enjoyed by such as would keep their brethren in physical bondage." Reynolds does not explicitly call out white prejudice in the children's book, but he permits an image of Herndon to point to Lincoln's legacy for black activists of the twentieth century. Again, I do not want to suggest that a child reader would identify Herndon, nor that his position as a Communist in the 1930s was emphasized either in the *Message* or in *Little Journeys*. However, as a labor leader who led an interracial march, Herndon is a provocative choice for a book that points to Lincoln as a model for social activism. Even if Herndon is not recognizable,[25] his position in the chair and the placement in sequence following the Lincoln Memorial image link him with the most prominent icon of social justice.

For Reynolds, Lincoln's revolutionary power is based in kindness, and further references to social reform point back to Lincoln's model. Further, the friendship approach dovetails suggestively with the interracial-brotherhood motif prominent in the midcentury intercultural-educational movement. Reynolds asserts with frequency the need for friendship and brotherhood, as in the chapter titled "Keep the Oil Can Handy," which describes the ocean liner *Carpathia*'s use of oil to calm the seas when rescuing the *Titanic*'s survivors. Reynolds belabors a bit the "oil of friendship" concept: "Let us bear in mind that a little oil will cover a large surface. A kind word, a cheery smile, a helping hand, just a little act of kindness may help someone through the storm. We, too, may strike stormy seas and need a helping hand. . . . [L]et us pour on freely the oil of love and brotherly kindness" (157–58). The choice of oil as a metaphor for friendship is somewhat unfortunate, as its associations with "oily behavior" and "unctuous smiles" might compromise the argument. Reynolds is more successful literarily when encouraging friendship between the races with specificity: "Have you had feelings in your heart against some particular race or nation? Have you been prejudiced against certain religious organizations? Have you criticized and condemned men and women before you really knew them? Don't be too hasty in forming opinions" (209). This is an especially optimistic perspective on race relations, positing that an obstacle to universal brotherhood resides in black expectation of white racism.

Again, the images make an argument for interracial friendship more powerfully than the language does. One significant image accompanies a chapter entitled "A Real Friend," which retells the Damon and Pythias myth and concludes with this advice: "But remember, to have friends you must be friendly—you must be a friend" (43 [Figure 2.4]). Although the chapter thus offers another iteration of the idea that racial goodwill would arise from eliminating bias against whites, the image, by African American photographer Gordon Parks, depicts two young boys, arm in arm, looking happily into the future. Parks photographed the children in Anacostia, a neighborhood in Washington, D.C., in 1942, in front of the Frederick Douglass housing project as part of Parks's OWI photographic work; the children had been swimming and were photographed shirtless and dripping wet. In the more tightly framed image in Reynolds's book, Parks's context is absent, for there is no indication that both children lived in the African American housing project. What remains is an image that likely would have been read as a picture of interracial friendship, much as were the images of Rex and his friends in Shackelford's *My Happy Days*. In Reynolds's text, the light-skinned boy has loose, curly hair, and their lack of shirts emphasizes the difference in their bodies' color. Coupling this photo with a Greek myth in

Loyalty between friends is an asset of lifelong value.

Figure 2.4. Two boys stand arm in arm. From Louis B. Reynolds and Charles L. Paddock, *Little Journeys into Storyland: Stories That Will Live and Lift* (Nashville: Southern Publishing Association, 1947).

which two young men "loved each other as much as if they were real brothers" (41), Reynolds suggests powerfully that the ideal of friendship transcends racial barriers. The boys in the image exchange an embrace that spotlights their differences through the image's physicality and yet allows the viewer to witness the effortless camaraderie that idealized "true" friendship brings (43). The brotherhood of humanity, heralded by Lincoln, the friend of "people of all nations" (22), becomes visible and material in the photographs Reynolds draws together.

Agents of Change: Technology and the Bible
Kindness, changing one's heart about others, and openness to friendship are all means toward better race relations for Reynolds, as his language details and the images illuminate. Reynolds also participates in the midcentury embrace of technology and science in literature for young people as a means toward explaining social progress as a logical inevitability. Just as Shackelford included images of Rex peering through a microscope in order to find out the truth about the world around him, so does Reynolds present images of black chil-

dren as budding scientists. In one such image, originally by Marjory Collins for the OWI, a group of children gather around beakers and Bunsen burners, some with half-suppressed smiles on their faces, as they await the results of their experiment. The caption reads, "Painstaking perseverance in life, as well as in the laboratory, is essential to achieving the greatest success" (120). The emphasis in the chapter that attends this image is perseverance, again hitting obliquely at racial prejudice by asserting, "Maybe you have spent long years in preparation for your life work, and now that you have your education, find no opening, no place in which to use your talents" (122). However, the laboratory suggests change is a result of scientific inevitability coupled with hard work. Racial progress becomes a foreseeable scientific result. Similarly, technological advances are linked with the movement forward in race relations through photographs. A chapter that encourages children to work even in the face of "jokes, ridicule and scorn" (197) includes a page that joins two images of aircraft. As the caption notes, "The lower picture shows the Wright brothers' airplane, the first really successful flying machine" (196), whereas the top photo, from the International News Service, depicts military men in a jeep gazing admiringly at a TWA commercial aircraft. The idea of progress becomes plain in the juxtaposition of these images. Technological development, that extension of scientific discovery, mirrors the progress that will inevitably happen in race relations, the chapter suggests. After briefly chronicling the experiences of twenty inventors, thinkers, and explorers who faced adversity, the chapter concludes, "You may have to stand alone, while the world looks on with scorn. To do this, one must know he is right. But when we feel we are right, we should be willing to stand alone if necessary. We cannot drift into goodness. We will have to face the wind, to battle with the tide" (202). The battle of goodness versus its adversaries will result in progress, as the descriptions and images of technological progress assert. Just as Reynolds treats race relations obliquely in all other instances, save that of Ralph Bunche and his grandmother, here he relies on a discourse of technological development to signal the inevitability of social change.

For this SDA author, however, the agent of progress in modern society is the Bible. Reynolds extends a colonialist perspective on non-Christian cultures, figuring the Bible as that which can transform both the (supposedly) backward indigenous communities in the South Pacific and the hard-hearted un-Christian people in the United States: "What the Bible has done on Pitcairn Island it has done and is still doing in all parts of the world. It will work just as wonderful changes in our towns, in our own lives" (105). The attached Acme Newspapers image of an airplane flying over an oxcart contrasts cultures through technology, however, as the text attributes modernity in all its facets to the embrace of Christianity. The airplane in the image connects, of course, to the Wright brothers / TWA image that comes a bit later in the text, revealing a teleology of progress (thanks to the Bible) that starts with the oxcart and ends with transcontinental air travel. Finally, for Reynolds, Jesus is ultimate friend as agent of social progress, because he eliminates divisions between peoples and draws all together. "Jesus is the Friend of all, rich and poor, high and low, white, brown, red, yellow, or black," Reynolds explains near the close of the book (215); and because the Bible enables social progress that leads to universal brotherhood, Jesus promises social equality.[26] There are no photographs of Jesus, of course (the book does contain an illustration), but the images that Reynolds amasses in referencing the "battle" against prejudice—whether it is the boys with arms around each other, the children in a chemistry lab, or the evolution of air travel—all indicate that the goodwill and hard work cultivated within the black community will come to inevitable fruition.

Conduct Traditions and the Politics of Picturing Joy

One can understand Reynolds's cautiousness when arguing for racial parity, given his fraught position as a spokesperson for the black Adventist community, coupled with the midcentury national insistence on celebratory depictions of race relations. He must be watchful in framing an argument for social change. However, Reynolds's text is most groundbreaking when it plays with the visual conventions of the black conduct book in order to articulate a new attitude toward child agency. Reynolds's book was marketed in the *Message* as a conduct book; an advertisement in 1947 proclaimed, "Nothing will help them more than good books in the developing of strong sturdy characters."[27] Of course, conduct and biography are related genres, given that frequently adults offer children historical biographical sketches as models of moral or economic success. The hybrid biography and conduct book makes sense, then, in combining accounts of individuals' lives along with direct behavioral advice. In the early part of the century, expectations for images within African American conduct books (and even children's images in newspapers like the *Crisis*) were quite stable: often publications included portrait photographs of well-dressed children, many of whom were performing middle-class accomplishment by reading books or playing an instrument like the piano or violin. Even in depicting dramatic episodes, the early conduct book often included images that appeared quite serene. For example, the photograph captioned "An Exciting Moment" in Silas Floyd's

AN EXCITING MOMENT.

Figure 2.5. An early conduct book depicts a moment of success at a spelling competition. From Silas X. Floyd, *Floyd's Flowers: Duties and Beauties for Colored Children*, 1905. Reprinted as *Short Stories for Colored People Both Young and Old* (Washington, D.C.: Austin Jenkins Company, 1920).

Short Stories for Colored People Both Young and Old (1920), a revised version of his popular *Floyd's Flowers: Duties and Beauties for Colored Children* (1905), illustrates a story about a spelling competition at school (Figure 2.5). The children appear decidedly unexcited, the only glimmer of enthusiasm coming from the hint of a smile on the face of the girl standing stiffly to the right. As Michele Mitchell explains, the approach of early twentieth-century black conduct books mirrored popular photographic practice: "Guidelines within advice literature not only depicted an upright race striving ever upward, but such depictions were, in and of themselves, a form of reproduction not dissimilar to staged studio photographs in which individuals projected desired selves for display and circu-

lation."[28] Conduct photos also typically demonstrated a severe degree of emotional control.[29] With this background in mind, Reynolds's figures of young
people take on particular weight.

Reynolds's most conspicuous revision of early conduct material comes in
the image of a child climbing a ladder (Figure 2.6). Accompanying a chapter
titled "Just Little Things," the image evokes the "upward climb" of Harlem Re-

Babies, though very small, can be very important, as any parent or brother or
sister will tell you.

Figure 2.6. A young child climbs a ladder with a joyful
expression. From Louis B. Reynolds and Charles L. Paddock,
Little Journeys into Storyland: Stories That Will Live and Lift
(Nashville: Southern Publishing Association, 1947).

naissance iconography, versions of which appeared in varied visual media, from paintings like *The Ascent of Ethiopia* (1932), by Lois Mailou Jones, to the cover of Monroe Majors's conduct book for children containing photographs, *First Steps and Nursery Rhymes* (1920). The "first steps" of Majors's title refer to steps on the path to collective black "development and progress" rather than simply to a baby's efforts at walking.[30] The cover makes this meaning clear in its depiction of three children helping each other up steps, each labeled with a value like "Obedience," "Courage," "Generosity," "Sacrifice," and "Education." The top landing is labeled "Success." The "upward climb" motif in black culture was treated pointedly by Langston Hughes in his famous poem "Mother to Son," in which a woman tells her child, "Life for me ain't been no crystal stair. / . . . But all the time / I'se been a-climbin' on." Reynolds's photograph clearly evokes the tradition of progress through movement upward, as the child is climbing the ladder. The caption reads, "Babies, though very small, can be very important, as any parent or brother or sister will tell you" (58). Reynolds's sentiment echoes back through the body of African American conduct books, for in the 1920s emphasis on youth leadership and on the "newest" Negroes embodying the "New Negro" potentiality, many conduct writers emphasized the importance of childhood, as Floyd had done when he addressed the reader in 1905: "Never think yourself, whoever you are, of small importance. . . . Every boy has his part to do in the great work of the world, and every girl has her part to do. Every boy and girl is of importance."[31] Reynolds shares this sentiment, this emphasis on the potential contribution of black childhood to the social landscape. The major difference in his figuration of the upward climb is that instead of representing it as laborious and difficult, he selects a photograph of a child with pure pleasure on his or her face. The child is in midstride, climbing the ladder of success with ease. Iconographically, this upward-climb image coheres with Reynolds's pictures of technology and science in the book; the inevitability of the child's success here becomes apparent through the child's blissful look.

Similarly, when Reynolds presents a sentiment conventional to conduct books, he employs an image that recasts its implications (Figure 2.7). A crowd of children stand over a bed on which two babies lie. The caption reads, "As big oaks from little acorns grow, so great men are made of little babes" (62). The weighty idea of "great men" emerging from childhood was quite typical of conduct literature, and could be read as a justification for the genre in general. Like the upward-climb image, this photograph refuses ponderousness, emphasizing instead the joy that the older children feel about the babies they are observing. Whereas the young people's lines of sight are focused on the infants, and in a

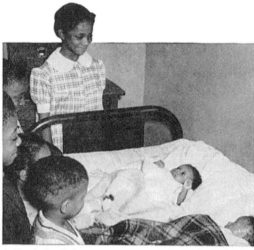

62   LITTLE JOURNEYS

As big oaks from little acorns grow, so great men are made of little babes.

the board. One of the boys was having trouble with his punctuation. The teacher rather chided the boy because he couldn't punctuate the sentence correctly. The visitor tried to encourage the lad. "Don't be discouraged, son," he said. "Those commas don't matter a great deal."

Thereupon the teacher asked the boy to write this sentence on the board: "The president of the school board says the teacher is a fool." "Now my boy," said the teacher, "please put a comma after board and one

Figure 2.7. Children admire babies in bed. From Louis B. Reynolds and Charles L. Paddock, *Little Journeys into Storyland: Stories That Will Live and Lift* (Nashville: Southern Publishing Association, 1947).

traditionally cropped image their sightlines would draw our focus to the babies alone, Reynolds crops the image so that the oldest child's head breaks the frame. She peers over the babies and over the photograph itself, permitting the reader to focus not only on the infants and their potentiality but also on the girl and her pleasure in observing the babies. The girl allows the reader to take joy in black childhood, a sentiment not usually associated with the severity of conduct material. Certainly Reynolds's text can be severe, particularly in its depiction of temptation, disobedience, and sin. In the images, however, we witness a new perspective on black childhood, one focusing on delight and ease in tandem with ideas of social progress.[32]

Other images within Reynolds's book provide powerful iterations of child resilience in the face of prejudice. Three playful images substantially revise the stilted and guarded photographs typically found in conduct books, as well as reinvent a vision of black childhood as natural, attractive, confident, and joyful. The first, which is attached to a chapter on farming, pictures two young people standing on farm property with their dog (Figure 2.8). The children smile comfortably at the camera, and their bodies fill the space of the image, suggesting their prominence and value, for the farm work is not the emphasis but rather their smiling faces and physical ease. The boy holds up his dog, extending its body alongside his in a gesture that speaks of affection and trust and the dog's pet status rather than worker status. The children are dressed attractively but not fussily, with the girl's hands breaking the line of the fence between them. The caption reads, "Bobby and Betty enjoyed living on the farm, and they were a big help to their parents with the farm chores" (108). In contrast to the many exploitative images of black children on farms, and in contrast to the FSA tradition of depicting rural poverty and dissatisfaction, these children work with their parents in a space they claim and enjoy.

The second image, showing seven children sitting in a line on a large tree limb (with another ready to climb up and join them), emphasizes the unity and contentment of the group of children (Figure 2.9). The conventional conduct caption offers a twist: "The successful and honorable men and women of tomorrow are found among the playful boys and girls of today" (134). Play, pleasure, and fellowship are all valued in this uncredited Adventist image, a moment that certainly diverges from the way in which black childhood had been figured visually before this point.

Finally, an image of children running down an urban street offers a sense of joy and movement rarely seen in public photographs of black children before this point (Figure 2.10). A Monkmeyer Press Photo Service image, it had appeared in the *Message* at least once before, in an April 1945 conduct article by Natelkka E. Burrell for parents, entitled "Our Parental Delinquency Problem." Reynolds's book tries to anchor the image to a chapter on obedience, linking it to a discussion of a child who was killed accidentally after not listening to his mother ("With him, disobedience was costly indeed") and a mention of "the electric chair or the gallows" for those who break the law (57). Even the caption

Bobby and Betty enjoyed living on the farm, and they were a big help to their parents with the farm chores.

Figure 2.8. Two children take pleasure in farm life. From Louis B. Reynolds and Charles L. Paddock, *Little Journeys into Storyland: Stories That Will Live and Lift* (Nashville: Southern Publishing Association, 1947).

Figure 2.9. Children sit together on a tree limb in an uncredited Seventh-Day Adventist image. From Louis B. Reynolds and Charles L. Paddock, *Little Journeys into Storyland: Stories That Will Live and Lift* (Nashville: Southern Publishing Association, 1947).

The successful and honorable men and women of tomorrow are found among the playful boys and girls of today.

Obedient children are safe and happy children.

Figure 2.10. The "obedient children" described in this image's caption run exuberantly down the street. From Louis B. Reynolds and Charles L. Paddock, *Little Journeys into Storyland: Stories That Will Live and Lift* (Nashville: Southern Publishing Association, 1947).

for the image strains to connect its energy with the message of the chapter: "Obedient children are safe and happy children" (55). The children in the image might be obedient; it is hard to say definitively, though, because their energy bespeaks a freedom of movement not typically associated with young people who are focused on obeying their parents. These children are happy, to be sure, and active and vigorous, in a rare depiction of urban black childhood. Their unity is suggested by their collective joy, as well as by the two girls who run together as one body with their arms around each other.[33]

These three images are not simply photographs of happy children. They are interventions in a racist visual landscape that insisted on urban child poverty and rural child despair, and as such they are deeply political. Within a context of a book that argues (however hesitantly) about the need for social justice in the face of prejudice, these images potently assert child resilience and capability. As bell hooks argues in *Art on My Mind*, "Though rarely articulated as such, the camera became in black life a political instrument, a way to resist misrepresentation as well as a means by which alternative images could be produced."[34] In the unattributed SDA photographs, one also senses the pleasure of the image maker in the process of reinvention, for, according to hooks, "Producing images with the camera allowed black folks to combine image making in resistance struggle with a pleasurable experience. Taking pictures was fun!"[35] A sense of joy in reclaiming the image has been overlooked in our consideration of early civil rights photography.

The liveliness of Reynolds's images also suggests a corresponding energy on the part of the viewer, a vitality that the black-child reader can witness in the photographs and recognize in herself. The forcefulness of these images might be associated with assertiveness, especially if we consider capturing these images as a form of political intervention. Sontag explains that "[i]mages which idealize . . . are no less aggressive than work which makes a virtue of plainness. . . . There is an aggression implicit in every use of the camera."[36] We might extend this understanding of aggression to an appreciation for Reynolds's editorial practice; even if his language is necessarily evasive and cautious, he encourages visually a vital engagement with the world surrounding the reader, one in which the "battle" for social equality was in full force. The cheerful and robust children in Reynolds's book model an attitude of confidence and courageousness for the reader. Not only do they extend the implicit agenda of social progress through transforming childhood found in the conduct tradition, but they also pattern a kind of assertiveness, resilience, naturalness, and ease that anticipate the visual aesthetics of the Black Arts Movement of the mid- to late 1960s. Change is inevitable, black childhood holds power and pride within itself, and joy in the face of prejudice becomes an assertion of integrity and power. Affirmative portraits like these opened up possibilities for new conceptions of black childhood.

By the 1950s, Reynolds could be more assertive about his embrace of civil rights. Reynolds's daughter, Dawn Reynolds, told me in an interview that the movement was, in fact, very important to her father: "In the 1950s, he had interviewed young Martin Luther King [for the *Message*], had a cover and a text, and the organization rejected it. My father saw King as a person of profound courage and someone who could make a difference."[37] Although there exists a theological basis to the church's general reluctance to participate in social movements, several black SDA members did work overtly for social justice, as Samuel G. London's *Seventh-Day Adventists and the Civil Rights Movement* explains. Reynolds was forthright in a 1952 editorial column in the *Message*, responding to the federal government's steps toward integration by saying, "It would not be a fair statement to declare that all U.S. problems based on color are being dissolved and that the brotherhood emphasis can be temporarily relaxed. Much more remains to be done before the effort can be viewed with a mood short of anxiety. But the front line has inched forward a long way in advance of what was years ago known to be forbidden ground. The march toward equal opportunities, evenhanded justice, and adequate public facilities is now, in the present group-betterment adventure, on many fronts and in many places."[38] In his April 1957 "March of Events" column, Reynolds praised "Martin Luther King praying for his enemies in Montgomery";[39] and although he could not offer the magazine's cover to King, Reynolds did include a photograph of the leader alongside his June 1957 "March of Events" column.[40] Even into the 1950s, photographs articulated Reynolds's desire that black SDA members recognize, visually, renewed iterations of black identity and possibility.

LANGSTON HUGHES AND MILTON MELTZER:
HISTORY AS INSPIRATION FOR ACTION

Less than a decade separates *Little Journeys into Storyland* (1947–48) and *A Pictorial History of the Negro in America* (1956), yet that period witnessed dramatic changes in the civil rights landscape for young people. The most transformative moment, perhaps, was the 1954 Supreme Court ruling on *Brown v. Board of Education of Topeka*, which overturned the 1896 "separate but equal" legislation of *Plessy v. Ferguson*. In March 1955, Claudette Colvin in Montgomery, Alabama, was arrested for refusing to give up her seat on a bus to a white person, as was Rosa Parks in December of that year, sparking the Montgomery bus boycott led by Dr. Martin Luther King Jr. The murder of fourteen-year-old Emmett Till in August 1955 triggered international outrage, particularly after Mamie Till permitted photographs of her brutally disfigured son to be published in *Jet* magazine and the *Chicago Defender*. *Pictorial History* predated Little Rock (1957), the Greensboro lunch-counter sit-ins (1960), and the Freedom Riders (1961), as well as the legislative and cultural accomplishments of the mid-1960s; the book emerged just as the civil rights movement started to catch fire, just before the "new, confrontational state of the Movement."[41] A harbinger of revolutionary change in black historiography, *Pictorial History* anticipated the 1960s black-nationalist commitment to popularized radical versions of African and African American history. Hughes and Meltzer were not black nationalists, of course, but their revisionist approach to history and their engagement with a large, popular audience forecasted a new approach in the 1960s to the shape of black history and its audience. In addition, one could consider *Pictorial History* as anticipating the experimentalism of the radical 1960s. Sara Blair explains:

> In the emerging institutions and communities that would coalesce later in the decade as a Black Arts movement, the commitment to auratic performance, collective experience, or community building and vernacular expression produced a powerful emphasis on antinarrative forms—jazz, experimental drama, stand-up performance, and spoken word. Novelists of all stripes, particularly those who had come of age as writers during the dawning of the civil rights era, shared a critical problem: finding resources to respond to the confusing, devastating, sometimes exhilarating challenges of an incendiary history in the making.[42]

To be sure, *Pictorial History* points toward many of the values of the Black Arts Movement, particularly community building and experimentalism. Although it might not expressly bear the radical stamp of the next decade, because *Pictorial History* is committed to the American identity of black history, its aim of popularization as a coffee-table history and its word/image experimentalism make it an important forerunner of 1960s populist expression. And the resources it offered to a movement in the making were nothing less than spectacular.

Although the engagement of trauma is not my project's primary concern, we might consider briefly the implications for the resources contained within Hughes and Meltzer's magisterial book. The text might be understood as a form of "postmemorial work," which, as Marianne Hirsch argues in *The Generation of Postmemory*, "strives to *reactivate* and *re-embody* more distant political and cultural memorial structures by reinvesting them with resonant individual and familial forms of mediation and aesthetic expression."[43] Given that black families had endured the pain of multiple displacements from the past, most prominently the erasure in public memory of enslavement, and having not much else but private memorials to the past through family remembrances, Hughes and Meltzer's work intervenes aesthetically as a monument to a history that could be mediated and concretized through visual artifact. Although the sections on enslavement rely more on illustration than on photography, the visual nature of *Pictorial History* aims to provoke and affect the reader with the "real" dimensions of history. Reading this text in a family setting, as it was intended, adds another layer to Hirsch's ideas about the "familial aspects of postmemory";[44] even if the text does not include family photographs and does not thus engender an affiliative response in precisely the terms Hirsch describes, a collaborative familial reading experience that examines the visual invocation of artifacts and individuals under enslavement would serve similar ends: "to diminish distance, bridge separation, and facilitate identification and affiliation."[45] The affective experience of history is at stake in such a family reading. The black family under enslavement was so rarely rendered photographically that the visual traces Hughes and Meltzer amass aim to reconstitute bonds and to embody history in terms emotionally appreciable to the book's family audience. Instead of looking at family photographs and considering the enduring life of history (as do Hirsch and other theorists of Holocaust visual representation), Hughes and Meltzer offer material traces of the past in order to nudge a family to recreate imaginatively its own historical presence. These are also moments that could be chaperoned, to use Joe Sutliff Sanders's term, as the reading situation permits exchange between adult and young reader.

Unlike Reynolds and Paddock, who shared the title page of *Little Journeys into Storyland* as coauthors in name only, as a signifier of interracial collaboration, Hughes and Melzer worked together on multiple dimensions of the book's production.[46] Meltzer was a Jewish leftist who was employed by the Works Progress Administration in the 1930s and collected printed ephemera on black culture during his travel in the 1950s for a pharmaceutical company. Later in life, he became one of the most prolific and influential nonfiction writers on social justice for young people.[47] Meltzer said of his experience collaborating with Hughes, "Strangers at the beginning, we became friends during the course of the work."[48] He and Hughes worked together to select the images for *Pictorial History* and together drafted an outline for the book. Hughes wrote the narrative, on which Meltzer offered comments, and the layout coordinator at Crown, Dan DeKoven, collaborated with Hughes and Meltzer on the text and image design.[49]

Although the book addresses the sweep of black history from the slave trade to the contemporary moment, space precludes an in-depth discussion of the thousand fertile images that recount Hughes and Meltzer's version of history. The reception of *Pictorial History*, however, can help us determine its role as a mediator in a national conversation about civil rights. In addition, my discussion focuses on the moments toward the end of the book that bring the civil rights context into relief, rather than considering the ample discussion of freedom fighters in the antebellum and Reconstruction eras. This is not because the latter discussion is irrelevant to the positioning of *Pictorial History* as a text that links history to the present moment in order to inspire action, for such a discussion would be quite relevant and would be important work for future scholarship. My attention will concentrate on the text's construction of recent history, the section entitled "Toward One World, 1941–," in order to address the intersection of text and image in the book's encouragement of civil rights action.

My emphasis on the reception of *Pictorial History* stems from an awareness of the need to situate photographs contextually, for black images risk misreading when dislodged from the framework of their use.[50] The uses of the black image transcend the moment a photograph is taken. For Hughes and Meltzer's text, the public context of a history text also influences my emphasis on reception; for unlike fictional photographic texts in chapter 1, which work to build a one-to-one connection of friendship between a reader and a subject, the photohistory emerges into a public space and claims an authority over a community's definition throughout history. The aims in transforming the reader's perspective are more wide-ranging than in the case of an intimate fictional photographic picture book: Hughes and Meltzer claim authority over the arc of black history, and although they might share ambitions with other writers in this study in connecting emotionally with young readers, their strategy differs fundamentally from those writers, for they speak directly of the injustices of history in order to reconstruct the community's view of itself and its potential for resistance to racism. Reception becomes, then, important to defining the cast of *Pictorial History*, for in understanding how the text was read in its moment, one can discern the text's public accomplishment and call to public action.

Coffee-Table Books and Family Reading
A Pictorial History of the Negro in America was a tremendously popular book, one of Hughes's best sellers, according to Arnold Rampersad.[51] Hughes, in correspondence with Meltzer, recognized the book's ubiquity, asserting, "I see our PICTORIAL HISTORY all around, even in Bermuda whence I've just come from doing a series of poetry programs, ending my season which took me across the country twice and from Tuskegee to Toronto and Vancouver."[52] The *New York Age*, an African American newspaper, reported in 1958 that the book was one of only two books by black authors given to Eisenhower's presidential library, the other being Marian Anderson's autobiography.[53] Embraced by Eisenhower, the book had a national, interracial profile, but it took on particular weight within black households. As civil rights activist Joseph McNeil explained, "You went to someone's home, had a seat, looked around in the front room and it wasn't unusual to see it, the *Pictorial History*. It was almost like a

badge of honor to have it."[54] Blair's volume on black writers and the photo-graph explains, "Everywhere throughout the *Pictorial History*, as it covers the experience of black Americans from the first settlements through the gathering civil rights movement, Hughes's belief in the power of the image—particularly the photograph—to render visible and to dignify its subjects is bedrock and self-evident."[55] The emphasis on the distinction and tangibility of black history rendered the book opportune, for American culture at that time was struggling to articulate a relationship between national identity and its African American population. *Pictorial History* made evident the long-standing participation of black people in American values, traditions, and historical events, serving as an articulation of African American citizenship during a time in which blacks and progressive whites (as well as governmental propaganda) desired a clear-sighted assertion of black citizenship. *Pictorial History* offered that affirmation, as well as identifying the ongoing process of the black freedom struggle, and its popu-larity bespoke its resonance within the larger American cultural milieu. As we remember Arthur P. Davis's comments about the moment of the late 1950s as an "interim between two worlds—between a world of dying segregation and one of a developing integration,"[56] Hughes and Meltzer's book appears even more courageous: their work intervenes in historical memory, insisting on black American investment in civil rights, and prods the reader to take action.

Briefly, it should be noted that the format of *Pictorial History* was part of an innovative trend in the 1950s. Pictorial histories from a variety of publishers appeared, addressing such topics as American presidents (1955), the American circus (1957), the American theater (1953), American sports (1952), American comedians (1957), the American West (1955), and so on. Crown, Hughes and Meltzer's publisher, issued several pictorial histories, including Lamont Buch-man's *Pictorial History of the Confederacy* (1951), which used a collage layout quite similar to that of *A Pictorial History of the Negro*.[57] Given Buchman's book and the popularity of the pictorial-history genre, Hughes and Meltzer's text was welcomed as an overdue contribution rather than something entirely new. Richard Bardolph's review in the *Greensboro (N.C.) Daily News* proclaimed, "At last we have a handsome and genuinely informative pictorial history of colored America, very much in the format of the numerous big picture books that in the past few years have been illuminating so many facets of our history and culture."[58] Hughes and Meltzer's book can thus be understood as less a novelty than part of a modern trend, one that would have been legible to middle-class Americans.

The argument about black American citizenship offered within *Pictorial*

History was imagined as being especially appropriate for an audience of young people. Two threads surface in configuring the audience of the book: some reviewers saw it as part of family reading, a coffee-table book, as Joseph McNeil encountered it, that would have been accessible to all members of a household and to visitors; other reviewers marveled over the book's appropriateness for classroom teaching. As family reading, not only did the book appeal to all, but it also was set in public space in order to inspire conversation and engagement with its subject, a feature of its communal identity and ethos. For black families, its visible household presence also testified to the parents' investment in instilling racial pride in children. Regarding its visibility within white and black households, the *Saturday Review* discussed Hughes's book alongside other pictorial histories, saying that the size of the text prevented it from sitting on a shelf: "[T]he handsome big picture books must be left out on library and living-room tables, and that is where they ought to be, as snares to the curious of family and guests." After explaining that children over the age of ten would appreciate the genre, the review asserts of Hughes's book, "Few of its pages can be read with pride by any white person, and most call forth a sense of shame and a corresponding awe that human beings can so well endure what has been the lot of the Negro in America."[59] The emphasis on childhood and family reading was even stronger in review and promotional material aimed at an African American audience. Horace Mann Bond, president of Lincoln University, where Hughes attended, rhapsodized about the appeal of the book to the young: "Its range and competence is such that it will be a gold mine for scholars, and, I think, an irresistible and inspiring treasure-store for the smallest child. To Fellow alumni, I say: 'If you do not immediately rush down to your bookstore and get this book, for yourself, your family, and especially for your children—you deserve to be expelled from the ranks of the alumni of Lincoln University!' Strong words, Mates: but that is just the way I feel about this wonderful, wonderful book."[60] *Pictorial History* is best placed within a household setting, Bond and others argued, because the story it tells is that of the family of black America across time. The popular African American newspaper the *Pittsburgh Courier* similarly connected purchase of *Pictorial History* with a parent's obligation to inculcate race pride: "Negro children of today and tomorrow would hold up their heads in pride if Negro parents of today would make 'A Pictorial History of the Negro in the United States' a part of the family library."[61] Owning *Pictorial History* signified black parental accomplishment, and the book served additionally as a conversation piece for socially minded adults, both black and white.

The other thread connecting *Pictorial History* to a child audience is its role as supplementary reading within classrooms. Mickenberg explains that "many school libraries purchased *A Pictorial History* because it filled a gap in children's book offerings; certainly no textbook provided this kind of information. The book's popularity with young people helped to convince Meltzer to devote the latter half of his career to writing books for young readers about the 'under-dog.'"[62] Reviews of *Pictorial History* sometimes considered its pedagogical use, as did Myles M. Platt in the February 1957 issue of the *Clearing House* (an education journal), who was frustrated that the book was bound and thus unable to be split up for teaching: "This reviewer believes that methods for wider use in the classroom should be found, simply because the total impact of *A Pictorial History of the Negro in America* is needed by our students."[63]

The book's appeal to young people is unsurprising, given its pictorial dimension (the *Worker* even said, "[I]n this age of comic books and television, it is a particularly attractive gift to consider for students and other young people who like their education visual") and its pedagogical subtext as a popular history.[64] But, perhaps more significantly, the book appealed to an inclusive audience of adults and children, black and white, because it was written by Langston Hughes. Throughout his long career as a poet, dramatist, children's writer, and newspaper columnist, Hughes strove to address a capacious American community, his signature artistic trait being a deep love for black people of all backgrounds and ages. More to the point, in December 1956, just after the appearance of *Pictorial History*, Hughes made his inclusive perspective visible in an essay for the *New York Age-Defender*. Hughes there suggested that the African American audience give books to schools and libraries as Christmas gifts, "or to some white social worker whose contacts with our people may be limited," arguing that "[i]t is up to us to help educate white Americans concerning ourselves. Books can help us do this." Books, he suggested, are part of the battle for civil rights, because being inclusive with black-authored literature could help change social relations: "To libraries, schools, lodges, community centers, or individuals, books make happy and lasting gifts. Many, many people can enjoy a book. If given to one member of a family, all the family can read a book. If given to a school or club, dozens of people may enjoy it. A little community gift-giving of books this Christmas can help to spread not only joy, but racial goodwill in whites, plus racial pride in ourselves. Give books for Christmas."[65] Given that Hughes encourages readers to purchase *Pictorial History* within this essay, the passage here reflects a number of applicable points, particularly the book's status as family reading, as a library book, as school reading, as a statement of racial identity, and (remembering the discussion in chapter 1 about the politics of friendship) as a means of changing the hearts and minds of white people. Books like *Pictorial History*, Hughes argues, can change the landscape of social relations, drawing children as well as adults into a reinvention of black identity through history. Hughes advocates for black textual self-representation to a white audience unfamiliar with African American historical accomplishment, and in doing so is more conspicuously interventionist than other authors of children's photobooks before this moment.

Reviews and Anticipation of Civil Rights Action

If children were prominent in the multiply constituted audience for *Pictorial History*, the book's emergence into a civil rights context spoke to the investment of young people in futurity. In particular, critics placed the history within the current civil rights movement by emphasizing the book's inclusion of Emmett Till. The *Newark (N.J.) News* was typical in noting, "It is perhaps an ironic commentary that the story must proceed from Crispus Attucks, first man to be slain in the Boston Massacre in 1770, all the way to 14-year-old Emmett Till, whose murderers are still free in Mississippi."[66] Other reviews called Till one of the "martyrs"[67] or commented expressly on the urgency of the civil rights effort. William Hogan, a white reviewer in the *San Francisco Chronicle*, described the immediate resonance of the book by saying, "It being a running history, the results of the Supreme Court decision on desegregation and the recent Montgomery, Ala., bus boycott are included. The 'trouble I seen' of the Negro's familiar lament, the authors suggest, is by no means ended."[68] Other reviewers were more direct in seeing the connections between history and the pressing modern civil rights moment, as in a December 1956 review among Hughes's papers, titled "The Negro": "[The book] portrays an era of wonderment. How could the white man have done these things to a fellow human being, and after doing them, how could he still persist in his illogical reasoning or give way to his primitive instincts? But as other men have said before and as others will say again, this thing shall pass. It will not always be this way. There will be more changes."[69] Even the show-business magazine *Variety* took interest in the text because of its civil rights import, saying, "The book is a must for those who have the slightest sympathy with a united America where all men are equal before the law and in the ballot box."[70] Sometimes reviews parsed out the civil rights activity of the past, connecting it with the present. For example, Myles M. Platt wrote in February 1957 to connect the historic attitude of nonviolence documented in the book with the current movement's strategy: "It is ironic that the pacific methods of Negro advancement should have been met with intimidation, riot, and the lynch mob, by those who in prejudice and bigotry insist on a status quo of subserviency."[71] Many of the reviews thus linked black historical responses to oppression with the techniques of nonviolent protest adopted by the civil rights movement in the 1950s.

Alongside Emmett Till and nonviolent protest, segregation was one of the main concerns of the reviewers of *Pictorial History*, for many readers connected the struggles of young people integrating schools in the 1950s with the difficulties facing historical African Americans as recounted in the book. Garrett D. Byrnes, in the *Rhode Island Sunday Journal*, noted, "Reminded as we are almost daily by stories out of Clinton, Tenn. [home to one of the first schools in Tennessee to be integrated], and other places of violent antagonism in the South that the struggle for freedom and equality for colored people continues to be an issue sorely trying for our democracy, this record will give the reader much that he probably never knew before. Certainly the book will put the present crises of racism in perspective as just one more action in a battle that has been going on within our gates since the Declaration."[72] Hughes himself retyped in his papers the following statement from the March 6, 1957, *Washington Star*, which suggests its significance to the writer: "Much of the turmoil going on in the minds of men over integration could be eased if more of the history of the Negro were taught in our schools to both white and colored children. This book should be available to every school and family."[73] In noting the connection between the current integration efforts and courageous black historic action, reviewers argued implicitly that Hughes and Meltzer's text offers an analogue to the present civil rights battle, one that would reshape a child reader's attitude toward black contributions to American identity and toward the civil rights movement.

In fact, drawing black contributions into an account of American history was understood by some as the practice of integration through art, a civil rights act in and of itself. One reviewer straightforwardly stated in February 1957, "Certainly the authors have spent their time well: their aim of *integrating* the American Negro with the mainstream of American history has been admirably fulfilled."[74] Crown's own advertisements for the book argued that it documents a long progress toward integration; the *New York Times Book Review* ad of November 1956 read, "Every milestone in the slow, painful road to equality in fact as well as theory is pictorially recorded. . . . As timely as it is important, this unique book portrays the rich heritage as well as the unquenchable spirit of the Negro people." In the December 1956 *Crisis*, Crown directly conflated the idea of describing historical civil rights efforts and practicing them: "And here are all the dramatic events . . . which are bringing America closer to the day when there will truly be 'liberty and justice for all.'"[75] Just as Hughes in his discussion of Christmas book-giving imagined texts as part of an arsenal in the battle for civil rights, in reviews and in Crown's own publication materials, the book enacts the kinds of effort it describes: it practices integration by weaving black experience into the fabric of the American past, and it itself wages war against a history that had excluded blacks.[76] Remembering these reviews, the context in which *Pictorial History* was read in its moment, can permit us to recognize more fully Langston Hughes's involvement in civil rights–era efforts. Deeply invested imaginatively and socially with the movement in the late 1950s and early 1960s, Hughes and his work were foundational to the early civil rights movement: his Harlem Renaissance–era poems, according to Rampersad, "were inspirational tracts" for many young activists.[77] Remembering *Pictorial History* within its context allows us to imagine Hughes, near the end of his life, as a vigorous proponent of and participant in civil rights efforts, as Christopher De Santis argues.[78] This is a facet of Hughes that should be emphasized in assessments of his contributions to the social milieu of the 1950s.[79] In *Sweet Flypaper of Life* (discussed in chapter 1) and *Pictorial History*, Hughes was a civil rights writer.

Brotherhood and the Camera's Impartiality

Hughes's approach to civil rights participated in the era's emphasis on camaraderie between African Americans and whites.[80] Remembering the writers in chapter 1 who struggled to articulate assertions of black agency and equality within a climate that relentlessly insisted on the success of racial relations, Hughes and Meltzer found their work read as promoting brotherhood and democracy through knowledge of black contributions to American historical events; but unlike the fictional texts' positive rendering of the domestic space, the text of *Pictorial History* contains harrowing depictions of historical injustices, like the middle passage, Margaret Garner's story, lynching, and more. Reviewers, however, preferred to highlight the way in which the text placed African Americans side by side with whites in shaping the nation. Reviewers mentioned black military accomplishments, for instance, and the way in which Jefferson edited the Declaration of Independence to exclude condemnations of slavery. A sense of the text as demonstrating and facilitating brotherhood dominated the reviews, even in African American journals. Benjamin E. Mays, the powerful black critic of segregation, explained in the *Pittsburgh Courier* that the book "says that many white Americans, such as Washington and Jefferson, had an uneasy conscience about slavery and many others fought for the emancipa-

tion of the slaves. Today, thousands of white Americans have an uneasy conscience about segregation and discrimination and are united with the Negro
in his efforts to be free";[81] a November 1956 book column in the same newspaper noted, "The cause of brotherhood and democracy would be inestimably
advanced if copies of this remarkable history could be placed in every public
school, college, and university in the United States."[82] One brotherhood review
by a prominent African American was republished in black newspapers across
the country: James Egert Allen, community coordinator for the Association for
the Study of Negro Life and History, argued for the book as a tool in facilitating
democracy and racial goodwill:

> The contents of this volume should lift the morale of our nation, break-
> ing down artificial barriers in our culture and society and paving a way
> for better communications among people of varied ethnic groups.
>   To place this volume in every library, every school, and, in fact, every
> home in America would add greatly to the moral courage and physical
> stamina of the entire country.[83]

Although "physical stamina" suggests physical engagement in the efforts of
the movement, the language here also partakes in the rhetoric of midcentury
American nationalistic unity. Part of this tendency in the reviews to emphasize
brotherhood comes from the frame Hughes establishes early in the text, in a
section entitled "Negroes as Americans," which concludes, "As citizens of the
United States, Negroes are Americans and their way of life is much the same
as that of other Americans."[84] The section is accompanied by photographs of
contemporary African Americans in occupations like teaching, science, sur-
gery, and factory work. Hughes calls for this American-brotherhood reading
of the text even as he and Meltzer include potent discussions of racial conflict
and resistance, like the *Amistad* revolt, Nat Turner's rebellion, John Brown's
raid, Reconstruction-era lynching and murders, and so on. The emphasis on
brotherhood might be understood as a necessary cover during a tense historical
moment.

Not all readers were happy with the book's alignment of blacks with whites.
Black historian J.A. Rogers, citing conservative editorialist George Schuyler,
believed that the book emphasizes enslavement rather than activism, arguing, "Now, the above is the habitual white viewpoint. And it is understandable.
Books got out by white publishers, even when by Negro authors, sell mostly
to white people and what the whites, even many of the most unbiased, want

on the Negro is generally different from what Negroes want on themselves."[85] Rogers concluded by resigning that "[u]ntil Negroes are ready to get out their books, 'A Pictorial History of the American Negro,' is the best of its kind." A Jewish intellectual offered a more radical criticism in the *American Examiner:* "[O]ne gets the feeling from this book that the Negro is trying to curry the white man's favor and appealing for his mercy. The illustration on the title page shows a chained Negro kneeling and asking, 'Am I Not a Man and a Brother?' I think it is time for the Negro to stand up erect and demand what is his by right."[86] To Hughes's credit, it appears as though he wished initially to include more information on the way in which whites had assaulted black communities, a perspective certainly not emphasized in the popular language of brotherhood and racial amity. A file in Hughes's papers titled "Comments on Hughes MS" contains the following from Meltzer: "A bit too much emphasis on the KKK and terrorist groups; notes in the margins indicate where they may be omitted." I do not include this archival evidence in order to criticize Meltzer, who became one of the most committed and important writers on the topic of social justice. I offer it in order to contextualize the production of the book, providing a sense of the discussions that led up to the book's publication in order to understand better the compromises Hughes had to make in order to bring the text to a mainstream audience.

In fact, reviewers read a nonconfrontational tone into the book, and this interpretation is, of course, debatable given the way the text recounts lynching, race riots, and murders, and includes poems like Claude McKay's "If We Must Die." But reviewers saw the text, as a history, presenting material objectively rather than through partisanship. John W. Parker wrote in the *Raleigh (N.C.) News and Observer,* "Steering clear of the propaganda angle, the book discloses the black man's inner being—his frustrations and hopes and desires to be one with a country to which he has given his blood. The authors have, therefore, proceeded on the sound assumption that the so-called Negro problem is but one segment of the larger problem of American minorities and those in far-flung parts of the world." This reviewer even denies that there is a "Negro problem" per se, but sees American racial problems as simply akin to worldwide ethnic tensions.[87] Arthur L. Cookman in Portland, Oregon, exclaimed, "If those who inspect the book expect to find its 9-by-11-inch format crammed with pro-Negro propaganda, they will be surprised to discover that it is free from bias and distortion. It is factual and authentic, I believe, in all particulars."[88] The *Cleveland Plain Dealer* praised the book for being "without hysteria,"[89] and the white literary editor at the *San Francisco Chronicle,* William Hogan, also commented on the impartial tone of the book: "What particularly struck me about the book is that the authors permitted not a shred of propaganda, ax-grinding or special pleading in their capsule history. They have done a sound job of research, no emotion involved, unless it be a tinge of sadness and embarrassment a reader might feel when coming to grips with some of the more bleak facts of our national background."[90] One might consider whether white-authored reviews in mainstream publications invoked terms like "Negro problem," "hysteria," and "propaganda" in order to steer white readers subtly away from reading this progressive articulation of black American history and identity. In other words, by evoking a white knee-jerk response to the book (even if reviews dismissed such a response ultimately), the reviewers indirectly warned white readers about the "embarrassment" and discomfort the book would provoke.

If we remember from chapter 1 the difficulty of speaking out against racial injustice during the Cold War, the reviews' repeated emphasis on the impartial, objective, nonpropagandistic tone of the book reminds us of the political uses of history and of the photograph generically. In an era during which straightforward critique of America was impossible within mainstream publishing venues, Hughes and Meltzer cannily employed both genres to make an argument about social injustice appear divorced from political bias, the "Negro question" of social equality and integration being a heated national subject.[91] The selection of images to document the history, particularly photographs when available, concretized the argument about black American citizenship by offering evidentiary "proof." Photographs appeared to have "no ax to grind," the favorite phrase of many reviewers, the image's objective nature being associated with the mechanics of the camera. Crown's promotional pamphlet emphasized the text's impartiality through the image:

> An authoritative, objective panorama of American Negro life from African origins, through slavery days to the present, covering all aspects—social, political and economic. There are concise pictorial accounts of all important events and developments and pictures of famous and important Negroes. The 1,000 pictures were selected from many thousands assembled during years of research from public and private collections, old manuscripts, obscure and forgotten publications. This is the first and only full-scale pictorial volume of Negro America ever published.

Of course, the text of *Pictorial History* makes an intensely partisan argument about the need for social equality and integration by re-presenting details from the past as a history that is significant to the present moment. As Alan Trachtenberg reminds us, "Images become history, more than traces of a specific event in the past, when they are used to interpret the present in light of the past, when they are presented and received as explanatory accounts of collective reality."[92] All photographic histories become histories when the images are selected and arranged in order to tell a story about how culture arrived at the current moment and to indicate pathways toward a reshaped future. The photograph makes this process appear objective, when in fact intentionality shapes the meaning around an image and its uses within culture to represent history.

Language and Photographs: Inspiring Action

For Hughes and Meltzer, the representation of history aimed to initiate social action, even if the text does not state its intentions outright. As noted in the reviews, readers recognized the connection of the history with the civil rights movement, drawing correspondences between the freedom fighters of the past and those of the current moment. But the use of language within and around the images in the last section of the book brings the imperative toward action to the surface. Regarding his own documentarian aesthetic in later works for young people, Meltzer commented on the significance of arrangement to meaning, explaining that a "designing narrator" arranges evidence and presents testimony in order to create meaning, arguing that "the truth comes through the ordering."[93] For the purposes of understanding the last section in *Pictorial History*, attention to the arrangement of language in conjunction with image enables recognition of the text's imperative that its readers act.[94]

In our examining the role of language in relation to the image in Hughes's text, Trachtenberg's ideas about the sociality of the image seem especially appropriate. Writing of Lewis Hine's modifications of the photographic survey and his experiments with text/image sequential presentations, Trachtenberg explains that Hine "enlarged the reformist idea of the social survey to embrace the *process* of communication itself, inventing presentational forms through which social information might become the viewer's own concrete experience—not facts 'out there,' in a distant realm, or facts to excite pity, but visual facts as the occasion for awakening the viewer's awareness of and imaginative empathy with the pictured others, and thus the viewer's own social being."[95] The result, Trachtenberg argues, was Hine's investment in the "sociality" of the image, for in being influenced by education reformists John Dewey and George Herbert Mead, Hine employed images in order to incite social dialogue, an internal response from a viewer that enables the viewer to recognize and engage the reality of the photographed subject, changing the social identity of the viewer as a result.[96] The role of text becomes directive: "The text draws from the image its connotation as a symbol of a social reality. Sympathy can thus be expanded to understanding, to responsibility, a sense (literally, an experience) of being implicated in the reality of which the picture is a concrete rendering."[97] Hughes and Meltzer employ language in order to inspire sociality, the engagement of the viewer with the subject in the photograph and the resultant transformation of the viewer's social implication. We must also remember that the 292 pages of images and text that preface the final section, "Toward One World, 1941–," have served pedagogically to instruct the reader in how to read history, how to see the images of the past. The book's emphasis on resistance, rebellion, and reform has prepared the reader to read images of black history as arguing for black agency, and the images that invoke language particularly engage a viewer in a sociality of the image that aims to spur engagement in civil rights assertion.

The first section within "Toward One World" is titled "In Action in World War II," a title that suggests combative agency. Images include a photograph of a casually confident Benjamin O. Davis Jr., son of the general in Reynolds's book, climbing into a fighter jet, along with an image of black troops aiming guns out of a tank and a photograph of two black soldiers firing machine guns on Bougainville. I mention this section because it picks up on the brotherhood thematic of much of the book, as these black troops are contributing to American military success and are internationally visible as Americans. But more to the point, as the introduction to the section, these images spotlight black militancy. They focus on action and potency. Perhaps in contrast to images of black men as victims of violence, these images frame the male body in action as hero and fatherly protector. The remainder of the section "Toward One World" turns toward civil rights progress and employs language conspicuously in order to draw a reader into a sociality with the image. Three main categories of word/image interaction emerge: photographs that incorporate language within them, images of ripped headlines from newspapers, and portraits conjoined with quotations.

On the page after the military section, an image appears of a group of men standing in front of a banner (Figure 2.11). The banner reads, "We must establish beyond any doubt the equality of man," a quotation by Republican politician Wendell L. Willkie. Willkie's signature also appears on the banner. Standing in front of the statement appears a group of white and black men, five of whom are in suits flanking a man who wears casual clothes and glasses. The caption reads, "Isaac Woodward (*center*), who was blinded in 1946 by a South

A helm watch aboard the submarine *Permit*. World War II brought racial integration to the Navy.

The Plaza 7- switchboard of the New York Telephone Company, whose operators are integrated.

An assembly line at the International Harvester plant in Louisville, where Negroes and whites work together.

WE MUST ESTABLISH BEYOND ANY DOUBT THE EQUALITY OF MAN.

Isaac Woodward (*center*), who was blinded in 1946 by a South Carolina policeman while on his way home from military service, with Walter White (*fourth from left*), who was then the executive secretary of the N.A.A.C.P.

Seesaw on the Home Front

On the home front, during World War II, race relations were like a seesaw, rising nobly in some aspects while sinking deplorably in others. Southern Negro workers poured into Northern and Western cities. More than 50,000 Negroes came to Detroit to work in the many defense industries centered there. Everywhere housing presented a problem, since white workers often resented colored families moving anywhere near them and violently opposed their integration into residential communities. Bombings and forced evictions occurred and serious race riots broke out in Detroit, New York, Mobile, Beaumont and other communities.

Figure 2.11. A blinded veteran, Isaac Woodward, stands flanked by NAACP leaders under a quotation by Wendell L. Willkie. From Langston Hughes and Milton Meltzer, *A Pictorial History of the Negro in America* (New York: Crown Publishers, Inc., 1956). Llewellyn Ransom News Features photograph; reprinted by permission of Victor and Pamela Ransom.

Carolina policeman on his way home from military service, with Walter White (*fourth from left*), who was then the executive secretary of the N.A.A.C.P." (296). White peers into the camera, as if asking for a reply to the situation, whereas the blinded veteran stares upward, standing stiffly as if in the pose of military attention. Given that the image follows immediately the discussion of black military agency, Hughes and Meltzer clearly transition toward injustice at home with this image. Woodward's image refutes the brotherhood thematic, a simplistic (but pleasing) argument that black military success speaks of racial equality. In the case of Woodward, military success did not preclude violence from the Southern police authority. The language here propels the reader into active response: "We must establish beyond any doubt the equality of man," the imperative language argues; suggestively, such a message appears within the photograph of the people, not outside of it as a caption. This unity suggests that the idea of equality cannot be separated from the injustice we have witnessed. The page facing the Woodward image depicts more effects of racial violence: two veterans within their bombed house in Los Angeles; a photograph of Harry T. Moore, an NAACP secretary who was murdered along with his wife on Christmas Day; and an image of Rosa Lee Ingram with her teenage sons in jail. Ingram had killed "in self-defense an armed white farmer" (297).[98] Hughes and Meltzer place the effects of racial violence in the foreground of their imperative to act.

What follows is a two-page spread of "Jim Crow signs," rows of photographs of signs that demarcated segregated spaces. These potent images include language within them, of course, and become a counterpoint to the idea of social justice embodied in the Willkie statement. If an audience is encouraged to make social equality a reality through the Woodward image, here Hughes and Meltzer underline through photography the illogic of racism made tangible through language (Figure 2.12). Such a layout reflects on the visibility of segregation, its rules apparently codified through the signs; the segregationist rules would seem intended to regulate behavior, to enforce white superiority through special designation, and to enforce racial separation. By placing the signs side by side, however, Hughes and Meltzer reveal the absurdity of such intentions and effects. Elizabeth Abel's brilliant book *Signs of the Times: The Visual Politics of Jim Crow* reminds us that photographs of these kinds of signs were exceedingly rare: "Jim Crow signs may have been commonplace, but their representation was exceptional. My research has uncovered fewer than two hundred photographs, a surprising underdocumentation that has been recognized by archivists and curators of historical collections in the South."[99] Hughes and Meltzer assemble

South of Washington, D. C., the Jim Crow signs which separate Negroes from whites vary from those on laundries which will wash "white" clothes only to exclusive whistle-stop privies. There are "white" benches and "colored" benches in municipal parks, "white" and "colored" water fountains in department stores, separate entrances and separate pay-windows in industrial plants. There are some theaters in the South which Negro patrons may not enter at all and others where they may gain admittance only via the "colored" entrance and where they must sit in the top gallery. Some roadside cafés have holes cut at the side for colored patrons who may not come in. Some coin-vending machines for soft drinks have "white" and "colored" slots. The "colored" booths in the rear of record shops where Negroes may play records often put up no restricted signs but post a photograph of Marian Anderson or Duke Ellington.

Figure 2.12. Hughes and Meltzer assemble various Jim Crow signs. From Langston Hughes and Milton Meltzer, *A Pictorial History of the Negro in America* (New York: Crown Publishers, Inc., 1956).

a kind of archive in these sixteen images, one that attests to the permeability of such signs and to their fundamental illogic.

Distinctions erode when reading the signs side by side. Both races rent rooms, as a sign advertising rooms for "colored only" is positioned next to an image of an older white woman under a "Room for White" placard. Several of the signs attempt to regulate black behavior through arrows: "Colored Area," "Colored Entrance," "Colored Parking," and "Rooms for Rent and Sleeping" are all marked by arrows. On the layout of the page, these arrows all point in different directions, suggesting a kind of absurdity in the notion of regulating and separating black bodies from white. The series of images most critical of segregation come through the single use of an arrow for "White," which points out of the frame to another image, this one of a country outhouse with the words "White Only" scribbled on its side. Making a scatological joke, Hughes and Meltzer point whites toward the space in which they belong—a rustic privy—which in turn sits beside an image of a billboard for a white laundry service, again associating filth with whiteness. Language appears to control, order, and separate, when in fact the idea it articulates is fundamentally illogical and defective. When language shapes the stable ideal of social justice, as in the Woodward image, it is not fragmented into more than a dozen images, here repeated to reveal the nonsensicality of codified racial segregation. A stable ideal articulated through language within an image—the Woodward conjunction of idealized language with the disappointment of social violence—instead aims to inspire reader action outside the frame. The illogical signage depicts the absurdity of prejudice.

A second major conjunction of language with image appears in images of ripped newspaper headlines. Hughes and Meltzer employ torn headlines throughout *Pictorial History*, and in truth other pictorial histories of the time also use headlines as shorthand to document historical events, drawing again on the evidentiary by invoking newspaper authenticity and credibility. Within African American literary culture, drawing on fragments of textual evidence to authenticate historical events has deep roots, particularly within black children's literature and culture. For example, children's history pageants in the 1920s and 1930s employed a verbal collage of quotations—from literature, historical and legal texts, and music—in order to substantiate revisions of American history and black identity.[100] Within Hughes's text, torn headlines testify to the progress of integration across the country, and are even conjoined with maps of the country specifying resistance to integration in the South (Figure 2.13). The layering of headlines suggests multiple sources of evidence of the trend, as

WHAT KINDS OF HOUSING DID OUR EARLY AMERICANS HAVE?

Camaraderie in a school cafeteria.

A Negro teacher in New York City, whose pupils are of varied racial backgrounds.

134,000 NEGROES IN MIXED SCHOOLS

RACIAL BARS DROP IN MANY SCHOOLS

SOUTH'S LIBRARIES OPENING TO NEGRO

Two Surveys Show Extensive Trend in Recent Years, but Urge Need to Expand It

t States and Washington
ve Some Desegregation,
porting Service Says

Special to The New York Times.
SHVILLE, Tenn., Oct. 1—
ce showing that 134,000

ter White Classes
ral Regions—
e Is Amicable

Negro children sat

Segregation's End On Buses, Trains Ordered by I.C.C.

INTEGRATION GAIN IN CAPITAL HAILED

Quakers Report Racial Bars Show a 'Startling' Drop, City Has a 'New Look'

By ALVIN SHUSTER
l to The New York Times.
NGTON, Oct. 6—A.

Applies To Interstate Passengers

Separate-Equal Policy Reversed

A map showing the reaction of the various Southern states to the edict on integration a year after the Supreme Court decision.

STRONGLY RESISTING INTEGRATION
AWAITING COURT ACTION
MOVING TOWARD INTEGRATION

307

Figure 2.13. Headlines focus on integration in schools, libraries, and transportation. From Langston Hughes and Milton Meltzer, *A Pictorial History of the Negro in America* (New York: Crown Publishers, Inc., 1956).

well as integration's temporal and geographic progress. The secondary headline that is fully readable states, "Two Surveys Show Extensive Trend in Recent Years, but Urge Need to Expand It" (307), another example of language within an image pressing for social action from the reader. Three headlines focus on integration within a national context, as they describe both the " 'New Look' " of the capital and the federal legislation that outlawed segregation on interstate transportation. All five headlines testify to the progress of integration from the South to the heart of national identity. The layered headlines also make visible a handmade aesthetic. Torn from newspapers, the images appear with rough edges and lie one atop another. One can imagine a hand at work arranging the evidentiary language, making present the "designing narrator," to use Meltzer's description of himself as a documentary author. For the purposes of inspiring civil rights action, the torn and layered headlines make it clear that history can be shaped by human hands, that a reader can arrange evidence in order to make a case about the outline of history and its projection into the future.

Finally, the ordering of portraits with quotations in the last pages of the book employs Trachtenberg's idea of sociality, calling the reader to respond in a dialogue with the images. Starting with illustrations of Phillis Wheatley, Benjamin Banneker, and John M. Langston, the sequence brings the voices of figures across history into the same space. W.C. Handy and Joe Louis claim their American identity; Dorothy Maynor and Louis Armstrong declare the beauty of black music; and Martin Luther King Jr. and Thurgood Marshall invoke the ideals of love, brotherhood, and justice. Mary McLeod Bethune splits space with the dome of the Capitol building and cries, "This is our day! Doors will open everywhere. The floodtide of a new life is coming in" (311). If we remember the idea of sociality in text/image interaction, this sequence draws a reader across the span of black history, demonstrating through the quotations a shared commitment to the American ideal of equality, and then asks the reader implicitly to respond. The last images are of contemporary young people: Gloria Lockerman, identified by her school in Baltimore, won a spelling contest on *The $64,000 Question* in 1955, an accomplishment with an academic cast during the heated debates over school integration;[101] and Margaret Walker, the young poet, who ends the sequence in a quotation from her poem "For My People," which speaks of commitment to education: "For the cramped bewildered years we went to school / To learn to know the reasons why and the answers to / And the people who and the places where . . ." The ellipsis ends the sequence, pointing the reader to the remainder of Walker's poem, which calls for rebirth of black culture through the young and a decided turn toward action (311):[102] "Let a race of men now / rise and take control," the poem concludes, the preceding ellipsis now suggesting that the words of the poem take shape in the mouth of the reader.

Unlike the images of Jim Crow signs, which appear in a hodgepodge arrangement, this last sequence suggests historical continuity and idealistic consistency. Speaking of Civil War sequences, Trachtenberg argues that "[o]rganized into a catalogue or sequence, single images can be viewed as part of a presumed pattern, an order, a historical totality. Moreover, in its own prosaic way, by delineating an emergent whole and projecting a totality, the archival catalogue reveals a literary motive: to comprehend this unfolding event as epic in scale and meaning."[103] The arrangement also reminds one of the way in which African American newspapers like the *Crisis* in the 1910s and 1920s had issued pages and pages of photos of middle-class children's faces as a testament to black material and social accomplishment; amassing the children's faces both speak of the particular locations of the children (they were often identified by city) and represent in toto the abstract commitment to middle-class ideals across the race. Certainly Hughes and Meltzer ask us to read the portraits on their last pages as individuals, because they feature famous people with particular specifying quotations. But there is a strong sense that in amassing these head shots—and in their similarity in size and framing—Hughes and Meltzer wish us to identify the images with each other in order to represent the abstract: the race's consistent commitment to social justice. The sequence thus embodies both the progress of ideals of equality across time and the permanent ideal of social equality within black culture. John Berger addresses the qualities of the photograph as art, saying, "All this may seem close to the old principle of art transforming the particular into the universal. But photography does not deal in constructs. There is no transforming in photography. There is only decision, only focus."[104] In the case of Hughes and Meltzer, transformation into the ideal takes place in the arrangement of the images, as well as in the shared concerns of the language. Both qualities call the reader to read the images both particularly and universally, a phenomenon that pushes the reader toward acting on the ideals that have been embodied before him or her.

The images in this final sequence also speak of the significance of black portraiture in inspiring social response. Richard J. Powell's argument about the dignity and inventiveness of black portraiture particularly applies, for he explains the variety of images in his book in language that connects to the portraits on these last pages of *Pictorial History:* "The people depicted in these works—enslaved, emancipated, anonymous, notable, or notorious—are as diverse a group as could be imagined, but their portraits have in common an idiosyncratic sense of *subjecthood:* the feeling that, beyond capturing likenesses, their respective artists were engaged in portraying real people and an embodied history and culture."[105] The integrity of the people in Hughes and Meltzer's portraits inspires respect but also obligation, for across history the commitment to self-determination and equality necessitates continued response.

The book's final image makes the call to action explicit. A photograph by Roy DeCarava of a child sitting on steps, looking seriously into the camera, the image is captioned in order to persuade: "This is Allen Turner, 1956. He wants to be a pilot when he grows up. The chances are, he *can* look forward to making aviation his career, or whatever else he may want to be" (312).[106] The image is crucial to my study for several reasons. First, it permits us to see the continuity between the photographic picture books of chapter 1, those which consistently employ close-ups of children's faces in order to forge a connection, a friend-ship, between reader and subject, one that would lead to greater racial goodwill. Here, the image of Allen Turner is much less sunny than those of Rex or David in chapter 1. Turner looks expectantly into the camera, becoming an instance of sociality that confronts with expectancy the action of the reader. Second, the Allen Turner caption links him to the "sky is the limit" motif found in repre-sentations of black childhood in chapter 1. He can expect to soar when he is an adult. Finally, the image uses the temporal nature of the photograph in order to make a case for the urgency of social change. As Sontag, Eduardo Cadava, Walter Benjamin, and others note, the photograph itself is always marked by loss, because it frames off a moment in time. As Cadava notes of the role of pho-tographs in history, "[E]very attempt to bring the other to the light of day, to keep the other alive, silently presumes that it is mortal, that it is always already touched (or re-touched) by death. The survival of the photographed is therefore never only the survival of its life, but also its death."[107] Sontag states the idea, fa-mously, in *On Photography:* "Precisely by slicing out this moment and freezing it, all photographs testify to time's relentless melt."[108] And there are images within *Pictorial History* that employ the temporal quality of the photograph in order to raise the dead: when representing Emmett Till, for instance, Hughes and Melt-zer include an image of Till before the brutality, rather than replicating the *Jet* magazine images of his desecrated body. In this way, Hughes and Meltzer frame off the moment in time when Till was young and whole by intimating the hor-ror of his future, which lies outside the frame, in other images.

In the case of Allen Turner, Hughes and Meltzer focus attention on a subject that foregrounds mutability—the child's body—and they are able to employ "time's relentless melt" to spotlight futurity. Unlike that of Emmett Till, Turner's future is unknown. Further, in specifying the time of the image's capture ("This is Allen Turner, 1956"), the authors emphasize the child's liminality, his position between a history that appears behind him in the pages of the book and the future that will follow 1956. Turner looks out into the eyes of the reader, asking for participation in building a world that promises possibility rather than death for black children. Reviewers noted the "candid and expectant face" of Turner,[109] terms that evoke the appeal of black-child innocence (the apparent innocence of the subject in tandem with the apparent innocence of the camera) within this particular cultural moment, as well as the expectation of social action in response to that innocence.

Pictorial History *and the Woolworth Counter Sit-Ins*

In fact, *A Pictorial History of the Negro in America* did directly inspire social action and helped influence the course of the civil rights movement. Langston Hughes's papers contain a clipping sent to him by Ezell Blair, one of the four African American students who started the Woolworth lunch-counter sit-ins in Greensboro, North Carolina, in 1960. The clipping reads as follows:

> CHICAGO, Aug. 21 (UPI)—The youth credited with starting the Southern sit-in demonstrations said today a picture book gave him the courage to do it.
>
> Joseph McNeil, 18-year-old son of a Wilmington, N.C., floor waxer, was in Chicago to receive the "Delta Youth Award" of the Delta Sigma Theta Sorority.
>
> He said he got the idea for protesting lunch counter segregation while he was in high school.
>
> "When I was a freshman at college," he said, "I thought it was finally time something was done."
>
> McNeil did not claim full credit for the sit-ins, but he said, "It was my compulsion and my impulse that got things started."
>
> The book that gave him the motivation was Langston Hughes' "The Pictorial History of the Negro."
>
> "I'd read how other fellows had made sacrifices," he said, "I remembered the kids at Little Rock, and I realized I hadn't made my contribution."
>
> McNeil said he felt the demonstrations had been successful. "When it started, there was an air of pessimism, we were told we would set commu-

nity relations back, but I now know more than ever that we were right," he said.

When he returns to North Carolina A&T College in Greensboro, McNeil said, "I'll find out the temperament of the other kids—we might sit-in on the holdout restaurants, or maybe the hotels."

McNeil quoted two lines from Langston Hughes' poem "Mother to Son."

"Life for me ain't been no crystal stair . . .
But all the time I'se been a'climbin' on."[110]

Following the sit-ins, Langston Hughes made a trip to Greensboro in 1960 to meet McNeil and to look at the lunch counter where the sit-in took place. I interviewed McNeil about the influence of *Pictorial History* on his sense of himself as an agent in history and on his decision to protest at Woolworth's. He was introduced to Hughes's poetry in high school and had seen *Pictorial History* in houses of friends and acquaintances.[111] He explained that "[h]istory is always exciting when it's oral, pictorial, or written. But it was the specialness of that book, its power because of its pictures and its words—this was crucial." He clarified that he and his friends had been reading the book in their dorm room, and that they decided to stage the protest. The images of racial violence in the book particularly influenced his decision to act: "These could have been done to me, my father, or my grandfather. . . . This kind of violence could happen to our parents, could happen to us, and, if we did not do something, would happen to our children." Like Allen Turner, whom Hughes and Meltzer set liminally between history and the future, McNeil saw himself at a juncture and was inspired to act by the depiction of historical freedom fighters.

The photographs were particularly inspirational to McNeil. He explained: "Pictures are a powerful way to communicate. When you can communicate a thought, either by writing or by looking at a picture—look at one and being able to imagine all that it connotes, what it means and how different people will see the same picture and come away with different impressions. Resistance was how I saw it, and in order to understand how we resisted in the past, Hughes captured all of that, smiling on the outside but crying on the inside. He was just masterful." "Smiling on the outside but crying on the inside" took on another resonance in the 1950s, when the popular emphasis on racial goodwill and brotherhood put pressure on articulations of civil rights action. Further, McNeil's reference to the "crystal stair" of Hughes's poem "Mother to Son" links social progress back to images from the Harlem Renaissance of the "upward climb," images that were determinative for Reynolds in his history/conduct book as well. As a bridge figure himself, Hughes enabled a sense of continuity between older conceptions of social progress and new articulations through image making.

If McNeil's experience is to be credited, young people were in fact inspired to change their communities by the images in Hughes and Meltzer's book. Reading *Pictorial History* influenced the course of the civil rights movement, as lunch-counter demonstrations became a cornerstone of nonviolent protest throughout the South. *Pictorial History*, furthermore, helped change the role of young people in the movement. Joseph McNeil and his three teenage friends made a substantive contribution to the movement through their unexpected lunch-counter protest. McNeil explained the context to me:

> The reality was one that not a lot of people had a lot of high expectations for us. They would have never imagined that 16, 17, 18, 19 year olds would take on something difficult—defiance, putting themselves on the line. On the first day, people were shocked that we were still sitting there hours later, and the next day there were more. Young people weren't expected to do much—in conversations with members of the local police and all of the store managers, years later, they were really taken aback by the fact that we had the gall to challenge the system. . . . The lesson to me is never to underestimate children and their capabilities. . . . Children have a sense of justice, fairness—that's not fair, that's not right. We didn't mind telling others that [segregation] was wrong.

McNeil and his classmates gave Hughes and Meltzer's history book new life. Inspired to extend the accomplishments of the freedom fighters in *Pictorial History*, they gave new life also to young people as agents within the civil rights movement.

The book played a part in black Muslim education in the early 1960s as well: an image from an unattributed June 9, 1962, article titled "Behind the Muslim Curtain," published in the *New York Amsterdam News*, depicts a child reading the book while being interrogated by educational officials. Chicago state senator Arthur R. Gottchalk was attempting to shut down Muslim schools, and the child in the photograph looks seriously at the camera while holding Hughes's book. The article concludes, "To the surprise of many the probing Senator found many conditions comparable and some even better than conditions in Chicago's Jim-Crow and Lily-White public schools some of which have been termed 'ghettos on wheels.'" Although the effects of Hughes and Meltzer's text on the movement and on black nationalism continue to emerge, what remains certain is a sense of the text as aiming to transform psychologically an audience of young people at a crucial juncture in history.

Both Reynolds's *Little Journeys into Storyland* and Hughes and Meltzer's *A Pictorial History of the Negro in America* permit new images of black childhood and new expectations for children's involvement in social change. Drawing on the reformative tradition of black conduct literature, Reynolds provides revivified photographs of young people, emphasizing confidence, beauty, and capability in the face of a social and religious culture that demanded conformity and silence. Reynolds's book, however masked its language, makes clear in its images a new sense of possibility for young readers. Hughes and Meltzer provided to families a book that would not sit quietly on the shelf. In the sociality of its text/image arrangement, *Pictorial History* provided an impetus to its readers to remake social relations. It resists palpably the idea that black children as potential activists are innocent and intuitive moralists, arguing implicitly for the need for deep historical awareness as a preface to action. By emphasizing the continuity between past and present, *Pictorial History* made manifest the need for readers to extend a tradition of social activism into the present moment. At least one reader listened, and helped start the sit-in movement that would give birth to the Student Nonviolent Coordinating Committee. By attempting to inspire its readership through a pastiche of word and image, *Pictorial History* emerged as a compelling forerunner to the more radical, populist texts that would arrive during the Black Arts Movement.

....

3

Today

Framing Freedom in Mississippi

"What do you want?"
"Freedom!"
"When do you want it?"
"Now!"
"Freedom now! Freedom now! Freedom now!"

  —Civil rights chant

I felt we were raising the next generation of movement children, self-confident, skilled, unafraid to be curious, and excited about learning.

  —Marilyn Lowen, "I Knew I Wasn't White"

A sequence in the documentary film *Chance for Change*, directed by Adam Giffard, shows a preschool teacher in the summer of 1965 leading her children on a walk across the Mississippi countryside. In the opening shot of the sequence, we view the scene at a distance, and the teacher seems to carry a banner or a flag over her shoulder. She opens barbed-wire fences so that the children can climb through, one by one, as they cross fields and pathways. Together as they march, they sing "We Shall Overcome," the anthem of the civil rights movement. Although the sequence evokes a protest demonstration, recalling perhaps the momentous walk from Selma to Montgomery, Alabama, in March of that same year, the teacher leads the children on a different type of civil rights demonstration: she leads them on a nature walk. As they climb through a wire fence meant to divide land and space, the children sing about freedom and make their way toward a lovely pond. As the camera closes in, the banner or flag turns out to be a fishing net, which the teacher uses to scoop up creatures from the water, much to the pleasure of the inquisitive children. Together they marvel at a baby frog erupting from the mud. With the evocation of civil rights protest, the children's nature walk becomes a political act, a resistance to the demand to stay in one's place and to the imperative to work the land rather than to see oneself as part of or enjoying the natural world. The freedom the children claim is psychological rather than legislative, a freedom of spirit, for their walk articulates a new way of seeing themselves. No longer demarcated as the impoverished children of sharecroppers, these young people define themselves as comfortable, curious, joyful inhabitants of the Mississippi landscape.

The preschool in the documentary film was organized by the Child Development Group of Mississippi (CDGM), one of the first Head Start programs in the United States and certainly the children's organization most committed to civil rights ideals in the mid-1960s. Although the CDGM existed for only two years (1965–67), it emerged at a turning point in the civil rights campaign in Mississippi; born from the Freedom Summer literacy campaign of 1964, and initiated after the Civil Rights Act of 1964 but before the Voting Rights Act of 1965, the CDGM aimed to train a new generation of children in the values of the movement. One of the tools it produced was children's books. The first children's book it issued was a photographic picture book. This chapter examines that photographic book, *Today* (1965), in order to discern the way in which it articulated the CDGM's political and psychological ideals, recognizing the book as just one star in a constellation of photographic and textual material available to young people during the civil rights movement. Containing images of children at play, reading, napping, singing, eating, and going to the doctor, *Today* depicts a day in the life of a CDGM preschool center.

In its process of composition, approach to visual representation, and engagement with the psychology of child readership, *Today* is one of a kind. *Today* intersects conspicuously with civil rights photographic practice: it is aligned with the perspective of the Student Nonviolent Coordinating Committee (SNCC) photography unit, which used photos to represent the investment of local people in civil rights efforts. As we will see, the temporal qualities of photography enabled the instantiation of "Freedom now!" in this children's text, a move that anticipated the more radical and community-based representational strategies of SNCC in the late 1960s. Although the CDGM may not have survived an onslaught of Mississippi racism coupled with governmental cowardice, *Today* exists as a testament to the inventiveness and adaptability of artists during the civil rights movement. Study of *Today* expands the archive of civil rights photography, adding images and moments to the field of civil rights representation, much in the spirit of *This Light of Ours* (2012), a recent anthology of community-based activist photography; but study of *Today* also expands our awareness of the range of photographic strategy and practice during the movement, adding another thread to the fabric of civil rights creative methodology.

As scholars of civil rights representation have charted with much subtlety, photographs of the movement range from the iconic newspaper documentary images, which were often created by white photographers uninvested in civil rights, to propagandistic and inspirational SNCC photographs and photographic books, like Lorraine Hansberry's *The Movement* (1964) and Julius Lester's posters, pamphlets, and calendars. In the past few years, scholars have expanded our knowledge about the range of subjects and approaches in civil rights photography: brilliant books like Erina Duganne's *The Self in Black and White: Race and Subjectivity in Postwar American Photography*, Leigh Raiford's *Imprisoned in a Luminous Glare: Photography and the African American Freedom Struggle*, and Martin A. Berger's *Seeing through Race: A Reinterpretation of Civil Rights Photography* have propelled new interest in wide-ranging movement representation. My approach to *Today* is certainly inspired by the expansiveness of these scholars, by the insights they have offered about figures like Bob Fletcher and Maria Varela (both of whom took pictures at CDGM sites), and by their reflections on the way in which the context of reproduction, along with verbal indices, helps determine the implications of images. In opposition to images offered to a white readership, those which Berger describes as "stuck to a restricted menu of narratives that performed reassuring symbolic work"[1]—work that emphasized the child passivity and silence in service to an idea of black victimhood—*Today*, in my reading, responds to Berger's call for an expansive canon of movement images and to his regret that children's voices were not heard in published narrations of civil rights photographs. Like Raiford, I wish to contribute to an appreciation of the malleability of photography during the movement. Images produced and articulated within black contexts become, in Raiford's words, an "opportunity and a challenge to reclaim, repair, remake, reimagine, and redeem" the integrity of African American experience during the civil rights moment.[2] My argument situates *Today* within a contextual framework that enables us to understand the book as a fundamentally utopian articulation, one that is both indexical and unreal, both a discrete product of a moment and an open-ended call for liberation. The book uses photography and text to "frame" freedom, a paradoxical notion in and of itself; shaping freedom with discourse both verbal and visual, the text solidifies improvisational play even as it insists on the fluid and labile experience of psychological freedom. In doing both—fixing representation through photography and narration yet insisting on the book as process rather than product—*Today* provides a new perspective on the exercise of visual culture during the civil rights movement.

CHILD DEVELOPMENT GROUP OF MISSISSIPPI: FREEDOM SCHOOL FOR PRESCHOOLERS

The CDGM originated through the efforts of a white psychoanalyst, Tom Levin, who had worked in the Medical Committee for Human Rights supporting the 1964 Freedom Summer voter-registration and education initiatives. During the winter of 1964 and spring of 1965, Levin began seeking collaborators for his idea of extending Freedom School ideals to the very youngest members of the black community. Levin was concerned that, in addition to needing literacy training and health care, the young would be overlooked by the movement. He explained in an interview,

> There were a lot of kids hanging around Freedom Houses—little kids. Many of them did not have stable families and they became like SNCC kids, you know like orphans of the movement. And I decided that we ought to start programs for them. That SNCC workers were doing it sort of spontaneously and one of the things [SNCC Mississippi project director] Bob Moses thought I might do is help get these schools going, for young kids, Freedom Schools. . . . I said we need to start schools where these little kids, who have no formative value system in which they feel they matter, where they would be trained to be the leaders of the Movement. I used to say, "The Movement will be their ego. The Movement will be their superego. The Movement will be who they are. They will spend their growing up using themselves to make the Movement work." . . . And I saw these kids as they would grow up to be the leaders of social change. We would provide them in the Movement, within SNCC, schools that taught them what their history was and where to go. It was a very ambitious idea.[3]

At the same time that Levin was formulating his idea, the newly formed Office of Economic Opportunity (OEO) initiated its Head Start educational grants as part of President Johnson's War on Poverty. The OEO had heard that Levin, along with the Reverend Arthur Thomas of the Delta Ministry and Jeannine Herron, educator and wife of SNCC photographer Matt Herron, was planning a preschool that would serve poor Mississippians. Matt Herron, whose images appear in *Today*, describes the atmosphere in the wake of the Freedom Summer:

> In the fall of 1964 as Jeannine and I evaluated the efforts of SNCC and the summer project to bring about political change, we reached the conclusion that the most effective and radical action we could take was to ensure that black children got a strong start in life, both educationally and personally. What we observed in the 1964 Freedom Schools of the growth and flowering of black children in that environment convinced us that permanent political change would flow naturally from creating a generation of young people with independent minds and expanded horizons. That insight led directly to Jeannine becoming one of the founders of CDGM.[4]

Although Levin was originally skeptical about taking government support, the OEO program analyst working on Head Start, Polly Greenberg, helped convince the group to propose a grant. Greenberg, a committed progressive educator, eventually left the OEO to lead the CDGM in Mississippi. The team developed a proposal, which was funded as the largest Head Start program in the country in the summer of 1965. More than six thousand children in twenty-four Mississippi counties were served by this first CDGM Head Start grant.[5]

Levin, Greenberg, Jeannine Herron, and other CDGM originators believed that a grassroots preschool program had to have the support of the poor, both theoretically, in their commitment to the project, and practically, in the investment of their children and families in the schools. They sought collaboration across civil rights groups, including the Delta Ministry, the NAACP, the Council of Federated Organizations, the Mississippi Freedom Democratic Party (MFDP), and SNCC. To a varying degree they received such support, if not officially, then through staff members and community organizers. SNCC is a case in point. Although SNCC administration resented the idea of governmental financial intervention in civil rights efforts, seeing the OEO as attempting to appropriate and contain the movement in Mississippi, individual SNCC members joined the staff of the CDGM, and others drummed up support for the preschools among their constituents. SNCC leader Frank Smith became the CDGM's director of community staff, a group that included SNCC members John Harris, Jim Monsonis, and Jim Dann.[6] To be clear, CDGM was not an arm of SNCC, nor was it an extension of any of the larger organized civil rights groups. But the CDGM and these groups shared many of the same individual workers.[7] Although officially it would be problematic both for a civil rights group to affiliate with the government and for government appropriations to go to a civil rights organization, many movement people saw the CDGM as a means to galvanize resources and motivation toward an area of development sometimes overlooked by traditional civil rights programs: the education and health of black children. Historian Charles Payne sees the CDGM's success as filling a need for larger community involvement in neglected dimensions of the movement and for grassroots political transformation: "By 1966, local women, say, who a few years before had not organized much more than church socials were arguing with Washington bureaucrats about how programs should be shaped. No matter what came out of the process, the activation of the local people was itself an important achievement."[8]

The CDGM aimed for grassroots control and sustenance of every preschool. Each of the original eighty-four preschools (along with additional preschools as the CDGM grew) was governed by a board consisting of local community members. The CDGM sought to institute black-owned, black-directed community centers through these preschools, offering training in early-childhood education to local women who had interest and talent and providing men with work in construction, maintenance, and security for the centers. Marilyn Lowen, a SNCC member who worked with the CDGM's Living Arts traveling performance outreach group, explains that "[m]any of the teachers and social service staff hired by the local communities were women who had previously been MFDP activists. . . . And the work was purposeful and immediately improved everyday life; the staff was helping to educate their own children and other children in their communities. Furthermore, community people were establishing their own institutions as they set up these schools, which also provided social services."[9] The CDGM supplied food and medical care to the children it served and offered its community workers a living wage, something that many, as movement people before CDGM, were unable to secure because of pervasive racism and white retaliation against activism. This was also an era in which black farm workers earned three dollars a day, whereas the CDGM paid teacher trainees and aides fifty to sixty dollars each week.[10] Community support for the preschools flourished across the state. As evidence of this commitment, when in response to political backlash the OEO withdrew the CDGM grant from September 1965 to February 1966, CDGM schools kept going, because the staff volunteered their time. Community investment was vital to the success of the CDGM.

In addition to community galvanization, the CDGM extended a vision of childhood education that aimed to transform psychologically children in the centers. If we remember that Levin was a psychoanalyst, it comes as little surprise that his idea about training movement leaders focused on shaping their frame of mind about themselves and their potential.[11] First and foremost, Levin and his colleagues believed in respecting the experience and perspective of black rural children. Greenberg, who was responsible for administering the CDGM program, describes in her fascinating account, *The Devil Has Slippery Shoes: A Biased Biography of the Child Development Group of Mississippi*, that the group wanted "to create a program that would build the iron egos needed by children growing up to be future leaders of social change in a semi-feudal state."[12] In order to do so, Greenberg insisted that teacher trainees encourage the children's curiosity and ability to question the world around them. For Greenberg, teacher training involved "encouraging children to talk, even if only in a structured conversation, instead of to sit quietly in their places; doing moving activities instead of paper and pencil activities; practicing remembering; offering ideas, even if only one-word ideas; involving teachers *with* the children, looking at them, listening to them, valuing the answers; being physically active, instead of gazing over children's heads from behind a desk; filling the day instead of waiting for it to evaporate."[13] Greenberg encouraged redirection of children's activities rather than any physical or verbal punitive response that would negate or humble a child. The goal was to encourage children to see themselves as valuable thinkers and contributors to their communities. Further, by seeing their mothers, fathers, and extended families as part of the educative effort, children would grow in respect for and commitment to their communities.

Play was the cornerstone of the psychological transformation encouraged by the CDGM, because play involves seeing the world and oneself in new ways. CDGM developed child confidence and autonomy through outdoor play on equipment built by community members, in rhymes and ring games the children brought from their home experience, and through indoor activities like art and block building. Greenberg describes a workshop offered in CDGM sites titled "Limits of Freedom," in which a staff member would start a dialogue with parents and teachers by asking, "What does freedom for children *mean* at this age, and are there ever limits to it?" Responses focused on developing the agency and confidence of children through play: "When I say free, I mean powerful and sunny. Make a kid feel important, and he'll feel big and strong. Like he can do things. Like he's good."; "Let him choose which song you sing when you sing a song. Ask him to choose. Freedom is when you get to choose"; and "In seven weeks time we can't do too much, but we can give him a taste of freedom. Maybe the only one he'll get, in this state! Let him alone to play like he wants."[14] I dwell on this perspective on freedom as play in order to unpack the significance for this community of practices like songs, games, art, and playground fun. These were not banal preschool activities. CDGM workers, teachers, and organizers saw these elements as crucial to building the black child's ability to adapt and to innovate. Imagination was necessary for children to survive racism and to become movement leaders who could reform society.

The CDGM faced hostility from white Mississippians and a weakening of resolve from the Johnson administration and Sargent Shriver, director of the OEO. The decline of the CDGM has been charted by Greenberg, Payne, Dittmer, and James P. Marshall in depth;[15] suffice it to say that the Senate Appropriations Committee chair happened to be a white man from Mississippi, Senator John C. Stennis, who vigorously opposed all civil rights legislation and led an unfounded "witch hunt" against the CDGM.[16] Shriver established an alternate Head Start program unsupported by movement workers and by the black community, the Mississippi Action for Progress, which deflected governmental support from the CDGM. Funding fluctuated during the two years of CDGM, and despite lobbying efforts that included a February 1966 meeting of children and teachers with the House Education and Labor Committee, CDGM disbanded after the end of its third grant, in December 1967.[17]

But while it lasted, CDGM drew in people like Roxy Meredith, the mother of James Meredith, the Air Force veteran who, in 1962 at age twenty-nine, was the first African American to integrate the University of Mississippi and who also led the March against Fear in June 1966. In a CDGM pamphlet, Roxy Meredith talks about the ramifications of James's efforts on his family, including the loss of her job and withdrawal of community relationships out of fear after the windows of her home were shot to pieces. She became a teacher trainee at CDGM, explaining, "Now I have heard many times that even if I didn't have an education, the way that we brought up our family was proof enough for me to work in Head Start. This was my chance to get sort of a Head Start too, and it really have helped me."[18] Marian Wright, who as Marian Wright Edelman would in 1972 found the Children's Defense Fund, was a board member of CDGM; according to Gordon K. Mantler, Wright's experience with CDGM led her to suggest to Martin Luther King Jr. what would become the Poor People's Campaign.[19] Though short-lived, the CDGM conveyed rewards for individuals and families, particularly those who had suffered retaliation for civil rights activism, and bore long-term implications ideologically as it helped to shape future populist movements.[20]

TODAY: BOOKMAKING AS LIBERATORY PROCESS

Some black children during the civil rights movement were able to access progressive reading material. As we have seen, young people during the movement read the *Pictorial History of the Negro in America*, for instance. In 1957, the Fellowship of Reconciliation, an ecumenical pacifist organization, published a comic book, *Martin Luther King and the Montgomery Story*, with an approximately 250,000-copy print run.[21] Herbert Russell's photographs of Freedom Schools in Mississippi in 1964 show young people reading photomagazines like *Ebony*, texts that allowed children to see black culture in new and exciting terms. SNCC produced *Negroes in American History: A Freedom Primer* (1965), by Bobbi and Frank Cieciorka, and an anthology of teenagers' creative writing, *Freedom School Poetry* (1965); the Freedom Summer schools, which served teenagers as well as adults, offered a developed curriculum.[22] But the CDGM sought material that would address emergent readers, the very newest to literacy, and found little that they considered appropriate for an audience of black rural children. According to Greenberg, the group wished to inspire a love of reading and to prevent a child from feeling alienated from a book's subject matter or approach. For CDGM, that meant that most children's books, especially those including white middle-class children, made apparent the exclusion of the black child from that landscape through his or her palpable absence.[23] Bookmaking became an extension of the CDGM's desire to value the black child's experience, language, and perspective. Philosophically, CDGM organizers believed that part of the process of becoming free psychologically involved demystifying print, so not only did they see a gap in black children's literature but they also were eager to involve children in the process of bookmaking so that children could see that books were simply people's ideas put on paper. Using Henry J. Kirksey, an African American printer connected to SNCC, the CDGM thus supported black-owned businesses and labor when creating its own readers, texts aimed to move an early reader toward competency.[24] Greenberg writes, "Using the material each child brought to the center with him, by making it into books for him to learn to read from, could help us work *with* him—not *on* him—toward evolving a strong sense of self that could cope and contribute in a manner that brought him satisfaction."[25] As an expression of their commitment to children's lived experience, CDGM workers took down the words of the children in their care when making books. Even though these texts were considered "bridge" books, meant ultimately to lead children to reading traditional texts, vernacular expression would be the first language in print that the children would read. By demystifying print and respecting children's language, the CDGM offered a truly revolutionary perspective on black children's literature. The CDGM produced seven books in total, many of which contained children's stories and children's illustrations.[26] The first was the photographic picture book *Today* (1965).

Greenberg and Maria Varela, the photographer and head of the "reading readiness" program at CDGM, both believed in the importance of moving children's stories into print. Greenberg said in correspondence with me that she organized the bookmaking process across centers.[27] *Today* appears to be largely the work of one CDGM head teacher, Doris Derby.[28] A black New Yorker who studied elementary education and cultural anthropology at Hunter College, Derby arrived in Mississippi in 1963 and developed adult-literacy materials in consultation with the SNCC voter-registration movement; she also spent 1964 and early 1965 researching historically black colleges and universities in the South. CDGM approached Derby because of her experience with literacy training. An amateur photographer since childhood, Derby brought her camera with her to the Newell Chapel CDGM center, where she worked as the head teacher during the summer of 1965.[29] The documentary film *Chance for Change* focuses on Derby's leadership, chronicling her approaches to positive interaction with children and her gentle encouragement and direction of teacher trainees from Mississippi. In recalling her work with CDGM, Derby emphasizes her practical approach. She oversaw the building of playground equipment just as she orchestrated the composition of *Today*. Derby explains:

> I saw that we did not have very many materials, we had a short period of time in the summer with the grant, and I wanted to get started. So my approach is looking at the experiences of the children and [thinking about] what we're going to work with them on and how we're going to do it. My idea was that I take pictures. I had my camera. At that time I just had a small camera, but I had my camera, and I took pictures of the activities of the children. . . . My idea was to take pictures of the children in their activities, and get them to react to those, record their words, and write them so that they can see the words and the pictures. And then make it into a book.[30]

Once the book left her hands and went to the CDGM headquarters in Mt. Beulah, Mississippi, Matt Herron's photographs were added, as were those by John Wallace, a local photographer who probably was involved in the Pilgrim's Rest Center in Durant, Mississippi. Most images within the book are Derby's, however, and reflect her hands-on experience in the daily life of a CDGM center.[31]

One particular image from the text allows us to understand how Derby's perspective on bookmaking permitted a new denotation for a familiar trope in child photographic books. Most of the text employs group photographs, a phenomenon I will discuss at more length later in the chapter. But toward the end of the text, an image of a beautiful young girl emerges, along with the first instance of a singular narrative voice in the text: "Thats me I ain't missed a day going to school" (Figure 3.1).[32] Considering the earlier photographic texts in this study, a child close-up might appear to carry particular connotations within a children's book with black characters. This child's eyes meet the viewer's in a kind of engagement that recalls Rex in *My Happy Days* or Allen Turner in *A Pictorial History of the Negro in America*. However, this expression of connection with a reader, this revelation of self, operates quite differently than in those earlier close-ups, which often appeared as ingenuous pleas for a reader to intervene in

Figure 3.1. A girl looks directly at the photographer.
From *Today*, Child Development Group of Mississippi, 1965.
McCain Library and Archives, The University of Southern Mississippi.

social relations. Here, there is no expectation of a reader unfamiliar with the life and experience of the subjects in the text, as in the case of the books examined in chapter 1. In fact, as Matt Herron told me, *Today*'s photographic work was not aimed to cross boundaries of race or experience, for it "was not meant to enlist others in the cause or to inform the wider public."[33] It was intended as a kind of mirror for the CDGM child, a reflection of self that would help articulate the child's value both aesthetically and politically. As Derby explains, "I wanted photographs of the children themselves so they could look, and they could say, 'This is me, I'm seeing my ideas written, I'm seeing my images in a book.' They don't care whether it's a book published by some well-known publisher."[34] From the perspective of Derby's philosophy, this close-up serves both a single child, offering her a profound sense of personal significance through the legitimating vehicle of the book, and her classmates, allowing them to recognize the beauty and value of their physical features and their experience at the CDGM. Thus, this movement image becomes not a public representation, not a call for action from readers of newspapers, newsletters, flyers, or posters; ideally, this is a moment of private exchange between the book and the group of children who seek to recognize themselves in print. This moment performs an inversion of the famous scene in Zora Neale Hurston's *Their Eyes Were Watching God* in which photographic representation concretizes blackness as stigma for six-year-old Janie. She initially cannot locate herself in the photograph of mostly white children, having never seen an image of herself. When she recognizes herself as black, she is profoundly disappointed. Janie's emergence into a raced subjectivity occurs through this visual engagement. In contrast, *Today* stages a radically constructive version of that same moment, for although no actual reader would be unaware of her own race in the implausible mode of Janie, a CDGM child might seek out a likeness of his or her own embodiment through the image and would discover there a picture that reflects back the joy of blackness.

It appears that this image is not one of Derby's original photographs but instead is an image added after the book left the classroom and entered the headquarters of the CDGM. It may not have been, then, literally a site of collaboration between Derby as teacher and one of her students. Although this is undoubtedly an image of a CDGM child, it may have been taken by Herron or by John Wallace rather than Derby, because Derby focused on group images and, moreover, the image's style and size suggest Herron; if so, the language attached to the image may not have come from a child at all and probably was added when the book left Derby's hands and went to the CDGM offices, where Herron's and Wallace's photographs were added to Derby's without any of the photographers' agreement. What does this mean for the idea of an exchange between the child and her own image? On the one hand, the child in the photo may not have ultimately held the book in her hands. We might then see the page masquerading as a child's voice and image aimed at a particular child reader, when in fact this moment was created by adults outside the classroom context and aimed to represent the CDGM as much as it served the population in Derby's school. We can see the adult hand behind this text/image coupling in other ways, too. In the language, its inconsistent punctuation (using an apostrophe with "ain't" but not with "Thats") nudges a reader to recognize the adult shaping presence behind the book, given that one adult wrote down this version of a child's language and another—probably Herron—took the child's image. This is not to say that other renderings of child language in the book appear more "authentic"—every representation of child language was written down by an adult—it is just that in this text/image moment the adult hand is more apparent. Further, the heavy pedagogical thrust of this text/image pairing—insisting on school attendance—evokes adulthood more palpably than other moments in the book do. This pedagogical moment makes sense: we are arriving at the end of the text, when the children disperse from school, and the adult voice may be intruding to insist on the children's return. We might sense an adult determining and arranging the page's placement and language as one of the final pages of the text. In this reading, then, adults stage the text's conclusion, and the intimacy of exchange between one child in the photo and the text becomes less probable.

On the other hand, actual CDGM children did encounter the book, particularly the children at the centers where Derby taught, so whether or not that particular child engaged her own representation, others certainly could read through the photograph the beauty of child blackness and appreciate print as a means of legitimizing reflection. Most of the other images in the book are of Derby's students and would have engendered specific identification. Further, considering the possibilities of the construction of this particular relationship among text, image, designer, and reader enables us to recognize the book as a deeply collaborative process. It may be that we will never know why CDGM headquarters altered Derby's narrative by inserting Herron's images. But in doing so, the book reflects a variety of imagistic perspectives, even those of the mysterious John Wallace, who is credited for images within the book on the copyright page although Derby is not.[35] One might suspect that in places where Herron's photographs are narrativized, as in the case of the beautiful girl, the book involves a kind of ventriloquism from an adult narrator of the child photographic subject. The ventriloquism is always present to some degree anyway in all of the text/image couplings, given that Derby moved language from oral into print form. Other Herron photographs are not captioned with language: the narrative pauses on a boy reading alone, children playing with blocks, and a boy sleeping on playground equipment at various points in the manuscript. These serve as documentary breaks within the narrative thrust of the book, moments that require a reader to step back and recognize that this is a world worthy of concretization and record but one that refuses full explanation or access through language. Even though all of the contributors to *Today* may not have been aware of each other and it may be impossible to chart fully the choices that determined the arrangement of the book, one gets an enlarged sense of community collaboration and investment by considering how, why, and when the beautiful girl appears in the book. Derby imagined the book as a site of intimate exchange—and certainly the text operates at this level, because it emerged from a particular group of children, focuses largely on those children, and was not mass-produced—and other players in the civil rights effort claimed and shaped the space of the text. The book evidences a collaborative ethos and outcome, a community investment in the work and representation of the Head Start effort. Derby's ideal of exchange among reader, word, and image may not literally hold for every page in the text, but we sense in the various contributors to the book a wide belief in the significance of the book as an articulation of CDGM ideals.

The intimacy and optimism of *Today* contrast sharply with other photographic representations of poor childhood in circulation during the early 1960s. The implications of *Today*'s close exchange between viewer and image come into relief when considering that the OEO, the office that funded CDGM, staged a photographic exhibition on poverty at the very same moment that CDGM was getting started. In fact, the exhibition was inspired by a Head Start publicity pamphlet created by Judith Friedberg, a former *Show* magazine editor who later organized the exhibition.[36] Erina Duganne's groundbreaking account of this *Profile of Poverty* exhibition in *The Self in Black and White* subtly describes a very different type of exchange of viewer with images of black rural children, some of which may have been taken by CDGM photographers.[37] Opening on May 12, 1965, *Profile of Poverty* exhibited 540 images by 102 photographers, including classic documentary artists Walker Evans and Dorothea Lange, as well as movement photographers Bruce Davidson and Bob Adelman. The images were hung on rusty scaffolding in a space at the new Smithsonian Museum of History and Technology, and arrows guided viewers through the sequence of captioned images. As Duganne explains, the exhibition argued for a common culture of poverty, one shared by poor people across time, race, and region; captions describing the nature and effects of poverty came from government officials like Johnson and Shriver, as well as from literary figures like Shakespeare and Victor Hugo. Given that actual poor people were not involved in the arrangement, production, or visitation of the exhibition, the effect was a sense of hierarchy and pity from the audience rather than connection and identification with the subjects in the photographs.

Further, Duganne reminds us that the elision of racial or regional difference among poor people represented in the exhibit was a product of the moment; the influential Moynihan Report, which argued for a distinctive pathologization characterizing poor black families, would not be issued until later that summer.[38] These *Profile* images were not considered aesthetic interventions but were envisioned instrumentally as creating sympathy for "the poor" as a group in need of government assistance. How striking that at the same time Derby was creating *Today*, the OEO—her funder—staged an exhibition fueled by a generalized stigmatization of poverty and its effects.[39] An awareness of *Today*'s divergence from this other photographic incarnation of the OEO allows us to recognize the independence of the CDGM's vision, its emphasis on an aesthetic that would confirm the beauty of the children who viewed the images, and the independence and integrity of this black community in creating a photographic articulation unmediated by the government. In fact, whereas *Profile of Poverty* aimed to make clear an imperative for the Johnson administration's war on poverty, *Today* set the government completely to the side. In this light, *Today* appears distinctive as a work locally situated, aesthetically interventionist, and politically audacious, the antithesis of, say, a fund-raising pamphlet aimed to convince whites of pitiable black childhood, or the totalizing stigmatization of poverty in the Smithsonian exhibition.

The photographic practice of *Today* maps more closely onto the work of the SNCC's photography unit, an arm of the "communications department" responsible for distributing a variety of information about SNCC efforts.[40] So many of SNCC's major photographers were taking images at CDGM, like Herron and Fletcher, who was married to Lowen.[41] Photographer Maria Varela directed the "reading readiness" program at CDGM and created literacy and farm-organizing filmstrips, as well as the photographic books *Something of Our Own, Part I* and *Something of Our Own, Part II* (1965), which resemble *Today* in production style.[42] One significant difference between SNCC's photography unit in the early 1960s and *Today* was a sense of audience. Matt Herron explains in a recent anthology about SNCC's activist photography: "And the movement, as [James] Forman so presciently understood, depended upon the word getting out to the wider nation. These events had to reach a much wider audience. And we were the agents of that, at least for these pictures, which carried the strongest emotional message."[43] However, 1965 marked a turning point both in the organization of SNCC, as it moved away from white participation and toward an articulation of black power, and in the photography unit, which, according to Leigh Raiford, became more invested in the artistic rewards of representation. Of course, the crossover between CDGM and SNCC photographers makes that aesthetic investment apparent. But although Derby insists that she was not part of SNCC's photo unit (she would become a documentary photographer in 1967 with Southern Media), her work—along with Herron's in *Today*—anticipates the perspective of Julius Lester, SNCC's photographic unit director beginning in the summer of 1966. As Raiford describes, Lester wished to use photography to represent black culture to itself; SNCC began prioritizing black media outlets for its images, and published calendars with images of rural people, postcards of black history, and other items aimed at local people. Raiford explains that Lester "most wanted to visualize to African American audiences, especially of the rural South, a narrative of themselves as strong black people in a world of their own making."[44] This goal is quite similar to that of *Today*, which created and represented its own universe to those who populated it. *Today* sits, then, liminally at a point in SNCC's transition both photographically and philosophically. Its aesthetic anticipated the valuing of blackness and reclamation of the vernacular that were so central to the Black Arts Movement, as well as the Black Arts Movement's emphasis on psychological liberation. Lester would become one of the most prominent black children's writers of the twentieth century; in correspondence with me, he wrote of his regret that something like *Today* was not available for his children, born in 1965 and 1967.[45]

Derby, CDGM head teacher and creator of *Today*, was part of a constellation of women initiating civil rights efforts in the mid-1960s. As the editors of *Hands on the Freedom Plow* attest, women led much community-based activism, particularly in Mississippi, where Derby worked, and offered support for student workers who were mobilized during the Freedom Summer of 1964. We might also place Derby within a populist photographic mode generated and supported by women, like Varela, whose images, filmstrips, and farm-labor photobooks aimed to generate activist and representational response.[46] Sara Blair reads Lorraine Hansberry's *The Movement* as an expression of an emerging lesbian feminist sensibility, one with a populist point: she notes the closing of Hansberry's book, in which portraits are captioned, "People do not always need poets and playwrights to state their case."[47] Blair sees Hansberry as "an archivist collating images, evidence, citations, and voices from the nation's past,"[48] an approach that reminds us of Hughes and Meltzer in chapter 2. Derby joins Hansberry as a kind of bookmaker and feminist archivist, for she gathers the language of Mississippi's young people and shapes through photographs a proclamation of psychological freedom. With the contributions of Herron and others at the CDGM front office, *Today* itself aggregates a variety of voices and perspectives. Alongside Varela and Hansberry, Derby helps constitute a female photographic practice within the movement, one committed to respecting the subjects before the lens and extending the possibility of further populist investment in representation.

The papers of SNCC contain a six-page typescript dated May 16, 1966, titled "Proposal for Use of Visual Education Materials in CDGM Programs." It outlines an ambitious plan for incorporating photographs into literacy programs for children and adults and activist efforts like involvement with the federal Agricultural Stabilization and Conservation Service. Part of the proposal encourages the development of filmstrips like Varela's; other sections emphasize the possibilities of each center's creating photographs for exhibitions in its center and for traveling exhibitions of photos from individual centers. The proposal describes the potential for these exhibitions: "Good photographs dignify what often seems commonplace, and makes beautiful usual things by letting people see them in a different way. Photo exhibits would enrich people's appreciation of what they're participating in, in CDGM centers." The proposal's overall argument melds utility (photographs serve literacy efforts and community activism) with politicized aesthetics (the desire for children and adults to see themselves and their efforts anew as beautiful). Three threads come together in considering *Today* in light of this SNCC proposal: first, this photographic book seems less insulated from the other textual productions of the CDGM, for the plans to employ photographs across group efforts signal that *Today* was more in step with the moment than an isolated production; second, the proposal helps make clear the intricate ties of SNCC to the CDGM, for although the civil rights group could not endorse the government program, its shared contributors intertwined the political and aesthetic goals of SNCC's photo unit with CDGM efforts; and finally, the memo makes clear that collective, grassroots ownership of the photographic process was of value to SNCC and the CDGM at this moment. Although the memo mentions that Bob Fletcher could make "professional" photographs for official representations of CDGM efforts, the community in each center could stage its own articulations of self. There is no evidence that SNCC and the CDGM were able to put the proposal into action. *Today*, however, had forged ahead in articulating the process of representation.

Bookmaking generally, and in particular through the making of *Today*, became a liberatory, egalitarian process at CDGM. Just as the SNCC proposal emphasizes the agency of each center in representing itself photographically, CDGM's book department, as we have seen, drew on the experience and language of children to create books children could claim as their own stories.[49] As a result, bookmaking became a democratic enterprise, accessible to all. Filmstrips were a similar venture, as Varela would write in a November 11, 1965, memo to SNCC staff: *"Anyone Can Make A Filmstrip* . . . . It's no big thing!! Just decide what you want to make a strip on and we'll (Fletcher/Varela) help you lay it out and shoot it. . . . We can either get you film—if you have cameras in your county—or we can come over and shoot whatever pictures you want in your strip."[50] However, what distinguishes CDGM's approach is the emphasis on process. Greenberg explains:

> It was my feeling that *the product*, the book, was not valuable. We should probably send no more than one copy to requesting groups, as a sample of the loveliness that can be captured. It's *the process*, the active instead of passive process, children telling stories and making books from them, and children learning to read first from their own creations, that's important. We would make little contribution if we disseminated our finished material, even though it's nicer than much available material. We might make a sizable contribution if we disseminated our process of preparing materials and teaching reading from them.[51]

For the CDGM, the course of creation, of taking control of narrative and representation and creating a version of oneself, bore more radical potential than the distribution of a self-contained representational product.[52] The CDGM process permitted teachers and young people to see themselves as creators, to take into hand the power of representation, and to feel satisfaction in owning the terms of print. This approach to process emphasizes democratic, inclusive involvement in representation, a value that is less often associated with civil rights photography than are, say, spectacular images of violence for white media or photographs of heroes. Such an emphasis on process values black experience, of course, and is connected to SNCC's trajectory in the mid-1960s. Varela comments about SNCC's approach to representation: "[O]rdinary people can and should speak for themselves and should represent themselves. Therefore, the elite should not be speaking for the so-called downtrodden. They speak for themselves with much more truth, facts, and realism than any interpreter could interpret who they are and what they're going through."[53] CDGM books, and *Today* in particular, anticipate the Black Arts Movement's "action-oriented" texts,[54] books that resisted commodification and insisted on generative aesthetic response and social action. But, further, CDGM's emphasis on process makes manifest a democratic creative theory. *Today* thus offers a new version of what civil rights photography can do. *Today* is not a call for action, making claims on the reader akin to SNCC newspapers, newsletters, flyers, or posters. *Today* is not even a book in the sense that SNCC's *The Movement* (1965) was a book: very few copies of *Today* were produced; it was not read outside the circle of preschools in the CDGM;[55] and it intended to germinate other texts rather than stand as a stable, final articulation of civil rights childhood. Its egalitarian ethos makes the process of psychological transformation through creativity, rather than through products controlled by singular writers or image makers, possible for all members of the black community. Instead of book as representational terminus, *Today* articulates the photobook as vision, as concept, as process, as possibility.

REPRESENTING FREEDOM: FRAMING AS A MEANS OF CONTROL

We are left in the contemporary moment with the artifact of that process, *Today*. In terms of the book itself, creators and CDGM thinkers would have considered the product as vital primarily to the children it reflected, the concrete result of the creative process and an engagement with print that enables a child to incorporate and identify herself, and an object to inspire other communal articulations. For readers outside that circle of exchange, we can reflect on the text as constructing the psychological freedom envisioned by CDGM. The joy that a reader sees on the face of the beautiful girl in the close-up constitutes *Today*'s version of life at the CDGM and of life as a black child in Mississippi. The close-up is one expression of the utopian desire of Derby and the group organizers to declare a sense of liberty in the readership. Framed on the page, the image shapes and secures a version of reality. In order to understand the photographic book as a defiantly constructed proclamation of freedom, an awareness of what is "off frame" at this moment in the daily life of CDGM schools becomes important. Children might not have been aware of the governmental bickering surrounding the centers' funding, which was certainly off-frame in *Today*, but the real threat of violence from local whites was conspicuous to young people. Historians have tracked incidents of cross burning and of whites shooting at CDGM schools; the most egregious, perhaps, was the early 1966 burning to ashes of a CDGM center in Valewood. Sol Gordon, who wrote the liner notes to a recording of CDGM children's freedom songs, explained that Valewood was unguarded at the time. (Derby speaks of men at each center with guns to guard the preschools.)[56] Gordon continues: "A year ago a cross burning would have been enough to halt any 'civil rights' activity; but that very day, the parents of Valewood meet and vow to continue the Head Start program under the open skies. They did so and completed the program."[57] Gordon and others note that most of the families at Valewood participated also in the Mississippi Freedom Democratic Party, an organization that incensed Mississippi whites by its challenge of the state's white delegation at the 1964 Democratic Convention.

The CDGM response to such violence appeared in its newsletter. After Valewood, early in 1966, an article titled "What Next?," in issue 4 of the *CDGM Newsletter* connected the violence at Valewood with aggression against the sites more broadly: "Some of your Centers have been shot at. Some of your Centers have been burned. Some of you have lost your jobs for working with CDGM. Some of you have been frighteningly threatened." The article then asks the reader what can be done for the schools, for parents' jobs, and for the overall freedom of life in Mississippi, concluding, "You have answers to these questions. You have the ability to act according to your answers. Is your community thinking about these things? Are you having meetings to discuss these and other things? What will you decide? What will you do?" I bring this essay to the surface because it makes apparent that Valewood was not a singular incident and that the CDGM leadership did not direct a response but hoped to inspire grassroots resistance to white violence. It also helps make clear that *Today* was an idealized space, a text that could frame off violence, aggression, and instability, and alluded to the political-organizing efforts of the adults only in a single image (Figure 3.2). Children play with blocks in the foreground, facing away from the camera as they make towers and other structures. In the background we see a few adult women in the corner left of the image, with rows of chairs on a small dais to their right. A lectern at the center of the background suggests that the floor where the children play also serves as a meeting space for adults. The image catches one of the children as she gently places the last block on top of a structure she has created, a fitting correlative to the formation of an

Figure 3.2. Children play with blocks while adults gather in the background.
From *Today*, Child Development Group of Mississippi, 1965.
McCain Library and Archives, The University of Southern Mississippi.

activist community taking place in this space after the school day.[58] Both the
women talking in the background and the children working in the foreground
are creatively building new structures for change. This image, an uncaptioned
photograph probably taken by Herron, also serves as one of the documentary
pauses that break up the children's narration, attesting to the simple existence
of the moment rather than to the children's interpretation of that moment. The
organizing and block-building image carries weight also because it assumes the
space of an entire page, serving as a record of the work the children and adults
perform.

Off frame is the sense of precariousness in fashioning these new structures,
the instability that every center experienced in the face of white threats. We
do not see, but can anticipate, that the blocks might eventually fall. *Today* takes
its images from two Mississippi centers, one in Holly Springs and the other in

Durant. Derby worked at both centers. She describes an incident that would otherwise go unrecorded except in oral histories of the CDGM:

> Durant was a rural area where there was strong black community support for CDGM and much opposition and violence from the white community. Early in my stay there, when the center director and I were returning from shopping in town and passed the church where Head Start was first held, I saw something strange on the ground. There was a fire slowly moving up a cord that ran up the path to the church steps, onto the church's porch, and through the doorway of the church. I yelled for the director to stop. We jumped out of the car, stamped out the fire, and headed back to the newly built center.[59]

Examining *Today* in light of Derby's account makes even more palpable the book as a conscious intervention in the life of Mississippi's black children, an idealized proclamation of psychological release from fear. In talking with me about *Today*, Derby pointed to the only hand-drawn illustration by a child in the book, titled "Lady Monster, by Sharon, Mt. Beulah Center." Derby said that she did not endorse or include such a picture herself; it came afterward, when the manuscript went to CDGM headquarters, also located at Mt. Beulah. Irritated, she said, "I didn't care about this. They [children] see a monster white man anytime they saw a white man with a shotgun, so they didn't need to see that." Although the illustration is nearly abstract and reflects no threatening details, the idea of including a "monster"— whether or not a child created it—in a text that staged freedom was objectionable to Derby. One might suggest that art permitted the child to engage the monsters surrounding the centers. But the book chooses to set such a context outside the frame, making psychological sovereignty a foregone conclusion rather than offering space to any version of white antagonism or to child therapeutic engagement. In the world of *Today*, freedom is a done deal.

In considering what the book *does* frame in order to articulate its vision, I focus on collectivity, play, and the role of time in the text. Until we meet the single child at the end of the book, *Today* is narrated in the collective voice of "we." That plurality suggests the shared experience of a community of children as they go about their activities. The text begins, "Thats the schoolhouse. We come every day and play around" (2), lines that swiftly announce the site, the group, and the focus of the children's day. Using a blocked letter for the *W*, this visual stress continues throughout the book, as nearly every instance of the word *We* becomes emphasized through that heavy font. The descriptions of activities are collective: "We go outside hopping like rabbits" (3); "Sometime we plays in the sandbox with the tires" (4). The images that attend the descriptions are largely group shots taken by Derby. In one shot, the group plays on the equipment built by the community (specifications provided in training manuals and newsletters by CDGM [Figure 3.3]). The language reads, "We climbing up on the posts[.] We jump down" (7). At the center of the picture, we see a child whose feet have left the play equipment, his fists clenched, a look of intensity on his face. But the arrangement of the image does not single him out as the leader or even depict him as performing a spectacular leap. One has to look closely to see that his feet are not touching the equipment, and he is crowded on either side with other children. The depiction here emphasizes collectivity, a shared purpose and experience in play, and a sense of communal strength.

However, the group shots in the book are purposeful beyond a straightforward assertion of belonging. Many photographic representations of children during the civil rights movement single them out, whether as objects of pity or sites of connection. Collectivity in *Today* suggests a kind of lack of accessibility for an outsider to the particularities of the children's existence. Readers will not get to know a particular child but can witness the group working, eating,

Figure 3.3. Children climb on equipment created by the school's staff.
From *Today*, Child Development Group of Mississippi, 1965.
McCain Library and Archives, The University of Southern Mississippi.

Figure 3.4. Children march playfully into the outhouse.
From *Today*, Child Development Group of Mississippi, 1965.
McCain Library and Archives, The University of Southern Mississippi.

and playing together. This book was never intended for outsiders, one might be reminded. A particular image evokes both the book's play against documentary uses of images and its insistence on the legitimacy of the children's viewpoint. The image of children heading into an outhouse might, in a conventional documentarian context, be employed as a marker of Southern deprivation or of degradation (Figure 3.4). Here, however, the photograph refuses access to the faces of the children. Their backs turned, they move as a group; as viewers, we thus do not focus on some kind of expected emotional effect of the outhouse on the children, but instead are led visually with the group into the space. Our vision thus conforms to their experience, and it is not disturbing in the least. A child on the right even seems to be at play as he enters, his arms in the air, his foot up in a jaunty stride. The details of the outhouse preclude the stigma of poverty in documentary photography; although the fence next to the structure is irregular, the outhouse seems newly built and freshly painted. To confirm its newness, construction materials appear on the ground next to the building. Derby described this scene to me pragmatically: "[The photograph] is [taken] there because that is what we all used!" Her perspective dovetails with the narration, which asserts, "We going to the toilet sometimes too" (21). The narration confirms the place of the image in the narrative; from the children's point of view, it is simply another activity the group completes. Free of the shame of images of documentary poverty, the photo and text make clear instead that, collectively, the group move through features of their day together, and even toileting is unproblematic.

In terms of the civil rights implications of group images in *Today*, the images insist on children as elements woven into the fabric of a community working together, rather than as singular figures advancing social change. This dimension takes on weight when we consider the way in which black youth sometimes were figured photographically in social-justice efforts: Elizabeth Eckford integrating a school at Little Rock and Emmett Till both before and after his murder, for example, are singular figures. Of course, SNCC's photography unit employed many images of children marching together and imprisoned together, even if in *The Movement* the conclusion lingers on the face of one young girl who was hit by a pickup truck. In truth, one could not argue that collective figurations of youth were rare during the movement, despite some iconic images of singular children. In images, we remember children on picket lines in front of Woolworth's, children marching in Selma, and children being imprisoned in Birmingham, as were adults. But Birmingham images are unsettling in part because jail as civil rights action was understood to be an endeavor of adults. As we see children behind bars, photographs demand reflection on the children's lack of fit with their environment. Although the Birmingham campaign is not my main concern, one could think about the way collective images of children interact with the objection of adults to children's inclusion in the movement (depending on the publication context, of course), even precluding the possibility that children could be viewers of the images. In *Today*, group photos insist on civil rights as a terrain appropriate for the young. *Today*'s group photos insistently frame a community of like-minded *children*, one that through play and invention will transform society together. As Thulani Davis explains of looking at the photo of Eckford, "We didn't need a lone icon facing abuse for all of us; we needed more bodies than could be captured in one image."[60] Although integration photographs do emphasize the isolation of children, in the black landscape of *Today*, collectivity articulates a shared vision and commitment that permit a freedom of mind accessible to the young. The ideal black community is here in childhood; white oppression is not. *Today* constructs childhood as freedom of mind and spirit, shared and affirmed in community.

In addition to Herron's uncaptioned photographs of singular children reading or sleeping, the only other instance of singularity in the book appears within a three-image sequence in which a child visits a doctor. Medical care was an important component of the CDGM program, and many children had not had experience with doctors before enrollment. One might expect to see an excited child happy for medical attention. In the first image, instead, a disembodied white hand pulls back the child's head, and his eyes and mouth are open (Figure 3.5). This image is cut out of the background, which makes it appear even more abrupt and aggressive, because we are severed from the context of the preschool. What we notice in this sequence is the child's frustration and sadness at the doctor experience; the narration for the last images reads, "He's crying cause he don't want the doctor to doctor on him" (16 [Figure 3.6]). The child resists, wailing at the doctor; this is no salvific white presence, even though the medical care was much needed and histories of the CDGM report that it saved children's lives. But within the context of *Today*, separation from the child community, as well as intervention—however helpful—from whites, provokes agitation. These doctor images are not Derby's and do not carry her warm, connected, communal sensibility.

But this shift in tone is purposeful and coheres with the text's ideals. If we consider that the CDGM headquarters inserted this sequence into Derby's story of a group of children, the radical implications become even more apparent. If CDGM management wished to use the book to promote their health-care efforts, the images might tilt toward the propagandistic. If this were a book meant for distribution to Northern supporters or to outsiders to the CDGM, the depiction of health care might appear more celebratory. But even the adults at CDGM headquarters selected images of children opposing the imposition of outsiders. Because they are resistant and disruptive, the medical images mesh perfectly with Derby's viewpoint: the images insist on respect for child experience and propel the recognition that within the world of *Today*, children are happy only when connected to each other.

In tandem with the brief doctor interlude, the book overall emphasizes the intensity and rewards of child play. In fact, the text's construction of freedom rests on the value of play as a kind of liberating psychological work. For instance, early in the book the narration explains, "We likes little Sally Walker. We twisting" (5 [Figure 3.7]). In the image, boys and girls, laughing, circle a boy who stands with his hands on his hips, performing the rhyme. "Little Sally Walker" was also one of the verses included on the CDGM freedom-songs album. The lyrics read:

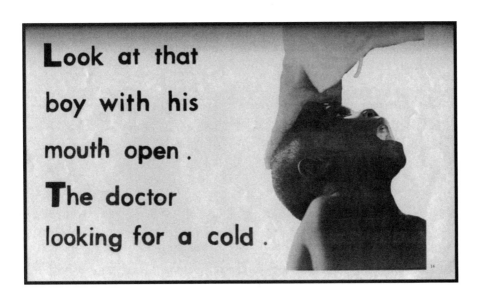

Figure 3.5. A boy undergoes a medical examination.
From *Today*, Child Development Group of Mississippi, 1965.
McCain Library and Archives, The University of Southern Mississippi.

Figure 3.6. A boy resists medical attention. From *Today*,
Child Development Group of Mississippi, 1965.
McCain Library and Archives, The University of Southern Mississippi.

> Little Sally Walker, sitting in a saucer
> Weeping and a-crying for a cool drink of water
> Rise, Sally, rise
> Gonna wipe your weeping eyes
> Put your hand on your hip
> An' let your backbone slip
> Shake it to the east, shake it to the west
> Shake it to the one that you love best.[61]

One might not think of this ring game as a kind of freedom song. However, Bessie Jones, the Georgia Sea Islands singer who collected black children's culture with Bess Lomax Hawes in *Step It Down* (1972), explains that although the song has British origins, it became associated in the United States with "the joys of release from shame."[62] The lyrics move from despair to physical release and include joyous sensuality in the dance the child performs. The children in the *Today* photograph twist their bodies as they circle the center child; again, a closed circle denotes the oneness of this child community. The liberation of play brings physical pleasure and joy to the group. There may not be the acknowledgment of shame within *Today*, which is unsurprising, given its argument for the triumph of psychological freedom, but the image of the ring game suggests that play enables children to expel any sense of disgrace or sadness.

Figure 3.7. Children play the ring game "Little Sally Walker."
From *Today*, Child Development Group of Mississippi, 1965.
McCain Library and Archives, The University of Southern Mississippi.

Figure 3.8. Children maintain the equipment they have helped to build.
From *Today*, Child Development Group of Mississippi, 1965.
McCain Library and Archives, The University of Southern Mississippi.

Play is also serious business in *Today*, an opportunity to demonstrate creative thinking. In one set of playground images, two boys work together on equipment: "We fixing a see-saw" (18 [Figure 3.8]). The physical involvement of the children in the effort becomes apparent. In the left photo, one child sticks out his tongue earnestly as he determines the problem, and in the right one, the other boy looks underneath the equipment, his leg balanced high in the air. The children's sense of responsibility and possession becomes apparent in these images. Play is a kind of work that allows children to demonstrate their inventiveness and capability. Inside play, like that depicted in the blocks image, also emphasizes the children's ability to generate ideas and make the ideas material. Another image in the book depicts two walls covered in children's art projects, from descriptions of colors to collages of images cut out of magazines and newspapers (Figure 3.9). As Derby describes, such a display offers a sense of the children's creative accomplishment: "They can see their artwork on the wall. 'OK, I want to see my things up, my artwork up. I did that.' Their names are on the pictures."[63] This kind of display could appear on the wall of any preschool today, and as a result may seem fairly innocuous. But in the context of 1965 Mississippi, in the context of white terror and black fear, the articulation of self offered in this pictorial display is anything but prosaic. It becomes a pronouncement of child facility as well as assertiveness, a way of marking the community's value through the grouping of names and a means to demonstrate the

Thems our pictures on the wall ,

what we been making.

Figure 3.9. Art projects adorn the walls of the school. From
Today, Child Development Group of Mississippi, 1965.
McCain Library and Archives, The University of Southern Mississippi.

way creativity helps transform a child psychologically. In fact, creating *Today* is akin to this play in art, a creative world building that assertively proclaims the community's integrity. Play is fluid and improvisational, and engages the impossible. Photography documents and fixes, and is attached to the real. Play and photography thus seem to be oppositional in some ways. But I see this tension as fundamentally productive in *Today*, because the book seeks more to inspire than to document; as a generative text inviting further creative constructions of psychological freedom, the text uses play images to argue for the possibility of the ideal.

Play as liberatory, as independent and generative, also dovetails with images in the text that suggest that play involves resistance. In addition to the child who opposes the doctor, subtle moments of rebellion arise through the course of the book. "We supposed to take a nap but we reading instead" (13), the narration to one photo explains, as the image of children lying in a line invites a viewer to look at each child to discover which ones are resisting the structure of the day (Figure 3.10). The arrangement of the image is humorous, for if one begins with the three larger figures in the front of the image, the children seem to be conforming; but as the viewer's gaze moves upward, beyond those three, it is doubtful that any of the rest of the children are asleep, except perhaps a child or two in the back. The rest of the children are reading or sneaking glances at the camera. This is the only image in the book of a group of children making

Figure 3.10. Children lie down for rest, some refusing sleep.
From *Today*, Child Development Group of Mississippi, 1965.
McCain Library and Archives, The University of Southern Mississippi.

such eye contact. No longer outside the ring game, the viewer is let in on the children's rebellion, caught and drawn in by their gaze. A reader becomes co-conspirator with the children. In another image, a child sleeps on playground equipment while others are gathered with teachers behind him. No one bothers the sleeping child; he is left to his own desire. All of the instances of rebellion in the book insist that independent thinking, in tandem with creative play, is of value within the CDGM program. Of course, the rebellion that the children stage in the group nap image is further reading and is in sync with the goals of CDGM's literacy program. At the top edge of the image, the viewer can see the legs of an adult who is also sitting on the ground, her ankles crossed casually, and we get the sense that adults give the children a sense of guidance but do not interfere with their desires. Child rebellion consists of resistance not to the ideal of freedom but to a rigid timeline for its expression. Within a stricter environment, structure would win over child-directed activity. In *Today*, freedom involves the ability to respond to desire for narrative, for physical play, for rest—all on the schedule of the child rather than of the adult.

The children thus play with the timeline of the school day, undoing a chronology that would hinder them. Similarly, the approach of *Today* plays against the temporal strictures of a photographic book. The photograph, as Barthes and others argue, insists on the pastness of the image. Images record that something happened, even as they pull that moment out of the past and reanimate it in the present. Through this lens, the image read in the present always mourns the past. But, as Sara Blair explains regarding photographs of the Harlem riots of 1935, assumptions about the elegiac nature of images crumble when photos emerge within contexts associated with immediacy; when images emerge outside of contexts with "daguerrean, characterological, or elegiac effects," fresh possibilities for the temporal dimensions of photography emerge.[64] In *Today*, the title insists on the accomplishment of psychological liberation within a current moment, a moment that has no closure. Certainly the present tense of the narration helps emphasize immediacy. The end of the text makes the temporal arrest clear; although the timeline of the school day has drawn to a close, the book and school exist in a timeless present, for as the children board a school bus, the narration reads, "We going home, but we going back too" (24). It is always ever "today" within the text. Using the framing of photography to focus on the accomplishment of the moment, on the achievement of freedom "today" in childhood, the book sets off-frame the violence against the centers, the dissent between movement and OEO members, and even the emotional ambivalence or fears likely experienced by actual children in Mississippi in 1965. Photography enables *Today* to frame space, representation, and the community within the current moment, and to insist that the moment remains alive and authoritative.

In fact, the result of that framing—the text itself—refuses the elegiac: the product recedes in importance when we consider the text's goal of inspiring children's ongoing representational authority and autonomy. As an act of resisting commodification, objectification, and representationality (rather than representation), *Today* is an egalitarian and democratic invitation to the young. Children become free in themselves in an ongoing psychological transformation rather than a single public event or intervention in representation. In fact, the last image in the book removes itself from time and space altogether (Figure 3.11). Reminiscent of the two adults holding hands on the back cover of *The Movement*, this image pictures an adult black hand gripping a child's hand in solidarity. But whereas the final image of Hansberry's book is set within a landscape of protest—bodies outlined in light frame the handshake—in *Today* the hands grip each other in a partnership that transcends particularities of a site or event. Just as the book argues for the continual "now" of the child's liberation, a move that further displaces the real physical threats to that freedom in the actual temporal landscape, the handshake exists in a realm of the ideal. *Today* as process and as product accomplishes the call of the civil rights cry "Freedom now!" Martin Luther King Jr. spoke with Robert Penn Warren about the frustration behind that popular chant:

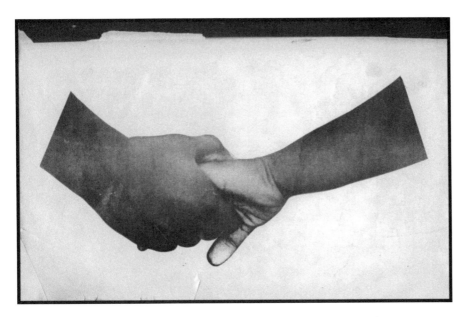

Figure 3.11. An African American child and adult grip each other's hands in a sign of partnership. From *Today*, Child Development Group of Mississippi, 1965. McCain Library and Archives, The University of Southern Mississippi.

Well, I find—it is a problem, and we have lived so long with this idea, of people saying it takes time, and wait on time, that I find it very difficult to adjust to this. I mean, I get annoyed almost when I hear it, although I know it takes time. But the people that use this argument have been people so often who really didn't want the change to come, and the gradualism for them meant a do-nothingism, you know, and a stand-stillism. So that it has been a revolt I think against the idea of a feeling on the part of some that you can just sit around and wait on time when actually time is neutral. It can be used either constructively or destructively.[65]

Today uses photography to insist on the urgency, the now, of children's psychological transformation. Waiting on time was an impossibility for Derby and others at the CDGM. Just as the children in the documentary film that opened the discussion crossed the landscape with confidence, enacting a freedom of spirit that denied boundaries of fence and barbed wire, *Today* insists on the immediacy of psychological transformation and the freedom that comes with confidence. Psychological freedom exists in the perpetual now of this photobook and in the transformative process of creation that it seeks to inspire.

4

The Black Arts Movement
Childhood as Liberatory Process

The black child is the era's black face. . . . In fact, the black child will
now reject the white playground and cavort about the less fashionable
but more familiar black slum yard, because the essence and fulfillment
of the pleasure that he seeks lies with familiar faces burnt by familiar
laughter in familiar places . . . and a unity of joy.
　—Lindsay Barrett, "The Tide Inside, It Rages!"

[Black power] can ultimately be defined only in action—in movement.
　—Larry Neal, "And Shine Swam On"

In Our Terribleness (1970), a landmark photographic book for adults by
Imamu Amiri Baraka and Fundi (Billy Abernathy), contains many images
of young people as members of a new nation forged by the Black Arts Movement of the late 1960s and early 1970s. Describing the need for a transformative
love of blackness, an early section culminates in an image of a boy emerging
from the doors of a building (Figure 4.1). Facing slightly left, the child looks
into the high distance with seriousness. His right arm pushes and his left hand
lightly grasps his hip; by the stance of his legs, one can sense the boy's body
weight pressing against the door. The child seems to be caught in the middle
of the movement, fixed visually in a liminal instant on the threshold between
two spaces. The image is placed transitionally as well, falling in between lines
of poetry. The first part of the poem leaves us with a line break of anticipation
and suspense:

> But
> the day
> to day
> always
> continuous exercise
> of

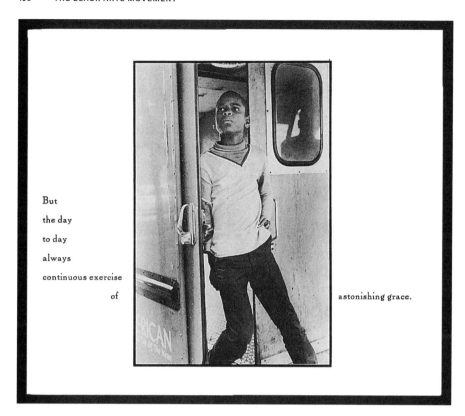

But

the day

to day

always

continuous exercise

of

astonishing grace.

Figure 4.1. A boy stands on a threshold and peers into the air.
From Imamu Amiri Baraka and Fundi, *In Our Terribleness*
(Indianapolis: The Bobbs-Merrill Company, Inc., 1970).

The poem concludes to the right of the image with a phrase that bears the finality of assessment: "astonishing grace." Black love is embodied in the image of the child in fluid motion. This child effortlessly incarnates the integrity and value of blackness, his body caught in a moment of motion and process. He opens the door to the black nation's ability to embody and affirm black experience.

Remembering photobook precursors, especially the Child Development Group of Mississippi's *Today* in its emphasis on process and indeterminacy, we can consider the place of the child in the Black Arts Movement (BAM) generally and can chart the emergence of a body of children's photographic books in the early 1970s. What was the relationship of the child to the ideals of the

BAM? How did literacy training and expectations about children's language inflect the rhetoric of the movement? Why were Black Arts writers invested in photobooks in particular? How did photographic texts for children adhere to the movement's emphasis on the oral, the performative, and the textual? Addressing these questions will enable us to consider children's texts as participants in a larger cultural conversation about the possibilities of the BAM.

During the Black Arts Movement, black childhood embodied both a nationalist ideal and its incomplete fruition. Three photographic books particularly reveal this potent perspective on childhood. Kali Grosvenor's *Poems by Kali* (1970), a tremendously popular collection written by a child poet with images by Robert Fletcher, argues for the child as both an icon of the black nation and a productively incomplete articulation of its possibilities. John Shearer's photographic picture book *I Wish I Had an Afro* (1970) responds to the genre of magazine exposé, which often focused photographically on youths in blighted city spaces in order to make an argument about psychological liberation as an ongoing process inhering in childhood. June Jordan's masterpiece of children's history, *Dry Victories* (1972), a text that is indebted to Hughes and Meltzer's *Pictorial History*, employs an oppositional aesthetic that poses moments in history against each other in order to construct the BAM child as creator of historical meaning. These are three dramatically different texts, but each draws on BAM configurations of childhood as icon and as process in order to argue for the child as embodying both black essence and futurity. My discussion focuses on both the place of the child in the BAM and the uses of childhood within photobooks for the young. By concluding with a brief discussion of *The Black Book* (1974), that monumental assemblage of text and image edited by Toni Morrison, we can consider briefly the wider circulation of the era's new emphasis on the possibilities of childhood. Like *Pictorial History* in the 1950s, the audience for Morrison's text was inclusive and expansive. If *Dry Victories* uses history to inspire activism, *The Black Book*, although not expressly a children's text but a book more suited to family reading, as are *Pictorial History* and *The Sweet Flypaper of Life*, establishes black childhood as the bearer of history into the future. Again, as inspiration and as process, the child articulates and enlarges the political activity of composing history, and again the book becomes a social-justice conversation piece for families. For Jordan, the child can become an archivist, much in the mode of Meltzer's "designing narrator," who can pull and arrange images in order to make meaning from the past. With the "astonishing grace" of Baraka's door-opening child in mind, we turn to three children's photographic texts that make plain the extraordinary function of the Black Arts child in emblematizing the values of the movement. As we remember, too, that the BAM emerged from the "black power" arm of the post-1965 freedom movement, we recognize that the children's texts here all engage expressly with the disappointments of the early civil rights movement.

THE BLACK ARTS MOVEMENT: THE PLACE OF THE FAMILY

The Black Arts Movement was connected ideologically with the push for black political agency in the mid- to late 1960s. Typically called the "black power" movement, this wide-ranging effort aimed to achieve economic and social self-determination.[1] Because it arose in cities across the country in response to pervasive cultural demands for increased active engagement with political struggle, the BAM as an aesthetic movement was configured capaciously.[2] Its first incarnation, perhaps, was Amiri Baraka's establishment of the Black Arts Repertory Theatre in Harlem, in 1964, and it gained energy in the late 1960s after the assassinations of Malcolm X, in 1965, and Martin Luther King Jr., in 1968.[3] The Black Arts Movement embraced ideological and representational reinvention, according to Larry Neal, who argued in 1968, "A main tenet of Black Power is the necessity for black people to define the world in their own terms. The black artist has made the same point in the context of aesthetics."[4] With an emphasis on rejuvenation through new and reconfigured versions of African and African American history and identity,[5] Black Arts thinkers began to consider the function of the family in relation to cultural definitions.

The emphasis on black childhood emerged from the idea of the heterosexual nuclear family as a metonym for the nation, itself a response (in part) to the degradations of the 1965 Moynihan Report, *The Negro Family: The Case for National Action*, and its uses in popular culture.[6] Despite the misogynistic tone of much BAM writing,[7] women wrote and created prolifically during the late 1960s and early 1970s, and many engaged the idea of children as constituting the future of the new black nation. To be sure, the issue for black women of family and child rearing (especially in relationship to their role in the revolution) was complicated, and it warrants a full-length study in order to understand fully the role of reproduction and childhood in the BAM. As Margo Natalie Crawford notes, writers in Toni Cade's landmark 1970 anthology, *The Black Woman*, grappled with the implications of the figurations of women as mothers of the race. Interest in the child, then, may have emerged as an extension of the "naturalization of family as race,"[8] a situation that consigned women to a relational role to men and that circumscribed the features of female identity and independence.

In some cases, however, it was the active presence of women in the movement, not simply an extension of a conservative gender role, that spurred attention to the young. Toni Cade resisted the idea that birth control was equivalent to genocide, for instance, and argued for a "healthy" approach to family: "It is a noble thing, the rearing of warriors for the revolution. I can find no fault with the idea. I do, however, find fault with the notion that dumping the pill is the way to do it."[9] Others in Cade's anthology insisted that "the need to politicize all Blacks, including children, has become so obvious"[10] and argued for a fundamental revision of the public school system, as did Maude White Katz.[11] The poet and playwright Sonia Sanchez is a case in point of female resistance to misogyny coupled with advocacy for children. Sanchez had been writing within the Black Arts Movement for years when she decided to join the Nation of Islam in 1971, turning away from her earlier belief in integration and her activity with CORE (the Congress on Racial Equality); she was a vital member of the Nation of Islam for five years, a period during which she helped develop the black studies program at the University of Massachusetts at Amherst. She left that post in 1975 to become "director of culture in the Nation," and began writing the children and women's page of the Nation of Islam's popular newspaper, *Muhammad Speaks*,[12] where she addressed gender inequities in the Nation and educated and inspired children.[13] In a September 5, 1975, column, Sanchez argued for collaborative responsibility for building the new nation through child rearing: "It is the Black family becoming the nucleus in the building of a Nation and a new civilization. . . . Come Black Man. Come Black Woman. We can begin it today, family style in our movement to the highest level of humanity."[14] It is not as though a repudiation of misogyny necessarily became a repudiation of motherhood for many female writers of the moment.[15] Children were valuable within the black community, within various familial configurations, and to women particularly. Although women were the most engaged artistically with childhood during the BAM, men also participated considerably in the process of educating (or reeducating) the young. Maulana Karenga established black-nationalist schools, youth organizations, and the Kwanzaa holiday;[16] the Nation of Islam also supported schools; and the Black Panthers offered education[17] and breakfast programs for children (Kali Grosvenor's mother, Vertamae Grosvenor, cooked for that program).

Whereas engagement with actual children was configured variously across black-power organizations, the aesthetic movement embraced the idea of childhood as an essential component of revolutionary formations, a means to a new epistemology and core identity. Don L. Lee (Haki Madhubuti), within Neal's 1968 essay "The Black Arts Movement," argued that intervention in systems of knowledge requires destruction of white-childhood artifacts. Aiming at American and children's literature, as well as the totalizing process of literacy training, he argued, "We must destroy Faulkner, dick, jane, and other perpetrators of evil."[18] In erecting a new epistemology, Black Arts writers launched an attack on white knowledge, presumed to be ordinary and uncomplicated, by questioning its children's texts. For these thinkers, rooting out corruption began in the language and lessons of childhood. But Stokely Carmichael saw in at least one non–African American children's text the potential for radical perceptual transformation, particularly in language. In *Black Power* (1967), Carmichael and Charles V. Hamilton wrote,

> Those who have the right to define are the masters of the situation. Lewis Carroll understood this:
> "When I use a word," Humpty Dumpty said, in a rather scornful tone, "it means just what I choose it to mean. Neither more nor less."
> "The question is," said Alice, "whether you *can* make words mean so many different things."
> "The question is," said Humpty Dumpty, "which is to be master. That is all."
> Today, the American educational system continues to reinforce the entrenched values of the society through the use of words.[19]

Childhood pedagogy became an ideal site to reorder systems of knowledge and to reify cultural literacy. Of course, a central endeavor of the BAM was redefining artistic language in order to reflect the vernacular rhythms of the black community. Black Arts writers thus turned to childhood as a site of Afrocentric teaching as well as a place from which to draw inspiration, as children were assumed to speak a language more "natural" than that of their elders. June Jordan wrote in 1973 of the corruption that school forced on children, saying, "[W]e sposed to choke our natural self into the weird, lying, barbarous, unreal, white speech and writing habits that the schools lay down like holy law."[20] Because language acquisition begins in childhood, Black Arts writers turned to young people—both through nationalist schooling and through literature—as a means of revolutionizing aesthetic expectations. Through these revised literacy and education efforts, BAM writers aimed for a literal undoing of corrupted language and texts. But in a more abstract sense, as an *ideal*, black childhood untouched by white literacy training became an aspirant state of consciousness in some figurations of the black nation.

Black Arts writers responded with passion to the idea of expressing (and forming) black national identity through childhood, offering a variety of publications for the young, including poetry, picture books, novels, histories, and autobiography. For instance, Gwendolyn Brooks's poetry is infused with youth as a topic and strategy, as Richard Flynn has adeptly argued.[21] Prominent black writers for young people of the 1960s and early 1970s included, in addition to Brooks and Sanchez, Nikki Giovanni, Mari Evans, Lucille Clifton, Rosa Guy, Alice Childress, Shirley Graham, Toni Cade Bambara, Tom Feelings, Julius Lester, Kristin Hunter, Sharon Bell Mathis, Virginia Hamilton, Eloise Greenfield, Jean Carey Bond, Sam Cornish, Mildred Pitts Walter, and Jean Pajot Smith, among others. A few critics trace threads between this upswing in black children's literature and the BAM, like Cheryl Finley, who notes of Tom Feelings, "Upon his return to New York [from Ghana, where he was teaching] in the early 1970s, he aligned himself with the BAM and began to illustrate Afro-centric children's books."[22] In tandem with the BAM, other forces helped propel the interest in black children's literature in the late 1960s. Dianne Johnson studies this moment, when "'black children's literature' gained weight and recognition within the publishing world, to a level which it has not enjoyed since."[23] Critics like Michelle Martin, Rudine Sims Bishop, and Violet Harris have charted the influence of the Council on Interracial Books for Children (founded in 1966) and the creation of the Coretta Scott King Award by the American Library Association (1970) on the rise in publication of black children's texts. Certainly, as Flynn, Johnson, and Judy Richardson note, the marketing demand for black children's literature, fueled by increased funding for underserved schools through the 1965 Elementary and Secondary Education Act, helped propel publisher interest in the subject. Black children's literature thus expanded appreciably during the Black Arts era, swelled by forces both within and without the movement.[24] Childhood suddenly offered the opportunity for Black Arts writers both to discover and to develop a black ideal: on the one hand, childhood became the epitome of the decolonized mind, a space for the black nation to express its "authentic" voice; on the other, childhood became the terrain for counterliteracy training, for undoing cultural degradation begun in white schooling, and for setting new foundations of black identity through authoritative histories of African and black American experience.

THE BLACK ARTS MOVEMENT AND
THE PHOTOGRAPHIC PERSPECTIVE

Children's photographic picture books were part of this groundswell of attention to black childhood. In order to understand the variety of approaches to photographic imagery in children's photobooks, we should be aware that in the late 1960s there was no singular aesthetic perspective on the relationship of photography to the race in general, or to the Black Arts movement in particular. Erina Duganne explores one of the most prominent photography collectives, the Kamoinge Workshop in New York, founded in 1963 and led by Roy DeCarava. In explaining that the group embraced no central, governing ideology of the black aesthetic, she observes that photographers moved away from the evidentiary and toward a vision of image as multivalent and evocative rather than indexical or documentarian.[25] Such aesthetic capaciousness may be a response to the documentary stigma that photography still bore in some circles during the late 1960s. In general, this was the era when photoessays in magazines became more personal than emotionally detached, as white photographers like Diane Arbus moved away from commercial work and toward the more intimate, suggestive, evocative, and disturbing. Arbus's work in the late 1960s helped dissolve the lines between photograph as art and photograph as document, since she turned toward using the camera to specify the features of social outsiders. Vietnam War photographers like Phillip Jones Griffiths, too, combined the aesthetic with the documentary, and their images were employed politically. But considering photography as art was a contentious move.[26] Black photography remained particularly controversial aesthetically, given its attachment in the public mind with the evidentiary, with documentation of blighted urban space and its desolate subjects. For example, the Metropolitan Museum of Art's January 1969 exhibit *Harlem on My Mind* was criticized by black visual artists for excluding painting and focusing on photography; the *New York Times* also dismissed the exhibit by suggesting it was an exercise in "sociological documentation," revealing the newspaper's bias against photography as a genre by suggesting that the exhibit "includes no art."[27] As Mary Ellen Lennon explains, black visual artists resisted the emphasis on photographs alone: "Where were the African American visual artists? Why *photographs?* . . . In response, under the leadership of Andres and Romare Bearden, Harlem artists organized themselves as the Black Emergency Cultural Coalition (BECC) and picketed the press preview of the exhibition on January 12, 1969."[28] Despite the fact that the exhibition included work by James Van Der Zee, Gordon Parks, and John Shearer, many black visual artists resisted the idea that the world would see black art as connected even implicitly with social science through photography.[29]

Thus, we remember in examining children's books that the photographic genre, although pervasive, carried the burden of being assumed to have a documentary sociological function, a weight intensified, perhaps, given the topic of urban youth. By embracing the black child photographically, the BAM flew in the face of white-created photographic representations of the decayed city and corrupt urban youth that were prevalent in the late 1960s in newspaper accounts of riots and social unrest. Cognizant of traditional documentary photographic depictions of the supposed pathology of the black urban family, Black Arts photographers and writers claimed black childhood instead as a site of emblematic potential. Just as poets like Baraka and Madhubuti embraced the cityscape as a site of beauty as well as of pain, BAM photographs of children claimed the urban site in ways that reflect children's place and value there, as well as the way the city evokes the child's inner landscape of potential and struggle. Children are at home in the city; the city becomes expressed through the spirit of the children. Books by Grosvenor, Shearer, and Jordan evoked and played with the expectation of photography as social document, resisting the mode of the exposé prevalent within urban journalism of the late 1960s: they defied the construction of black youth as a social problem and incarnated the ideals of the BAM through the body of the child.

Of course, black magazines had staged a long-standing visual counterculture to the journalistic exposé in images of black material success; and African American photojournalists made tremendous strides during the 1950s and 1960s, another important component to the rise of photography during the BAM. Most prominent of these was Gordon Parks, the first black staff photographer at *Life* magazine.[30] John Shearer, a close friend to Parks and author of *I Wish I Had an Afro*, was the second. In the 1950s and 1960s, magazines like *Ebony, Jet, Negro Digest/Black World*, and others were dominated by photographs, many of young people, and undoubtedly children's books like Shearer's and Grosvenor's were influenced by the popularity and attractiveness of black periodicals. These magazines contained photostories about black communities and the civil rights movement, images of black celebrities, and black photo advertising, all of which influenced an age in which "black is beautiful" came into public consciousness. Black public figures in, say, *Jet* magazine in the 1950s may not have been wearing Afros and dashikis, but two decades of expansion in positive visual imagery (though often politically and aesthetically conservative) anticipated the 1960s spirit of racial pride.

Although Black Arts photographers did not share a unified perspective on the black aesthetic, they did embrace certain core values. Foremost was a commitment to self-determination through a variety of expressions. The larger BAM thus offered artists the freedom to chart their own paths, to articulate their conceptions of black integrity and visibility, in ways that had not been imagined before. This freedom accounts for the variety of photographic perspectives in children's books during the movement.[31] Some photographers gravitated to the idea of "black light," as Crawford defines it: "Dark-skinned blackness, in so many Black Arts Movement texts, became an embodiment of the 'black light' that many of the poets and visual artists were discovering."[32] A black-light aesthetic would become important for professional photographers like Shearer, who embraced darkness in *I Wish I Had an Afro*.

Yet despite the controversy around photography as an aesthetic mode during the late 1960s, the genre connected explicitly with the goals of the Black Arts Movement. In seeking articulation of cultural distinctiveness, the photograph enabled a concretization of ideals, such as "black is beautiful" and the family as nation. Further, photographs' association with truth telling (however precarious, given the constructedness of photographic images) enabled black artists to stage what they saw as "real" and effective revolutionary statements. Toni Morrison, who has spoken about her indebtedness to the photographic image,[33] composed the unpaginated foreword to the first issue of the *Black Photographers Annual*, a 1973 collection self-published by photographers who were upset at the absence of venues in which to show their work. Morrison writes,

> This is a rare book: not only because it is a first, but also because it is an original idea complemented by enormous talent, energy and some of the most powerful and poignant photography I have ever seen. . . . It is also a true book. It hovers over the matrix of black life, takes accurate aim and explodes our sensibilities. Telling us what we had forgotten we knew, showing us new things about ancient lives, and old truths in new phenomena.
>
> Not only is it a true book, it is a free one. It is beholden to no elaborate Madison Avenue force. It is solely the product of its creators and its contributors. There is no higher praise for any project than that it is rare, true and free. And isn't that what art is all about? And isn't that what *we* are all about?

Not only does this passage become important in appreciating Morrison's long-standing investment in the form of photography, but it also reminds us of the self-determination of black photographers during the BAM. The emphasis on honest images bespeaks the idea that the new—in images of the young—could speak of "old truths." Morrison suggests a revised vision of "truth" in images: truth inheres within the idea the image evokes rather than within an indexical representation. "[R]are, true and free" photography embodies that which is best about the black community: "And isn't that what *we* are all about?" Image becomes metonym for the people. Child can stand in for the truth of the nation.

If the Black Arts Movement intensified interest in pedagogy, language, narrative, and childhood in an attempt to materialize black epistemologies, artists also discovered that coupling words with photographic images linked revolutionary concepts to their expression in the world. There was a productive traffic between word and image within the BAM, with language often evoking the visual in, say, a poem's layout on the page, and images speaking in collages that conjoined paintings with words, as in June Jordan's *Who Look at Me* (1969). Considering the BAM's commitment to participatory and public articulations of revivified black identity, marrying word and image did not happen only in books. Perhaps the most prominent example of this multimedia strategy was South Side Chicago's *Wall of Respect*, a mural created in 1967 by several artists from the Organization of Black American Culture, which included photographs, poetry, and paintings.[34] Edward Christmas painted Amiri Baraka's poem "SOS" into the mural, including these memorable, age-inclusive lines: "Calling black people / calling all black people, man woman child / Wherever you are." As Crawford explains, photography was a prominent component of the project: "The photography of Robert Sengstacke, Darrell Cowherd, Billy Abernathy, and Roy Lewis was framed and mounted on it [the mural]. The mural became a gathering point for Chicago Black Arts Movement photographers."[35] One of the photographs depicted young girls singing and praying at church; there were other children figured within paintings on the wall. Because the *Wall of Respect* combined aesthetic forms, qualities of each form infused the others: poetry took on the tangibility of visual art, and painting and photography became narrativized through language.[36]

Childhood had a major place in the most important and critically overlooked Black Arts photographic book, Baraka's *In Our Terribleness* (1970), with images by Fundi (Billy Abernathy).[37] In a brilliant gesture enabling audience participation, the title page of Baraka's book is in flat, reflective silver, becoming a mirror into which the reader peers. The reader's face thus appears as an image on the page, becoming part of the text, one with the other "terrible" faces in the book.[38] As Crawford has noted, the book evokes a handmade quality, because that mirror seems pasted on.[39] The apparent constructedness of the book recalls the Child Development Group of Mississippi's *Today* as an act of handmade, collective, resistant literacy. Baraka writes,

> Terribleness
> Bloods!
> Brothers
> Hipsters
> Old Folks
> Kids
> Roots
> A LONG IMAGE STORY IN MOTION[40]

These are lines that call out to the book's inclusive community, one that incorporates the reader, too—regardless of age—as another image within the mutable story of the black community. Given that Baraka, as in "SOS" and other poems, acknowledges and embraces the role of childhood in nationalism (in the photobook even saying, "Man woman child in a house is a nation"),[41] it is unsurprising that photographs of children populate *In Our Terribleness*, adding concrete form to his claim that young black faces reflect "[n]ot cuteness but realness."[42] Also fundamental to Baraka's book and to the representation of children in Black Arts photography is the emphasis on movement, on process. "A LONG IMAGE STORY IN MOTION" permits us to consider the black nation as a body in developmental process, both growing out of childhood and returning to it as an ideal of a decolonized blackness of "astonishing grace." Blackness becomes articulated through an ongoing process of becoming, and the child's body as mutable permits recognition of its limitless potential.

Additionally, photographic books seem a perfect fit with the era's embrace of oral performance and its relationship to textuality. Remembering that performances of poetry, plays, political speeches, and social protest dominated the Black Arts era, one might imagine photobooks as joining that participatory, "real" form of art. Photobooks are images that speak, with photographs drawn from life. Further, there is a sociality to the form of the photographic book that distinguishes it from other printed texts. Often a photobook is large, too big to fit comfortably on a shelf, and is left on a coffee table or in a social space to pick up, read, and share with others.[43] The public nature of photobook reading may have contributed to its popularity during a moment invested in the oral and communal. Certainly the vernacular voice on the page asks to be considered as a version of the oral, even if it is not to be read out loud in public settings.[44] The success of photographic books at this moment drew on the energies of the vernacular as well as on the assumption that photos testified to the lived experience of the community, revealing its "true" values and ideals, becoming a double for the valued components of black life.

Of course, the success of 1960s and 1970s photographic books extended beyond the oral, given that they emerged during an era of black desire for publishing autonomy, as Morrison's slam on Madison Avenue confirms. Aldon Nielsen warns of the "dangers to our understanding of African-American literary history implicit in the construction of an idealized orality in opposition to a devalued writing," a risk apparent in reductive critical evaluations of the performative in the Black Arts tradition.[45] African American publishing houses took off during this period, including Dudley Randall's Broadside Press and Haki Madhubuti's Third World Press, as well as journals like *Black Dialogue*, *Soulbook*, *JBP*, *Liberator*, and *Negro Digest/Black World*; the journals in particular brought together visual art and language in arresting ways.[46] In addition to the era's emphasis on pedagogy, language, and cultural idealization and continuance through childhood, the children's photographic picture book spoke to the aesthetic threads of the moment that had come into relief: the ascendance of photographic experimentation, an emphasis on performance and orality that cohered with the vernacular voice of the photobooks, and a vigorous interest in a print culture that combined visual and verbal forms.

THE "KINDERGARTEN OF NEW CONSCIOUSNESS": PHOTOGRAPHIC CHILD AS ICON AND PROCESS

As we have seen, childhood took on representational weight as both a source of black possibility and its incomplete fruition during the BAM. As symbol of the new nation in progress, children were employed iconographically in publications like the Black Panther newspaper, in which Emory Douglas, the minister of culture, used children in back-page posters to represent the principles and stakes of the movement; and metaphorically in the wide-ranging poetry of Sonia Sanchez, Nikki Giovanni, Lucille Clifton, and others. But photographs of children within books articulated the ideals of the movement—in particular, the "consciousness-raising" that emphasized black cultural and aesthetic integrity—in ways that permitted both reproduction of those ideals in texts and insistence on their ongoing, productively incomplete articulation. Like the

Child Development Group of Mississippi's resolve that its photographic book serve as generative inspiration rather than as commodified representation, photographic picture books within the BAM embraced the idea that black childhood could embody both the abstract and the concrete, both the idea of the black experience and the call to create that experience. Photographs allowed writers to point both to the ideal and to the particular, to the absolute and to the unfinished, through the body of the child.

In large part, photographs of children could represent both the abstract and the concrete because they focused on childhood as a BAM ideal as well as on particular details of the subject's experience. Within the context of the BAM, childhood as an ideal became analogous to a revitalized perspective on black culture, one stripped of white cultural corruption, as we have seen in the resistance to white versions of literacy. An image of a BAM child evoked an essential aspirant state for the black nation, one untouched by miseducation and psychological colonization. Imagined as the kernel of black potential, childhood embodied a state of limitless possibility. That aspirant state was always in process, always the goal of the black nation's progress toward what Gwendolyn Brooks called the "kindergarten of new consciousness."[47]

If childhood pointed backward to an ideal of the nation's essential state of limitless potential, it also alternately enabled an emphasis on change, movement, and progress toward the fruition of that potential. Aesthetically, in photographs, the child evokes blackness as constant change when images focus on the child's body as an unfinished, nascent figure, or on the child in the midst of movement, as in the case of Baraka's door-opening child. A photograph of a child's body during the BAM often incurred projectural meanings: for example, the August 21, 1971, *Black Panther* back-page poster offers Emory Douglas's collage of photographs of children under the title "We Shall Survive. Without a Doubt." The large central child wears sunglasses, and in each glass frame is an image of children at Black Panther breakfasts. Rays of light fan out like inspiration behind the main child's head. The "we" of "We Shall Survive" becomes more than the central figure of the child, encompassing the idea that the black nation will endure through the growth and success of youth. Through photographs, then, childhood could embody both the ideals of the nation (as the child was the best vision of the nation's unlimited potential) and the unfinished culmination of those ideals through the imagined process of the child's growth. The unfinished state of the nation (as child) thus invited collaboration, development, and continuance, values especially embraced by artists of the BAM.

I dwell on the idea of child both as icon of nation and as incomplete liberatory process because this framework enables an appreciation of the role of the children's photographic book in the Black Arts Movement. As Crawford explains, the BAM carried a suspicion of the textual as a site that would concretize and arrest the process of cultural transformation: "The danger tied to the *textualization* of movement, gesture, sound, and performance is dramatized during the Black Arts Movement. As writers in the Black Arts Movement fought against the textual taming of radical black processes and actions, they produced texts that performed the packaging of the unpackagable."[48] At the same time, writers understood the need to create an artifact, a venue through which people could share the poetry and ideas of the BAM. Photographic books became a vital site for containment of the uncontainable, for representing the process of change and transformation in ways that invoked and demanded an open-ended response. Sometimes employing the tension between child as icon and child as incomplete national process, sometimes dramatizing the decolonization of young subjects' minds, photographic books for young people enabled BAM artists to accomplish both the stabilization of the potential of the movement photographically and the insistence on the mutability of the child subject and the possibilities of transformation of the new nation.

POEMS BY KALI: CHILDHOOD AS NATURAL SITE OF RESISTANCE

Poems by Kali became a sensation when it hit the streets in 1970. The author, Kali Grosvenor, was then eight years old, and the book contains poems written when she was six and seven. According to *Ebony* magazine, the book became "an 'in' item among the literati";[49] Kali herself became something of a media figure as a result of her work. She appeared on the television programs of David Frost and Dick Cavett, sold a thousand copies per week of her text,[50] and gave poetry readings with Baraka, Sanchez, and others.[51] When she told the editors of her volume that her mother, Vertamae Smart-Grosvenor, was an exceptional cook and writer, the mother's literary and public career was born: she published *Vibration Cooking; or, The Travel Notes of a Geechee Girl* (1970) and began a successful career as a radio journalist.[52] *Poems by Kali* contains photographs of Kali, her sister, and her friends taken by Joan Halifax, a Columbia graduate student in anthropology, who Grosvenor believes was a late addition to the book, as well as photographs by one of the most prominent photographers of the early civil rights movement, Robert Fletcher, the African American photographer who worked with SNCC from 1964 to 1968 and who took photographs of the Child Development Group of Mississippi.[53]

In the media and among BAM writers, Kali embodied the idea of the black-power child as gifted visionary. Studying her book permits us to recognize the interchange between adult investment in the image of black childhood and its representation within children's literature. In fact, one could argue that *Poems by Kali* is not strictly a children's book because it had a substantial adult readership and became a kind of fashionable literary asset. However, adults were buying the book for their children as well as reading it themselves. For instance, African American children's writer Rita Williams-Garcia, author of the novel *One Crazy Summer*, which takes the BAM as its subject, remembers reading *Poems by Kali* as a child; in conversation, Williams-Garcia joked with me that Kali, as *the* child artist of the BAM, "stole my thunder!"[54] Grosvenor's book appealed to the black community across age. In *Poems by Kali*, the child is constructed, in word and image, as an agent of psychological decolonization for the black community: such a process positions Kali as more in touch with that which is natural about blackness because she is a child. She thus embodies a kind of Edenic perspective on beauty and language, a call back to origins through the image of childhood. The uses of Kali for decolonizing the mind also involve Kali's insistent questioning about systems of power, a resistance that the text argues every reader should also espouse. The photographs within the text place Kali in relationship with an urban context, insisting on her ability to shape that landscape. Kali embodies both icon and process, the source of essential black goodness and the inspiration for ongoing transformation. Photographs aim to capture Kali and, in doing so, stabilize her iconographically within the image but also suggest the continuance of her efforts through her body in motion.

Because physicality—in handshakes, hairstyles, clothing, and so on—was ideologically revelatory during the Black Arts Movement, photography took on particular significance. If the black body was sacred, especially in the wake of its violations in the early civil rights movement, then photography became a vehicle for announcing and stabilizing the values it evoked. In the case of Kali, these values were associated with the "natural," meaning that the child appeared closer to the core values of blackness by virtue of not having been socialized into adulthood. Of course, there is a certain contradictory nature to the Black Arts embrace of the "natural" in hairstyle and clothing, because such elements were cultivated and displayed, and were far from being intrinsic, undemanding, and essential. But allowing a child to represent the "natural" elements of black culture permitted such an effortless staging. The speaker opens the book with these words, from "Black Is Black": "I am Black / I Know I am / Black do you?" The attendant image, by Halifax, places Kali behind a chain-

Figure 4.2. Kali stands behind a city fence, her eyes meeting the viewer. From Kali Grosvenor, *Poems by Kali* (New York: Doubleday & Company, Inc., 1970). Photographs by Joan Halifax and Robert Fletcher. Copyright 1970 by Joan Halifax.

link fence, suggesting her urbanity and separation from the African American she challenges in the poem (Figure 4.2). The fence horizontally bisects Kali's face, placing the emphasis on her unsmiling eyes; her hands, which are clenched with tense energy; and (most prominently) her loosely styled Afro. The image focuses, then, on her looking back with confrontation. She knows who she is, the image and the poem assert, by virtue of her youth. The poem then moves into a consideration of the order she must inhabit:

> But This
> World is Wite
> I'll tell you
> Wite Book White Milk
> Wite Dolls
> Wite everything
> no Black no Blacks![55]

In linking the Afro photograph with the disbelief at the cultural disorder Kali witnesses, the text emphasizes the ease with which a child can testify against white hegemony. In *Poems by Kali*, we again find the assumption of the camera's innocence working in tandem with the assumption of innocence in the child subject; the truth telling that the camera supposedly effects is echoed in the truth of the child's uncolonized perspective. In this poem and photograph, we see both Kali's claim of essential blackness and her challenge to the reader to remake a distorted world.

Kali's vernacular voice attaches her to the aesthetic ideals of the Black Arts Movement, particularly as it opposed models of white literacy. Just as poets Baraka, Sanchez, Giovanni, and others played with diction and spelling in order to convey the spoken language of the streets within print texts, Kali also includes innovative sentence and word construction that contribute to the idea of childhood as essential blackness, its voice supposedly unfiltered and untouched by white pedagogical structures. For example, at the end of her poem "My People," in which she announces that her family has "all kind of / colores Black yellow Bash / and Brown red," she includes the following: "Joke: I am e / largick to White" (20). Breaking up and spelling *allergic* differently emphasizes Kali's sense of power and her size ("larg[e]ick") in relationship to whiteness. Certainly the misspellings and neologisms appear to be the unaffected expressions of a child and permit, by extension, a confirmation of naturalness of the innovations in form within the work of adult poets. Kali does work in modes apparent within the printed texts of other poets of the era, a practice that might suggest one cause of her popularity. In fact, the publisher of *Poems by Kali* refused Kali's later plea to correct the misspellings. Kali indicated several times that she was embarrassed by them, and in the *New York Times* article on her book, Kali asserted defensively, "You can tell I was 6 years old when I wrote these. . . . I misspelled a lot of words."[56] As an adult, Grosvenor explained to me that "the publisher published the poems exactly as I had written them. . . . [T]hat was *so* disappointing to little me. But they talked to me about that and I saw they were going to do what they wanted to do. To get through that I calmed myself and imagined the poems were sort of 'dialect' poems of a kid."[57] Grosvenor acknowledges an aesthetic terrain that demanded a version of the "real" invested in neologism as well as in the materiality of the word through its conspicuous misspelling. Grosvenor's book does not play with word/image interaction as do other Black Arts texts that render words imagistically or intersperse language within images. The language is always set by itself, separate from the photographs. Instead, I suggest that the misspellings and deliberate arrangement of letters, as in the case of "e / largick," draw attention to the physical presence of the word as well as call for communal identification with the vernacular. Cheryl Clarke's observations about women poets during the Black Arts era apply to the child poet, too: "For the Black Arts women, black vernacular speech was the always already, essential signifier of a black poem."[58] As the authentic representative of blackness, Kali was required to use a language that demonstrated her commitment to the common people. In addition, authenticity demanded a voice untrammeled by white education. Using a language that springs from a basic identification with black value, Kali as visionary poet becomes a sign of blackness itself.

Kali interrogates systems of knowledge in order to spur a reader's reinvention of self. She turns to childhood lore as the primary site of socialization away from black identity. If we remember Don L. Lee's proposal to kill "dick, jane, and other perpetrators of evil," Kali's poetry becomes even more insistent on the way in which psychological corruption begins in childhood. She addresses child lore in "What Happing to The Heros":

> anunt jemina Dead
> Mother goose is dying . . .
> Clark Kent can't turn
> in to Superman Because
> Superman can't fly.
> Tonto went back to his
> people and lone ranger is
> all alone
> That's whats happing (33)

The destruction of whiteness and white power begins at the roots, the poem suggests, in the figures idolized in childhood, including the stereotype of Aunt Jemima. The game of cowboys and Indians places black children in the place of white police authority in persecuting people of color, an idea that is echoed in Nikki Giovanni's "Poem for Black Boys." Issued within *Ego-Tripping and Other Poems for Young People* (1973), Giovanni's poem asks children to question the ideology of role-playing games: "Where are your heroes, my little Black ones / You are the Indian you so disdainfully shoot."[59] In Kali's poem, observations on the death and decline of childhood heroes are coupled with an image by Halifax of

Figure 4.3. Kali points at her peer's mouth. From Kali Grosvenor, *Poems by Kali* (New York: Doubleday & Company, Inc., 1970). Photographs by Joan Halifax and Robert Fletcher. Copyright 1970 by Joan Halifax.

Kali with another female child (Figure 4.3). The friend's eyes are closed, nearly squinting with effort, while Kali points with both hands toward the child's lips. Kali appears here even more intensely an agent of change, as she scrutinizes and reshapes the language that falls from the friend's lips. Significantly, Kali's hands take the form of guns as she points to the child's mouth. The language of white childhood must die, the image suggests, as revolutionary culture erects new champions for its young people.[60]

Kali's approach is characteristic of the BAM, because revising the elemental in children's culture appeared in a variety of forms and publications. Racial abecedaries surged during the BAM, including Lucille Clifton's *The Black BCs* (1970), Jean Carey Bond's *A is for Africa* (1969), Jean Pejot Smith's popular *Li'l Tuffy and His ABC's* (1973), and Muriel Feelings's landmark *Jambo Means Hello: A Swahili Alphabet Book*, with pictures by Tom Feelings (1974).[61] For the purposes of our discussion, Third World Press's children's photobook *I Want to Be* (1974), by Dexter and Patricia Oliver, is particularly salient as a radical photographic abecedary containing images of children performing adult labor in service to the black nation, with child as plumber, nurse, X-ray technician, and so on. (The book resists ideas about the photograph as elegy and insists on the tangible futurity embodied by the child subject.) As the site through which readers learn the building blocks of written language, the ABC book became a vehicle for cultural definition and for opposition to racist representations normalized in conventional English and in traditional pedagogy. For both Grosvenor's treatment of child lore and the radical ABC books, revolution takes place at the grassroots, at the fundamentals, and in erecting a new epistemology, these texts launch an attack on a white system of knowledge that has been presumed to be natural and uncomplicated. What is natural, for Kali, is revolutionary resistance, an ongoing process of linguistic reinvention with limitless possibilities.

Kali's most famous poem, "Lady Bird," also plays with child lore to create radical possibilities. The poem riffs on a nursery rhyme:

> Lady Bird, Lady Bird
> Fly away. Home
> Your house is on fire
> And Rap's on the phone. (35)

Kali read "Lady Bird" in 1972 at the Apollo Theater in Harlem with major poets of the BAM, including the Original Last Poets, Stanley Crouch, Larry Neal, Imamu Amiri Baraka, and others. The reading was recorded by Motown Records and issued as *Black Spirits: A Festival of New Black Poets in America*. (In fact, William Melvin Kelley's introduction to *Poems by Kali* stages the book as performance poetry by inviting adults at the "Apple-O Theater" to listen to the child's words.)[62] Of course, part of the "Lady Bird" poem's appeal is its memorable reworking of the nursery rhyme "Lady Bug" into a catchy slam on the Johnson administration, attacking implicitly its political diffidence and the ineffectuality of civil rights legislation.[63] The "house is on fire" line alludes to the Watts Riots of 1965, in which "Burn, baby, burn" became a call to action; H. Rap Brown, the Black Panther activist who argued that "[v]iolence is as American as apple pie," popularized the phrase "Burn, baby, burn." Kali is not peculiar in alluding to violence within a children's poem during the Black Arts moment; Giovanni was working in the same mode in her "Poem for Black Boys," which reads,

> a company called Revolution has just issued
> a special kit for little boys
> called Burn Baby
> I'm told it has full instructions on how to siphon gas
> and fill a bottle.[64]

Kali may not explicitly advocate violent resistance, as does Giovanni, but her poems are suffused with allusions to the agency of the black community during the Watts Riots.

Kali injects revolutionary, nearly violent, potential in revising a traditional religious song, "This Little Light of Mine." Her poem of the same name concludes with these lines:

> this littlle [*sic*] light of mine will burn so bright that
> not only my people but all people will see
> it burn
> burn baby burn. (28)

The image, by Fletcher, that adheres to the poem, Kali's favorite picture of herself in the book,[65] could be read as a straightforward, positive, uplifting image, somewhat like the photographs of black children in the 1940s and 1950s (Figure 4.4). Its implications are, of course, positive, because Kali is no victim and is not threatened in the urban space. But the image comments on the way urban youth reshapes the landscape. Kali's body aligns with the apartment building in the distance, her arms echo the horizontal bisecting line of the rooftop just behind her, and her legs parallel in size the vertical lines of bricks toward the left side of the image. She becomes icon and architecture, revolutionary idea and urban structure. Considering the final statement of Kali's poem, the image uses exuberance to render the possibility of her body in resistant activity. Her stance may echo the solid buildings, but her body is suffused with energy as she turns a triumphant smile skyward. The best part of Kali, her "little light," can set the city afire. Kali cannot be contained, for her body is the spark of revolution. The city and the child are one: her body becomes a building, just as the city is structured by youth revolution. The phrase "burn baby burn" locates radical potential within the body of the urban child.

Kali's embodiment of blackness as process is best articulated through the critique her poems offer. In the poem "Our World Is Ours," the speaker proclaims,

Our world is ours!
Ours is the world.
It is ours
Because we built it
With our bare hands.
Why did you take it?
Why? why? (39)

Figure 4.4. Kali exuberantly embraces the city space.
From Kali Grosvenor, *Poems by Kali* (New York:
Doubleday & Company, Inc., 1970). Photographs
by Joan Halifax and Robert Fletcher.
Copyright 1970 by Robert Fletcher.

Figure 4.5. Kali leads her peers in a circle. From Kali Grosvenor, *Poems by Kali* (New York: Doubleday & Company, Inc., 1970). Photographs by Joan Halifax and Robert Fletcher. Copyright 1970 by Joan Halifax.

The attendant image, by Halifax, emphasizes Kali's role as agent of black be-coming: she sits on the grass outside apartment housing, extending her hands to form a circle with her sister and other black children (Figure 4.5). The poem might reach into history, suggesting the collective accomplishment of "we built it / With our bare hands," but the image establishes a circle of youth, a place where Kali smiles and becomes both inspiration and race organizer.[66] With the poem's return to the child's simple questioning of the social order: "Why? why?," Kali's interrogatory stance models social resistance for her peers and her readers. Another poem, "It's a New Kind of Day," picks up on a common phrase during the late 1960s ("It's a new day") in order to emphasize the pride that fuels ongoing revolutionary transformation. The last stanza reads,

> It's a New Kind
> of D. It's a New kind
> of day. It's a New
> kind. love. help us with
> this love. lord we love
> to much. (53)

The "new day" of the race comes through the child, whose body and ingenuity point both backward, to origins, and forward, to transformation. Some Black Arts poets configured the "new day" as the instantiation of a precolonial, essential Africa in the body of the black child. In *It's a New Day: Poems for Young Brothas and Sistuhs* (1971), Sonia Sanchez writes to her sons Morani and Mungu,

> the world
> awaits you
> young
> blackness
> sun
> children
> of our tomorrow.
> Here is my hand
> black
> warriors of
> our dreams.
> . . . for u my loves
> will be the doers.
> and yo
> deeds
> will run red with ancient songs
> that play a continuous chant of
> it's a new day.
> it's a new new new day
> It's A NEW DAY![67]

The boys' "deeds / will run red with ancient songs," as though the voice of a core African identity streams through moments of violent action or resistance. In Sanchez's poem, locating ahistorical Africa in the body of the child impels "continuous" political action, an escape from history into an identity that will enable ongoing accomplishment. In Kali's "New Day," the child takes strength from love of herself and love of her people. History, Africa, conflict, all retreat (and do not in fact surface at all within her poem) when Kali considers that "It's the love that make / a New kind of day" (53). Through love of blackness, children will be able to shape society, offering both inspiration and a challenge for the reader to experience blackness as the process of becoming.

Perhaps the best example of the book's emphasis on the process of mental decolonization appears at the end of the text. The poem "Were Is My Head Going" reads:

Were is my head Going
Were is my head Going
up Down arond Sidways
Black White turning
Were is it Goning
its Going Black
that's were. (62)

Racial perspectives structure consciousness, or should structure one's mind-set, for the poem argues that "Going Black" is an ideal state. By ending with "that's were," it sounds as though the speaker were in a conversation with another person, pointing him or her to the actual location of decolonization. A black state of mind has a space to inhabit, a place accessible through the process of shunting off corruption. The photograph of Kali, by Fletcher, emphasizes the sense of "Going Black" as a locale: shot with an angle from below, the child's head appears as monumental as the two urban buildings that frame it (Figure 4.6). The photograph places Kali's mind, her "Going Black," in an urban space and suggests that her uncolonized mind embodies a physical place in the city, much as in the image of Kali that accompanies "This Little Light of Mine." The "Going Black" photograph is quite dark, with Kali's face almost in an outline, just as the buildings are outlined by a setting (or rising) sun. The details of the image thus point to the abstract, to the black limitlessness of Kali's mind. If we remember also the photographic aesthetic of "black light," an embrace of darkness that signifies racial pride, the image of Kali's head as a building establishes the child's mind as a solid, bottomless urban space and place. Amiri Baraka, then LeRoi Jones, wrote about the linkage of poetry and social reality in "Black Art" (1966):

We want a black poem. And a
Black World.
Let the world be a Black Poem
And Let All Black People Speak This Poem
Silently
Or LOUD[68]

Figure 4.6. Kali stands between skyscrapers. From Kali Grosvenor, *Poems by Kali* (New York: Doubleday & Company, Inc., 1970). Photographs by Joan Halifax and Robert Fletcher. Copyright 1970 by Robert Fletcher.

Kali's poem and image speak explicitly to the Black Arts Movement's attachment of poetry to the concrete and to the physical, to bringing idea into action. "Let the world be a Black Poem" seems especially apt in considering the assertion of "Were is my head Going" in both text and image. The child's body, rendered in photographs, becomes the black poem in the world, an object both idealized and mutable, always expressing the process and potential of black becoming. The revolutionary world (and poem, and image) is a black child's mind, which is rightly aligned, rightly positioned on the urban landscape, and limitless in possibility.

In recalling her ambitions for her book, Grosvenor explains that she saw her work within a black photo-text tradition: "My favorite poet at this time was Langston Hughes, and I had *Sweet Flypaper of Life* and those photos made sense. My all time, to this day, favorite poem is 'When Dey Listed Da Colored Soldiers' by Paul Laurence Dunbar; it was in a book my mother used to read to us called *Candle-Lightin' Time*. It is a beautiful book with photographs that depict the poems. So, I thought my book should be like that."[69] Grosvenor's statement asks us to consider the presence of children as an audience for signal photographic texts, and their sensitivity to possibilities of narrative through photographs.[70] Leigh Richmond Miner's gentle photographs from the Hampton Institute, which illustrate Dunbar's *Candle-Lightin' Time* (1901), emphasize the homey satisfaction in African American life, offering readers like Kali, nearly seventy years later, a sense of photographs' potential to validate black domestic bonds of intimacy and affection—the love, perhaps, that Kali sees at the heart of a revolutionary sensibility. The fact that Grosvenor references two domestic photobooks—one published nearly seventy years before hers—speaks to the consequence of published images within black families and to the longevity of their effects. Declaring the health and value of black domestic arrangements, books like Hughes's and Dunbar's served as testaments and reference points for young people seeking affirmation, connection, and beauty.

In terms of the social purpose of her text, Grosvenor turns to an earlier moment as a cause for her work: "I was always haunted by what happened to Emmett Till and horrified by the Birmingham church bombings that killed the four girls in 1963. I was too young to remember when these events happened, but I grew up with these stories and they influenced my childhood. I felt children were fair game and should be engaged in the 'struggle' because they were targets of hate and were so vulnerable that for the most horrific crimes, they were the easiest victims."[71] Child social and artistic action results from such loss, a phenomenon made explicit in *Poems by Kali*, which contains this dedication: "This book is dedicated to Addie Mae Collin[s], Denise McNair, Carol Robertson, and Cynthia Wesley, killed in Sunday school in Birmingham, Alabama, on September 15, 1963." The child questioning social authority becomes a means to mourn Till and other child victims of the civil rights campaign. For Grosvenor, staging images became an assault on a white culture that would victimize children. As she suggests, "*Poems by Kali* is proof of a child's social power.

It showed adults that kids were aware of what was going on and were deeply affected. . . . I would hope children who read the book remember that they have a
voice and can speak about whatever affects them. It can be very powerful."[72] For
a sense of the child's significance to the Black Arts Movement, *Poems by Kali* also
permitted readers to engage with the structures of mental colonization at the
site of their inception. Revolutionizing the mind takes shape through interro-
gating systems of power, pedagogy, and language. As an icon of the "New Day,"
Kali embodied in word and image a resistant and resilient spirit, being both
the epitome of "natural" blackness and the inspiration for readers to pursue the
ongoing transformative process of "Going Black."

I WISH I HAD AN AFRO: JOHN SHEARER'S DOCUMENTARY INTERVENTION

"Going Black" is the subject and photographic mode of John Shearer's picture
book *I Wish I Had an Afro. Poems by Kali*, with its palpable adult audience, carried a certain cachet during the BAM, in that it explored ideas about childhood
that connected explicitly to creative work by other BAM artists. Kali's book
allows us to understand more about childhood as a concept in the late 1960s. In
contrast, Shearer's text addressed children exclusively, and, as he explained in
conversation with me, his goal was to reach urban and suburban African American boys in language they would respect: "I was absolutely all about the child,
all about the child wanting to pick it up and read it and it be in a meter they were
familiar with. This was first and foremost in my mind. It was very important
to me." Shearer does not idealize the black child in service to black-nationalist
ideals, but his work—like Grosvenor's—connects the process of freeing one's
mind to the site of childhood. Kali's mind may be already liberated, but the
main character of Shearer's book, Little John, recognizes that he should seek
such freedom. The two texts, so different in tone and approach, thus share the
idea that psychological liberation is fundamental to reconstituting identity and
to political action; and both Grosvenor and Shearer embrace the photobook as
a means to articulate that liberation. Little John is framed by his environment
but yearns to become politically active and to express his pride in his blackness
and in his family.

The urban setting dominates *Poems by Kali*, as the black child's revolutionary viewpoint claims the high-rise, the chain-link fence, and the city street as
sites of beauty and power rather than of despair. *Kali* thus stages child agency by
interacting implicitly with assumptions about urban blight, disintegrated black
families, and black children as social problems. As Richard Flynn explains,

black childhood "was defined in sixties journalism and documentary photography as the absence of 'normal' childhood."[73] Shearer's text also counters the urban-pathology story but this time by placing Little John in the suburbs and having him attend an integrated school in a poor section of Westchester, New York.[74] The book uses multiple voices, including the perspective of the child, his mother, and his father, to tell the story of the family's economic and social frustrations; like other Black Arts texts, the prose uses the vernacular, although it does not engage the materiality of the word as does Grosvenor's book. Shearer's gritty photographs play with shades of darkness in order to evoke the child's determination to struggle toward black pride.

A protégé of Gordon Parks, Shearer wrote the book as a young photojournalist quite sensible of mainstream audiences' expectations for a black boy. Although he is associated with magazine work, Shearer does not invoke the intractability or permanence sometimes associated with the journalistic photo-story, which confines through text and image a particular community or location, seeking to document social reality rather than to intervene in representation. Instead, Shearer subverts the stability of photo-textual representations of black city sites in order to inspire black economic and psychological transformation; like Grosvenor and Fletcher, Shearer is interested in the photograph as part of the process of change, a means to display both the accuracy of the idea he explores and the need for that idea to come into fruition. Working in abstractions and shadings of meaning, Shearer's photographs emphasize and encourage resistance to limitations, blurring hard edges in order to suggest fluidity and possibilities. The tone of his text differs substantially from the exuberance of *Poems by Kali*. Grosvenor's energy, courage, and confidence pronounce her book's approach to black possibility; in contrast, Shearer's quiet, somber, guarded tone (both visually and in the narrative) fittingly articulates his exploration of psychological constraints and the child's anger simmering underneath.

As the son of cartoonist Ted Shearer, John Shearer grew up immersed in discussions of visual racial representation.[75] At age seventeen, Shearer became a staff photographer at *Look* magazine, a post he held from 1964 to 1969, covering civil rights demonstrations and SNCC meetings as well as Martin Luther King Jr.'s funeral and the Harlem riots resulting from King's assassination.[76] In addition, Shearer was the second black photographer at *Life* magazine, after Gordon Parks. Shearer's career was inspired by Parks, and his perspective influenced by H. Eugene Smith and Henri Cartier-Bresson. He explains the origins of *I Wish* in connection to Parks:

I guess the genesis for the book really goes back to my relationship with Gordon. Gordon always wrote and took pictures, and as a young kid I kind of idolized him and wanted to do the same kinds of things. I was lucky enough in my late teens to start working for *Look* magazine. I went out and covered a lot of stories on the movement and entertainment and other things, but primarily the movement. That led to my wanting to do something like *I Wish I Had an Afro*. . . . And it was really because of Gordon. Gordon said, "You have to look at your grandmother and your grandfather aesthetically." He is the one who pointed me in the direction of Cartier-Bresson and Gene, because they were the fathers of photo-journalism at the time.[77]

Shearer photographed the black community with tenderness and respect but without forgetting the injustices of social circumstance, an approach he imag-ines as derived from his close relationship with Parks.[78] Shearer evidences a fundamental affection for black individuals (especially when facing difficult circumstances) and uses shades of darkness to convey the emotional depth of the characters he depicts. The reference to grandparents recalls the tenderness and complexity with which Roy DeCarava photographed older people in *Sweet Flypaper*, like Mary, the book's narrator.

In aiming for a sense of trust and solidarity between himself and a black public, Shearer participated in an ethos galvanizing black journalists of the late 1960s and early 1970s. When race protests and riots blazed across urban cen-ters, often newspapers sent their few African American journalists to cover the events. After the FBI pressed black journalist Earl Calwell to become an infor-mant on the Black Panthers—Calwell was covering the Panthers for the *New York Times* in 1968—and Calwell refused, African American journalists came together to form the Black Perspective, an organization that issued a statement in the *New York Amsterdam News* in February 1970 defining the investments of black journalists: "We will not be used as spies, informants or undercover agents by anybody. We will protect our confidential sources, using every means at our disposal. We strongly object to attempts by law enforcement agencies to exploit our blackness. . . . [F]rom our perspective, black and white report-ers are not interchangeable. For one thing, when the black reporter leaves the office to cover a black story he goes home. Home is the black community."[79] Reaching out through the black press, the journalists confirmed their allegiance to their home groups, and although they asserted that "[w]e are not spokes-men for the black community," they emphasized their "sense of responsibility to bring about a greater understanding and clarity of the dynamics and nuances of the black revolution."[80] The statement was signed by Shearer, Parks, and a number of other prominent journalists, including Gil Scott, Ed Bradley, and Ted Poston. Shearer's participation in the Black Perspective group and his allegiance with Parks strongly signal his desire, in 1970, to respond to the black community with a realism shaded with empathy and compassion. Black Arts photography, in the hands of Shearer, took on an intimacy and tenderness not always associated with the public exuberance of, say, Chicago's *Wall of Respect*. In fact, in 1972, Parks himself commented on Shearer's aesthetic in a foreword to Shearer's second photographic picture book for children, *Little Man in the Family*. Describing Shearer as a child who once brought "sensitive" images to Parks for review, Parks concludes, "He is still young, still the keeper of those traits that set him significantly apart. And already he has learned the most important thing about his craft—great photographers see mainly with their hearts."[81] Shearer's photographs in *I Wish* are not sentimentalized; rather, his compassion for his subjects and his desire to effect change in society and in representation draw his images beyond the evidentiary and into reformation.[82] Not only does *I Wish* uncover the presence of a vital black community within suburban settings, but it also permits a fresh examination of the effects of poverty and racism on the black psyche and permits Shearer to address the failures of civil rights efforts, like integration.

Three main threads surface in Shearer's unpaginated *I Wish*, all of which react against white tendencies to envision the black community through journalistic stasis: Shearer conspicuously rejects the idea of the black family as fatherless and failing, a cliché that came into prominence after the 1965 Moynihan Report; instead of offering a single narrative of a black family's story, Shearer offers multiple voices; and, through the photographs, Shearer pushes the main character's anger, articulated verbally, into a visual call for social action. In the book's vision of the black family, the story of Little John's life is narrated through his own voice, as well as through sections voiced by his mother and by his father. Such an approach permits Shearer to explore the causes and impact of the family's lack of money based on the father's intermittent employment. Little John first explains that his father, a construction laborer, "can't work in the winter" because of the weather, but that otherwise "[h]e has a truck an' he leaves the house early about five every mornin'—every day but Sunday. He builds cellars for the Man." Next, the child's mother, Rena, mentions her worry about her husband's lack of work off-season; and then Big John, the father, tells his own story, one that emphasizes his ingenuity and drive: "I'd like one day to start my own business. Right now, in the winter I can't work, an' in the summer Uncle Sam, he takes too much money. If I had my own thing, I could do cement work in the summer an' in the winter I could do some kind of inside jobs, like puttin' up that wallboard or maybe do some floor waxin'." The images in this section depict the man at work: he rakes concrete in a full-page picture (Figure 4.7) and pours water into a mixer in a smaller image. Big John tells us that he is fifty, and the large image points toward further signals of maturity; not a muscle-bound, youthful construction worker, John is slight, wears glasses and a warm hat, and is dressed in a V-neck sweater and button-down shirt. The visual emphasis on the quality of John's labor and the worry his family shares in words about the consistency of his job all rebut any derogatory assumptions about poor, underemployed black fathers.

Further, Big John is completely committed to his family and its survival. We see this not only because he says so but also because the other family members speak of his dedication. Shearer, in my interview, spoke

Figure 4.7. Big John labors in construction work. From John Shearer, *I Wish I Had an Afro* (New York: Cowles Book Company, Inc., 1970). Courtesy John Shearer. Copyright 1970 by John Shearer.

of his distaste for what he sees as the hollowness of pejorative characterizations of the black family: "During that period people always talked about black families as though they were fatherless. It was very important to tell a story in which, 'Hey, here's dad and this is what he thinks about it, and what he is doing.' I thought that was really important." The richness of Shearer's text comes through the interactions between the perspectives of the three voices, as each talks about his or her personal history—going back to childhood in the South for Rena and Big John—a strategy that gives flesh to their relationships and characters. The book becomes as much about the parents as about the child. This narrative strategy echoes that of Toni Morrison's *The Bluest Eye*, published the same year as Shearer's book; for both texts, the story of a young person cannot be told without the stories of the adults, and understanding the histories of the adults enables a reader to understand both the predicament of a child in poverty and the predicament of the larger community, one burdened with the psychological, social, and economic effects of racism.[83]

Much as Shearer breaks the story into sections voiced by each character, he offers photographs of the three main characters in close-up range. Remembering the way in which earlier photographic picture books use the child close-up to build a sense of friendship between reader and subject and to convince the reader of the innocence of the narrative voice and visual perspective, we note that the three close-ups in Shearer's text draw a reader into each character's sensibility. The close-up of the father, Big John, prefaces his description of his childhood in the South, an idealization that finally emphasizes the family's economic stress in Westchester; and that of the mother, Rena, shows her collapsed in exhaustion after a day of work. The close-up of Little John, also used for the cover, reminds one of the last image in Hughes and Meltzer's *Pictorial History of the Negro in America*, in which Allen Turner gazes unsmiling into the camera, challenging a reader to remake the world by continuing the civil rights struggle. For Shearer, the image of Little John appears at the moment at which black power explicitly surfaces (Figure 4.8). Little John has listened to his teenage sister's friends talk about "what the white man is doin' wrong," and his father argues with them about their militant approach. Little John says, "They don't let nobody push them around. Sometimes I think, deep inside Dad he really agrees with them. I wonder, though, if he agrees with them, why don't he go along with them an'

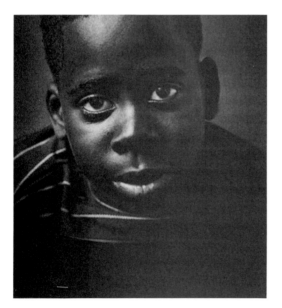

Figure 4.8. Little John gazes with gravity at the viewer. From John Shearer, *I Wish I Had an Afro* (New York: Cowles Book Company, Inc., 1970). Courtesy John Shearer. Copyright 1970 by John Shearer.

why don't he let me grow my hair like theirs. They sure do dig bein' black. I wish I could be like them. I wish I had an Afro." The pages preceding the close-up picture Little John getting his hair cut reluctantly at the barber, and his father asserting, "I'm not sayin' black power is a bad thing. I'm just sayin' long hair don't make you any blacker than someone with short hair." The child longs for the visible sign of his identity, whereas the father recognizes racial multiplicity, as well as the idea that pride does not need to be expressed through styling the body. The fact that Shearer includes both perspectives and leaves them unresolved suggests again the text's emphasis on the black community's diversity and signals Shearer's capaciousness in meaning making through visual signs. The only figure in the book of a person with a black-power Afro appears within a painting held by a student toward the end of the book; the Afro as signifier exists only in the imagination, whereas Little John struggles to articulate a sense of dignity through lived experience. There is no easy path toward liberation through external signifiers. The image of Little John offers pride without the Afro: luxuriating in blackness, the photo reveals shadows playing across the boy's forehead, cheek, and nose; his cheek blends into his shirt, and the shirt fades into the background, becoming nearly indistinguishable from darkness itself. The chin line on Little John's face melts away, becomes fluid, suggesting that boundaries between the idea of blackness and the boy's face begin to evaporate. To return to Crawford's idea about black light, darkness here becomes revelatory. Little John may grasp for simple signs of a black-power identity, but the photo reveals that he already embodies beauty and self-respect. Shearer's photograph confirms the child's immersion in blackness.[84]

The text contains only a few images of decay that one might associate with the urban-blight photographic genre, and those picture the child's dog rather than the child. But in one arresting picture, Shearer subverts the urban documentary tradition in order to point toward the process of psychological transformation. Little John stands in front of his mother's laundry line, with an empty lot behind him (Figure 4.9). We note the empty lot and the associations with black degradation and despair it carries. But the light passing through the laundry encircles the child's head like a halo, and the child's gaze addresses the viewer directly and seriously. His arms are symmetrically posed, with hands at his hips. The line of his arms and his flared fingers frame an open fly. One could see the empty space as signifying absent manhood, or incipient manhood awaiting the eleven-year-old child as he grows older. The image suggests an idea of blackness as process; whereas Kali embodied black essence and called others to transform their minds, here the child exists on the cusp of transformation himself: the

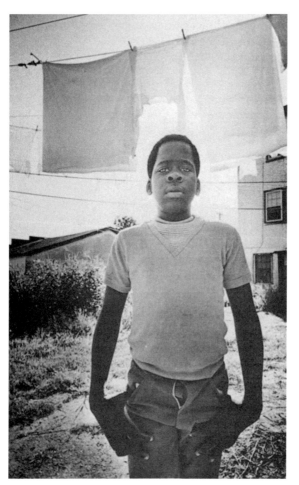

Figure 4.9. Little John stands under the laundry line, his fly undone. From John Shearer, *I Wish I Had an Afro* (New York: Cowles Book Company, Inc., 1970). Courtesy John Shearer. Copyright 1970 by John Shearer.

image suggests the need for that gap of black manhood to be filled, for Little John to grow into wholeness and maturity despite the poverty that surrounds him. Rena's voice accompanies the image, emphasizing the subject of manhood for this text/image interchange; neighborhood children take Little John's lunch money, and his mother states, "I had to make the boy go out an' fight. He didn't do too bad, either." Little John has begun his struggle toward manhood. Although the image at first glance seems one of humiliation, with the successful fight in mind we can read in the empty space of the open zipper that Little John's growth is inevitable. This image permits us to recognize the lack that poverty has created while insisting through the language that the black boy will grow into black manhood.

Late images in the book confirm Shearer's approach of invoking ideas about urban blight only to emphasize the child's dawning resolution to create himself differently. Little John describes a friend who died of a heroin overdose, saying, "I don't ever want to die!," then begins a consideration of the way the American military recruits and relies on black soldiers during Vietnam. Little John asserts, "Someone told me once that they want to put all the people like me in the army. I wonder if he was tellin' the truth." Shearer emphasizes Little John's emergence into knowledge through the child's questioning (a strategy shared by Grosvenor as she critiques the foundations of American culture). Shearer pairs the discussion of death with a potent image of the boy running across a graveyard (Figure 4.10). The image recalls Vietnam combat photography, for the silhouetted figure in motion appeared in Associated Press mainstream coverage of the war.[85] Here, however, Shearer plainly critiques the trope of the anonymous soldier on the battlefield by coupling the figure with the graveyard.[86] Little John is entirely composed of blackness, running downhill, away from both the white light of the sun and the threatening grave markers. By rendering Little John an abstract figure, Shearer is able to render the boy's resistance as a representation of overall attitude: faced with a larger culture that wishes to consign him to the graveyard, Little John resists, placing his body into motion, rushing away from the symbols of death, away from the setting sun, and toward the dark shadow his own body casts across the ground. Remembering the BAM idea of black childhood as limitless possibility, the boy is entirely composed of the blackness that will propel him away from death and toward life.

Figure 4.10. Little John runs through a graveyard, thinking about Vietnam. From John Shearer, *I Wish I Had an Afro* (New York: Cowles Book Company, Inc., 1970). Courtesy John Shearer. Copyright 1970 by John Shearer.

This run echoes the most daringly critical image in the text. Feeling anger about his surroundings and about his exclusion from his sister's black-power group, the child runs in a football struggle with two other children (Figure 4.11). The image is particularly courageous in light of the history of Greenburgh, the Westchester community depicted in the book. Greenburgh was widely known at the time as being one of the first communities to integrate schools willingly. In 1951, the Board of Education voted, with the support of community groups, to

Figure 4.11. Little John bests his peers at football. From John Shearer,
I Wish I Had an Afro (New York: Cowles Book Company, Inc., 1970).
Courtesy John Shearer. Copyright 1970 by John Shearer.

reorganize Greenburgh's segregated schools in order to follow a Princeton
Plan, which involved placing all children in the same schools by grade level
rather than by area of residence. As Mary Ann Lachat explains, Greenburgh
"pioneered efforts which became associated with its emerging philosophy of
'quality integrated education.'"[87] The first lines of Shearer's book name Greenburgh as the text's setting, invoking associations with the Princeton Plan. The
book, however, does not celebrate the supposed rewards of school integration.
A main subtext of the narrative is Little John's difficult experience in school,
because he is placed into a special education program. Because the narrative
does not name any disabilities, saying only that Little John "had problems in
school," and because Little John's voice is quite perceptive, the text pushes a
reader to consider whether the boy has been placed in special education because
of his race and poverty. Little John also mentions that he does not get enough
rest to be prepared for school, because he does not have a bedroom in the house
and must sleep in the living room. "When I have to get up for school I be real
tired," he says.

The image of children playing football takes on particular weight as a counterpoint to Greenburgh's positive associations. Although the narrative does not name conflicts or tension between the children, in this image we see Little John being pursued by the other children, one of whom wears a shirt torn by Little John's tackle. While the text tells us that the white boy ripped Little John's pants, suggesting parity in roughhousing, what we see in the image is a determined black child vigorously running in a contest against nonblack children, one of whom he has damaged. This image appears in the same section that describes Little John's anger at being prevented from joining his sister's black-power group earlier in the chapter; as a result, the image can be read as a demand for child social action. If Little John cannot join a black-power group, at least he can strive for power in a context that pretends to have achieved racial parity. When Little John runs, whether on the field or in the graveyard, the narrative visually calls out for movement, for resistance to the constraints that seek to fix and limit the black child's authority and possibilities. Throughout *I Wish*, the child struggles to resist; in images of movement and abstractions in blackness, Shearer characterizes the incipient anger and questioning of Little John as a means of productive transformation for children faced with inequity and hypocrisy. "Going Black," to use Kali's term, involves this ongoing process of resistance, one that Little John has just begun.

Shearer's sensitive book carefully and generously explicates Little John's and his parents' perspectives on the budding transformation in the community's sense of itself. This care was, perhaps, too understated for white audiences; in the *New York Times* review, for instance, Margaret Berkvist praised the book's "fine photographs" and "authentic atmosphere" but concluded that "[i]ronically, the author's honesty in refusing to manufacture sensation results in a book that is almost too low key."[88] Black audiences saw the book differently, as Charles G. Hurst Jr., the founder of Malcolm X College in Chicago, explained in the *Chicago Tribune*: "A black reader will feel nostalgic without regret and anger without rage. A white reader may feel only wonder. For most it will be a glimpse of a new and strange world, one they ought to know much better."[89] In Greensburgh, the black community responded with euphoria. As the *New York Amsterdam News* reported, the town threw a massive block party for Shearer; the paper proclaimed, "When a hometown boy makes good—especially today—there is dancing in the streets."[90] The black press reported that Shearer and the boy pictured in the book, John McDuffy, did book signings together; such signings acknowledge the creative contribution of young people in the early 1970s, as do Kali's poetry readings with Black Arts figures.[91] The joint readings also recall the spirit of adult–child collaboration so important to the CDGM's *Today*. Part of the accomplishment of *I Wish* for black audiences at the time was the way in which it presented an impoverished child with complexity. Lucille Clifton described her work in the 1970s with the Everett Anderson series: "I write about poor children. . . . Not having any money has nothing to do with character. One does not have to be poor in spirit because he is poor economically."[92] Like Clifton, Shearer spotlights courage within the context of poverty; in the process of articulating black pride and social engagement, Little John and his family permit Shearer to offer a multidimensional portrait of a black community, one that offers no straightforward answers to the demands of black power (like the easy sign of an Afro) but that depicts the growing determination of a child—through images of gaps, shadows, and movement—to articulate himself and his cultural value. Will Little John be able to survive all of the threats against him, including poverty, racism, special education classes, and the possibility of wartime service and being sent (as an infantry private) to the front lines? The book offers Little John's courage and determination as the only response to the child's difficult life circumstances. Like Kali, whose questioning voice expresses frustration with social injustice, Little John at the end of Shearer's text will not be still when faced with the limiting expectations of those around him.

Shearer explains that his experience during the civil rights movement inspired his depiction of Little John's resistance: "Certainly I was influenced by Emmett Till, and I did a story on King and Michael Schwerner and James Chaney, who got killed. . . . I covered the Kennedy assassination. So certainly all the events that surrounded me had a great impact. . . . It was an incredible, amazing time, and what was happening was tragic—the church bombings. And America was going through a lot."[93] Shearer expansively identifies the sources of inspiration for his activist child character, whereas Grosvenor explicitly dedicates her book to the children killed in the Sixteenth Street Baptist Church bombing. In seeing Little John as a response to a larger milieu of social violence, much of which affected children, Shearer permits his book to be read as an intervention both in representations of urban youth and in images of black sacrifice from the civil rights movement. By claiming agency, reinvention, and value for young people, Black Arts children's texts responded to the powerlessness young people felt when faced with the devastation of the 1960s.

JUNE JORDAN'S CHILDREN REWRITE HISTORY

June Jordan's *Dry Victories* (1972), a brilliant and courageous pastiche of narrative and visual forms, challenges its child reader to join the project of interpreting and narrating history. This version of BAM childhood retains the emphasis on black child as visionary, one who can understand the "truth" of black identity like Kali and Little John. The stakes here are quite different, however. Responding to the era's embrace of revolutionary pedagogy, Jordan's book articulates a perspective on education that demands an actively critical viewpoint from children and an interrogation of sites of knowledge—whether in legal documents, photographs, or history books—by a knowing child capable of understanding historical atrocity and misinformation, wielding texts in order to uncover bias, and making new versions of history through research and questioning. Jordan metatextually encourages the reader to pursue the academic grounding for the book's argument, offering a "list of other books you can check into" at the text's conclusion.[94] Like Kali, who probes the distortion of black culture by asking, "Our world is Ours! . . . Why did you take it?/ Why? why?,"[95] the children in *Dry Victories* assume a questioning stance. In all three photographic books—Grosvenor's, Shearer's, and Jordan's—the BAM child seeks the roots of corruption and injustice and aims to remake the world.

The textual component of *Dry Victories* reads as a film script of a conversation between two boys, Kenny and Jerome, who discuss what they have learned about American history in preparing for a presentation for their parents and the community. In her "Note to the Readers," Jordan brings to the surface the correspondences between two points in history: "This is a book we make because we think there was two times, Reconstruction and the Civil Rights' Era, that still be hanging us up, bad."[96] Three quarters of the boys' discussion focuses on violence and dispossession under Reconstruction; only in the last few pages do they make (in language) explicit connections between Reconstruction and civil rights. Jordan, throughout the children's discussion, intersperses images from both the nineteenth century and the 1960s, most of which are documentary and portrait photographs. If Kenny and Jerome wrestle with the disappointments of history, Jordan as visual director works through a confrontational aesthetic, one that poses images against each other in order to destabilize single-minded narratives of history. Whereas Shearer uses Little John in order to question the stability of assumptions about black children, Jordan arranges photographs in order to subvert historical authority and temporal linearity. Her text demonstrates black power over images, and it calls for children to take a role in the shaping of historical narrative.

Best known for her poetry and political essays, Jordan was also deeply immersed in children's literature. She wrote the first children's novel entirely in the vernacular, *His Own Where* (1971), and edited an influential anthology of poetry that included adolescent authors, *Soulscript: Afro-American Poetry* (1970), as well as *The Voice of the Children* (1970). Her work in the late 1960s and early 1970s connects with a community of writers interested in visual texts for young people, including Milton Meltzer, coauthor with Hughes of *A Pictorial History of the Negro in America*. When Hughes died, in 1967, he and Meltzer were developing another text/image book to focus on black painters; Meltzer then asked Jordan to write poetry to accompany the images he selected, which became Jordan's mesmerizing children's book *Who Look at Me* (1969). In December 1968, Jordan began work on a script for a documentary film titled *The Victories Neglected*, which eventually became the book *Dry Victories*.[97] *Dry Victories* thrilled Kali Grosvenor's mother, who wrote to Jordan in October 1972: "[J]ust got 'Dry Victories.' Read it! Looked at it! Loved it! And wanted to let you know that at once. It's wonderful. Write on."[98] Participating in a web of authors who supported visual texts, Jordan herself had a long-standing interest in camera work as an amateur photographer. In fact, several of the powerful urban images in *Dry Victories* were taken in New York by Jordan. If, given her complicated feminist and political writings, Jordan is "hard to 'classify'" in any simplistic way,[99] an awareness of her investment in photography can only enrich our appreciation of the astonishing range of her creative commitments. As an artistic act, *Dry Victories* can be understood as contributing to the variety and vitality of BAM visual art, contributing to our appreciation of the array of aesthetic responses to black self-determinism.

The book is also distinctive as a literary text that engages American history. Much BAM poetry and drama tended to leap over historical event into an idealized African past. Smethurst argues that "in the academic discipline of history . . . a surge of nationalist-influenced and nationalist-inspired work did take place. . . . However, generally speaking, such an interest with respect to the arts did not occur for the most part—not directly anyway."[100] Representations of history, like the *Wall of Respect*, tended to forge alternate history through heroes rather than through event.[101] Jordan's book, in contrast, focuses exclusively on historical processes and documents, offering through the child narrators extensive detail about the major figures, conflicts, compromises, and disappointments of Reconstruction. Jordan's text adheres to generic impulses within BAM creative writing, because its structure is a script, an oral exchange between Kenny and Jerome, and it draws together the visual and the verbal in textualized form.

Jordan is fundamentally groundbreaking, however, in using photographs to interrogate "truth" about history rather than to concretize knowledge: her images ask us to question what we think we know about the past. The images themselves alone, therefore, become suspect as stable conveyors of "truth" and can exist meaningfully only in relationship to other images and to the language of the book. Often Jordan juxtaposes the familiar with alternate photographic versions of the past in order to unsettle assumptions about history. Jordan wants readers to recognize these alternate versions as easily as they do the iconic: the "Note to the Readers" tells where in the book to find identifying information: "We hope you dig the pictures and get into the truth behind them terrible things you need to know. And, if you don't know, right away, what these pictures mean, then check them out, page 76. Please" (viii). A text that begins by repeating and inverting images of the Declaration of Independence set in black and white, *Dry Victories* engages expressly the documents that have registered promises of civil rights, as well as the idea that documentation—whether in image or in legal papers—can "prove" the facts of history.[102] The text's photographs become analogues to the legal documents that have framed ideals of social equality, documents that fail to accomplish ideological work by themselves.

Exploring the consistency of America's failure to live up to its ideals, Jordan pulls images out of time and sets them side by side in order to push her reader to question the power of iconographic and documentary images. Her images exist in dialogue with each other, as in the set of images she couples with the boys' discussion of the failures of the Thirteenth, Fourteenth, and Fifteenth Amendments (Figure 4.12). Abraham Lincoln and Coretta Scott King face each other in the two photographs, which appear on facing pages. Both portraits are framed by circles, which lend a kind of familiarity and intimacy to the portraits, as though they were family portraits on a wall; and, indeed, both are major figures in the historical family of African Americans. The two appear to look at each other, and the weight of the exchange falls on the reader's recognition that King's image is taken from her husband's funeral. The pairing asks us to think about why Lincoln would be invoked here; the reader questions, then, the ideal that this image of Lincoln evokes, concluding that his efforts had not produced any solution to racial violence or inequity either in his day or in the present, given King's death. Both images evoke negation and death, and, set in relationship with each other, both critique the power of ideology and image to frame truth and progress. The widow of Martin Luther King points toward his absence, for if Lincoln was the (failed) hero of the nineteenth century, King was the martyred hero of the twentieth. King is replaced by an image of his absence, his loss, that of his mourning wife. Perhaps Coretta Scott King is here also in the position of mourning for Lincoln, or by invoking Lincoln a reader

Figure 4.12. A portrait of Abraham Lincoln juxtaposed with an image of Coretta Scott King at Martin Luther King Jr.'s funeral. From June Jordan, *Dry Victories* (New York: Holt, Rinehart and Winston, 1972).

might free-associate with, say, Martin Luther King's 1963 speech at the Lincoln Memorial. The fact that Jordan does not dictate the terms of the photographic exchange permits a range of associations.

But, perhaps in order to settle the reader's concentration on King, it appears as though the evocation of his loss conjures King for the reader, because Jordan then presents an image of King in life in the set of images on the next pages, where he is paired with Frederick Douglass (Figure 4.13). Jordan moves from critiquing the iconic white president to demonstrating the ineffectuality of traditional black leadership. Frederick Douglass faces the reader, whereas Martin Luther King, pictured accepting the Nobel Peace Prize, appears turned toward Douglass. Underneath each is an image of the devastation that their efforts have

Figure 4.13. Frederick Douglass is linked to Martin Luther King Jr., as cotton labor is linked with urban unrest. From June Jordan, *Dry Victories* (New York: Holt, Rinehart and Winston, 1972).

not prevented: exploited agricultural laborers in Texas, who recall conditions of enslavement (the photograph is undated), and an image taken by Jordan of an overturned, burned-out car in New York, which evokes rioting. The text itself says nothing about Douglass, King, agriculture, or urban unrest at this point; the reader is left to consider how Jerome's description of Reconstruction's legislative failures attaches to Douglass and King. Jordan does not explicitly critique the methods of Douglass and King; neither does she advocate in language an alternative path of black radical politics. The form demands that the reader instead enact this critique, by yoking the leaders with failed results. Such a strategy makes sense within a text that confronts the myth of documents and questions the stability of documentation. Historical truth—the recognition of

America's failure across time to make substantive racial and economic change (especially because, in the text, the boys emphasize the legal inadequacies as the pictures appear)—must come through the reader's discernment of the relationship between the artifacts Jordan presents. The reader stages the critique, joining the process of meaning making.

For Jordan, documentation in legal text and image proves inadequate as a form of truth telling. Instead, the "truth" of history emerges through a reader's ongoing engagement with the past as archive of information. Further, Jordan is more invested in the idea behind the image than in the indexicality of the image. Like Toni Morrison, who embraces "rare, true and free" images that represent an idea of the black nation, Jordan works toward the conceptual and the abstract when speaking the truth through photographic arrangement. For instance, a strategy of cotemporality enables Jordan to emphasize the persistence of features of black American life, pulling moments out of time in order to make clear their commonalities. Jordan spotlights three steady features of black experience through cotemporality: military service, education, and political confrontation. Before the dialogue between Jerome and Kenny begins, Jordan sets images of black Civil War troops alongside photographs of African American Marines in Vietnam. But most affecting compositionally is a collage of images that appears in conjunction with the text's discussion of the "60,000 Black soldiers" who died "for they own freedom, in the Union Army" (15). The collage repeats three separate images of black soldiers in Vietnam with two images from the Civil War, one of a dead Confederate soldier and one of white bodies at Gettysburg (Figure 4.14). The images are fractured, with repeated close-ups of black soldiers camouflaged in reeds in battle, holding smoking grenade launchers, and positioned behind a loaded machine gun. Jordan also manipulates images from the Civil War in order to offer varying perspectives on dead white soldiers.[103] What the collage suggests, instead of indexicality, is a repeated insistence on the idea of military action, on the power of black men with guns in the field. The images of dead white soldiers offer material evidence of black military action in the Civil War, working in tandem with the narrators' insistence on black sacrifice. The images could have been set whole, side by side, but instead the collage creates an almost dizzying effect, as though a reader cannot find a single focus or a single authoritative image to represent each conflict. In fact, the manipulation of the material evidence permits Jordan to lift the idea of black military conflict out of the concrete and into the abstract; this brilliant strategy enables a reader to absorb the concept of activism rather than the specifics of a single image or paired images. Through these fractured, cotemporal

Figure 4.14. A collage of images from the Civil War and Vietnam War. From June Jordan, *Dry Victories* (New York: Holt, Rinehart and Winston, 1972).

Figure 4.15. Four images of African American education, two contemporary and two from the nineteenth century. From June Jordan, *Dry Victories* (New York: Holt, Rinehart and Winston, 1972).

images, we envision military success as an unwavering feature of black identity. Jordan asks us to focus not on a single image but on the idea that structures them all: black military potency.

Cotemporality also characterizes the depiction of education in Jordan's text. Although not as ambitious visually as the war images, a conjunction of images from the nineteenth century to the present (77) suggests that Jordan rejects an evolutionary sense of black educational accomplishment, one that might have emerged if the images had been presented in sequence to reflect linear time (Figure 4.15). Jordan may include a photograph of the first black school in the South, "Penn School, St. Helena Island, South Carolina" (77), along with a classroom from the nineteenth-century Tuskegee Institute, but she does not

40   41

Figure 4.16. Malcolm X yoked to Booker T. Washington. From June Jordan,
Dry Victories (New York: Holt, Rinehart and Winston, 1972).

place those images in a line that would suggest growth from the teacher and
students of St. Helena to the VISTA teacher leading an integrated classroom
in Chicago.[104] Instead, the images all affirm black investment in education not
simply as learners but also as teachers; as in the war collage, the four images
work together to point toward a stable value: here, command of the classroom
as a consistent feature of black communal character.

The next set of images points toward the third quality Jordan emphasizes as
a stable feature of black experience: political engagement. In full-page images,
Jordan offers photographs of Malcolm X and of Booker T. Washington (Figure
4.16). As with the images of Abraham Lincoln and Coretta Scott King, here
the two figures appear to face each other, as if in dialogue. Malcolm X's finger

appears to point toward Washington accusingly, whereas Washington's face reads as tough and solemn. Malcolm X looks as though he is lecturing a hostile or at least skeptical audience in Washington, producing a drily funny awareness of the variations in black activism.

Jordan offers no simple resolution to these two images. One might expect in the Black Arts era a valorization of Malcolm X, for instance, or a visual critique of Washington. Instead, Jordan gives them equal visual emphasis. Their bodies are the same size, and Jordan offers a sense of parity in the seriousness of their poses. The figures may be equally weighty, but they are certainly posed as oppositional. In retaining the idea of two strong, insistent points of view, however they might disagree, Jordan asserts the constant presence of political engagement, regardless of time period, and the demand that readers make their own choices and not be told by an authority—the book, in this case—what to think about the two leaders. Political engagement is the constant; an interpretive argument is up to the reader. (For instance, one could stage a traditional reading and see the figures as oppositional, given that Washington evokes a conservative approach to racial development, and Malcolm X a more radical approach; alternately, one could stage a reading that sees the two as unified in their emphasis on black economic nationalist integrity, even if they disagree profoundly on how to get there.) In this open-ended visual exchange, Jordan refuses any reductive statement about national icons, any simple and straightforward didactic or propagandistic historical interpretation. Instead, the book offers a sense of the significance of black political engagement generally, in all of its variety, complexity, and ambiguity.

The images that follow emphasize visually the value of a strong political stance for African Americans. Elizabeth Eckford integrates Central High School in Little Rock, Arkansas, in 1957, and George Wallace vows to stop integration at the University of Alabama in 1963. Just as the Civil War is echoed in the Vietnam War, here the persistence of the Civil War conflict becomes the subtext of the integration movement, as Jordan positions a handmade American flag (from the Smithsonian) underneath Eckford and a nineteenth-century Confederate flag above Wallace. The two sides are posed oppositionally, of course, as the purpose for black political engagement across time becomes clear. Not much has changed in the South, Jordan argues; political resistance becomes necessary for black survival.

All of the paired and quadrupled images suggest not only the material presence of the past as well as the abstract values that remain constant to black identity, but also Jordan's power over images in order to construct a narrative of history, one that resists simplification through linearity or through mythologizing key figures. Jordan manipulates images from history; as a photographer, she adds her visual artifacts at times, but for the most part Jordan creates a narrative out of fragments from the past and asks the reader to make sense of it. Jordan permits us to extend our expectations for power over the image during the Black Arts moment; we can consider the way in which Jordan takes control of representation through presentation rather than solely through framing an image with a camera.[105] Nowhere is this control over imagery more potent than in Jordan's inclusion of newspaper images of racial violence. In the dialogue between Kenny and Jerome, Jerome discusses the murder of his ancestor Mississippi state legislator Charles Caldwell in 1875, which Jordan couples with images of slain Mississippi civil rights activist Medgar Evers and his grieving widow and son. Two pages of images taken from newspapers follow (Figure 4.17). The titles of the articles suggest that the images replicate the content of the articles, that they represent evidentiarily an Alabama KKK rally and a Birmingham Klan meeting. In fact, the newspaper articles are from the 1960s, but the images are from Georgia in the 1940s; yet Jordan has reconstituted them, arranging her own argument about the persistence of race hate. She is not deceptive, for she explains the composition in a captions-and-credits section and is therefore not trying to trick the reader with a documentary argument.

Jordan thus announces her control over newspaper images in offering her counterhistory. Although these text/image pairings invoke the authority of reportage, they exist only in the pages of Jordan's book. The pairings are her creation, for she has brought the reader "inside" the Klan rally, making the reader a "witness" to cross burning by viewing both images. Also telling is the repeated presence of the American flag in each photograph she selected, a gesture that echoes the book's questioning of America's faithfulness to civil rights. In a text of historiography, one which queries the narratives that have structured civic identity, manipulation of newspaper articles and photographs permits Jordan to emphasize the constructedness of historical narratives. For Jordan, this is a fact of historiography, for constructedness invests the historian with social power. As she argues in an author's note, "History is the business of choose and show" (75)—not choose, show, and explain, one might add, given the text's urgent insistence (by withholding explication) that the reader join in the interpretive process.

As Kenny and Jerome turn toward the 1950s and 1960s civil rights era in the last quarter of the book, Jordan includes many images that evoke journalistic coverage, including classic images of the bombed Sixteenth Street Baptist

Figure 4.17. Jordan uses newspaper accounts and photographs to comment on the persistence of racial terror. From June Jordan, *Dry Victories* (New York: Holt, Rinehart and Winston, 1972).

Church, the 1961 Freedom Rider bus on fire in Alabama, police officers fire-hosing young people in Birmingham, and Bull Connor at a 1963 meeting of Tuscaloosa's White Citizens Council. Jordan includes pages of headlines, again largely resisting chronological presentation, although the two-page assemblage ends with the murder of King.[106] These images adhere to Jerome and Kenny's explaining in the text that "the second Reconstruction was the Civil Rights' Decade" and that "the President, the U.S. Supreme Court, the U.S. Congress [have been] reconstructing reconstruction over and over and over" (57). The children list the civil rights acts of the nineteenth century along with those of the mid-twentieth century. Such iconic newspaper photographs and the plain-spoken catalog of failed civil rights legislation offer more than simply documentation. If it were simply documentarian, then it would be easily explained and contained, and the "truth" would be limited to a particular event or moment. Jordan makes plain the way in which meaning comes through the arrangement of facts and images across time. She undercuts our knowledge about the stability of documentary versions of history, arguing instead for meaning making as an interrogative and participatory process of interpreting the fragments of the past.[107]

The book ends with a photograph, taken by Jordan, of a graveyard in Brooklyn, and the children speak sarcastically about what they will see when they walk out onto the street: "Let's go on outside. Look at some fair housing. Dig the free and equal scene: today. Say hello to some up-to-date poor people. People hanging on" (73). Just as the book's engagement with history has taken place through images, the boys will continue to register their surroundings visually by looking at the "scene" on the street. At this point, Jordan makes plain the activist intent of the text: Jerome asks, "What do you think the parents and them other folks will do? After they hear all this?" Kenny responds, "Hard to say, brother. But maybe they do something. Be about time. About time to do something" (73). Jordan addresses the reader through the boys' comments here, demanding the reader incorporate the ideas within the text and a move toward social action. Jordan speaks extensively in the author's note about children's need for knowledge in order to act: "Kids may want more of the same ammunition, and teachers may want different points of view, *after* reading these *after-words*. That's the idea; go and find out for yourself. Check into it. It's important. History don't stop to let nobody out of it. So go ahead, and get into the facts. Then we can move on" (75). The real implication of the text comes through making the book live, moving beyond the book and toward a vision of the child as archivist, historian, interpreter, activist.

The final image is of a young black girl holding the American flag as she weeps at Robert Kennedy's funeral. And if Kenny's exhortation that it is "about time" for action does not suffice, Jordan extends her author's note on the following page:

The Publisher is worried. He wants me to write something, besides this book. Call it An Afterword. This whole book is an "afterword." It is written *after* the Civil War, *after* the Reconstruction Era, *after* the Civil Rights' Era, *after* the assassination of Malcolm X, the Kennedys, Dr. King, little girls in a Birmingham Sunday School, and *after* the assassination of countless hopes and acts of faith.

The Publisher is worried, but I'm not. I'm angry, and you should be too. Then we can do something about this after-mess of aftermath, following on so much tragedy. (75)

Writers imagined child activism variously during the Black Arts era: Kali becomes inspirational to adults and children as she naturally embodies and enacts resistance; Little John seeks avenues for articulating his sense of pride even when his parents and environment envision him through limitation; and Kenny, Jerome, and (Jordan suggests) the child reader of *Dry Victories* need a base in historical artifact in order to know what to change. Jordan is less interested in black pride per se than are Grosvenor and Shearer; she seeks black economic and social victory, the promise of America as it defines itself in the Constitution. Jordan's book can be considered a masterpiece of social-activist literature in large part because she presents not only a progressive version of history but also the method through which a child can take historical event and assemble new meanings.

Richard Flynn notices a consistent respect for childhood's capacities in the work of Jordan, and an attention to poor children that we can link to Shearer: "While attuned to children's real suffering, she [Jordan] resists the ways in which the child (and particularly the 'disadvantaged' child) is reified as an object of pity, preferring to emphasize children's agency by helping them to become writing subjects."[108] Although Flynn describes, in part, Jordan's contribution to developing child poets in her Poetry for the People program, his perspective might be extended to the idea of historiography in *Dry Victories*. Children can be agents in making history and potent interpreters of the past, for, as Jordan states in the author's note, "History don't stop to let nobody out of it" (75). Sharon Bell Mathis wrote of *Dry Victories* in a 1972 article issued by a black bookstore, "Black children have never had a history book like this one. The photographs alone are worth the price of the book—photographs that put you in a mood to yell and scream and man guns."[109] Although Jordan does not specify militancy as a response, she does insist that the reader incorporate the book and take action.[110] Her approach connects expressly to a Black Arts aesthetic. Haki Madhubuti argued in 1971, "Black art, like African art, is *perishable*. This too is why it is functional. For example, a black poem is written not to be read and put aside, but to actually become a part of the giver and receiver. It must perform some function: move the emotions, become part of the dance, or simply make one act. Whereas the work itself is perishable, the *style* and *spirit* of the creation is maintained and is used and reused to produce new works."[111]

Madhubuti's remark that "[b]lack art, like African art, is perishable" recalls the CDGM's *Today* and the theorization of book as active process and not passive, settled, commodified object. In many ways, Jordan recognizes that photographs can be perishable, too, for she seeks the "*style* and *spirit*" of the idea that photographs assembled side by side can convey out of time. For Jordan's text, one containing images of loss and atrocity as well as images of military, educational, and political courage, the perishable quality of the photograph confers hope: that the documentary details will retreat, and that the black child will enact the "*style* and *spirit*" of a living, resistant history. We return again to the idea of Black Arts childhood as ongoing process of becoming, of child as enacting a black critical position that is always in motion and always in relationship with the material world.

ENDING WITH BEGINNINGS:
TONI MORRISON'S *THE BLACK BOOK*

June Jordan's *Dry Victories* dovetails with Toni Morrison's edited compilation *The Black Book* (1974; credited to Middleton A. Harris), the most influential word/image book of the Black Arts era. Morrison's text pieces together various visual media—movie stills, photographs, patent applications, illustrations, musical scores, advertisements, and much more—in order to give an account of the history of black people in America. *The Black Book* focuses not on heroes or celebrities but on the cultural milieu shared by ordinary enslaved, newly freed, and modern African American people. Cheryl A. Wall talks about the book as "a scrapbook," one that "documents the history of African Americans."[112] Although the book certainly has a documentary thrust, it also intervenes in representation simply by gathering various public constructions of black culture (those widely circulated in the mainstream media and in material culture) and by circulating less familiar images: some taken from Morrison's own family albums, as well as rare photographs of enslaved and working-class individuals. *The Black Book* reconfigures the visual imprint of black culture by giving shape to a lost history, one previously unchronicled visually. One can easily imagine *The Black Book* as drawing on the methodology of Hughes and Meltzer's *Pictorial History of the Negro in America* and *Black Magic: A Pictorial History of the Negro in American Entertainment* (1967).

The *Black Book* also strategically follows Jordan's *Dry Victories*.[113] Both texts exploit the generic qualities of photography to demonstrate the presence of the past. Although Morrison's text moves through history in a loosely chronological way and Jordan gives form to the concepts of American inconstancy and black resistance through cotemporality, both texts are committed to the visual as a means of argument and a form of solace for historical losses (as well as the loss of black history itself). Both texts also invoke and involve young people. Jordan's text situates the power to create and act in childhood, whereas Morrison's text begins with an unpaginated preface by Bill Cosby that imagines the book as a record of childhood memory: "Suppose a three-hundred-year-old black man had decided, oh, say when he was about ten, to keep a scrapbook—a record of what it was like for himself and his people in these United States." Cosby's formulation recalls the impulse among Black Arts writers to revisit childhood as originary source of blackness and site of pedagogical reinvention. It also con-nects to Hughes and Meltzer's *Pictorial History of the Negro in America*, because both texts construct social justice as emerging from a kind of family album—photographic and textual—of black American experience. Cosby then reflects on the uses of the book for young people by regretting its absence in his youth: "I sure wish I'd had it when I was in school. Then I'd know what to say when Mrs. Broadbird said my speech was slang. I sure wish I'd had it in my house back in Philadelphia—then whenever I played the 'dozens' I'd know where they came from." Cosby's frame allows us to appreciate Morrison's text as a form of reeducation for the colonized child's mind, a child who questions like Little John, Kenny, and Jerome. As a scrapbook of sorts, *The Black Book* also sought an engaged response from the reader, one that echoes Jordan's, Shearer's, and Grosvenor's insistence on child social activism. As Wall observes, "A scrap-book reproduces a series of images in response to which readers construct their own narratives. Images elicit different stories from different readers at different times. Images in *The Black Book* provoke a kind of storytelling that is participa-tory, improvisational, and collective. The number of possible stories is infinite, but their sum would total a black history 'truer' than that available in archival documents or scholarly texts. In their collectivity, these stories would indeed constitute *the* 'black book.' "[114] As a young person, Wall herself brought *The Black Book* home to her parents, and found that the images inspired the parents' storytelling, drawing out of the adults rich family histories that had been buried by time and by pain.[115] For Wall's parents, gazing at images provoked a narrative response, helping create a form of resistant memory work that they then shared with their child and that the child carried into the world.

Given the Black Arts Movement's reinvention of cultural definitions, child-hood became a dynamic site for framing a new nation across audiences and me-diums. In word, sound, and image, BAM artists aimed to remake black identity; children's photobooks became one venue for articulating the idea of blackness as unlimited potential. Rebutting the idea of the blighted urban space involved rebutting the idea of black childhood as spiritually, economically, and intellectually impoverished. Claiming black power included reframing origins, turning to the child who embodied pure blackness untouched by white degradation, as well as the promise and potential of the black nation in the world. As essence and as process, as stable site of value and as nation in motion, the child enabled black creators a means to explore the incarnation of new forms of identity. Photographs too, paradoxically, both stabilized ideas and registered the mutability of the subject. The BAM offered new ways of thinking about the black child in the wake of the early civil rights movement, and new ways of employing the photograph conceptually within written texts.

5

Blurring the Childhood Image

Representations of the Civil Rights Narrative

... wherever I looked that summer
I learned to be at home with children's blood
with savored violence
with pictures of black broken flesh
used, crumpled, and discarded
lying amid the sidewalk refuse
like a raped woman's face....

    —Audre Lorde, "Afterimages"

Audre Lorde's 1981 poem on Emmett Till explores the effects of experiencing violence through the visual. Lorde implies that the medium of newspaper photographs contributes to Till's violation, for even as the visual details of the boy's brutalization stick with Lorde, she recognizes that the ephemeral and public quality of newspaper publication destabilizes the tragedy of his loss. Lorde sees that such images untethered in the public press could be used to confirm racist power, inspiring in white viewers the "secret relish / of a black child's mutilated body / fingered by street-corner eyes." The newspaper's transient quality promises a further loss, when the images lie "used, crumpled, and discarded" in the trash on the street. Although Till's photographs wound the speaker, becoming "etched in [her] forever," the pervasive media presence of the images at the same time inure her to their tragic implications, teaching her "to be at home with children's blood." Lorde's poem permits us to consider the multivalent implications of publication frames, particularly for those images associated with the civil rights movement. Many critics, movement participants, and historians rightly note that media publication of photographs—particularly of children, whether they are subject to violence, like Till, or on the front lines of integration, like Ruby Bridges and Elizabeth Eckford, or facing dogs and fire hoses in Birmingham—became turning points in the civil rights movement; yet the effects of such images are both long-lasting in our visual memory and essentially fleeting in the impact of their documentary function. At the same time, by the mid-1960s, such images were "old news" of a sort, as the movement turned northward and more intensively toward issues of poverty, anticolonialism, and black nationalism.

Yet early movement images became iconic in memory, specifically those originating from the 1950s to 1965,[1] and remain alive in photographic picture books for young people. How do iconic photos, so powerful and yet so particularly of a moment, function when set within books that narrate elements of the movement to an audience of children? Set at a distance—both in time and memory—from the movement, child readers encounter many of these familiar images (familiar to adults, anyway) for the first time in the pages of a photographic book. How do texts shift or play with the meaning of images originating within newspapers and periodicals in the 1950s and 1960s? Further, once the images are narrativized within books, what political uses does the civil rights narrative serve? And how do books for children reflect explicitly on the process and challenges of representation? These texts make choices as they represent the movement in various ways, whether by focusing on a particular feature, figure, or moment, or by broadly reviewing the movement across time; but they also become more generally representative as typifying *the* African American story, or even presenting themselves as *the* representative story of American identity. Such questions of form, politics, and representation are at the heart of this chapter and seek to open a dialogue about the possibilities of the contemporary children's civil rights photobook. We might note that contemporary texts are of a different type than the photographic books that appear earlier in this study; whereas early civil rights photobooks made social justice the implicit rather than explicit subject, the books in this chapter address the movement directly. The construction of history and memory functions differently here, too, with the movement itself functioning as both history and the prototypical American story, in contrast to texts like *A Pictorial History of the Negro* that embrace black history at large as constituting the civil rights movement. There are texts that draw on that tradition, as in the case of Walter Dean Myers's *One More River to Cross* (1995), but overall the contemporary civil rights photobook focuses expressly on an American history encapsulated in the early movement of the 1950s and early 1960s. Contemporary texts reflect upon the movement, considering it through iconic images, and are often more concerned with creating memory than agitating for change.

The chapter begins by considering generally the explosion of civil rights photographic picture books from the early 1990s to the current moment. Although a few civil rights photobooks appeared in the 1980s,[2] it was not until the 1990s that the civil rights moment became a pressing topic for a child audience. Why the 1990s? Why do civil rights photobooks remain popular? What does the upswing in civil rights photobooks suggest about the possibilities of the form within our cultural landscape? In addressing these issues, I will consider Leigh Raiford and Renee C. Romano's argument about the "consensus memory" of the civil rights movement in order to present the most frequently accessed figurations of the movement.[3] A brief overview of the political and social landscape of the 1990s will allow me to speculate about the sudden surge of interest in civil rights photo narratives for young people. Reflection on the cultural moment permits us to understand the political uses to which a photobook may be put, both by progressives and by conservatives. As we will see, the movement is an especially protean site, a place claimed politically by the right and by the left, and civil rights photographic books thus often articulate contending and contentious versions of the national story. My goal is not to offer sweeping generalizations about the politics of all photobooks but rather to limn the features of cultural debates on ethnicity and multiculturalism in the 1990s and 2000s in order to conjecture about the form's malleable ideological potential. Such ideas are admittedly speculative. However, an awareness of the sociopolitical milieu fostering the popularity of these texts will allow us to consider the implications of themes that pop up regularly within children's civil rights stories, such as Martin Luther King Jr. as dominant hero, friendship as a path to peace, and integration as a solution to social ills. In the final section of the contextual material, I consider the way in which photobooks generically reflect on the possibilities of representation, turning especially to the book as a means to render civil rights action continuous work. How do photobooks render civil rights unsettled and unfinished rather than seeking documentary closure? The chapter then analyzes four photographic texts: Walter Dean Myers's *One More River to Cross* (1995), Ruby Bridges's *Through My Eyes* (1999), Toni Morrison's *Remember: The Journey to School Integration* (2004), and Carole Boston Weatherford's *Birmingham, 1963* (2007). My readings of the texts focus on particular, salient elements rather than exhaustive close readings. Setting facets of the texts into dialogue with each other will permit us to understand how texts play with and against history, ideology, and the form of the photobook.

CONTEMPORARY CIVIL RIGHTS NARRATIVES:
TENDENCIES AND TRIUMPH

The civil rights story contains several tangible markers in the popular imagination, signposts that inflect narratives with meaning and resonance. As Raiford and Romano argue in *The Civil Rights Movement in American Memory*, "While there are many constituencies that lay claim to being bearers of the 'true' memory of the civil rights movement, there exists today what we might call a consensus memory, a dominant narrative of the movement's goals, practices, victories, and, of course, its most lasting legacies."[4] Romano and Raiford's critical anthology documents the vitality of the movement as a site of imagination, its legacy wielded in art shows, novels, poems, street signs, and memorials, as well as in commerce and politics. Even in the face of the variety of uses and expressions of civil rights narratives, the idea of a consensus memory rings true, for although the political and cultural uses of civil rights icons might vary, the icons themselves remain. Consensus about the civil rights era might be most clearly expressed in classrooms across America, spaces that frequently articulate the struggle through images beloved by adults: students learn about the evils of segregation, the triumphs of boycotts, and the grand leadership of Martin Luther King Jr. His birthday may be a national holiday, but nowhere is it celebrated with more regularity than in children's classrooms. Childhood becomes the site on which this consensus is formed.

For Romano, Raiford, and other critics of civil rights cultural production, certain salient features emerge out of this consensus. King, of course, is the most prominent personality, with Rosa Parks his female analogue; but King is imagined largely through images of his "I Have a Dream" speech and his assassination, rather than, say, through his resistance to the Vietnam War or through his Poor People's Campaign. In other words, representations truncate King; he is knowable only through his early integration protest and his martyrdom.

One element frequently cited in this nationally palatable story of King and of civil rights is the popular interpretation of his 1963 "I Have a Dream" speech, the climax of which seems to invoke childhood futurity rather than contemporary action. As King's speechwriter and activist Vincent G. Harding observes, the antipoverty context of the speech has been erased in the popular mind and the speech's emphasis on immediacy and tangibility (on realizing "the promise of democracy") elided in favor of a vision of black and white children stepping hand in hand into a romanticized future. "Indeed, his references to our children are among the most misused and misunderstood elements of the speech," Harding argues.[5] The most famous lines from the speech become abstracted when taken out of context: for instance, the line "I have a dream my four little children will one day live in a nation where they will not be judged by the color of their skin but by the content of their character" has been invoked by the political right as an argument *against* considering racism as a factor in evaluating the nation's moral status, when King in fact was arguing for a consideration of race and poverty's effects on children's lives in the present. The second favored quote from the speech is often replicated without any reference to social and material injustice. I offer a fuller passage here: "I have a dream that one day, down in Alabama, with its vicious racists, with its white governor having his lips dripping with the words of interposition and nullification, that one day, right there in Alabama, little black boys and black girls will be able to join hands with little white boys and white girls as sisters and brothers. I have a dream today!" Remove the virulent racists, their hateful rhetoric, and the pressure of Southern government, and what remains is an American utopia founded on a sentimental vision of childhood. That is the vision of King's speech that populates the American imagination. Interracial amity becomes placed in a nowhere land of the future, based not on struggle to consider one's character but on an idealized, race-blind, imaginary culture.

Further, relying on King to emblematize the movement brings certain compromises. The singularity of King as leader erases the hard work of countless individuals who sacrificed profoundly and acted courageously for the cause of equality. It minimizes the importance of networks of people facilitating social action. For children, however, valorization of King maps nicely onto the narratives in which they are immersed: a singular individual battles the evils of racism, solving the problem of oppression, changing the political and social landscape for a community he loves. It sounds like a fairy tale, or a children's book.[6] King as individualist harmonizes with American ideals, both politically, in conservative circles, and culturally, in popular news investment in celebrity and personality, as Edward P. Morgan and other critics have cogently argued;[7] but King's singularity also speaks to young people trained in tropes of children's literature. Even though King was martyred for the cause, his life changed the world, such consensus memory argues, and we arrive at a happy ending in which good triumphs over evil for schoolchildren celebrating his legacy in integrated classrooms (or in classrooms that could in theory be integrated but in practice are not).[8] He cannot be forgotten there, because he is written into the school calendar. He is the legitimate face of the civil rights movement for young people.

The other main site of consensus memory attached particularly to childhood is integration, an idea apparent in the dearly held trope of little black boys and girls walking hand in hand with little white boys and girls. It is school, however, that stages the practical accomplishment of the theory of integration, an accomplishment fulfilled in consensus memory if not in national practice. We remember the image of Elizabeth Eckford surrounded by shouting racists at Little Rock, and Ruby Bridges being ushered into a Louisiana elementary school by federal marshals. (Other than in group photographs of the Little Rock Nine, black boys are not typically at the center of school-integration representations.) School integration becomes a site of child courage and child accomplishment, dominating popular configurations of civil rights action. School integration makes material the details of King's dream, becoming a first step toward national harmony, one that can be witnessed, documented, photographed, and remembered. School integration enables social integration in this consensus narrative, as children's supposedly color-bind vision of the world teaches adults to see beyond their prejudices. It is not only the site of school, then, that brings this dimension of consensus memory into relief for children. It dominates because it is evidence of the fulfillment of King's dream; its closure on questions of equality and struggle permits the ultimate "happy ending" for American schoolchildren, whether or not the classroom in which they sit actually contains the "other."

THE 1990S AND 2000S: THE PROMISE
OF THE CIVIL RIGHTS NARRATIVE

The 1990s spurred a renewed cultural interest in the civil rights moment, as many critics have noted. For instance, Jennifer Fuller compares the low-key celebration of the thirtieth anniversary of Little Rock by Arkansas governor Clinton in 1987 with the exultant tone of 1997: "[T]he national media and federal government seized on the fortieth anniversary of this event as an opportunity for the nation to take stock of how far it had come and how far it had to go in race relations since the 1950s."[9] Central to the fortieth anniversary was a photo-op around a reunion (of sorts) between Elizabeth Eckford and a white woman, Hazel Bryan; they had featured prominently in an iconic photograph of Eckford walking to school with Bryan standing behind her in a crowd, her open mouth shouting racial epithets.[10] At the 1997 meeting, Bryan was appropriately penitent, and the two posed for another photo in front of Central High School. The image, with the two smiling together, was sold as a poster with the title "Reconciliation." If images structured response to the original civil rights moment, in this case new images appeared necessary in order to document its fruition through friendship. (In fact, the two women developed a friendship that would prove temporary.) Children's books joined the renewed interest in civil rights, as the surge in publication of photobooks from the middle 1990s to today evidences. The cultural milieu of the 1990s offered a particularly ripe setting for movement photobooks. It is not my intention to offer a comprehensive overview of cultural politics in the 1990s and 2000s; critics like Romano and Raiford have superbly outlined the connection between the culture wars and the appropriation of civil rights images, narratives, and discourse. Instead, I hope to signal some of the features of the milieu in order to speculate on how children's texts particularly could connect with the energies of the moment. As I say in the introduction to this chapter, the ideas here are admittedly exploratory. In discussing politics, it is not my goal to engage reader-response criticism. My thoughts here instead indicate the protean character of the movement for modern children's narratives.

Min Hyoung Song's *Strange Future: Pessimism and the 1992 Los Angeles Riots* (2005) and James Kyung-Jin Lee's *Urban Triage: Race and the Fictions of Multiculturalism* (2004) both discuss the prevailing sense of American cultural despair from the 1980s to the beginning of the 1990s. Focusing particularly on the political and popular treatment of urban populations, both texts acknowledge that under Ronald Reagan and George H. W. Bush, poor people and people of color suffered greatly from the absence of governmental acknowledgment, a lack manifested through hostile public policy and the withdrawal of civil rights supports. Even as public structural foundations for urban citizens were crumbling, politicians bemoaned the state of the cities, and popular culture depicted people of color through images of urban decay and destruction. The state of the cities became the proving ground for definitions of American identity: politicians and the media characterized immigrants as essentially foreign, affirmative action as the cause of the economic decline of the white middle class, and black people in cities as "welfare queens" or living "off the system," evidence of their failure to adhere to ideals of American individualism. Antagonism toward the poor extended into the 1990s, with the Clinton presidency's emphasis on welfare reform, for instance. As Song explains, "Both major political parties in the United States in the 1990s, while paying homage to the language of racial equality, converged in their hostility to programs designed to facilitate access to higher education, better-paying jobs, adequate housing, and even clean food and water."[11] Despite the variety of people living in cities, urban decline was associated with African Americans primarily, and the immigrant other in their wake. The 1992 Los Angeles riots appeared to conservatives to be evidence of black people's refusal to access American values; burning their own neighborhoods and destroying businesses, black people were publicly stigmatized as violent, socially alien, and fundamentally ungrateful for the freedoms America supposedly extended. As Lee suggests, the pervasiveness of the term "underclass" in political discourse in the 1990s indicates the displacement of blame for poverty onto poor people rather than acknowledging the political abandonment of the inner cities.[12]

Civil rights photobooks for children emerged in this moment of profound despair and contention about the reasons for the material and social collapse of the urban community. The popularity of civil rights texts for children speaks of the desire for an uplifting narrative of social progress, a happy ending that would reinforce the viability of American ideals. The popularity also speaks of a cultural desire to redefine and restructure characterizations of black Americans, to tell the "truth" (through photographs) about both America and black communities. These goals have been and remain accessible to writers and readers of various political and ideological stripes. For neoconservatives in the 1990s, the turn to civil rights narratives might serve what Song suggests was the overall temperament of conservative discourse in the face of ideas about national decline: "Let's stop feeling guilty about the problems of black people, since we as a country have already done more than is required by common decency to make up for the abuses they have suffered."[13] Civil rights photobooks might serve for some as evidence of all that has been done for black people, with the federal officials in images representing the role of the state in enforcing the accessibility of American ideals. America becomes heroic in these narratives, and certainly it is rare for a children's book to question the extension of American democratic values to all citizens, with works like June Jordan's *Dry Victories* being rare exceptions. In the face of simplistic versions of a racial nightmare in the early 1990s, civil rights photobooks might permit (for some) a kind of denial of the real economic and social difficulties faced by children. They might present civil rights as a solved problem, a told story, easily accessed, compartmentalized, and dismissed.

African Americans resisted a teleology that blamed the poor for a decline precipitated in large part by neoconservative policy. Black writers and photographers, then, can be understood as gravitating to civil rights stories as a means of articulating, conspicuously, the "truth" of black identity and black cultural life. The turn to images of clean-cut, earnest, courageous children walking determinedly into schools might respond to the pervasive media representations of black youth as gangbangers, sexually and morally corrupt. Or, for some, civil rights narratives might assert a core black American identity, countering ideas that the urban "underclass" has turned away from American ideals of individualism, integrity, and morality. As Lee notes, writers engaged the dismissal and abandonment of people of color, working to "reflect on, take issue with, and at times participate in the tragic consequences for those who are, literally and figuratively, written off the map of power."[14] Civil rights texts for children by people of color are a response to being "written off the map"—the map of social power, of cultural dignity, and of American identity. In photographic picture books, the civil rights movement serves as an origin story for black communities, featuring images documenting the tangibility of the movement's players, courage, and accomplishments.

In the 1990s surge of interest in civil rights photographic picture books, the first main cultural factor, then, is the sense of urban decay and the dominance of pejorative constructions of black communities in political rhetoric and popular culture. The second key factor influencing the form's popularity is the ascendance of multiculturalism as a value in publishing and education. Curriculum reform in schools and colleges emerged in part from the culture wars of the 1990s, which focused on whether literary studies should adhere to the "great books" in order to defend against cultural degradation, as Allan Bloom's *The Closing of the American Mind* (1987) asserts,[15] or whether the progressive curricular push of the 1970s and 1980s (articulated in the founding of black studies and women's studies programs, for instance) could culminate in the inclusion of creative voices other than those of white men. As Bethany Bryson argues, both sides of the cultural debate invested text selection with ideological significance: "[E]very time an English teacher put together a reading list, the future of the nation hung in balance."[16] In addition to English curriculum, elementary school academic performance became a major site of argument regarding approaches to minority populations, with policy makers on the right like William Bennett publishing texts like *The De-valuing of America: The Fight for Our Culture and Our Children* (1992).[17] Photographic picture books about civil rights were certainly a product of the intensified curricular interest in writers of color, a response to the desire for depictions of African Americans and, perhaps, for evidence of black investment in American values.

However, multiculturalism became a vexed proposal for Americans, as critics like Lee and Jodi Melamed explore: emerging from such canon debates about representation and inclusivity, literary multiculturalism permitted representation and, to a large degree, codification of cultural production by people of color. Although writers, progressive educators, and scholars had advocated for texts by African Americans (as well as for texts by other ethnic groups, women, LGBT writers, and others), the move toward inclusion led also to an emphasis on representationality and on aesthetics.[18] First and foremost, multiculturalism as an idea enabled readers to understand communities of color through literature. This utilitarian tendency was not new, for at least since the 1920s, with white interest in the Harlem Renaissance, and gaining steam with the race novel in the 1930s and 1940s, white readers were attracted to literature about black people as a means of understanding the "truth" of the culture. And certainly photographic books generally participate in the desire to "know" communities and their authentic ethnic and racial identities through images and their explanations. Melamed calls this tendency in multiculturalism "literature as information retrieval."[19]

Although in the 1920s, 1930s, and 1940s, race novels (and photobooks) could be authored by writers outside of communities of color, the rationale of multiculturalism as representationality in the 1990s intensified the emphasis on truth and the authentic, valuing writers who belonged to the groups about which they wrote. The argument about inclusiveness made narratives emphasizing "authentic voice" even more attractive, books in which characters articulated themselves and their culture in the face of opposition; this thematic tendency echoes the movement of multicultural texts from exclusion to canonicity. Importantly, texts became even more utilitarian as evidence of multicultural liberal achievement: in university, high school, and elementary classrooms, reading a text by a person of color could enable the reader's sense of competency regarding culture. Read a text by Maya Angelou, say, and know black America, the logic went. Literature became product, as definitions of race relied on aesthetics and voice rather than on politics, as Melamed argues: "A work of multicultural literature was understood to be an example of the value of different racialized cultures and a commodified form of racialized cultural property. The idea of culture as property owned by people of color functioned within a consumer economy in which antiracism could be expressed by a desire for diversity, which consuming racialized cultural property presumptively fulfilled."[20] Civil rights photobooks for young people drew on the energies of liberal multiculturalism, becoming one of the most acceptable forms of stories to tell about black identity,[21] offered within institutional settings like school to an audience being trained in citizenship. In this way, texts that already told the "right" story—of minorities not as an underclass, of the extension and embrace of democratic ideals to and by black people, of the guaranteed success of the American integration story—became positioned even more steadfastly as the truth of black culture, easily consumed, for a young readership.[22]

Although much time has passed since the 1990s, liberal multiculturalist ideals shape our contemporary vision of the potential of civil rights children's texts. The movement remains the right story to tell, offering a malleable set of images that can be used variously in response to ideas about urban decline, the vitality of democracy, the success of the American project, and culture as commodity. After September 11, 2001, the second anxious site of urban identity after the black underclass—that of the perpetual foreigner, the immigrant store or restaurant worker, for instance—became more pronounced in articulations of national anxieties about race and identity. As desires to concretize the alien other in our midst led to intensified racial profiling and anti-Muslim sentiment, interest in civil rights narratives for children continued. Such interest could speak to cultural desire for a simpler, apprehensible, containable time in cultural history. Evelyn Alsultany argues that popular culture post 9/11 exercises "simplified complex representational strategies" that work in binaries of good ethnic subject versus bad ethnic subject, in order to make facile arguments for America's multicultural accomplishment and postracial identity.[23] Cultural desire for binaries expresses itself in superficial representations of civil rights history. In the face of racial multiplicity and mutability, old models for understanding cultural and racial difference might appear more attractive, like the sociological mode that underpins photographic narratives; stories that conceptualize "race" as black versus white, good versus evil, might become more attractive in a time period structured by a lack of understanding of Muslim cultures and a fear of immigrants. Civil rights narratives return also to a moment of success that, on the one hand, serves the state, even as the "American ideals" espoused by neoconservatives are purportedly apolitical; and, on the other hand, it can serve the idea of blacks as Americans, as embodying the American story. Civil rights narratives can thus be used to conservative ends in order to cement state narratives and erase the presence of the immigrant other, becoming a return to a time when race and conflict were more apparently clear-cut. For some black writers since 1990, asserting Americanness might assuage African American anxiety about a sense of place within a moment of multiplicity and turmoil. Returning to the civil rights story can confirm a kind of black exceptionalism, one that might evade the multiplicity of racialized experience and social claims, becoming a proclamation of black national incorporation in the face of suspicious foreign identity. For other African American writers, a return to the civil rights story might extend a promise to those groups excluded from the frame, because writers can suggest larger implications and make connections between the evidence of the civil rights campaign and the dynamics of the current moment.

But whether texts reify state control, assert black exceptionalism, or extend and apply the civil rights story, many photographic narratives for children rely on friendship as a means of accomplishing social change, particularly when discussing integration. The idea of racial amity fits perfectly into the political dynamics of the 1990s, as the earlier example of Elizabeth Eckford and Hazel Bryan indicates. Further, friendship as a mode of social rectitude became more prominent in the wake of the 1992 Los Angeles riots and Rodney King's plaintive question at the acquittal of the police offers who beat him brutally: "Can we all just get along?" Certainly, on the surface, Rodney King's plea calls for friendship as a solution to urban violence and despair. But King's desperation might indicate cultural desire for social progress based on collaboration, on consensus. The civil rights children's photobook responded to this moment; its teleology, apprehensible meaning, and intentionality (with participants working toward a common goal) suggest that black political action can be logical, concerted, and morally just. Movement texts not only represent consensus memory but also seek to build consensus around the way in which the major figures and events of the movement are depicted. Rodney King's desire for social progress based on friendship might also suggest a cultural desire for consensus about the economic and cultural success of urban communities.

The withdrawal of governmental civil rights-based programs in the 1990s corresponded with the state's emphasis on racial harmony through friendship. This governmental approach dovetails with the long tradition in American children's literature of using relationship rather than politics or social action to resolve racial troubles, a strategy that sometimes elides the hard-wrought political efforts of civil rights movements. As an approach in children's books, the "solving" of civil rights through interracial friendship has deep roots, going back at least to the multicultural movement of the 1930s,[24] gaining steam and governmental endorsement during the 1940s. Mary Dudziak discusses the United States Information Agency pamphlet *The Negro in American Life* (1950), explaining that the government perspective, shared by a majority of white Americans in the 1940s and 1950s, was that "[t]he problem of racial prejudice ultimately could not be eradicated through law, for it was essentially 'a question of evolving human relations.'"[25] Friendship, therefore, has frequently been the terrain on which civil rights could be won; certainly photobook writers like Ellen Tarry, Jane Dabney Shackelford, and Louis B. Reynolds wielded friendship as the main weapon in a struggle for social change. In the 1990s and beyond, we find that racial amity as an ideal cohered with the governmental and cultural insistence on relationship as the dominant mode of social progress, a tendency that recalls the 1940s racial liberalism behind *My Happy Days* and *My Dog Rinty*. Fuller calls this the "friendship orthodoxy" at the heart of the 1990s: "The belief that persistent racial problems such as discrimination and economic inequality are caused by personal attitudes and are not a matter of public policy became 'common sense' in the nineties. The 'friendship orthodoxy' of race was endorsed by the left as well as the right."[26] That orthodoxy did not evaporate after September 11, 2001. Popular films like *The Help* (2011) evidence the continued belief that if white and black women, particularly, would talk together and become friends, then racial progress could be accomplished.[27] And friendship between white and black children becomes a site of great national pride, evidence of the goodness that America makes possible.

Revitalizing the conversation about the civil rights movement, texts by African Americans grapple with how to position its conclusiveness, whether with the "happy ending" of school integration or civil rights legislation. Civil rights narratives thus risk closing down dialogue about the actual state of minority childhood in the United States; the school-integration story has been one of the most popular narratives in part because it places inequities about education squarely in the past, rendering injustice, of course, but confining it safely and neatly through imagistic evidence of its supposedly stable place in history. It seems paradoxical that the actual retraction of civil rights programs by the state coincides with an influx of civil rights narratives for children. But considering the potential uses of the civil rights story, such an influx could insist on the completion of the project of democracy in the face of racial anxieties; or rather the influx can be understood as an intervention, a reminder that civil rights work began at a particular moment in history and remains unfinished. Texts that insist on the unfinished state of civil rights work employ photographs productively, exploring their ability both to place an event in time and to resurrect that event and its demands within the current moment.

PHOTOGRAPHIC BOOKS AND MOVEMENT REPRESENTATION

Photographic picture books became popular in the 1990s largely because of their ability to concretize race relations, for, as we have seen, the ideological malleability of the form takes its power from the "truth" the images and text describe. With democratic ideals at stake, the "truth" as articulated within a book thus becomes the "truth" of national identity. In order to consider how texts grapple with photographic books as a means to close down or open up dialogue about the civil rights efforts, past and present, of African Americans, we should briefly consider the form as a site of representational performance. Leigh Raiford's *Imprisoned in a Luminous Glare: Photography and the African American Freedom Struggle* (2011) brilliantly considers the effects of repro- ducing civil rights images within contemporary frames, asking questions like "What happens when these images travel through time? Why and how does social movement photography resurge in particular moments? What messages and meanings does it carry in these new contexts[?]"[28] For the purposes of ex- amining children's books, we might remember the presumption of innocence that photographs bear with them, a mechanistic truth telling that corresponds with popular constructions of childhood innocence's unfiltered feedback on the world. We might also remember that photographs render heroes and heroic moments iconic, fixing them within a particular conflict, speech, or action that emblematizes particular values.[29] Iconic images perform in their ability to con- jure up a set of meanings that can be interpreted within a text. The fact that the images appear within a book also bears significant interpretive weight. To return to the Audre Lorde poem that opened this chapter, images within a newspaper at a moment in time can pass away, become yesterday's news, but still can haunt like a memory. Placing those images within a book invests the story with the weight of solidity and of currency. It is a story to be read now, consid- ered important enough to be permanent within the present moment as well as significant to the past. Words sutured to images and published within books make an argument about reality—what we need and what race means—within the cultural moment.

By reproducing movement images within photobooks, however, the stability and consumability of black identity—whether within neoconservative or mul- ticultural rubrics—become somewhat unsettled. For although one might seek the "truth" of black or national identity through the consumption of these im- ages, the books themselves make clear that the arrangement of images on the page reveals the maker's hand, the shaper who intervenes to re-create meaning around ideological figures (like those of lynching or the KKK)[30] or the archivist who amasses and juxtaposes images in order to erect a new "truth" in the face of misinterpretation or elision. Language, too, bears responsibility for the political and social meanings of a particular text.[31] Language might play an even more intensified interpretive role within contemporary photographic texts, because

the images are so familiar. Whereas children's texts in the 1940s and 1950s relied heavily on the image to speak the unspeakable, contemporary photographic
texts rely not only on the iconic image to conjure up a site of meaning but also
on the interpretive explanation and the arrangement of the images on the page.
These factors shape the meaning of the images, and, in the process, the idea
that meaning is constructed, that "truth" about civil rights is shaped by the
presentation of the "facts," becomes more apparent than in earlier photographic
books. In short, the familiarity of the images places more pressure on the way
the text asks us to see them anew, whether through language or arrangement on
the page. Such self-consciousness permits us to see the presentation as a performance of certain ideals, a representation that reflects on representation and our
shaping of memory. The photographic book thus offers authors the potential
to depict race as a performance, to deny that images themselves offer an essential, consumable version of blackness by the very fact that they have been conspicuously edited and narrativized. Readers might seek civil rights narratives
in representationality or positive images, but the books themselves, by being
books that use photographs, reflect on the process of representation. Just as the
form of photography is intrinsically metatextual by drawing attention to image
making through the frame of the image, even more self-reflexive are collages
of word/image, or even, I would argue, texts that employ fictional narratives in
collusion with photographs, a move that draws attention to the constructedness
of both forms. Photobooks thus represent and resist the confinement of representationality by revealing its constructedness.

   As in the 1940s and 1950s, some books do not draw attention to the essentially metatextual status of the photographic book. These straightforwardly
claim to tell the truth about the subject at hand. But other photographic books
draw attention both to our desire to know the truth and to the final instability
of representation. Certainly June Jordan's *Dry Victories*, with its collage of images and drawing together of film script, book narrative, and photograph, found
an ideal form to explore the failures of simplistic American summations of truth
and justice. Such critique via self-reflexive form can function as an expression of
critical black memory; according to Raiford, "African American political uses
of photography as a site of memory suggest a mode of historical interpretation
in which African Americans mobilize the medium's documentary capacity, its
function as historical evidence, in order to critique the 'truth-claims' of history that have worked to classify, subjugate, and marginalize black life."[32] But it
is more than just alternative truth telling through photographs: for children's
photographic texts, critique comes when there is a self-consciousness that the

images presented are historical and have been arranged; also, when a fictional-ized voice interprets the images, we can recognize that the voice is an act of creation. In the best of these books (such as Jordan's book), the openness of the form enables a call to action to the reader to intervene in the representation of history. This call can also challenge readers to recognize the unfinished nature of civil rights in their own lives. Reframed in books, the abject child martyr can signify something other than passivity and sacrifice; the martyr can live again to challenge the reader to accomplish something new.

WALTER DEAN MYERS'S *ONE MORE RIVER TO CROSS*: FRAMING THE FAMILY

The readings that follow of four photographic books focus on issues of form, politics, and representation. Myers, Bridges, Morrison, and Weatherford re-spond to the pressures on the civil rights narrative, a consensus story that has been used to stabilize, confine, and commodify social progress. I am particu-larly interested in considering whether these books, authored by major literary and cultural figures, consider unfinished the project of the civil rights move-ment. Like Jacquelyn Dowd Hall, I am looking for indications that civil rights is a more complicated narrative than that which has been presented in public discourse. Hall asserts, "I want to make civil rights harder. Harder to celebrate as a natural progression of American values. Harder to cast as a satisfying mo-rality tale. Most of all, harder to simplify, appropriate, and contain."[33] How do children's texts use the photobook form to reinterpret iconic images? Do they make representation conspicuous in order to offer a critical perspective and encourage a critical readership? How do they contend with the insistence on a "happy ending," both in civil rights consensus narrative and in children's texts more generally?

Walter Dean Myers's *One More River to Cross* (1995) appeared at the cusp of renewed interest in the civil rights movement. Myers presents black civil rights activity across time, from enslavement to the current moment, in the form of a family photographic album; in doing so, he joins Hall's project of remember-ing the "long civil rights movement." Most of the images Myers offers come from his personal collection: he refreshes the narrative of black American social progress by juxtaposing familiar photographs with those of unknown figures. Although Myers offers an index at the back of the book that sometimes speci-fies the identities and contexts of the original photographs, he never within the language of the narrative signals individual identity within a photograph. As an archivist, Myers assembles images of forgotten, unnamed black people, setting them in an equalizing position with the "great men and women" of black history. This juxtaposition enables a reader to value the unvalued, to remember those whose names are not present in mind but whose images live on the printed page. A reader might recognize, say, photographs of Duke Ellington, James Baldwin, and Mary McLeod Bethune, but Myers does not specify them within the text's language. They sit side by side with individuals whose identities have been lost over time. Further, such a strategy demands critical practice from the reader: the reader seeks to identify figures within images, and discovers the frustration of trying and failing to identify and specify those who are nameless. Thus, the reader recognizes both the desire to concretize history and the loss of being unable to connect with people who are just as valuable as the well-known (equalized through placement alongside recognizable black heroes and heroines) but whose contributions have been erased. Both famous and anonymous, then, become specific through the image yet abstracted through a narrative that refuses to name but instead invokes ideas and ideals and speaks in the collective "we." By assembling a visual public archive from the fragments of his own personal collection, Myers enables black readers to reposition imaginatively their own family photographs among the story of African American civil rights efforts. His strategy not only makes apparent "the maker's hand" in arranging the text, but also demands reader involvement in the rewards of identification and of joining Myers's project, as well as in the bittersweet recognition that countless nameless individuals contributed to civil rights efforts across the sweep of history. Such a reading situation might propel conversation between child and adult, creating the kind of "chaperoning" exchange that can build community and draw out threads of family memory.[34]

Myers also reframes historic images of racial violence, countering sentimentalized versions of the movement story that elide violence or truncate the time period in which civil rights efforts took place. He offers a two-page spread of a Ku Klux Klan rally in Washington, D.C. (an image from August 1925, though Myers does not indicate the time period), linking visually white supremacy with the nation-state: we see the Capitol looming like a ghost behind the marchers, its whiteness reiterated in the Klan's hoods and robes (Figure 5.1).

The image that immediately follows brings racial terror from the abstract into the concrete: a mob with dogs stand for a picture in front of a lynched black man (Figure 5.2). Adults may be familiar with lynching images, but young people (the audience for the book) may not be. The image itself is confrontational, given that all members of the mob face the camera; the central figure has a particularly menacing look, and white hands pass into the frame on the left to

And the people who

hated us because of our color

Figure 5.1. A Ku Klux Klan rally in Washington, D.C. From Walter
Dean Myers, *One More River to Cross: An African American Photograph
Album* (New York: Harcourt Brace & Company, 1995).
Photograph from Library of Congress, Underwood & Underwood, Inc.

touch the post on which the man hangs, desperate to attach themselves to the
site of violence that confirms their power and ideology. The effect of violence
remains present in the hanging man, just as its threat emerges across the photograph into the space of the present-day reader. Myers's narration emphasizes
racism as a conscious choice; he narrates the Klan and lynching images with a
phrase that breaks in the middle: "And the people who hated us because of our
color / WERE PROUD OF THEIR HATE."[35] Ideals of amity become impossible to stage on this terrain.

Introducing a Klan march at the Capitol and a lynching photograph into a
"family" photographic album specifies the sources of racial violence quite con-
cretely. Published in the mid-1990s, shortly after the Los Angeles riots, the

WERE PROUD OF THEIR HATE.

Figure 5.2. An African American man, lynched, and the white mob.
From Walter Dean Myers, *One More River to Cross: An African American Photograph Album* (New York: Harcourt Brace & Company, 1995).

book insists that violence inheres in whiteness and has been overseen, if not legitimated, by the ghostly symbol of governmental power looming behind the hate group. Just as the NAACP mobilized images of murdered black Americans to advance an antilynching campaign,[36] Myers refocuses through language our attention onto white hate rather than black victimhood. Critics like Amy Louise Wood have offered cogent readings of the details of this particular lynching image, paying special attention to the resonance of the sign "Please do not wake" in the light of ideas about death as sleep.[37] But Myers does not name the murdered man (Charles Hale), the date of the image (1911), or its place (Georgia). His reframing of the lynching photograph abstracts Hale; Myers does not name any of the subjects of the book's photographs, because it is impossible to name the forgotten photographic subjects. Instead, the lynching image focuses on the idea of white hatred rather than on the specifics of one man's loss. Because the image focuses so intensely on the gaze of the white men holding the dogs, Myers involves his readers in returning a resistant gaze. Raiford discusses the reframing of black lynching photographs by activists in the 1920s in order to "reconstruct the black gaze back at [the] injustice" of the lynched individuals as they faced white mobs;[38] here, Myers places his reader in the oppositional space. The namelessness of the victim of the lynching does not diminish the crime; instead, the abstraction of time, subjects, and place enables a reader to confront the image. We are not pinned into a specific moment or focused on a particular loss, for the image launches our reaction against white hate and white violence no matter the time period. The reader thus stages resistance.

When Myers turns to photographs of the 1960s civil rights movement, he includes those which argue for black communal inclusivity and continuity. Offering a two-page spread of the 1963 March on Washington, Myers brings the image to the edges of the page (Figure 5.3). The image represents the number and diversity of people involved in the march, particularly in terms of age and class. Unlike the Klan image, which stands back from the individuals, declining to engage their faces in a way that refuses to condone the ideology of that march, this image permits a reader to consider the details of the people involved in this march as well as to appreciate their number. Although most are facing the camera, looking into the distance toward the speaker, some turn their faces to the side or even their backs to the camera in order to talk among themselves. The multiplicity of subjects' gazes, then, speaks to the dynamism of the scene: the particularity of the subjects' engagements reflects their individual considerations. One might notice the effect of this image in contrast with the singularity of gaze in the mob-lynching scene. There, the single-mindedness of white hate evokes simplicity, whereas multiplicity in the march scene suggests complexity, individual commitment, and thoughtfulness. The sign in the image marks continued commitment to civil rights: "We Will March as Long as We Can and Demand the Rights of Everyman." Although the image is located in time and space, the language insists on an enduring movement toward equality, one that reaches into the space of the contemporary reader. The caption Myers offers to the image also points to continuity across time: "It had taken so long and still we had to struggle" (136). The caption resists truncating civil rights efforts (as, for example, between 1954 and 1965) as it offers a sense of the people's frustration at having to struggle still for civil rights after hundreds of years of resistance, a sentiment that might be applied to the contemporary reader's

had taken so long and still we had to struggle.

We Will March AS LONG AS WE CAN *and* DEMAND THE RIGHTS of EVERYMAN

Figure 5.3. The crowd at the 1963 March on Washington for passage of the Civil Rights Act. From Walter Dean Myers, *One More River to Cross: An African American Photograph Album* (New York: Harcourt Brace & Company, 1995).

experience as well. The idea that the struggle continues is, of course, central to liberation campaigns of the mid- and late twentieth century.

Just as he represents mass investment in civil rights, Myers also refuses to valorize particular individuals, a move that, in lesser books, often flattens the complexities of figures like Martin Luther King Jr., Rosa Parks, and others. Because Myers aims to reflect the black family's investment in civil rights, he humanizes the heroes of the movement, offering both King and Malcolm X (who are often portrayed as ideological adversaries) side by side, both smiling, with King embracing his wife tenderly. When Myers offers images of the 1963 March on Washington, he presents a crowd rather than the iconic image of King giving his "I Have a Dream" speech. Malcolm X is neither angry nor confrontational, as he is typically represented in descriptions of the civil rights movement that compress its complexities. Myers refuses to transform either leader into an icon; they become individuals, much like the people on the mall, set in relationship to others. Tenderness and joy characterize these leaders; although Myers alludes to the iconic "I Have a Dream" speech, he appropriates its language rather than rehearses it: "There were people to lead us, people willing to take us to the mountains" (138–39). Much as Myers's refusal to identify particular black heroes pushes the reader to recognize and name the photographs as they appear, the allusion to King's speech asks the reader to remember the ideal of the mountaintop but will not parse out its meaning for the reader. The allusion nudges the reader to remember the speech, but the reader must dwell on her own reading of "take us to the mountains." Again the language of the text points toward openness and collaboration with the reader, a process that resists the already told, easily consumable consensus narrative of civil rights discourse.[39]

Myers's depiction of civil rights efforts is fundamentally communal. He represents movement leaders, like King, not through a journalistic, evidentiary photographic frame but rather through the familial. Even the collective "we" voice of the narrative insists on a collective effort within the family album of black America. Admittedly, Myers documents the black "family" by offering repeated images of heteronormative nuclear families, a gesture that might speak to discourse in the 1990s about the absence of black fathers within home life. The families Myers presents are compellingly heterogeneous in terms of class, however. One could also consider whether the framework of family participates in the era's insistence on social change based on personal relationship rather than on institutional movements; in this, however, Myers emphasizes collective efforts to intervene in institutional power, whether in images of Negro League baseball players, or the postmaster and his family in the black town of Littig, Texas, or the sailors on the USS *Herbert*. In the final section of the book, which follows the civil rights images, Myers weaves photographs of unknown historical children and families with images of contemporary ones (Figure 5.4). His narration dislocates the narrative of civil rights from the early 1960s, arguing that the struggle for equality has extended from enslavement and continues into the present day: "Our tears have been washed away, allowing us to see with our eyes the stories that have been told / and with our hearts the ones yet to come. And through it all there is the sweet triumph of life, / a triumph we have nourished like a sacred flame through the centuries" (142–45). Myers places the struggle for civil rights into a long view, making it a persistent feature of black

Figure 5.4. Images of girls across the twentieth century. From
Walter Dean Myers, *One More River to Cross: An African American
Photograph Album* (New York: Harcourt Brace & Company, 1995).

life rather than something peculiar to the 1960s; he also emphasizes the victory of life complexly and wholly lived. Just as struggle is a continued feature of black life, Myers argues, so is that "sweet triumph," that victory of self-love sustaining black families. Myers alludes to Langston Hughes and Roy DeCarava's photographic book *The Sweet Flypaper of Life* in this phrasing, and certainly one can see the affinities between the two explorations and celebrations of black family life.

One More River to Cross insists on civil rights as an enterprise of the heteronormative black family, of mothers, fathers, and children together. Marianne Hirsch theorizes the role of family photographs in terms that I would like to extend in order to discern the text's activist effect. Hirsch argues, "Recognizing an image as *familial* elicits a specific kind of readerly or spectorial look, and *affiliative look* through which we are sutured into the image and through which we adopt the image into our own familial narrative."[40] Following Hirsh, witnessing a family image has an affiliative effect: we place ourselves into the family image, or at least consider our own families in relationship to the images we read. In Myers's book, readers witness hundreds of black families living what he calls a story of "triumph and endurance" (151); in doing so, we recognize that, as Myers says, "the journey continues" into the present day. The text calls out to an African American reader to recognize the continuity of her family's experience with those of other black families. Integration is absent from Myers's narrative, a move that locates activism in the black home (rather than in white acceptance and incorporation) and dislocates activism visually from images of black-child victimhood and sacrifice so familiar to civil rights discourse. Further, Myers's text includes images of segregated living spaces—black towns in the West and South, urban sites in northern cities, rural communities in the South—a move that resists the teleology of integration as a solution to civil rights struggles. Segregation is not necessarily evil, but it can be generative.[41] For Myers, segregated spaces, including the black family unit, become the source of civil rights triumph. Myers courageously resists the civil rights consensus narrative, particularly its insistence on integration, interracial amity, and the closure of the civil rights story. Considering the popular stigmatization of black neighborhoods and communities in the 1990s, Myers's text radically asserts the viability of black collectivity as a means of social change.

TONI MORRISON'S *REMEMBER*: IMAGINING INNOCENCE AND AMITY

Toni Morrison's *Remember: The Journey to School Integration* (2004) permits us to recognize the hazards facing writers who recount the movement for young people. Aiming to engage a young audience emotionally and imaginatively with the integration movement (figuring it as a shared memory that no twenty-first-century child could literally possess), texts like Morrison's wish to avoid the confinement and stasis of documentary photography; as Morrison's preface insists, the struggle for integration should matter to young people: "So remember. Because you are a part of it. . . . In every way, this is your story."[42] Although Morrison includes a preface to the book, brief introductions to each section, and informational appendixes, the bulk of the book consists of individual fictionalized narrative glosses on images of the civil rights movement. In her response to particular evidentiary photography, her fictional glosses elide particularity and insist, somewhat problematically, on universal child desire for interracial friendship. Such friendship is not a destructive ideal in and of itself; but Morrison frames history through that lens and, in doing so, sometimes smooths over the bumps in the rough road to social progress. The focus here on friendship in rendering history also provides an accessible, uncomplicated solution to questions of inequality.

Morrison's *Remember* participates in that long tradition of imagining racial progress through amity, and of offering photographic depictions of friendship that bear the weight of evidentiary truth. Her book stages interracial friendship as both the cause and reward of school integration. In doing so, the book harks back to texts that use photographs in order to locate black children as potential friends of white readers. Just as Jane Shackelford's white child reader at a book signing pleads with his mother to support his friendship with Rex, the black protagonist of *My Happy Days* (1944), calling out "Look at him . . . ! He's *almost white!*," Morrison's book asks its reader to embrace interracial friendship by looking with care at the similarities across races between children (in terms of affect rather than, in Shackelford's case, skin color). But in contrast to Shackelford and other earlier photobook writers, Morrison explains history through the lens of friendship rather than employing images of amity to spur social change. In focusing on affect, her book elides the complexities of children's actual political investments in civil rights activities in favor of a representation of childhood (black and white) as essentially innocent, welcoming, and somewhat naive. Because her book is structured as a "journey" toward school integration, as the title suggests, my reading will first consider the text's construction of innocence and then move linearly through the narrative. In the journey recounted by the book, the topic of education becomes nearly incidental; instead, the book permits us to consider the risks of emphasizing child friendship within contemporary civil rights discourse. Here, friendship erases the particularities of history and the agency of individual civil rights workers, leaping over the real challenges of the struggle as well as any discussion of hard-won political rights. Sweet, innocent, untrammeled friendship trumps all else in Morrison's text.

Robin Bernstein's discussion of the uses of racialized innocence applies particularly well to *Remember*. Bernstein describes the severing of blackness from sentimentalized innocence in the nineteenth century, explaining that "angelic white children were contrasted with pickaninnies so grotesque as to suggest that only white children *were* children," resulting in the "exclusion of black youth from the category of childhood."[43] Bernstein explores the way in which black civil rights figures in the 1920s and 1950s resisted such exclusion, focusing on the installation of childhood innocence in the black-child body through performance; Bernstein is particularly interested in the affective power of black children's tears resulting from the Kenneth and Mamie Clark doll-play experiments prefacing and sustaining the *Brown v. Board of Education* decision in 1954. Black children during the civil rights era, Bernstein argues, performed innocence in terms appreciable to white culture; their performance of innocence offered evidence for political and social change, and as black children demonstrated their suffering under racism, the civil rights movement established that "children's daily lives are political" and destroyed the idea that children "exist in a state of holy ignorance."[44] Inherited from nineteenth-century cultural texts and practices, "[i]nnocence was not a literal state of being unraced but was, rather, the performance of not-noticing, a performed claim of slipping beyond social categories."[45] Although Bernstein is interested in Little Eva as an example of this imperviousness, I see Morrison's text staging a similar kind of "holy ignorance," one in which the slippage outside of social boundaries comes not through a total ignorance of race—for certainly the children in the book are aware of their raced status—but through questioning and undoing the fact of white-child racism. White children's racial imperviousness is necessary for friendship orthodoxy to work.

Remember begins with a black child asking about white-child racism: "The law says I can't go to school with white children. Are they afraid of my socks, my braids? I am seven years old. Why are they afraid of me?" (8). The book moves further into questioning the nature of white-child feeling when the first day of integration arrives. The child narrator asks, "I thinks she likes me, but how can I tell? What will I do if she hates me?" (23). The photograph of a classroom in Fort Myers, Virginia, in 1954, foregrounds two girls, one black and one white, both with indeterminate expressions (Figure 5.5). Although their bodies face each other, they do not look into each other's eyes; the white girl scrutinizes the

Figure 5.5. Two girls look at each other in a school integration scene.
Copyright by Corbis Corporation.

black child, objectifying the black girl and placing the potential of the friendship in the hands of herself, the white child. Even the narration, which seems
to offer the black child interiority, focuses instead on the judgment of the white
child and on the black girl's inability to know whiteness or handle rejection:
"What will I do if she hates me?" This black innocent, in Bernstein's terms,
anticipates performing emotional pain that might come through rejection.

Happily, that rejection does not come, as the next few pages depict interracial groups of children studying and playing together. The image that follows
the photograph just described resolves quite easily the tension of "What will

Figure 5.6. White students endorse an integration poster. Copyright by Corbis Corporation.

I do if she hates me?": a white girl points to a phrase on a display board, "Let's All Work Together," while looking again at a black subject who does not meet her eyes (Figure 5.6). As the reader turns the page, then, the question of white-child racism gets answered swiftly, for the book announces white ingenuousness and partnership.

When white children are depicted visually as racist in documentary photographs from the integration moment, Morrison questions the children's certitude and offers prose that complicates the "truth" of the photos. Two linked images of children in protest action permit a consideration of the effects of language and of framing on the documentary image. The first, from Clinton,

Tennessee, in 1956, offers an image of children objecting to desegregation at their high school. This image is tightly framed, suggesting the confinement and limitation of the children's perspective. The next image, from Hillsboro, Ohio, in 1956, depicts a group of black children and adults marching in protest of exclusion from white schools. The photograph fills the page, leaving no borders to suggest the limitation of what is framed within. Morrison's caption to the white-boy protesters places their conviction into question by offering the imagined voice of one of the children: "I don't know. My buddies talked me into this. They said it would be fun. It's not, but these guys are my friends and friends are more important than strangers. Even if they're wrong. Aren't they?" (28). Reframing the documentary record, Morrison enables a recognition of the form's exteriority, insisting on the surface nature of photographs: they represent a moment in time but cannot speak, except visually, of the interior life of their subjects, for that life must be imagined. White children here may participate in protests, but they do so in terms of loyalty to friendship and not in terms of racial dynamics. Ending with a question of camaraderie suggests that the white boy is confused about his role in racial politics. He may not be as impervious to social categories as Bernstein's white innocents, but Morrison saturates the scene with a sense of the white child's confusion over the implications of alliances. The approach to white childhood here recalls the claims of innocence made by white adults regarding the integration protests at Little Rock that they witnessed as children. At the 1996 reunion of the Little Rock Nine with white students on the television show *Oprah*, one white former student, David Sontag, declared ingenuousness in describing his daily harassment of the black students: "I am genuinely sorry for any negative things I did at that time. I was really acting as a child that was not prepared."[46] The reduction of the political implications of white children's actions to innocence is a potent means to deny complicity, of course; but it also can be wielded to minimize the experience of black young people in order to facilitate a narrative of friendship and forgiveness. After apologizing and claiming child innocence, Sontag and one of the Little Rock Nine shared a hug.

Remember's insistence on white-child simplicity recasts another of the few images in the book that evoke child racism. A boy and his sister peek out of the back window of a car (Figure 5.7). The boy is dressed in the garb of the Ku Klux Klan, and the sister sticks her tongue out and looks into the distance. Neither the boy nor the girl offers physical gestures demonstrating racism. Even the girl's tongue is not stuck out aggressively or even teasingly but, rather, hangs there in a way that suggests her own dislocation from using her body for mean-

SOUTHERN WHITES ARE
THE NEGROES' BEST
FRIENDS BUT
NO INTEGRATION

Figure 5.7. White children at Ku Klux Klan activity. Copyright by Corbis Corporation.

ing. The boy in the KKK garb crosses his arms easily and offers a crooked smile. His face depicts no aggression, no hostility. He appears unaware of the social implications of his dress, and instead looks eagerly out toward the viewer of the book. The image is jarring, in fact, because of the dissonance between the children's innocent gazes and their context. Even white children raised by bigots appear protected by their status as children. The language on the page across from the image emphasizes parental responsibility for segregation and hate: "When they let us in the school, none of the white students came. Their parents made them stay home" (31). Reflecting back on the child Klan member, we notice that the car is piloted by the children's mother, who sits in the front and refuses to engage the camera. She is the shadowy force behind child racist practice; the children themselves seem unaware of the meaning and practice of segregation. The car image also includes language that hints of the overriding theme of Morrison's text: "Southern Whites Are the Negroes' Best Friends but NO INTEGRATION" (30). White friendship, then, supposedly structures the South; it's a friendship deployed by white adults, however, who mask prejudice with paternalism and insist that bigotry is in everyone's best interest. In friendship, adulthood becomes a version of failed childhood.

Innocent children, both black and white, know better how to stage interracial friendship. I should note that teenagers in *Remember* seem to inhabit a different space from young children, because twice the book pictures teens in conflict with African American students. Given that the book is structured in three sections ("The Narrow Path," "The Open Gate," "The Wide Road"), I will pull out particular moments from each that present the text's progress toward racial amity. In "The Narrow Path," a black child sits in a chair on a porch, braiding the hair of a white doll (Figure 5.8). Such an image bears multiple resonances, of course: first, the Clark doll experiment, in which black children preferred white to black dolls, comes to mind, and Morrison's gloss on the photo in the appendix makes her intentionality clear: "During the *Brown v. Board of Education* trial, an expert in child development presented studies done with children and dolls, which showed that African American children identified white skin as preferable to black skin" (74). The image reifies the Clark critique, as the ghostly white of the doll, framed by the child's dark legs and highlighted by the child's gaze, becomes the center of the focus. The image suggests, as did the Clarks' research, that black children focus on white dolls. Morrison's language, however, adheres to Bernstein's reinterpretation of the Clark experiment by suggesting that the child sees the doll as a doll, and not as an evocation of her negative self-image. The child begins with a discussion of the doll's renaming: "Her name was Betty when she belonged to my cousin. Then her name was Alice when my sister got her. Now she's mine and I call her Jasmine" (12). Ownership conveys power to the child, which she employs in order to reinvent the doll's identity. This play with the doll as a doll, rather than as an indication of the black child's rejection of self, enables the child to perform interracial friendship. As she reinvents the doll's identity, she formulates its racialized relationship: "I like playing with her. She doesn't stick out her tongue

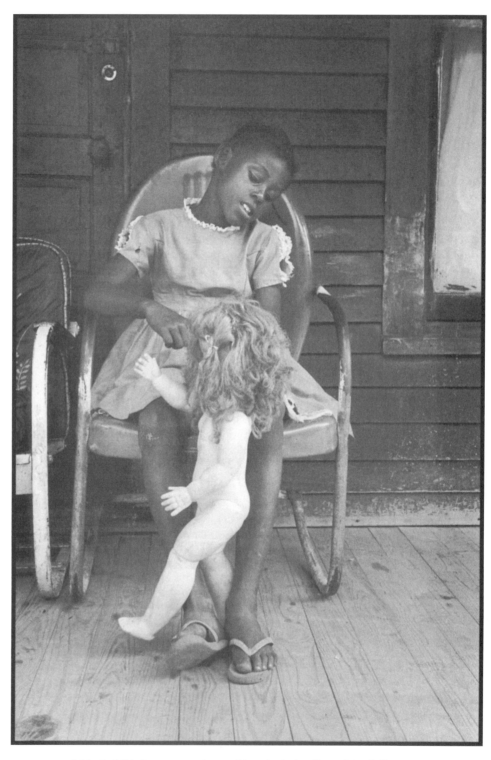

Figure 5.8. A black child sits on a porch, combing the hair of her white doll.
Copyright Bruce Davidson/Magnum Photos.

or call me names. And she doesn't hide behind her mother's dress, pointing at me, when I go into town" (12). Here, in language filtered through doll play, we get some sense of the actual virulence of white-racist childhood. We hear about it secondhand, however, through the child who herself describes the white child as hiding behind the mother and therefore attached to the mother's ideology. Finally, the girl reinvents the white doll as a living white child, the child of the girl's dreams: "She's a good friend, my Jasmine" (12). Black desire for white-child friendship is never under dispute in *Remember*.

The second implication of the image results from the very fact that a black child playing with a white doll appears within a Toni Morrison text. Morrison famously explores the psychologically devastating implications of desiring white childhood through dolls in *The Bluest Eye*, in which girl characters yearn for and puzzle over Shirley Temple dolls. The passage in *Remember* alludes conspicuously to Shirley Temple in the language the child offers about the doll's clothing: "I think her dress was red with white dots and I remember she had a white underslip with lace, and panties too" (12). The doll apparently was wearing the famous polka-dotted dress of Temple's film *Baby Take a Bow* (1934), which was reproduced on Shirley Temple dolls throughout the second half of the twentieth century. In *Remember*, however, Morrison calls up this Shirley Temple allusion only to dismantle it. After describing the clothes, the child says, "They got torn and thrown away. She can't cry Mama anymore. All she has now is yellow hair and green eyes" (12). Tossing aside the costume, the girl has stripped the doll of cultural implication. The doll can then be reinvented, becoming the girl's "good friend" rather than that which should be emulated or desired.

I dwell on the doll passage because conceptually it propels the integration story. The black child imagines white friendship, creates it through doll play, and then moves into the space of integration. She dreams a new world of play with a white friend. Even the image of the daughters of Oliver Brown that closes "The Narrow Path" erases racial conflict by emphasizing parental choice, framing political action as an extension of domestic success: "Our parents sued the Board of Education not because they hate them, but because they love us. They are full of hope but they are determined, too. No matter how narrow the path or how long the journey, all of us are on it together" (16). Racial tension evaporates when the terms are reframed through the domestic; litigation becomes an expression of model parenting. The girls' last statement, "all of us are on it together," suggests again collaboration, a shared path for people across races.

Black-child identity is structured by its impulse toward amity, an impulse that relies on reciprocation from the unbiased white child.

The book's second section, "The Open Gate," focuses on the Supreme Court decision by offering the front page of the *New York Times*, on May 18, 1954, followed by a photograph of the nine white men who prepared the decision. Ordinarily such a photograph might not be troubling, if it were provided in the context of a biography of the court or balanced by images of black litigators; but in a text so insistent on white friendship and the white scrutinizing gaze, an image of nine kindly white men in power takes on a different valence: like the newspaper page that attests to the reality of the decision, the photograph asserts the visual sympathy of white masculinity toward black children and, perhaps, is in tune with conservative reliance on governmental authority in a post-9/11 moment. The remainder of "The Open Gate" offers images focusing on space: a black teenage girl sits at a lunch table while a group of white teen girls sit at an adjacent table. The text reads, "I eat alone. No one looks at me. I can't (won't) look at them" (40). As the reader turns the page, the narrative progresses from sharing space together to budding interracial friendship: in the first image, a black and a white teenage girl smile at each other as they finish lunch (the tension of the page before of sitting alone in the lunchroom becomes effectively resolved), with the caption "I see in her face just a girl. She sees in my face another girl. Maybe not friends, but simply girls together" (42). In the second image, a black and a white girl share space in a bathroom and put on makeup together. The movement toward friendship thus appears afoot, when suddenly the narrative is interrupted with images from Montgomery, New Orleans, and New York City, which depict very small children being harassed by crowds of adults. The child narrative voice wonders, "But didn't grownups used to be little kids who knew how it felt to be scared?" (45). This puzzlement is quite telling, for it points to the disparity between child and adult perspective on race (reiterating the superiority of innocent childhood and asking for readers to mourn its loss) and insists on affect rather than justice as a rationale for integration.

In the last section, "The Wide Road," interracial friendship takes flight. As the scope of the integration effort expands from schools to workplaces and restaurants, we witness interracial friendship on the picket line, at restaurant protests, and in freedom marches. An image of a white and a black woman at a lunch-counter demonstration features the women alone, side by side, as though it were the two of them against the world. The text reads, "[I]t's not all that easy. You can feel the eyes, the silence, the hate. What makes it worth it is we are going to change things; what helps is doing it with a friend" (55). The text moves to a close by pointing back to images of child interracial friendship: a group of students pledge allegiance to the flag, two boys work together on a school project, and two girls smile as they eat together in the school cafeteria. Martin Luther King Jr. and Rosa Parks appear briefly in celebratory images, framed by language that figures the civil rights struggle as the resolution of loneliness: "[I]f I ever feel helpless or lonely I just have to remember that sometimes all it takes is one person. Then the loneliness melts away" (62, 65). The attendant image is of King's "I Have a Dream" oration, a speech that serves here to assuage child loneliness; such a move erases all particularities of the struggle, placing King within the rubric of friendship alongside many of the whites in the text. This move also emphasizes the suffering black child, one who might experience fear and isolation, the possibility of distress pointing again to the black youth's status as innocent. The book concludes by first showing a black child drawing figures on a chalkboard, with the narration explaining, "I am drawing a Magic Man. He can make anything happen. Anything at all. Just wait and see" (69). We have just witnessed King on the mall in Washington, a friend to the wounded child, and he here becomes, by implication, the "Magic Man" who eliminates racial tension, making friendship possible, understood in terms appreciable only through child fantasy. The narrative concludes with an image of two girls, one black and one white, holding hands through the bus window, and the statement "Anything can happen. Anything at all. See?" (71). The "Magic Man" fulfills the black-child desire for interracial friendship, permitting the willing white child to reach across the boundary of the bus-window frame to grasp her friend's hand. Public discourse in America still often constructs race relations as a "problem" to be solved, the resolution of which in integration narratives like Morrison's often permits a false version of American democratic victory.

Morrison's narrative voice is fictive. Her narrator imagines intimate, personal voices for subjects within images. This strategy is fundamentally self-reflexive, for by yoking together a form associated with nonfiction—the photograph—and a voice conspicuously fictional, Morrison nudges readers to recognize the constructedness of her narrative, to recognize the stitches and seams in this hybrid representation. We can then reflect on the process of representation, because our attention has been drawn to the constructedness of both forms. Morrison herself suggests that her reader be aware of the authorial invention in her preface: "To enliven the trip, I have imagined the thoughts and feelings of some of the people in the photographs chosen to help tell this story" (3). The preface subsequently offers the kind of specificity, factuality, and balance one might seek in a rendering of the complexities of the civil rights effort. The introductions to each section also offer concrete information on the shape of the movement, as do the appendixes. These apparatuses enhance the productive tension between the fictional voices within each section and the nonfictional photographic form. Such a tension permits readers to recognize that Morrison's voice is that of her imagination. Morrison's emphasis on interracial friendship thus becomes one element within a range of possibilities, one version of the internal lives of the subjects, as we become more aware that we have access only to the surface of the subjects through the images. Despite the limitations of emphasizing interracial friendship as a solution to civil rights problems, the book's generic hybridity enables an openness regarding the imagining of history. In giving voice to "ordinary people" (5), Morrison's book propels readers to imagine the inner lives of those anonymous individuals in photographs of the civil rights movement, to connect with them emotionally. Morrison asks in the preface, "Why offer memories you do not have? Remembering can be painful, even frightening. But it can also swell your heart and open your mind" (5). Although the selection and interpretation of images within the book might emphasize, for good or for ill, the liberating possibilities of friendship, Morrison asks the reader himself to become engaged in representation through the imaginative process. "Memory" becomes a construction, a creation that can be staged by the reader, and that staging engages the surface—a surface potentially generative and potentially inhibitive—offered by photographs.

RUBY BRIDGES'S *THROUGH MY EYES*:
MYTH AND NARRATIVE FRUSTRATION

One of the most influential nonphotographic images of the civil rights movement depicts young Ruby Bridges integrating William Frantz Elementary School in New Orleans, Louisiana, in November 1960. *The Problem We All Live With*, Norman Rockwell's 1963 oil painting of Bridges, first appeared as an illustration in the January 14, 1964, issue of *Look* magazine. In the painting, Ruby walks to school flanked by four U.S. marshals whose faces are cut off by the top edge of the image; smashed tomatoes and the scrawled word *Nigger* appear on the wall behind her. Bridges is not mentioned by name in the painting's title or in *Look* magazine, but photographs of the child being escorted to school by federal agents circulated widely in the media, rendering her image—a lone girl in a white dress with a bow in her hair—iconographic and inspirational to Rockwell. Bridges's photographic picture book *Through My Eyes* mentions that Ruby herself was unfamiliar with the piece. She explains, "It wasn't until

I was eighteen that I even found out that the artist Norman Rockwell had made me a subject in a painting."[47] Similarly, Bridges describes her inability to identify herself in filmic and photographic representations of her integration experience: "As a grown woman, I watched the public television series *Eyes on the Prize*, about the civil rights movement, and my mother had to point out that some of the old film footage was of me" (60). Unable to see herself in images representing the movement, even if those images were coded as documentary, Bridges, in an epilogue to her picture book, admits, "It's taken me a long time to own the early part of my life" (60). She offers a photograph of herself with the two U.S. marshal escorts, holding a poster of Rockwell's painting as a form of reconciliation with the past and with public representation. Her early life articulated, mediated, and circulated through images, Bridges resolves her text by offering a photographic reunion with the white men, faceless representatives of state power in Rockwell's painting, here rendered familiar and avuncular. This concluding photograph not only makes the marshals visible but also reconciles Ruby to the role that images have played in the public articulation of her civil rights activism.

Through My Eyes reconstitutes history by reproducing and narrativizing iconic photographs. If Bridges was unaware of Rockwell's painting and unable to see herself in documentary coverage, her photobook becomes an effort to engage the images that have defined her to a larger public, and to intervene through language and images—some from her own personal collection—in order to describe her experience of school integration and national notice. My attention to Bridges's rich text focuses on three areas. First, by amassing representations of Ruby's history and yoking them to a version of her child voice, the book intimates Bridges's frustration with her role in the movement, a daring articulation that emerges by reading her narrative voice alongside the iconic images. Second, the structure of the book demonstrates, purposefully, Bridges's inability to tell the story wholly "through her eyes," because public mediations bear certain inevitable valences of sacrifice and courage. Bridges plays with those expectations in order to reveal an oppositional experience, one that emphasizes her powerlessness and her very real fear of physical violence. Finally, her story operates expressly within the context of the ethos of friendship narratives in the mid-1990s, as it emphasizes her attachment to Mrs. Henry, her teacher, and her parallels to courageous white children. However, the accomplishment of the text is in its foreclosure of friendship as a solution to racial and educational inequity. As a book that serves Hall's desire for an unfinished civil rights project, *Through My Eyes* stresses Ruby's abandonment after the moment of integration and offers an afterword that stresses the persistent difficulties of education and urban life in New Orleans.

Through My Eyes is a quietly furious book.[48] Bridges begins by constructing her younger self as an unwilling and unknowing participant in the integration effort. She says, "When I was six years old, the civil rights movement came knocking at the door. It was 1960, and history pushed in and swept me up in a whirlwind" (4). After Ruby performed well on a school-board test, the NAACP contacted her family and then visited her house to urge the family to volunteer Ruby for integration. Bridges subtly suggests that the civil rights organization impelled the choice: "They pressured my parents and made a lot of promises" (12). On the first day of school, Ruby's mother expects to find at her door members of the NAACP, but instead four stern U.S. marshals, white men, escort her and Ruby to the school. Bridges constructs the moment of integration in terms evocative of celebration, only to suggest her complete lack of understanding about the moment's political implications and the threat to herself and her family: "There were barricades and people shouting and policemen everywhere. I thought maybe it was Mardi Gras, the carnival that takes place in New Orleans every year. Mardi Gras was always noisy" (16). The language continuously marks Ruby's inability to comprehend the situation, for she is impressed by the size of the school and concludes, "The policemen at the door and the crowd behind us made me think this was an important place. It must be college, I thought to myself" (16). Bridges's understated misapprehensions, coupled with the critique of the NAACP, bring into relief a sense of Bridges's frustration at being employed in this effort.

The images attached to her naive language make plain the threat to the child and her family. Although Ruby may not have understood the crowds, policemen, and noise, a reader witnesses these scenes in the images attached to her description. The first depicts lines of white police officers (shown outside another school at which integration protests took place, McDonogh), and the next depicts a crowd of white male segregationists. Both of these images suggest that the integration debate is white men's terrain; also, Bridges refuses at this point to offer an image of herself climbing the steps into William Frantz School on the morning of November 14th, an iconic image of the civil rights movement. Instead, just before her description of the day, she offers a photograph of white children and mothers entering the schoolhouse. Not only do these images refuse triumphalism, they also place the focus not on the little black girl in the white dress but on white terrain, white debate, and white hatred. By absenting herself visually, Bridges affirms her own sense of dislocation from the

Figure 5.9. Ruby Bridges leaves the William Frantz School, in New Orleans, Louisiana, November 1960. Copyright by Corbis Corporation.

political and social implications of the event. When Ruby finally appears in the school context, the image focuses on her, and the language again reveals the child's experiential disconnection (Figure 5.9). She misunderstands the commotion resulting from white mothers who came to the school to remove their children ("All I saw was confusion. I told myself that this must be the way it is in a big school" [18]) and concludes, after spending the day with her mother in the principal's office, "I had thought my new school would be hard, but the first day was easy" (18). The images in this section insist on the reader's awareness of racial tensions and the threat to Ruby, whereas her own narration and visual absence—except when departing the school—create the child as uninformed and suggest the author's dissatisfaction with being employed politically.

A turning point in the book occurs after Ruby exits the school after her first day. The narration continues to position Ruby as uninformed about the tumult around her; she teaches a friend to jump rope to a chant she heard and repeats: "Two, four, six, eight, we don't want to integrate" (20). Her father concludes the section "Going Home" by using terms familiar to conventional representations of Ruby's experience: "That night when he came home from work, he said I was his 'brave little Ruby'" (20). The section ends with that comment, Ruby's silence on her supposed bravery suggesting her inability to engage directly or deny her public construction. Directly across from this narration appears the most disturbing image in Bridges's book. A crowd of children and adults, carrying the Confederate flag, segregationist signs, and what appears to be a burned cross, stand outside the school (Figure 5.10). The photo's striking element, however, is that it contains a black baby doll in a coffin. Decorated with fake flowers, the coffin is carried by a white boy whose face is half obscured. This image makes palpable the threat to Ruby, as she observes when considering the events of her first day at school: "Many of the boys carried signs and said awful things, but most of all I remember seeing a black doll in a coffin, which frightened me more than anything else" (21). Bridges tells us outright of her terror, which had not been a consideration in her previous naive narration, and as readers we consider what it would mean for Ruby to face an avatar of herself, ironically eulogized by the white crowd. Many of the figures in this photograph are smiling. They seem to take pleasure in the idea of the dead black child. They celebrate her death.

What does this image suggest about the trope of the martyred child that is so central to consensus memory of the civil rights movement? First, it focuses our attention on the objectification of the child, here transformed into a doll, a plaything for a white mob. It also turns on its head the uses of the martyred child for African American activists. This martyred child directs us explicitly toward white menace rather than noble purposefulness. It evokes the legacy of abuse of black dolls, as Robin Bernstein's work articulates, here taken to confront its human analogue in Ruby, and her emotional response makes plain the way the civil rights movement exploded the "whiteness and obliviousness" model of childhood innocence.[49] The scene announces both a real threat to Ruby's life and the anticipatory joy of white masses, including white children, in destroying the black child. No sense of admirable martyrdom can emerge from

Figure 5.10. A segregationist protest includes an African American doll in a coffin.
Copyright by Corbis Corporation.

this devastating moment. And the reader's recognition of Ruby's fear, offered through her admission coupled with the potency of the image, chafes against the father's concluding platitude. Why should a child—an innocent—have to be brave in the face of incomprehensible racial terror? Why should a child take on the role of warrior when she does not understand the political landscape? These real questions are made tangible by the juxtaposition of this photograph and Ruby's naive school story.

This alarming image fractures Ruby's narrative. Whereas the page layout before this image includes text boxes containing quotations from Bridges's mother as well as *New York Times* and *Good Housekeeping* coverage, after the image of the doll in the coffin, the narrative turns expressly toward other voices and additional participatory subjects. The palpability of racial violence in that image renders impossible a celebratory narrative of exceptionalism, that of the single brave child facing racist mobs. Bridges turns to offering others' stories instead of glorifying her own participation in any uncomplicated integration story. The next chapter is titled "My First White Teacher," which focuses on Mrs. Henry, the Boston transplant who agreed to teach Ruby. The narrative then turns toward mediated versions of Bridges's story in an effort to destabilize the first-person-narrative perspective. Bridges describes John Steinbeck's attendance at the scene of integration and quotes the section of *Travels with Charley* that describes Ruby. She reproduces here Rockwell's painting alongside Steinbeck's words. This fracturing of perspectives allows a reader to understand the way in which popular culture mythologized Ruby. The quotation from Steinbeck emphasizes Ruby's objectification in the public eye: she is "the littlest Negro girl you ever saw," with a "face and little legs . . . very black against the white" of her dress. Her fear is described through the animal and the object: "[T]he whites of her eyes showed like those of a frightened fawn. The men turned her around like a doll."[50] Objectification becomes constelled in the narrative, as we witness the whites constructing her as a dead doll-child in a coffin, then see Rockwell's inspirational child marching into the schoolhouse, and finally observe Steinbeck's fawnlike fearful doll. Later in the story, we hear from Robert Coles, the psychologist who studied and wrote about Ruby's experience; the text box attending Bridges's description of his interview with her emphasizes Coles's interpretation of Ruby's resilience: "Ruby had a will and used it to make an ethical choice; she demonstrated moral stamina; she possessed honor, courage."[51] All of these totalizing interpretations of Ruby's life appear within the text alongside a range of constructions of the event drawn from media sources and individuals. This assemblage of public mediations of her story is intentional, given that, particularly after the doll in the coffin, she moves away from telling her story and into describing others' impressions of the events. The phrase "through my eyes," the book's title, refers, then, both to the early sections of the text, which offer a construction of Bridges's naive perspective, and her adult recollection of the way in which her experience became an outline onto which the media, writers, and artists could inscribe meaning. She offers multiple public constructions of her experience, rendering fragmentation through her eyes. Ruby as a child in the story remains powerless, not only in sitting "quietly huddled with Mrs. Henry" as riots shake New Orleans (32) but also against the scripting of her story by others. Even though she did not see Rockwell's portrait until she was eighteen and did not read Steinbeck as a six-year-old, the adult author employs pastiche strategically in order to demonstrate the way in which her child experience became common property.

This narrative fracturing involves not only media representations of Ruby's story but also reflections on others' experience of the moment of integration. Bridges offers analogues to her experience by describing three black girls, Leona Tate, Tessie Prevost, and Gaile Etienne, who integrated McDonogh Elementary School in New Orleans on the same day as Ruby, in November 1960. She also describes two white families that permitted their daughters to attend Frantz School with Ruby, only to be harassed by mobs. Bridges describes receiving support from people in her neighborhood, from affluent African Americans, and from Eleanor Roosevelt. But after the image of the doll in the coffin, the bulk of her narrative and the weight of her affection fall on her teacher, Mrs. Henry. A six-page sequence of narrative and photographs emphasizes Bridges's perception of the differences in perspective between herself as a child and the vision of Mrs. Henry. These differences erect interracial friendship as the trope through which Ruby initially survives psychologically. In the first sequence, Ruby describes the "fun" she and Mrs. Henry had together: "She was more like my best friend than just an ordinary teacher. She was a loving person, and I knew she cared about me" (40). Ruby adopts Mrs. Henry's Boston accent, explaining again through naïveté, "I didn't sound like my brothers and sister, but I didn't know why" (41). She concludes the section by emphasizing her affection for her teacher: "Little by little, I grew to love Mrs. Henry. We became very attached to each other" (41). If we consider the place of interracial friendship to teleologies of integration success in the 1990s, Bridges's strategy here seems quite deliberate. Ruby loves Mrs. Henry, and the teacher feels affection for her student. Bridges constructs here a sense of hope for racial reconciliation through friendship. Even the images presented elide the political and highlight the personal. Ruby's close-up photograph, with broad smile revealing missing front teeth, recalls a school photograph and is captioned "Mrs. Henry's Only Student"; Barbara Henry's photograph emphasizes her beautiful dress and a decorative domestic space. The images, framed neatly as though they were portraits for a mantelpiece, sit alongside each other, separated only by the gutter between the facing pages.

The next sequence of photographs and narrative draw outward from the intimacy of Ruby's narrative. A two-page quotation from Mrs. Henry describes her affection for Ruby in terms that seem to surprise the woman: "It was a joy to go to school each day and to have her as—well—my child. . . . I think Ruby became 'my child'!" (43). Mrs. Henry then spends much of her narrative talking about her own sense of exclusion from the other teachers and administrators at the school and her inability to talk about her experience with Ruby's mother or with her community. She concludes by admitting of Ruby, "I knew she was lonely," and turning to abstraction when describing Ruby to contemporary children: "They feel they finally have a hero who is like them. Ruby's story allows children to feel they, too, can do very important things and they, too, can be heroes. . . . Ruby was a star" (44). The images that appear here, late in the book, finally depict Ruby entering the school; they are full-page, iconic images of the tiny child accompanied by U.S. marshals. Through Mrs. Henry's eyes, Ruby has become that hero, that star who acted with courage. The relationship Ruby seeks becomes overpowered by the politics of her role in this sequence. These iconic photographs, unframed and bleeding to the edge of the page, signal the impossibility of the intimate containment of friendship and anticipate the failure of the friendship orthodoxy to solve interracial tensions.

In the last pages of the narrative, the friendship that sustained Ruby suddenly evaporates when Mrs. Henry fails to appear as Ruby's teacher in second grade. Mrs. Henry explains her return to Boston in a text block: "[I]t was very hard to let go of Ruby. Even so, I wasn't sorry to leave New Orleans. Integration had been a shattering experience. After New Orleans, Boston seemed like a very appealing, uncomplicated place" (52). For Ruby, the loss of Mrs. Henry became her most shattering experience: "I felt very alone again. There was no one to talk to, no one to explain things. My heart was broken"; Bridges describes "losing my teacher and best friend" as the major devastation of that year (52). The silence around that confusing, traumatic year of school was paralyzing: "No one spoke about the previous year. It was as though it had never happened. At home, there were no NAACP people coming to visit, no packages in the mail" (52). Her new teacher then mocks Ruby's adopted Boston accent, and Ruby attempts to form her words differently, to assimilate back into a southern drawl. The text concludes with subtlety and elusion: "William Frantz School was integrated, but the long, strange journey had changed me forever" (53). Ruby's understatement becomes more devastating by virtue of Mrs. Henry's distance and mythologizing; in a text box, Mrs. Henry talks about looking at her photograph of Ruby—the gap-toothed image of Ruby that emblematizes their friendship—over the course of years. Searching the picture as though that representation summoned an actual child, Mrs. Henry suggests, "I would check every once in a while to make sure Ruby was still there." Her language suggests loss in terms that render Ruby dead, memorialized in image, rather than school-aged and alive in New Orleans: "Over the years, I told my children about her again and again. I had to keep the memory alive." Finally, Mrs. Henry suggests that the school wouldn't welcome a visit from her, and she devastatingly concludes, "But I used to wonder how Ruby was doing" (52). The effect of yoking Ruby's despair with Mrs. Henry's inaction yields a potent critique of the 1990s friendship orthodoxy.[52] In spite of her avowed affection for Ruby, Mrs. Henry sees through her own eyes a difficult, politicized landscape to which she would not return. Ruby is stranded in that landscape.

In the afterword, "Let Me Bring You Up to Date," Bridges stages her most direct critique on the Ruby Bridges mythology. She describes her survival of integration as dependent on obedience to her mother and on her familiarity with responsibility, concluding, "Still, I sometimes feel I lost something that year. I feel as if I lost my childhood. It seems that I have always had to deal with some adult issues" (56). Shadowed by an ideal of childhood insularity and safety, Bridges mourns her politicized youth. Although she does not address the political stakes of black children generally, when she discusses her own difficulties getting into college and the death of her youngest brother in a 1990s shooting at a housing project, the text suggests that post-integration black youths still tread a rough path. She does speak more generally when she reflects on the condition of William Frantz School, which her nephews attend: "As is true of most inner-city schools, there's never enough funding to keep William Frantz up to current standards or to offer the students the same opportunities they would receive in some of the suburban schools I've been fortunate to visit. The kids are being segregated all over again. There aren't enough good resources available to them—and why is that?" (58). If Bridges participates in the values of integration and imagines herself an activist, it is only in adulthood, the afterword argues, with the establishment of the Ruby Bridges Foundation: "For a long time, I was tempted to feel bitter about the school integration experience, not understanding why I had to go through it alone. Now I know it was meant to be that way. People are touched by the story of a black child who was so alone" (60).

Bridges may be right. In the consensus narrative of the civil rights moment, the single child determined to change the world bears significant sentimental and individualistic valences; these ideals serve the same purposes as do conservative representations of Rosa Parks as simply a tired seamstress who wanted to get off her feet, rather than an activist trained by the Highlander Folk School. The "child will lead them" motif also patronizes the considered investment of adults in the civil rights movement. Further, individualism becomes the value, rather than collective social action. Of course, collectivity in practice placed Ruby at the center of its effort, with devastating effects for the child. The sense of Ruby's aloneness, appealing for conservative and sentimental attraction to the myth, might be said to call on the reader's sympathy. But Bridges resists in her picture book the kind of sympathy that would sentimentalize child political action; in fact, there is no willing child political action to critique or patronize. Bridges denies any celebratory version of school integration in depicting her frustration and alienation in and with the early 1960s. For Bridges, the refractions of her story, shattering the first-person narrative, violate the integrity of her childhood. She does pragmatically recognize the power of the sentimental in versions of her life, offering a preface to her own book by Harry Belafonte that concretizes her meaning for many Americans: "By this simple act of courage, Ruby moved the hearts and opened the minds of millions of people. Her story was and is an inspiration."[53] But unlike children's texts that spotlight willing participation of children in the movement, like Cynthia Levinson's *We've Got a Job: The 1963 Birmingham Children's March* (2012) and Ellen Levine's *Freedom's Children: Young Civil Rights Activists Tell Their Own Stories* (1993), Bridges daringly constructs herself as a confused but obedient child who did not understand the implications of her efforts, and she stunningly argues that the time to act on behalf of black children in schools is now.

CAROLE BOSTON WEATHERFORD'S *BIRMINGHAM, 1963*: ANIMATING LOSS

Although Bridges does not envision herself as a martyr with intentionality and willing commitment, consensus memory nevertheless frames her history in terms of courage. Of course, the four children killed at the Sixteenth Street

Baptist Church in 1963 are most insistently framed in memory as martyrs for the movement. Morrison's book ends with a dedication to the four little girls; their photographs spread in an arc across the page, and Morrison speaks in their collective voice: "Things are better now. Much, much better. But remember why and please remember us." The narrative voice then shifts into third person: "Their lives short, their deaths quick. Neither were in vain."[54] Morrison leaves these four iconic girls as the last images in the book, proposing that readers embark on the kind of memory work Morrison has enacted in the book by considering imaginatively the lives and deaths of these particular girls. Unlike Bridges, who specifies involvement in underserved schools as a way to extend the movement, Morrison imagines the four little girls calling out for the reader to consider their lives; but implying that to "remember why" social progress happened relies on remembering the children as sacrificial. Morrison asks for a kind of partnership between the viewer and the four girls in photographs in which the viewer will respond empathetically and imaginatively through memory work, keeping memory alive while at the same time fixing the girls as a group in death. Softly curved, framed photographs of the girls in a gentle arc place the children in a state of memorial.

Carole Boston Weatherford's photobook *Birmingham, 1963* takes up Morrison's proposal—remember us—differently, by constructing a fictional poetic voice to describe the events around the bombing. For Weatherford, the losses of Birmingham include but extend beyond the children's deaths. Her narrator, a child who is turning ten years old and who has been involved in movement protest, offers a consistent perspective across the story, unlike the multiple voices in Morrison's text that respond to each image. Weatherford's narrator is pointedly *not* one of the girls killed by the bombing but, rather, a fictional surrogate, a peer who witnesses and connects emotionally to the events. The book's cover features an image of the church in rubble, set next to a vertical line of photographs of each of the girls. A sense of dread thus shadows Weatherford's depiction of black childhood, complicating any assumption of childhood insularity. Further, unlike Morrison in her somewhat static version of white-child innocence and unwavering black desire for white friendship, Weatherford tracks her narrator's growing awareness of the brutality of racism and the risks of political involvement. In truth, part of the power of Weatherford's text lies in its quiet, controlled poetic voice. As Angela Sorby, Joseph T. Thomas, and Richard Flynn explain in their essay on the 2008 *Lion and Unicorn* Excellence in North American Poetry Award (Weatherford's book was an honor book), the "deceptively simple, skillful free-verse" bears emotional weight through its economical and sure-handed diction.[55] The first lines of the book emphasize not childish naïveté but social commitment and its palpable effects. The narrator begins,

> The year I turned ten
> I missed school to march with other children
> For a seat at whites-only lunch counters.
>
> Like a junior choir, we chanted "We Shall Overcome."
> Then, police loosed snarling dogs and fire hoses on us,
> And buses carted us, nine hundred strong, to jail.[56]

The attendant photograph shows young people on the picket line during the Birmingham "Children's Crusade" of May 1963. The central figure, a young woman, looks directly at the camera, holding a sign that reads "Can a Man Love God and Hate His Brother?" Considering the book's later exploration of faith lost and the atrocity of murder committed at a church, the sign seems thematically effective. We begin, then, with young people's investment in the movement, with their sense of solidarity in the face of state oppression, and with the narrator's choice of activism over conventional schooling.

When Weatherford does draw on symbols of innocent childhood, she uses the visual to question innocence's solidity. The narrator often describes herself in relationship to her family. For instance, in recounting her tenth birthday, the narrator seems liminal, set between playful scuffles with her younger brother and her parents' gentle recognition of her growth: "But Mama allowed me my first sip of coffee / And Daddy twirled me around the kitchen / In my patent-leather cha-cha heels" (10). The images drawn together in the birthday scene follow a pattern we find in the book: the layout places a photographic token of an item associated with childhood on the same page with the narrator's language, and sets on the facing page a full-page photograph of events from 1963 drawn from documentary accounts. The text thus pulses between the documentary record and the perspective of the fictional child, offered through her voice and material relics characterizing her life—here, in the birthday episode, the shoes she wore to church,[57] and in other places her white gloves, white-lace bobby socks, pencils and erasers, Motown 45s, jacks, doll clothes, and so on. That conjoining of personal and public sets a rhythm to the text, as the reader moves back and forth between the narrator's private experience of the tragedy and the public documentary record. This rhythm unsettles a reader's sense that the child's private life could be set safely aside from public engagement. As much as we might wish, seeing the bobby socks, birthday candles, and barrettes, that as a child she might escape the horror that we know is coming, given the book's title and cover, such insularity becomes unattainable. We long for that impossible insularity. The yoking of material artifacts with the child's poetic voice, set against documentary photography, permits an awareness of the intricate sensibilities of a child invested in history, a child who fights with her little brother after practicing church songs and who recognizes injustice and acts, through protest and jailing, to resist. Bernstein argues that the civil rights movement "acknowledged that children's daily lives are political, that children do not exist in a state of holy ignorance";[58] Weatherford articulates this complicated lived experience by fusing material evocations of innocence with the child's daily political implications.

For instance, Weatherford yokes the birthday dance/shoe image with a photograph of a sign indicating a segregated waiting room. In one sense, the photograph visually emphasizes the birthday description and the child's voice; its arrow literally points our attention backward across the page. The content of the image might also suggest a revaluing of segregated spaces, like the family's home, because the family lives in a "colored" room populated by black people joined together not through the force of segregation but by love. The "waiting" of the "waiting room" could signify, in the context of the book, both the movement's anticipation of justice and our own expectation as readers of the culminating events of the book, our sense of dread in waiting for the inevitable. The sign also, of course, draws attention to the South's codification of prejudice through Jim Crow signs; that we have a photograph of the sign insists on the truth of prejudice, for the image makes social codes of the South material, as well as the reader's affirmation that the signs are worthy of reportage, that the facts of southern bias should be remembered.

The final visual element that destabilizes insular childhood innocence in the text is the repetition of fragments of red photographic frames. The fragments appear between the colored-waiting-room sign and the prose birthday description; they appear, in fact, somewhere on every page of the narrator's narrative alongside the images of material culture associated with childhood. Indeed, they appear even on the cover of the book, where they lie on top of the photograph of people marching in civil rights protest. The individuals carry a placard with an image of the church bombing labeled "No More Birminghams." The complexity of this cover image permits us to understand the presence of the red fragments throughout the text. The cover image makes plain the act of construction that takes place in telling history. In order to access the site of the bombing, a viewer must move through nested images: innermost is the image of the church ruins, nested within an image of protesters, framed by an archivist's black border with an identifying number, 9771, written by hand above the photograph. In order to reach back through memory, one much reach back through constructions of history. The red framing fragments intimate two things: the inexorable shaping of historical events through narrative (whether visual or verbal) and the way in which Weatherford's treatment, as its own construction, aims to annihilate the familiar frames that have shaped the already-told story of the four little girls. The fragments of these frames lie scattered across the pages of the narrator's story. Weatherford signals to the reader that she is aware that telling history through image relies on representation shaped by a photographer's (and, in the case of prose, an author's) framing. But shattering those frames permits Weatherford to indicate that she is doing something new in telling the story through a fictionalized child. The shattered frames also suggest the failure of framing, in narratives both visual and verbal, in conveying the heartbreaking loss of four young lives. Red fragments scattered across a black-and-white text suggest bloodshed spilled across the pages of the story; Weatherford described the fragments to me as signifying "the violent and bloody shattering of innocence."[59] And although history, to be shared, must be framed through narrative, the crimson fragments suggest the impossibility of any representation to articulate fully human loss.

Typically, the pattern for remembrance of the deaths of the four little girls stems from Martin Luther King's "Eulogy for the Martyred Children," delivered at the funeral of three of the girls. In the speech, King transformed the individuals into religious icons, suggesting that the children's deaths were best understood as serving the movement: "These children—unoffending, innocent, and beautiful—were the victims of one of the most vicious and tragic crimes ever perpetrated against humanity. Yet they died nobly. They are the martyred heroines of a holy crusade for freedom and human dignity." King describes childhood's new power through a metaphor of voice. "[T]hey have something to say to each of us in their death," King explains, and one might wonder whether such a phrasing suggests that children find the possibility of political expression only in death. Civil rights children have been visually useful as victims of race hatred in a stasis that echoes the fixed location of the subject within photographic images.

Weatherford refuses utility and symbolism in describing the loss of the four girls. First, her fictional narrator places the reader into the mind of a child participant rather than as one looking back through history from a distance. As the narrator waits to sing a solo at a Sunday church service, a shock rattles the "quiet" church (14): "The day I turned ten / Someone tucked a bundle of dynamite / Under the church steps, then lit the fuse of hate" (18). Weatherford offers an image of a Ku Klux Klan member at this point in the narrative, a banner over his head reading "Tonight," rendering the threat of racial violence imminent (Figure 5.11). In turning toward white hatred as the cause of the destruction, the text refocuses attention in a strategy similar to that of Walter Dean Myers when he provides images of lynching and KKK battles. The cause

Figure 5.11. A Ku Klux Klan member stands before a sign that threatens immediate violence.
Courtesy of Birmingham, Alabama, Public Library Archives.

of violence is hatred—both texts take that hatred out of time through the framing of the photograph. Myers does not date or specify the lynching or protest, a mode that launches white hatred out of the confinement of a particular moment in history. For Weatherford, the word *Tonight* performs a similar dislocation, for we anticipate the continuance and immediacy of white hatred rather than see it as confined photographically to a moment that has passed. "Tonight" may be a part of an image from history, but within a narrative propelled by dread, the term suggests continuance outside the frame of the image, perhaps even into the space of the contemporary reader.

Weatherford employs documentary images of the destruction at this point, the familiar becoming new in the poetry attending the images:

> Smoke clogged my throat, stung my eyes.
> As I crawled past crumbled plaster, broken glass,
> Shredded Bibles and wrecked chairs—
> Yelling *Mama! Daddy!*—scared church folk
> Ran every-which-way to get out. (20)

Figure 5.12. The stained-glass window of Jesus at the Sixteenth Street Baptist Church in Birmingham, Alabama. Courtesy Birmingham, Alabama, Public Library Archives.

The narrator then names the four children who were killed, adding a recognition that places them within familial frameworks: *"This is my sister,* a boy cried. *My God!"* (20). The text offers an especially familiar documentary image, that of the stained-glass window with Jesus's face blasted out (Figure 5.12), an image that speaks of the feeling of religious abandonment—both visually, through the gap of Jesus's face, and verbally, through the brother's call out to God and the pastor who reads Psalm 23 on his megaphone: *"The Lord is my shepherd"* (22). Weatherford directs the reader's attention to another dimension of the image, calling the window "the one where He stands at the door" (22). Such a move recalls the narrator's experience, for by offering an image of liminality—Jesus at the threshold—the text points to the idea that the narrator has crossed over into a new sense of herself and the world. Again, documentary images become personalized and particular. The narrator concludes her section of the book by announcing her own loss: "The day I turned ten / There was no birthday cake with candles; / Just cinders, ash, and a wish I were still nine" (28). Like Ruby Bridges, who mourns the loss of her childhood, the speaker looks back through time and seeks a version of childhood set apart from political implication. But though that longing is real, *Through My Eyes* and *Birmingham, 1963* assert from the start that innocence of social implication for a black child, particularly during a moment of social conflict and danger, is an impossibility.

The book concludes with four elegiac poems about the girls who were killed in the blast. Again, Weatherford works against a totalizing estimation of the "four little girls" who became martyrs for the movement; in these poems, the children are individuals with particular families, styles, and interests. Each poem bears with it a photograph of the child subject (Figure 5.13). They are all tightly framed with the caption "In Memoriam" underneath, language that recalls Morrison's employment of the photographic arc to signal the children's location in death. The frame indicates the circumscribed possibilities of their lives, and the close-up on the girls' faces evokes the kind of affective connection generated between photographed child and reader in the texts explored in chapter 1. The frames ask us to linger on their faces. The last two poems project Denise McNair's and Carole Robertson's lives into the future: "Niecie, who always smiled for cameras / And would have been a real go-getter" (34), and "Carole, who thought she might want / To teach history someday / Or at least make her mark on it" (36). These are the final words of the narrative (although there is an author's note on the bombing that follows); the poem points clearly both into Carole's aspirations and into the irony of their achievement, for Carole's mark on history is certainly palpable. Carole's frustrated desire concludes

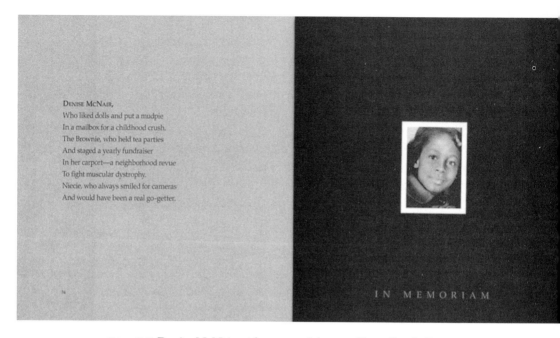

Figure 5.13. Denise McNair with a memorial poem. From Carole Boston Weatherford, *Birmingham, 1963* (Honesdale, Penn.: Wordsong, 2007). Poetry courtesy of Carole Boston Weatherford.

Weatherford's meditation on the disappointments and losses for young people of the civil rights movement. The final section of the book moves beyond the teleology of social change built through martyrdom, the idea that, as in Morrison's text, "[t]heir lives [were] short, their deaths quick. Neither were in vain"; in our being asked to think about what might have been in the lives of each girl, the poems lead us inexorably back to the fact of their deaths, the deaths of valued individuals rather than of a group of martyrs. We impossibly long for their lives just as we impossibly long for childhood insularity. The losses here recall Ruby Bridges's strategy of trying to get the reader to see her as herself, to see through her eyes. Both texts struggle to undo the knot that ties an individual to a mythology, recasting through language iconic images in order to imagine the life of the individual. That struggle to wrest the individual from the myth may be unwinnable, as in the case of Ruby's narrative, fractured by other voices, but the attempt offers a more complex and more considered version of politicized civil rights childhood than the myth alone.

I began with a question: How do photobooks render civil rights unsettled and unfinished rather than seeking documentary closure? The bare tension—between myth and individual story, for instance—nudges the reader to consider history as more open-ended. Focusing on loss, Weatherford draws her story into the current moment, calling us to recognize each individual girl not as a martyr but as a fully human subject. The bombing makes clear the inability of black children to exist in a separate sphere from politics, and the text also refuses the comfort and simplicity of nostalgia (the idea that before the bombing black children were safe), because the narrator is never separate from politicization; the book begins with her commitment to social justice and weaves images of white threat throughout the narrative. Weatherford's book offers no image of American triumph or democratic equality; we are left with the sadness of faith and lives lost. A profound loss for the narrator is in the assumption that civil rights could be achieved peacefully through protest, and perhaps the book troubles the idea that the goals of the civil rights movement were achieved at all. Weatherford dedicates her book this way: "To all who made the ultimate sacrifice for freedom. The struggle continues." Morrison's *Remember* aims to connect the contemporary reader with the integration story, but in doing so the book advances constructions of childhood and of the movement that "solve the problem" of race through friendship and that frame social justice as resolved by the "Magic Man" of Martin Luther King Jr. In contrast, Myers, Bridges, and Weatherford, who also seek to connect the reader with the movement, insist that the progress toward equality continues in the present day. These books construct the black child as always already implicated in politics, and although the texts might seek a safe space for childhood, each book argues that such political implication bears rewards as well as burdens.

Returning to the epigraph that begins this chapter, Audre Lorde's meditation on the losses that result from documentary uses of civil rights photographs, we can consider the implications of photobooks for children. In newspapers marking events, such images become attached to a moment; they are indexical gestures that, when repeated, may inure readers to the horrifying events they track. And yet, paradoxically, these indexical images persist iconographically in memory. When the children's photographic book reappropriates what was once indexical and is now iconic, reframing images through narration, sequence, and juxtaposition against other images, new meanings come to life. Myers makes plain the relationship of civil rights action to everyday people across time by setting unidentified photographs alongside the iconic and narrating the specifics of neither in order to argue for the value of all social-justice efforts. Bridges, in contrast, makes plain the implications of the iconic. Assembling images and narratives of her young life, Bridges illuminates the devastating effects of having one's story told by others. Representations both visual and verbal dissociate Bridges from her own life. Children's books like Morrison's and Weatherford's reinterpret particular photographs in order to reflect on the demands of narrative representation. We become more aware of the implications of image making and of telling stories about those images, more aware of the limitations, compromises, and accomplishments that can result from imagining civil rights. As storytelling fractures the frame of the image, a strategy apparent in the brilliant red fragments scattered through Weatherford's book, we become aware of the new implications that can emerge from the civil rights story offered in a modern context. The friendship orthodoxy so prevalent in children's literature generally, and in photographic texts particularly, has continued to bear weight in the 1990s and 2000s, in part because adults still long for an ideal of childhood innocence. But, as Myers, Bridges, and Weatherford make clear, the politicized experience of children in the past can help shed light on the politicized position of children in the present. These books ask children to recognize the losses of history so that they might participate in the continual communal march toward social justice. The struggle continues, both in word and in image, on the pages of the photographic picture book.

CONCLUSION

A Text for Trayvon

As the Introduction to this book noted, Emmett Till became a child with two photographic identities, one as a dressed-up schoolboy and another as a mutilated body. These paired images echo each other both in print, where they were often coupled, and in memory. Till as schoolboy has been incorporated into children's photographic picture books as a reminder of the "real" child, one associated with innocence and respectability, a characterization that insists on the outrage of the violence committed against him. In the contemporary moment, the death of Trayvon Martin, in February 2012, at the hands of George Zimmerman has similarly spurred two images: one of the boy in the gray hooded sweatshirt and another of the smiling child in the red Hollister T-shirt. Activists and concerned individuals have been drawn to the hoodie image, in large part because the murderer cited the sweatshirt as a reason for his aggressive action (because of its supposed association with criminality). The hoodie has become a central symbol of the injustice of Trayvon's death and has spurred demonstrations of identification with the youth. In protest marches after the murder and in countless blog and Facebook postings, individuals proclaimed, "I am Trayvon Martin," while wearing hooded sweatshirts. Bobby Rush, a congressman from Illinois, was ushered off the House floor in March 2012 for wearing a hoodie in protest of racial profiling. Just as Till's images inspired a generation of activists and ignited the civil rights movement, the image of Trayvon in his sweatshirt has become a rallying point for people concerned about the practical, devastating effects of racism in American culture.

The other image of Trayvon, that of the child in the red Hollister T-shirt, has also prompted controversy. It depicts Trayvon sometime before the murder, but because his age in the picture is unspecified,[1] critics have taken issue with its evocation of childhood innocence. People who wish to create Trayvon as a teenage thug have objected to this photo because it pictures a young man with a warm, nonthreatening, casual confidence. It suits a narrative of childhood ingenuity and virtue. By yoking innocence and blackness in terms legible within popular culture, the red-T-shirt photograph prompts recognition that the murder of a young black male should violate our shared ideals about the protection of childhood. This image reminds us of the upbeat photographs of black children in many of the books analyzed in this study, and the way in which those images have been wielded for civil rights purposes. Although to date there is no children's photographic picture book about Trayvon, his parents are planning to publish an account of their experience, one that will provide "the full picture of their son while tracing their own experience of shock and sorrow."[2] The truth of a childhood lost to racism becomes, again, a narrative that urges social change. That truth becomes material in photographs.

Young protesters have claimed these two photographs and created their own word/image texts as social-justice arguments. In a July 20, 2013, image, a teenage boy in Chicago participated in a protest of the acquittal of Zimmerman (Figure C.1). He held up a sign that brings together both the hoodie photograph and the T-shirt image. His placard offers this coupling three times for emphasis, and with each pairing he links the images to a single word in his message: "Stop Gun Violence." The young man displays and repeats these images and attaches them to language, much as do the writers and editors in the books in my study, who assemble and interpret images in order to argue for social action. The repetition in the boy's poster also evokes the reproduction of images in the media, and by pairing and repeating the two photographs, the boy intervenes in representation. He claims these images—so widely circulated as to become common cultural property—as his vehicle, his means of granting authority, to his perspective. The repetition continues in the boy's dress and affect. Refusing to engage the camera, his disappointment at Zimmerman's acquittal is palpable, but although he seems too exhausted to stand, he remains dedicated to the presentation of his message; he holds the sign up with two hands. His commitment to the images is echoed even in his dress, for he wears clothing that unites the two images explicitly: a hoodie the color of the T-shirt, and, like the T-shirt, the hoodie is emblazoned with the brand name Hollister. Like many of the people who took protest images of themselves in hooded sweatshirts, this young man sees himself in Trayvon, but he pictures himself both as potential victim of violence and as incarnation of youthful virtue. Like the paired Till images, here the boy himself draws together two versions of child identity, one associated with vulnerability to violence and the other with the innocence and confidence of youth. Imani Perry reminds us of another form of innocence violated, that

Figure C.1. In Chicago, a young protester shows disappointment at the acquittal of Trayvon Martin's killer in July 2013. Copyright by Corbis Corporation.

of Trayvon's innocence of criminality: "The bitter truth is that Martin's innocence was eclipsed by the ever-present presumption of Black guilt."[3] In response to the annihilation of Trayvon's childhood innocence and legal innocence, protesters assemble texts and images in order to reframe the black image, to teach us how to see black youth.

Considering the alignment of books with protest posters is one way to think about the implications of the texts in this study. Like protest signs, many of the books in *Civil Rights Childhood* articulate themselves as interventionist, as voices in the movement and not just as reflections of it. Many books, like the signs, are affective endeavors, aiming to generate response in order to move a reader to consider her relationship to the world around her. Photobooks also play with the temporal strictures of the image and the unfolding of a narrative over time in order to generate a sense of urgency, much as did the signs at Trayvon Martin protests that demanded "Justice for Trayvon" and asked "Trayvon Today, Who

Tomorrow?" Like signs, many photographic books urge civic action, a critical involvement in the images that constitute black identity and history. They urge readers to feel, to think, and to act.

But, more than a particular text/image document offered within a moment of protest, these photographic books, by virtue of being books, aim to stabilize and authorize a perspective on representation. They resist the long history of textualized and photographic degradations and elisions of black character advanced in a variety of print forms. They reject the distortions and inventions of black character and history found in white newspapers, magazines, film, comics, and books across the twentieth century, and deploy new incarnations that bear the weight of photographic "truth." Unlike the protest poster, these photographic books are often slippery and subtle. We remember the way children's photographic books in the 1940s and 1950s worked through masking and indirection, offering layered meanings that unsettled any supposition of stable sociological knowledge of black childhood. In fact, by embracing joy as a political stance, many books—especially those before 1970—argued for the resilience and vitality of black youth as a site of resistance to constructions of black passivity and abjection. In the wake of the early civil rights movement, in the early 1970s, children in photobooks retained that resilience, but child characters became fierce in the face of disappointment. We remember Kali's claim on the streets, as she stands with solid confidence between skyscrapers. We hear the fury and determination in the voices of June Jordan's narrators.

That resilience and determination continue in contemporary texts. The best photographic books of the late twentieth and early twenty-first centuries bear the frank recognition that social justice is incomplete and that children can participate in the ongoing process of cultural critique. Just as the early books insist that the "American creed" is an unfulfilled promise, and books of the Black Arts Movement expose the failures of civil rights legislation, modern texts mourn the losses of children under violence and demand further action, as they ask children to see themselves as an extension of black history's commitment to social change. All of the books in this study imagine black-child readers as thoughtful, critical, engaged citizens. Remembering the photograph of the boy at the Trayvon Martin protest, we may see that black children in photographic books and black-child readers become more the protesters at the march than they become Trayvon himself, more activist thinkers than victims.

Photographic books do not imagine that children go it alone. Community building happens through the very site of family reading, of exchange between adults and children. Many texts encourage child readers to witness the continuity between contemporary social action and the past, as does Myers's *One More River to Cross*, in a way that imagines the long civil rights movement as a fundamental component of black identity and history. None of the books in this study argue that social justice has been completed. In this way, they resist the documentary strictures of the photograph in order to push toward continued action rather than offering evidence of achievement. The photographs themselves, sutured to words, point toward the need for dialogue about the world around the child. Especially in texts that engage history, like Reynolds's *Little Journeys* and Hughes and Meltzer's *Pictorial History of the Negro in America*, or that aim to recount the movement, like Weatherford's *Birmingham, 1963* and Jordan's *Dry Victories*, the collision of word and image triggers a reader to ask questions about history and how it is constructed. These texts implicitly (and sometimes explicitly) reveal that history is constructed through the assemblage of "evidence," some of it photographic, and that children can become critical arbiters of representation. Not only do civil rights remain unresolved, but the depiction of black history and identity is similarly open to black children as readers and interpreters.

The books in this study often invite participatory responses, with the child reader posed as critic and as creative agent, just as the Child Development Group of Mississippi's *Today* imagined the photographic book as an invitation to the ongoing process of psychological liberation. The texts here take energy from the idea of childhood itself, attaching the inevitable growth of the child's body to the inevitability of change. A kind of urgency inheres in the images of children in this study, particularly those with bodies in motion; these children will move, will grow, will play, will act, and the world will respond. This is one way in which the black photographic book about civil rights resists the nostalgic. The texts are more than simply reflective. The early books constitute voices in the civil rights movement as they advocate for integration, housing reform, and psychological strength; and even those that reflect on history (whether black experience across time or a version of the early 1960s moment) seek to connect the present with the past in order to inspire a continual awareness of the stakes of representation.

The photograph of the Trayvon Martin protester calls us to think about the importance of textualization to social change. Not only do words coupled with images create a demand for justice, but the flooding of social media—that new landscape of text/image—intensifies the urgency of that demand. What is missing, though, in that protester image and in the case of Trayvon in the media is the aesthetic permanence and provocation of book publication. What of a Trayvon Martin children's book? Would it be like Weatherford's *Birmingham, 1963*, a poetic destabilization of mythology that enables access to real loss? Would it be like Myers's *One More River to Cross*, offering images that connect Trayvon to other children across time, a move that might propel recognition of the commitments of Trayvon's family and his culture? Would it celebrate Trayvon's beauty or imagine his anger, as do Black Arts Movement texts, or ask questions about the public construction of Trayvon's history? Perhaps, instead, it would remind readers, as do so many of the books in this study, of the impossible yet poignant desire for black-child insularity, with the appeal to childhood innocence leading to the only viable mode, a stance of social action.

ACKNOWLEDGMENTS

Civil Rights Childhood owes an enormous debt to individuals who spoke with me about their involvement in the civil rights movement and in the creation of photographic books for young people. Joseph McNeil offered great insight about the influence of *A Pictorial History of the Negro in America* on the movement, as well as inspired observations about the relationship of the visual to social justice. Dawn Reynolds, daughter of Louis B. Reynolds, shed light on her father's important work and his investment in painting and photography. Doris Derby, the activist and author of *Today*, uncovered the context for the production of the book and offered me invaluable encouragement at a crucial moment. I am proud to count her among my friends. Photographer Matt Herron and educator Polly Greenberg were also tremendously helpful in describing their experience with the Child Development Group of Mississippi. I am thankful for their contributions to this project. Julius Lester provided encouragement and assistance in discerning the relationship of SNCC to child representation. My gratitude to Kali Grosvenor Henry is boundless. She shared with me her experience as a child poet and got me thinking about the continuity of images within family spaces. She offered complexity and nuance to my understanding of children's aesthetic investment in the Black Arts Movement. I can't thank her enough. Robert Fletcher and Joan Halifax were also quite generous in sharing their photographs and insights. John Shearer not only talked with me at length about his work with Gordon Parks and as a journalist but also offered terrific ideas about shifts in image making during the early 1970s. I am so grateful to John. I thank Carole Boston Weatherford, whose *Birmingham, 1963* helped inspire this project. She, too, offered sharp ideas about violence and the visual. Thanks to Victor and Pamela Ransom, son and granddaughter of Llewellyn Ransom, for their support and encouragement. Arnold Adoff, poet, continues to inspire and enrich my work, and I am grateful to know him. If I could thank

June Jordan, I would. Her work for young people was part of my life as a child, and I would not be the same person or scholar without her.

Many extraordinarily kind and generous librarians facilitated this work. I thank Richard Bleiler at the University of Connecticut for his support of all of the faculty members and graduate students in the Department of English. He is a tremendous resource and fantastic scholar. Not only did Benjamin J. Baker, archivist for the General Conference of Seventh-Day Adventists, read through my chapter on Louis B. Reynolds to check for historical and interpretive accuracy, but his own work informs my perspective on the church and its civil rights involvement. Thank you, Benjamin, and thanks also to Carol Barry at the Review and Herald Publishing Association. Thank you to Sylvia Cyrus and Karen May at the Association for the Study of African American Life and History for their support of this project. Two of the kindest and smartest archivists ever, Ellen Ruffin and Jennifer Brannock, at the University of Southern Mississippi McCain Library and Archives, helped me locate and reproduce *Today. Civil Rights Childhood* would have a gaping hole in the middle without their contribution. Jana Hill at Mississippi State University, Susan Klein at Yale's Beinecke Library, and Nicole C. Dittrich at Syracuse University Special Collections were very helpful. Jim Baggett and Don Veasey at the Birmingham Public Library Archives offered thoughtfulness along with assistance.

The project was sustained by a sabbatical leave at the University of Connecticut and funding from UConn's Human Rights Institute and the Office of the Vice President for Research. I thank the English department, particularly its leadership, including Bob Tilton, Wayne Franklin, Margaret Breen, and Bob Hasenfratz. At UConn, I am surrounded by brilliance: Lisa Blansett, Lynn Bloom, Alexis Boylan, Mary Burke, Ellen Carillo, Eleni Coundouriotis, Tom Deans, Clare Eby, Brendan Kane, Kathy Knapp, Ellen Litman, Rachael Lynch, Veronica Makowsky, Jean I. Marsden, Micki McElya, Brenda Murphy, Penelope Pelizzon, Tom Recchio, Fred Roden, Lisa Sánchez González, Greg Semenza, Tom Shea, and Jeffrey Shoulson all have nurtured this project in one way or another, and their camaraderie sustains me. Very special thanks to Margaret R. Higonnet, Victoria Ford Smith, and Anna Mae Duane, my children's literature community in Storrs, for offering laughter and friendship along with major brainpower. Susannah Richards, Lisa Rowe Fraustino, Pegi Shea, Cora Lynn Deibler, and Patti Argoff make life in Connecticut tremendous fun (and they know a few things about children's literature!). I am grateful to Sam Pickering for his compassion and warmth and for making me smile just by appearing in the department hallway. How can I adequately thank the

Americanist Reading Group at UConn? They read nearly this entire project at the draft stage and offered exceptional feedback along with good humor and wit. Martha Cutter, Sherry Harris, Shawn Salvant, Cathy Schlund-Vials, Chris Vials, and Jerry Phillips are the best colleagues and friends one could ever have. Cathy, I owe you particularly, because you have made the stakes of this project clear every step of the way. My thanks to Ivy Linton Stabell, Wendy Glenn, Jason Courtmance, Abbye Meyer, Pam Swanigan, Toni Fellela, Zara Rix, Patrick Lawrence, Michelle Resene, Catherine McKenna, Emily Cormier, Michelle Maloney-Mangold, Alysa Auriemma, Sarah Austin, and Christiana Salah for their lively investment in children's literature and culture.

The Children's Literature Association has been a formative organization for me. Not only have I joined an incredible network of scholars by attending the ChLA annual conference and editing the *Children's Literature Association Quarterly*, but also I count myself very lucky to be surrounded by these friends, who are as kind as they are smart. Richard Flynn and Kenneth Kidd, our original *Quarterly* gang, make life so sweet. Anne K. Phillips and Christine Doyle, UConn alums, are my true ChLA buddies, and every year is a joyous reunion. Julia Mickenberg and Nathalie op de Beeck provided useful and generous readings of the manuscript, and the book is so much better for their feedback. Annette Wannamaker and Michelle Abate, my sister editors, help me through each year. Yvonne Atkinson has enriched my work on Toni Morrison tremendously. Many ChLA scholars helped me formulate my ideas for this project, including Michael Joseph, Lissa Paul, Robin Bernstein, Marah Gubar, Phil Nel, Karin Westman, Claudia Nelson, Michelle Martin, Mark West, Beverly Lyon Clark, Paula Connolly, Teya Rosenberg, Naomi Wood, Thomas Crisp, Dianne Johnson Feelings, Lance Weldy, June Cummins, Debbie Reese, Ebony Thomas, Sarah Park Dahlen, Jennie Miskec, Chris McGee, Katie Peel, Karen Chandler, Naomi Lesley, Karen Li-Miller, Michelle Pagni Stewart, Erica Hateley, Gregory Eiselein, Laura Wasowicz, Joe Sutliff Sanders, Katie Strode, Joseph Thomas, Mike Cadden, Roberta Seelinger Trites, and Gwen Tarbox. That's a long list of names, but every single one has been important to this book.

Generous, gifted scholars in American studies informed my work. Aldon Nielsen, James Smethurst, and Margo Natalie Crawford provided much insight and feedback about the Black Arts Movement. Erina Duganne, Shawn Michelle Smith, Sara Blair, and Laura Wexler helped me immeasurably with photographic theory and practice, and Patricia Crain and Angela Sorby enhanced this discussion with their deep knowledge of childhood studies. Charles Hatfield and Gene Kannenberg helped me with text/image history and theory and welcomed me into their circle of comics scholars. I thank Imani Perry and Pier Gabrielle Foreman for their encouragement and their groundbreaking scholarship. Gerald Early and Wendy Love Anderson deserve special thanks for bringing me out to Saint Louis several times to talk about my work. Gerald has been extremely supportive and bighearted. Laurie Langbauer has cheered this project on, and I am grateful. Rita Williams-Garcia came to UConn twice to talk about Black Arts childhood. We were lucky to have her. I am thankful for warm conversation with Leslie Bow and helpful feedback from J. J. Butts. Cheryl Hudson, Jason Low, Bernette Ford, A'Leila Bundles, Daphne Muse, Nancy Tolson, Myisha Priest, and Zetta Elliott reminded me at various times how much black children's literature matters, and this has been a salvation. Richard Morrison at the University of Minnesota Press had faith in this project from the outset. Thank you, Richard, for sticking with me, and for all of the invigorating conversations across the years.

My family has been the biggest support for this project, whether that be my brother Dan sending me text messages with images from the Smithsonian and other museums, or my sister Liz appreciating *I Wish I Had an Afro* with me. My brother Ted is a truly inspirational man, a real leader in the world of black youth, and my sister Jane offers me love and perspective when I need it most. My siblings make me laugh and help me understand how to celebrate life. Their partners, Linnea, John, Angel, and Jon, are encouraging and upbeat, and I am glad that they are part of our family. Their children bring us all joy. I thank my mother-in-law, Marie, for her enthusiasm about art and her emotional nourishment. My mother, Eileen, is the most beautiful spirit on the planet, and I am thankful to her and to her husband, Jerry, for believing in me. My father, Frederick W. Capshaw, has been by my side in spirit through this project. My children, Joe, Grace, Liam, and Finola, make me happy every day. Oh my, they are a blast. My incredible husband, Steve, knows more about art than I will ever hope to know, and his perceptiveness informs this book. He taught me how to read images. His commitment to Haiti offered me a model for social justice work and pushed me to think about the role of representation to survival. Our love gives life meaning, and I am so very grateful for his humor, intelligence, and tremendous patience and generosity. Thank you, Steve.

NOTES

INTRODUCTION

1. Hughes and Meltzer, *Pictorial History*, 308.
2. Martin Berger describes Till's coverage in the black press: "Depictions of Till's corpse and/or open casket appeared in the following black newspapers and periodicals in either September or October of 1955: *Afro-American* (Baltimore, MD), *American Negro, Chicago Defender, Crisis, New York Amsterdam News, Michigan Chronicle, Pittsburgh Courier, Philadelphia Tribune*, and, most famously, in back-to-back issues of *Jet* magazine" (*Seeing through Race*, 127–28). Berger argues persuasively that white venues refused to publish graphic images of children as victims of violence, whereas such images were present in black periodicals.
3. T. Davis, foreword, xiii. Also see Metress, *Lynching of Emmett Till;* and Pollack and Metress, "Emmett Till Case and Narrative(s)."
4. According to Steven Kasher, "The leading black periodicals, including *Jet* and the *Chicago Defender*, juxtaposed earlier photographs of the bright-eyed youngster in shirt and tie with the horrific picture of his bashed and bloated face" (*Civil Rights Movement*, 11). Hughes and Meltzer's book features a photograph cropped so that only Till's head appears. In the *Jet* magazine September 15, 1955, issue, the full photograph, of young Till with his mother, appears.
5. J. Berger, "Understanding a Photograph," 293 (emphasis in original).
6. Joyce Ladner, quoted in Maurice Berger, *For All the World to See*, 109. According to Martin A. Berger, "[A] number of observers and scholars have labeled the youths radicalized by the photographs the 'Emmett Till Generation'" (*Seeing through Race*, 128).
7. The most potent example of child activism during the civil rights era was, perhaps, the "Children's Crusade," in 1963 Birmingham. Maurice Berger describes the controversy over Martin Luther King Jr.'s involvement of young people in the movement: "While organizers were reluctant to place children in harm's way, they came to believe that the compelling spectacle of black youth pleading for their rights—and being mistreated by vicious segregationists—could most effectively sway public opinion. . . . For some critics, white and black, the drama was being sought at too high a cost. 'School children participating in street demonstrations is a dangerous business,' warned U.S. attorney general Robert F. Kennedy. 'An injured, maimed or dead child is a price none of us can afford to pay.' Malcolm X dismissed the idea as cowardly and reckless: 'Real men don't put their children on the firing line'" (*For All the World to See*, 120). According to Steven Kasher, "Boys and girls went to jail by the hundreds. At one boisterous

mass meeting, King urged some third- and fourth-grade volunteers to sit down, but they wouldn't be kept from the front lines" (*Civil Rights Movement*, 94). Kasher then describes May 2, 1963: "By four o'clock, 959 children had been sent to jail. In terms of the Gandhian imperative to 'fill the jails,' it was a glorious day" (95). Much of the testimony from young people in Ellen S. Levine's *Freedom's Children* insists on children's willing and active involvement in social-justice protest.

8. Howard Zinn emphasizes the youthful character of the civil rights campaign in *SNCC: The New Abolitionists* (1964): "For the first time in our history, a major social movement, shaking the nation to its bones, is being led by youngsters" (1), and he continues by explaining their contribution in terms of potential evidentiary sacrifice: the youngsters consisted of "Negroes who make their pleas to the nation more by physical acts of sacrifice than by verbal declamation. Their task is made easier by modern mass communication, for the nation, indeed the whole world, can *see* them on the television screen or in newspaper photos—marching, praying, singing, *demonstrating* their message" (7–8 [emphasis in original]). Language—or art—is not the forte of youth, Zinn suggests; young people succeed by silently offering their bodies. As Martin A. Berger notes (*Seeing through Race*), images of tranquil and passive children were the images attractive to the white press; white publications were not interested in picturing children in active resistance, or in depicting child bodies mutilated by violence. Black audiences, however, were well aware of photographic constructions of children both as agents and as victims through the black press.

9. See Dudziak, *Cold War Civil Rights*.

10. Steven Kasher and Maurice Berger cite Hansberry's *The Movement* as the first civil rights photographic book. Six years before *The Movement*, Jewish writer Dorothy Sterling had issued *Tender Warriors* (1958), assisted by Donald Gross and with photographs by Myron Ehrenberg. Sterling's photobook focuses on school integration and draws on interviews Sterling and Ehrenberg conducted with black and white children and their parents in several states across the South, as well as transcripts of a student forum at Little Rock. Sterling states, "In the spring of 1957, we took a trip through the mid-South—to Kentucky, Tennessee, Delaware, West Virginia, Virginia, and into South Carolina—to meet the children in the thousand and one schools where integration has just begun or is about to begin tomorrow" (24). Sterling's book is an accomplishment that deserves critical attention in histories of the movement. Roy Wilkins, executive secretary of the National Association for the Advancement of Colored People (NAACP), wrote the advertising blurb in the *New York Times* ad of April 27, 1958: "It speaks through the mouths of children of the effects of the Great Change" (Wilkins, advertisement). Sterling's book could be considered the first photo text of the civil rights movement; but because neither Sterling's nor Hansberry's book bears a child readership I have been able to trace, whether in family settings or individually, my project does not engage these rich texts.

11. Morrison was *The Black Book*'s editor at Random House; Middleton A. Harris and assistants are credited on the copyright page. Scholarship typically credits Morrison for her organization of the book.

12. J. Jordan, *Dry Victories*, 75.

13. Sanders, "Chaperoning Words," 59 (emphasis in original).

14. The field of children's literature includes a large body of scholarship on text/image relationships within illustrated picture books, as demonstrated by the work of Maria Nikolajeva and Carole Scott, Perry Nodelman, Ellen Handler Spitz, Lawrence Sipe and Sylvia Pantaleo, and many others. Yet there is very little theory within children's literature on the photographically illustrated children's book. But photographic picture books for the young flourished in the twentieth century and continue in popularity, as Mus White's invaluable bibliography *From the Mundane to the Magical* attests.

15. op de Beeck, *Suspended Animation*, 43.

16. Sontag, *On Photography*, 15. See Eduardo Cadava as well on the connection of the photograph to an elegiac meaning: "In photographing someone, we know that the photograph will survive him—it begins, even during his life, to circulate without him, figuring and anticipating his death each time it is looked at. The photograph is a farewell. It belongs to the afterlife of the photographed. It is permanently inflamed by the instantaneous flash of death" (*Words of Light*, 13).

17. op de Beeck, *Suspended Animation*, xvi.

18. Blair, *Harlem Crossroads*, 15. Many of the thinkers cited in this study have been influenced by Walter Benjamin, particularly Barthes, Sontag, and Cadava, but any discussion of the "modern" camera and our relationship to it is shaped by Benjamin to some degree. As Dudley Andrew writes, "Walter Benjamin stands at the entryway to any discussion of modernity that takes into account the shifting methods and roles of representation" (introduction, 3).

19. Blair, *Harlem Crossroads*, 5–6.

20. Hall, "Long Civil Rights Movement," 1235.

21. Willis, "Search for Self," 107.

22. See Sara L. Schwebel's terrific *Child-Sized History* for a discussion of the political uses of historical fiction and the rise of multicultural education in the 1990s.

23. I recognize that I am truncating the definition of documentary photography and its multiple permutations. See Blair, *Harlem Crossroads*, 268–69, for a full discussion of the various uses of the category "documentary."

24. Stott, *Documentary Expression*, 62.

25. Ibid., 275.

26. Rabinowitz, *They Must Be Represented*, 18.

27. *Skyscraper* was published with Elsa Herzfeld Naumburg, Robert Egolf, and Clara Breakey Lambert. *Manhattan* was published with Clara Breakey Lambert.

28. Blair, *Harlem Crossroads*, 271. See Willis, *Family History Memory: Recording African American Life* and *Reflections in Black: A History of Black Photographers, 1840 to the Present* for the self-generative dimension of black image making. Willis offers a road map to landmark photographers, studios, and production contexts.

29. In *Photography on the Color Line*, Smith interprets Du Bois's photographs in order to demonstrate "how contested, mutable, and flexible visual culture has been as a site through which race is posed and challenged" (3), a concept that has influenced the capaciousness of my study. I am also particularly indebted to her idea in *American Archives* that "visual culture is not a mere reflection of a national community but one of the sites through which the narratives of national belonging are imagined. In other words, I suggest that photographic images not only represent but also produce the

nation" (158). I am also influenced by Anne Elizabeth Carroll's revelatory *Word, Image, and the New Negro.*

30. See James Allen, *Without Sanctuary;* Apel, *Imagery of Lynching;* Apel and Smith, *Lynching Photographs;* and Raiford, "Consumption of Lynching Images."

31. Hirsch, *Family Frames;* Willis, *Reflections in Black;* Wexler, *Tender Violence;* Abel, "Domestic Borders, Cultural Boundaries"; Liss, "Black Bodies in Evidence"; and others explore the implications of such pictures, particularly the Cook family photograph "Nursemaid and Her Charge."

32. Wexler, *Tender Violence,* 84.

33. Family photographs often include children, and although critics have negotiated the racial and gendered identities of adults in such images, black childhood as a topic of discussion continues to be erased. Hirsch, for one, notes the centrality of children to the family photograph: "This predominance of images of children, and the looks exchanged with them, . . . allow us to recognize the energies and fantasies, the fears and vulnerabilities we project onto family pictures" (Hirsch, "Familial Looking," xxiv). For many critics of the family image, childhood primarily enables readings of adult investments and desires.

34. Higonnet, *Pictures of Innocence,* 224.

35. Several critics' work has commented on the prominence of the image within civil rights campaigns, including Kasher's influential *Civil Rights Movement;* Maurice Berger's *For All the World to See,* and Martin A. Berger's *Seeing through Race.*

36. Only in the twenty-first century have critics begun to consider the creative output of the civil rights movement in terms that depart from the evidentiary. Maurice Berger explains: "[D]espite books, exhibitions, and documentaries on [Gordon] Parks and other artists, photographers, filmmakers, designers, and television producers and directors of the civil rights era, the story of the remarkable role played by visual culture in shaping and fortifying the movement remains one of the least understood in recent American history" (*For All the World to See,* 3).

37. hooks, *Art on My Mind,* 60.

38. Raiford and Romano, "Struggle over Memory," xiv.

I. FRIENDSHIP, SYMPATHY, SOCIAL CHANGE

1. My awareness of the child participant in the photographic exchange is influenced in part by Ariella Azoulay, who argues that "[a]nyone who addresses others through photographs or takes the position of a photograph's addressee, even if she is a stateless person who has lost her 'right to have rights,' as in [Hannah] Arendt's formulation, is nevertheless a citizen—a member in the citizenry of photography. The civil space of photography is open to her, as well. That space is configured by what I call the civil space of photography" (Azoulay, *Civil Contract of Photography,* 85). Azoulay sees the site of exchange in a photograph—between subject, photographer, and audience—as a new civic territory where the oppressed demand a response.

2. Barthes, *Camera Lucida,* 80–81.

3. Bernice A. Pescosolido, Elizabeth Grauerholz, and Melissa A. Milkie study a large sample of books, including Caldecott winners and Honor books, *Children's Catalog* compilations of books, and Little Golden Books, arguing that from "1937 through the

mid-1950s, Blacks are present in modest though declining proportions" ("Culture and Conflict," 450), and then either in stereotypical or biased representation or alongside white children in "family of man" images (451).

4. Preer, "Guidance in Democratic Living," 679.

5. Dudziak explains that "World War II marked a transition point in American foreign relations, American politics, and American culture. At home, the meaning ascribed to the war would help to shape what would follow. At least on an ideological level, the notion that the nation as a whole had a stake in racial equality was widespread" (*Cold War Civil Rights*, 7).

6. Melamed, *Represent and Destroy*.

7. Myrdal, *American Dilemma*, 1022.

8. According to Melamed, race literature was envisioned as "a helpmate to the social sciences: literature was thought to present racial experience with the same truth content as social-scientific studies, but with more emotional impact and presumably a greater ability to arouse sympathy" (*Represent and Destroy*, 67).

9. Ibid., 52.

10. The legacy of racial liberalism in children's texts is not this book's main concern, though certainly further study is necessary in charting the pervasiveness of friendship as a reductive solution to racial "problems" in American children's literature.

11. Rex Manuel Sr. was listed as "mulatto" in the 1910 census and as "Black" or "Negro (Black)" in the censuses of 1920, 1930, and 1940.

12. Dudziak, *Cold War Civil Rights*, 23.

13. Natanson, *Black Image*, 40–41. Natanson's overview of one series of photographs emphasizes the upbeat character of such government representations: "Howard Liberman's 'Americans All' series, taken at a California bomber plant for the OWI in July 1942, epitomized the trend. . . . Soaring camera angles, close-ups highlighting determined faces and skilled hands, underline the point: New Deal beneficiaries had turned into national assets, the 'uplifted' black into the 'valuable' black" (39–40).

14. Shackelford, *My Happy Days*, 116. Subsequent citations of this book appear in the text.

15. Dudziak, *Cold War Civil Rights*, 12.

16. Ibid., 13. Dudizak offers a number of fascinating portraits of African American activists during the Cold War and their attempts to negotiate the pressure to be silent about civil rights failures. NAACP executive secretary Walter White is a case in point: "White had earned the credentials to criticize, within the walls of the White House, racial violence and segregation. When sent abroad, however, he would emphasize racial progress in the United States and argue that persons of color had nothing to gain from communism" (67).

17. May, *Homeward Bound*, xviii.

18. As May points out, suburbia midcentury was a vexed space for black Americans: "Americans of all backgrounds rushed into marriage and childbearing, even though many of these newly formed families—most notably Americans of color—were excluded from suburbia, the site of the 'American way of life'" (ibid., xvii).

19. May explains: "American leaders spoke loudly and often about the efforts the nation was making to eradicate institutionalized racism, claiming that the situation for black Americans was improving" (ibid., xix); she continues by explaining that the government "allowed racial segregation to prevail in the suburbs, where the Federal

Housing Authority and lending banks maintained red-lining policies that prevented black Americans from obtaining home mortgages. . . . The long-term effects of these policies and attitudes were devastating. Black Americans were excluded from the suburbs, even if they could afford to live there. That exclusion denied them the opportunity for capital accumulation and upward mobility that home ownership provided. So while white working-class Americans prospered and joined their middle-class peers as suburban homeowners, African-Americans lost ground economically. They were forced to reside in substandard urban housing, left out of postwar prosperity, and denied the government subsidies available to whites" (xix–xx).

20. In life, Terre Haute, Indiana, was not hospitable to housing integration. Shackelford describes in her papers resistance from both whites and blacks to her attempt to buy a house in a white neighborhood. She does not describe the purchase in terms of an attempt at integration but, rather, suggests that the house was close to the school at which she taught. She discovered resistance from realtors and sellers as well as from black community members, who suggested that improving her original house in a black neighborhood—as they had done—was not "good enough" for Shackelford.

21. See my chapter on Woodson's publishing house in K. C. Smith, *Children's Literature of the Harlem Renaissance*.

22. Myrdal, *American Dilemma*, 752.

23. In *Children's Literature of the Harlem Renaissance*, I talk about how Woodson during the 1940s sometimes removed references to race in publications for children, hoping that the books would appeal to a white audience. Although the marketing impulse for these kinds of erasures seems obvious, given the economic struggles of his publishing house, the ideological implications within a context of race liberalism have not been explored by scholars.

24. Woodson critiqued Myrdal in a 1944 review of Otto Klineberg's *Characteristics of the American Negro*, saying, "His picture of the conditions obtaining among Negroes is mainly what he could see only through a glass darkly" (234); but later that year, in "Books of United States History," Woodson suggests that *American Dilemma* should be translated and distributed internationally (494).

25. Suburban domesticity as evidence of antiracism also emerges, if briefly, in the black popular press in the 1940s. The household emblematizes national peace in *Ebony* magazine, which published a March 1947 photoeditorial entitled "Goodbye Mammy, Hello Mom." The editorial credits World War II for drawing black women out of the kitchens of white households and into war work; when that form of employment ended, the editorial argues, black mothers returned to their families as housewives, with reassuring results: "Domestic peace seems to be the order of things since she came home" (36). The editorial does not imagine the turn toward domesticity as constrictive but, instead, advocates individual choice: "Not that a woman's place is in the kitchen necessarily. Nobody wants to tie a woman to her hearthstone with hackneyed phrases and ideas about where her place is. . . . And every woman should be able to choose whether she wants to devote her days to her children and her home or to a career girl's job" (36). May reads this article as embracing household work wholeheartedly: "For black women, domesticity meant 'freedom and independence in her own home.' People of color longed for the 'good life,' just like anyone else. But their exclusion from the opportunities most citizens took for granted intensified their desires" (*Homeward Bound*,

18). Given this nod to professional work, the article then insists that black domesticity has produced healthier and happier children and fathers. The accompanying image places the mother at the table, cutting potatoes as she watches over her two small children in the backyard through a window. The mother's face is turned away from the camera, as her charges are framed by the window, enclosed in domestic safety even when outside the house. Shackelford's photographic book coheres with this strong domestic impulse within the black community at the close of the war. Although the turn toward domesticity "has not made headlines in the Negro press," according to *Ebony*, it "certainly stacks up with the biggest news of the past decade" ("Goodbye Mammy," 36).

26. Kozol notes that "*Life*'s narrative . . . divides into two strains: one tending to depoliticize the public sphere by directing attention to domestic dramas, the other tending to politicize the private sphere by depending on domestic ideology in stories about political issues" (Life's *America*, 137).

27. Coverage of Jackie Robinson typifies the way in which the magazine employed domesticity in order to transform an exceptional black individual into one who represented all African Americans and, by extension, America itself. The August 1, 1949, editorial is entitled "Negroes Are Americans: Jackie Robinson Proves It in Words and on the Ball Field." Kozol (in ibid.) discusses at length the way in which the editorial emphasizes Robinson's refutation of Paul Robeson's political activism. The editorial figures Robinson's mainline democratic political ideals—he refutes Paul Robeson's endorsement of the Soviet Union—through an emphasis on the domestic. Robinson's commitment to democracy is an extension of his role as a father in a middle-class family: Robinson says, "I know that I've got too much invested for my wife and child and myself in the future of this country, and I and other Americans of many races and faiths have too much invested in our country's welfare, for any of us to throw it away because of a siren song sung in bass" (22). The editorial essay concludes with a full-page photograph of Robinson and his wife and two-year-old son sitting on the steps outside their house in Brooklyn. *Life* refigures the exceptional Robinson as a "normal" American father, one whose patriotism and befuddlement at radical politics are an extension of his commitment to his domestic role. In general, the 1940s saw an increase in interest in black life stories that metonymically represented the citizenship, accomplishment, and potential of African Americans, as biographies of public figures like Lena Horne and Ralph Bunche appeared in international periodicals as well as at home (Dudziak, *Cold War Civil Rights*, 35).

28. Shackelford, "Message to Parents."

29. Dudziak discusses the United States Information Agency pamphlet *The Negro in American Life* (1950), explaining that the government perspective, shared by a majority of white Americans in the 1940s, was that "[t]he problem of racial prejudice ultimately could not be eradicated through law, for it was essentially 'a question of evolving human relations'" (*Cold War Civil Rights*, 51). In the 1940s and 1950s, representations of African Americans focused less on the structural causes of inequity and more on the need for understanding and individual rights. Kozol explains that *Life* magazine "presented civil rights protests by focusing on personal crises and responses. This attention to personal experiences legitimated social struggles but it did so at the expense of criticizing the structural foundations of racism in American society. The magazine

focused on issues of individual merit or failure in character rather than addressing the hierarchies and power relations that structure society" (Life's America, 11).

30. Benjamin DeMott (The Trouble with Friendship) applies the phrase "friendship orthodoxy" to cultural production in the 1990s; it is useful here as well.

31. May, Homeward Bound, 17.

32. Selig, Americans All, 267.

33. Ibid., 262.

34. Samuel H. Flowerman, quoted in Mackenzie, "Inquiry Group," 18. Flowerman was also coeditor of the five-volume series that included Theodor W. Adorno's influential The Authoritarian Personality.

35. Bettelheim and Janowitz, Dynamics of Prejudice, 105.

36. Flowerman, "Portrait of the Authoritarian Man," 31.

37. See K. C. Smith, Children's Literature of the Harlem Renaissance.

38. Mickenberg, Learning from the Left, 185.

39. Betty Bacon, quoted in ibid., 191.

40. Mickenberg explains that there was a particular demand for science books at the time of the publication of My Happy Days: "Thanks to growing concerns about 'manpower shortages' and the need for technological innovation, there was a thriving market for science books by the mid-1940s and not enough well-written, realistic, and scientifically accurate books available" (Learning from the Left, 190).

41. See ibid., 114.

42. The erector set may also signify preparation for a career in engineering or industrial management, especially if read through the "shop theory" described by John Stilgoe in his foreword to Mary Liddell's Little Machinery (vii).

43. K. C. Smith, Children's Literature of the Harlem Renaissance, 210–11.

44. "Music Appreciation Hour" ended in 1942, two years before the publication of My Happy Days.

45. Denning, Cultural Front, 9.

46. Robeson, and the composter Robinson, had not yet been stigmatized by being associated with Communism, so the invocation of "Ballad for Americans" places Shackelford squarely within the progressive left rather than in any more radical tradition.

47. Mickenberg, Learning from the Left, 129.

48. Ovington, "Revisiting the South."

49. Shackelford's papers at the Vigo County Library in Terre Haute, Indiana, list twenty-three newspapers from across the country that reviewed her book, and sixteen magazines. Her papers also name twenty-nine book lists of recommended titles on which My Happy Days appeared.

50. From Roosevelt's January 6, 1941, State of the Union speech, the Four Freedoms were freedom of speech, freedom of worship, freedom from want, and freedom from fear.

51. Garrison, "Race Relations."

52. Robeson, "American Family Portrait." A review by Esther Popel Shaw, African American children's writer and dramatist, in the Journal of Negro History reads, "From still another angle the book is significant. Perhaps it was not the intent of the author to do so (though one would hesitate to make such a statement without equivocation, for Jane Dabney Shackelford is wise with the wisdom that abides in teachers of youth and

mothers of children of their own), but she has produced a document which, in the field of race relations in present-day America, will go far toward furthering understanding and respect between the majority and minority groups so torn and biased by prejudice, misunderstanding and fear at the present time. For this book portrays Childhood in wholesome, average situations, and any reader, old or young, white or black, cannot miss the impact of these facts: that average human beings, in normal every-day situations, react in the same way, regardless of pigmentation, to the same stimuli, enjoy with equal pleasure the happy experiences of life, and grow to a full and rich appreciation of the things about them which make life beautiful, when given the incentives and the opportunities for so doing" (221).

53. In *Children's Literature of the Harlem Renaissance*, I mention a January 16, 1944, letter from Shackelford to Carter G. Woodson in which she insists on modeling the production of *My Happy Days* on *Tobe*. She writes, "This book will be a failure unless it is printed on the best grade of thick, smooth paper like 'Tobe.' It will be a tragedy to ruin it with cheap paper. Do not do it. The type must be the same size as that used in 'Tobe' also. . . . May I suggest that the book be manufactured by the Kingsport Press, Inc., Kingsport, Tennessee. They did an excellent piece of work with Tobe."

54. Sharpe, "Autobiographical Material."

55. Farrell, "Story Back of the Publication."

56. Farrell, "Comments on Photographs."

57. Natanson, *Black Image*, 201.

58. Stott, *Documentary Expression*, 213.

59. G. W. Johnson, letter to Charles Anderson Farrell.

60. Hughes, "Books and the Negro Child," 110.

61. Shackelford, "Langston Hughes Statement."

62. Shackelford, "My Books."

63. Farrell's papers reveal that the father of the family represented in *Tobe* wished to sue Farrell, Sharpe, and the University of North Carolina Press for a share of the profits of the book. The lawsuit was resolved in part because Couch sold the books at a low price (one dollar) that did not generate large profits for the book.

64. Shackelford, "Book Signing."

65. See Robin Bernstein's discussion of the role of innocence in the civil rights movement in *Racial Innocence*.

66. Alexandra Alland, Alexander's wife, is also listed as a photographer for the book, though the level of her involvement is unclear.

67. See Tarry's autobiography, *The Third Door*, and her insistence that "this [the two books] is the 'here and now' thing, too, at work. The basis of these stories for children came out of experiences" (K. C. Smith, "From Bank Street to Harlem," 276).

68. Tarry considered writing literature for children to be "very serious business" and believed that adults did not respect children's literature because of a "general disinterest in the affairs and problems of children and the dreadful tendency toward thinking that children don't have real problems" (quoted in Carter, "Meet Ellen Tarry").

69. Tarry, *Third Door*, 136.

70. K. C. Smith, "From Bank Street to Harlem," 274.

71. As Mickenberg explains, "The pedagogical trend toward student-generated learning complemented the new anti-fascist common sense for it rejected an authoritarian model of adult-child relations and emphasized freedom, democracy, and cooperation as desirable traits" (*Learning from the Left*, 93).

72. See Nathalie op de Beeck's discussion of modernist picture books in *Suspended Animation*.

73. Mickenberg, *Learning from the Left*, 41.

74. K.C. Smith, "From Bank Street to Harlem," 275.

75. Ibid., 281.

76. Ellen Tarry, quoted in Carter, "Meet Ellen Tarry."

77. K.C. Smith, "From Bank Street to Harlem," 279.

78. Ibid., 278.

79. The boy's name was David De Brecourt, and Rinty, the dog, was Alland's pet. See Carter, "Meet Ellen Tarry."

80. K.C. Smith, "From Bank Street to Harlem," 279.

81. Augusta Baker (1911–1988), one of the most prominent black librarians of the twentieth century, began as children's librarian at the 135th Street branch of the New York Public Library and, in the 1960s, became the first African American administrator in the NYPL system as coordinator of children's services.

82. Tarry, *Third Door*, 253.

83. Alland's attention to urban communities may have been shaped by his work recovering Riis, because Riis documented the city and offered images to wealthy donors in order to propel social reform. Of course, Riis focused on the ghetto and on stereotypes of the poor, whereas Alland was much more invested in treating ethnic communities as members of the American community.

84. Denning, *Cultural Front*, 448.

85. Alland, interview by Edward Applebome, 24.

86. Alland, *American Counterpoint*, 17.

87. Ibid., 18.

88. Ibid., 57.

89. Ibid., 46.

90. Buck, introduction, 14. Alland, in an interview, describes the origins of *American Counterpoint*: "Here I did text and photography. And Pearl Buck's husband, Richard Walsh, was the owner of the John Day Publishing Company. So they made an appointment for me, they looked at my pictures, and she fell in love with my work. She wrote an introduction. There is an 11 page introduction here by Pearl Buck, which characterizes me very well. But I have to open the book and you get annoyed every time I go back to the book. She calls the introduction, 'Land of the Noble Free.' And it's a long story and in the end she says. I'm sorry, taking your time, but she speaks of me, she says, 'The man who took these pictures was born in Russia, but he's an American, and he is showing you America through his camera. He has understood that to find America you have to look into many faces of many colors and kinds. This man has found an even greater variety in our country than most of them ever knew existed. Assyrian and Welsh as well as English and German, and Scandinavian, Italian and French, but try the test of Americanism. Speak the word freedom to anyone of them and the same look comes into their eyes.' This book was chosen as one of the 50 best books of the year,

which is quite a distinction because we published a billion books every year, and I had two books selected as one of the 50 best books of the year" (24).

91. *The Springfield Plan* is also distinctive as a photographic text of the early 1940s in its inclusion of a statement from the Committee of Education for Democracy, which recognized that democratic values had not been put into practice in the classroom. Although Alland's photographs demonstrate the success of those ideals in Springfield, the authors include this statement: "One of the major weaknesses of previous attempts to inculcate democratic ideals was the fact that the teaching had been too idealized. Youngsters were given to understand that we in this country had already achieved a perfect democracy. This teaching and idealization did not coincide with the realities of the youngsters' experiences. The committee decided therefore that issues should be faced squarely; that, while a positive and affirmative position on democratic ideals would be taken, it should be emphasized that we had not yet achieved the perfect democracy that is our goal; that the weaknesses in our democratic processes should be pointed out, and the question how these weaknesses could be corrected, and how our democratic processes could be strengthened, should be discussed realistically" (Wise, *Springfield Plan*, 11).

92. Selig, *Americans All*, 2.

93. Wise, *Springfield Plan*, 46.

94. Alland, *American Counterpoint*, 22.

95. Ibid., 49, 77.

96. Selig argues, "It [the cultural-gifts movement] represented a process of exchange in which groups would share traditions in order to create a larger, richer culture that would incorporate people from diverse backgrounds, encourage civic participation, and bring minorities into the democratic system. These innovations set the stage for what came to be called intercultural (and then multicultural) education. The focus on the child, as both the victim of prejudice and the hope for racial understanding, lasted throughout the century, emerging in the *Brown v. Board of Education* decision, the moral appeals of Martin Luther King Jr., and efforts to enlist support for work against racism through a focus on children's needs. Cultural gifts placed childhood at the heart of American liberalism—where it remains today" (*Americans All*, 17–18).

97. Selig discusses the objections of Alain Locke and other African American intellectuals to this upbeat approach, one that diminished the cruelties of black experience in America and was finally, in the words of Locke, "well-intentioned but rather ineffectual" (quoted in ibid., 220).

98. Mickenberg describes the effects of progressive perspectives on children's publishing: "At least two dozen of the Newbery Medal and Honor books published between 1922 and 1940 concerned children in other lands . . . or minority characters in the United States, such as American Indians and Alaskan 'Eskimos.' Other books, like Annie E. S. Beard's *Our Foreign Born Citizens*, which contained biographical sketches of distinguished immigrants . . . were self-consciously geared toward the Americanization of foreigners and breaking down anti-immigrant sentiment among native-born Americans" (*Learning from the Left*, 47).

99. op de Beeck, *Suspended Animation*, 66.

100. May Massee, quoted in ibid., 62. Massee references Maud and Miska Petersham's *Miki* (1929).

101. Maren Stange explains, "Previous studies such as the Photo League's 'Harlem Document,' undertaken in the late 1930s under Aaron Siskind's direction, had followed the documentary model set by the New Deal's classic Farm Security Administration (FSA) project, which linked photographic coverage to statistical and economic data, seeking to produce a thematic, even scientific, whole. The most extensive such photo-study of black Americans by the mid-1950s may have been *12 Million Black Voices*, published in 1941 with pictures primarily from FSA files and a text by Richard Wright" ("'Illusion Complete within Itself,'" 79).

102. Nicholas Natanson reminds us that not all of the coverage of African Americans by documentarians in the 1930s and early 1940s was dismissive, reductive, or exploitative: "The 'Harlem Document' and 'The Most Crowded Block' passed lightly over the black business elite in favor of street vendors and small-store employees—immediately appealing subjects, given a particularly noble cast by Aaron Siskind and the other photographers; the more inclusive FSA coverage moved from sidewalk stalls to a prominent insurance firm. . . . These quantitative measures do not tell the entire story, but they do suggest an FSA commitment to exploring the diversity described in the Cayton-Warner studies" (*Black Image*, 148).

103. Maren Stange says Wright's book offers "overall a relentlessly chilling image of Northern urban life, where, he writes, the death rate exceeds the birth rate, so that 'if it were not for the trains and autos bringing us daily into the city from the plantations, we black folks who dwell in northern cities would die out entirely over the course of a few years'" ("Illusion Complete within Itself," 79).

104. Butts, "New World A-Coming," 650.

105. Ibid.

106. Natanson, *Black Image*, 250.

107. Ibid., 251.

108. Tarry, *Third Door*, 149.

109. K. C. Smith, "From Bank Street to Harlem," 272.

110. Tarry, "Native Daughter," 524, 526. A devout Catholic (responsible for the conversion of Claude McKay to Catholicism toward the end of his life), Tarry courageously asks her *Commonweal* readership, "There may be Catholics who will not read 'Native Son' because its author is a communist. But, did you ever stop to think that Catholics may be among those who are responsible for some of the conditions that have led Richard Wright and scores of others into the ranks of the reds?" (524).

111. Jane Dabney Shackelford, author of *My Happy Days*, did focus on the image's details, however, commenting in her papers, "Look—Look—Look. Negroes are lazy—untidy —sloven. It made me furious. My Dog Rinty. Buttons missing from front of mother's dress. Hem of mother's dress ripped and hanging down. Laziness—slovenliness of Negroes" ("Rinty Comment"). I attribute Shackelford's response to her intense desire to represent black home life positively and to her personal anxiety about the lower class's habits and tendencies. See K. C. Smith, *Children's Literature of the Harlem Renaissance*, for a fuller discussion of Shackelford's class bias.

112. Another dimension of the text that aligns Harlem with celebrity culture is the dog, Rinty, who evokes two of the most famous movie canines of the 1930s and 1940s: the name alludes to Rin Tin Tin, the German shepherd, and Rinty's breed and look re-

mind a reader of Asta, the wire fox terrier star of *Bringing Up Baby* (1938) and the Thin Man movies (1934–57).

113. Wright, *12 Million Black Voices*, 139.

114. One could argue that the Joe Louis line is also a metonymic gesture, with his success standing in for the success of Harlem.

115. Stott, *Documentary Expression*, 62.

116. Stott argues, "Social documentary deals with facts that are alterable. It has an intellectual dimension to make clear what the facts are, why they came about, and how they can be changed for the better. Its more important dimension, however, is usually the emotional: feeling the fact may move the audience to wish to change it" (ibid., 26).

117. See Dunlap, "At Fifty"; and Butts, "Writing Projects."

118. See Butts, "Writing Projects."

119. May, *Homeward Bound*, 150.

120. Tarry explains in her autobiography, "The housing shortage in Chicago became insignificant in comparison with the living conditions I found when I returned to New York in 1944. . . . Various friends joined me, and we walked the streets hoping to see a 'for rent' sign. We went to real estate offices, we advertised and told everybody who would listen that I had to find a place to live before my baby was born. My doctor, who became disturbed over my anxiety, begged his patients to notify them if they heard of any vacancies" (*Third Door*, 250–51). Tarry eventually found a place through a friend, "a fourth floor walk-up, with few of the comforts I would have wanted for my child, but it was a home" (251).

121. Butts, "New World A-Coming," 651.

122. Christine Jenkins notes that *My Dog Rinty* was included in the bookselling effort of the American Library Association's International Relations Committee for CARE-UNESCO, and thus was part of the Cold War effort at presenting American childhood to an international audience. See Jenkins, "ALA Youth Services Librarians."

123. Reviews generally did not invoke the text's plea for housing reform, preferring to focus on the liveliness of the story and the dog's personality. If they did mention Harlem, comments were vague, like that of Arna Bontemps in the *New York Times*, who wrote about Rinty's mousing abilities: "[A] talent like this was not to be scorned in a part of the city where buildings are old and mice often a problem" ("For the Young Reader's Bookshelf").

124. I allude to Melamed's use of "race-radical" (*Represent and Destroy*, xvii), a category of texts addressing material conditions and causes of oppression, often with an international emphasis.

125. C. Curtis, "About Books and Authors," 11.

126. Dudziak explains, "The cases leading up to *Brown v. Board of Education* did not involve a concrete federal interest. Instead, the federal government was interested in the abstract concept of justice at stake in these cases, and in the well-being of the plaintiffs" (*Cold War Civil Rights*, 91).

127. See Galassi, *Roy DeCarava*, for instance, who emphasizes the tenderness of DeCarava's approach.

128. Stange, "Illusion Complete within Itself," 78.

129. Ibid., 82.

130. Blair, *Harlem Crossroads*, 52.
131. Roy DeCarava, quoted in Rampersad, *Life of Langston Hughes*, 249.
132. Ibid.
133. Willis, "Picturing Us," 3.
134. Ibid., 4.
135. Langston Hughes, quoted in Rampersad, *Life of Langston Hughes*, 202.
136. Chuba Nweke, quoted in ibid., 239.
137. Hughes, quoted in ibid., 240–41.
138. Mickenberg, *Learning from the Left*; and Scott, "Advanced, Repressed, and Popular," 35.
139. See Sonia Weiner, "Narrating Photography," on the history of the text's production.
140. Hughes and DeCarava, *Sweet Flypaper of Life*, 7. Subsequent citations of this book appear in the text.
141. Priest, "Flesh that Needs to Be Loved," 65.
142. Ibid., 68.
143. Hughes, quoted in Rampersad, *Life of Langston Hughes*, 244.
144. Rampersad discusses Hughes's spring 1950 essay in *Harlem Quarterly*, "How to Be a Bad Writer (in Ten Easy Lessons)," as evidence of Hughes's distaste for the gritty urban realism of Wright and Himes. See ibid., 207.
145. A. Davis, "Integration and Race Literature," 145.
146. Ibid.
147. Ibid., 146.
148. Rampersad, *Life of Langston Hughes*, 199. Rampersad discusses the middle class's desire for literature that did not mention racial issues, and uses the Karamu Theater's refusal to stage Hughes's *Mulatto* as evidence of the cultural inclination away from texts that spotlight blackness. Rampersad also explains that "Hughes's harping on blues and jazz and the beauty of black folks was an archaic position many were eager to repudiate in the dawn of integration, whose glorious sun would be the Supreme Court's 1954 decision" (207).
149. The representation of the family is not wholly celebratory in Hughes's text. See Erina Duganne on DeCarava and the psychic self, where she argues that Hughes uses the tension between text and image in representing Rodney's neglectful parents to offer a nuanced response to the sociological charge of familial disintegration (Duganne, *Self in Black and White*, 149).
150. Alan Thomas reads these political images as conforming to the spirit of the overall narrative: "The impression conveyed is that of political struggle as part of Harlem's very rhythm—no more obtrusive in DeCarava's eyes than stick ball or parades or family ritual, but no less integral to black American existence" ("Literary Snapshots," 21).
151. Priest also notes the liminality of children in *Flypaper*'s photographs, but reads liminality through the body; children allow the reader access to a new version of physicality: "In many of the pictures of children, they stand, literally, in the vestibules and borders within the pictures—in doorways, windows, and on stoops, or as with Ronnie Bell, on the very threshold of the text—because they are the gateway between the discovery of the flesh both pained and beloved" ("Flesh that Needs to Be Loved," 68). Sonia Weiner offers a terrific reading of the "no place" child, seeing the X of the crossroads as a gesture toward treasure maps, and the manhole cover in the image as covering up the

"social unrest bubbling just beneath the surface of Harlem and beneath the surface of *The Sweet Flypaper of Life*" ("Narrating Photography," 168).

152. Stange asserts, "Like [Dorothea] Lange, DeCarava uses the found text of a billboard and the iconography of travel; like [Gordon] Parks he places a dignified black woman against a discordant setting. Parks complicated his meaning with iconic reference to Grant Wood's self-denying and self-righteous farm couple, and DeCarava evokes, with equal resonance, the myth of Cinderella. There seems no doubt that social statement is intended. But DeCarava's title is without the pointed irony of those that name the FSA photographs. Rather, the word 'Graduation' refers us to a familiar, virtually universal ritual, whose regular, cyclical recurrence is dependable. Despite the poignant juxtaposition of a figure symbolic of hope and beauty against an environment that appears vicious in its indifference to her, DeCarava's title directs us toward neither the 'anecdotal descriptiveness' of photojournalism, nor the social instrumentality of documentary" ("Illusion Complete within Itself," 85).

153. Stange explains, "Even as the word 'graduation' 'explains' the image literally in relation to such an occasion, it becomes itself a marker of ambiguity. The title both denotes the sharp, ritually-defined difference between childhood and adulthood that a graduation ceremony marks and that seems to be signified visually in the image, and it connotes a transition that is all but imperceptible, as in the related terms 'gradual' or 'gradation,' and this second sense of the word is directly contrary to the sharp contrast that is visually signified" (ibid., 86).

154. Ibid.

155. In an interview, DeCarava discussed his decision to name the image "David," as a reference to David and Goliath, and he assented that he aimed to evoke an African mask in representing David's face (I. Miller, "If It Hasn't Been One of Color," 855). The naming of an image as it appears outside a text should not necessarily inflect its interpretation within a photo narrative. In other words, DeCarava may employ the David-and-Goliath myth for his own interpretation of the piece but, when one reads the photobook, there is no uplifting certainty that this child will strike down a giant of the streets.

156. A. Davis, "Integration and Race Literature," 142.

2. PICTURES AND NONFICTION

1. Barthes, *Camera Lucida*, 88.

2. Sontag, *On Photography*, 10.

3. It seems as though there was a first edition published in 1947 by the Tennessee Southern Publishing Company. My edition, with a copyright page dated 1947 and no mention of a new edition, describes the assassination of Folke Bernadotte, which happened September 17, 1948.

4. Robert Simon, quoted in Rampersad, *Life of Langston Hughes*, 248.

5. Mickenberg, *Learning from the Left*, 233.

6. Ibid., 256.

7. Reynolds edited the *Message*, the monthly publication for African American Adventists, from 1944 to 1959 and from 1977 to 1980. A biography of Reynolds published in *Youth's Instructor*, the Adventist youth magazine, asserts, "While a student of Oakwood

College and of Fisk University, he earned school expenses by working on a farm, in a sawmill, and as a rock crusher. Before entering boarding school he worked at sign lettering, a skill he continued with profit in college. A district minister for six churches in Kansas before becoming editor, he had also pastored churches in St. Louis and Sedalia, Missouri, and had raised up or organized churches in St. Joseph and Kansas City, Missouri. He has edited a column for the Kansas City *Call;* written the book, *Dawn of a Brighter Day;* collaborated on *Little Journeys Into Storyland,* and *Modern Home Counselor;* and contributed to many religious publications" ("Editor's Note").

8. Paddock published a variety of children's books for the SDA community.

9. Although it is possible that Paddock mentored Reynolds in writing for children, Reynolds's daughter, Dawn, told me in an interview that Paddock had virtually nothing to do with the composition and content of the text. The work was wholly Reynolds's, and Paddock, as a white children's author, served as a kind of endorsement of the work. Paddock was also manager of the book department of Southern Publishing Association, the press that issued *Little Journeys,* a situation that might have contributed to his name's appearing on the book (Reynolds, "Introducing in This Issue").

10. Baker, "Precursor to the Sabbath," 25.

11. See Baker, *Crucial Moments,* 118–25.

12. See Baker on James K. Humphrey's Utopia Plan ("Precursor to the Sabbath," 25–27); and R. C. Jones, *James K. Humphrey.* See London, *Seventh-Day Adventists,* 142–44, on Byard's death and its effects for Seventh-Day Adventists.

13. Samuel G. London describes black Adventist James McElhaney's proposal to the General Conference Committee in Chicago in April 1944: "[H]e provided the denomination's white leaders with two choices: integration, or the creation of black regional conferences—allowing African Americans to exercise more control over their affairs. Unable to stomach the idea of a fully integrated Church, Jay J. Nethery, president of the Lake Union Conference, persuaded most of his white colleagues to vote for the establishment of semi-independent regional conferences for blacks. On April 10 the measure passed, and the black regional conferences came into being" (*Seventh-Day Adventists,* 144–45).

14. L. B. Reynolds, We Have Tomorrow, 321.

15. L. B. Reynolds, "Brighter Horizon Beyond," 6.

16. See London, *Seventh-Day Adventists,* on the theological sources of Adventists' reluctance to participate in civil rights efforts. Not all Adventists retreated from engagement with the cause. London describes the contributions of black Adventists: Matthew C. Strachan, a minister and NAACP member (93); Irene Morgan, plaintiff in the 1946 *Morgan v. Virginia* Supreme Court decision desegregating interstate travel (106); Alfonzo Greene (NAACP leader and Southern Christian Leadership Conference [SCLC] member), Terrance Roberts (one of the Little Rock Nine), and Frank Hale (a founder of the Laymen's Leadership Conference, which in 1961 pushed the Adventists to desegregate [107]). He also discusses at length black ministerial involvement in civil rights, as in the case of Warren St. Claire Banfield Jr., founder and director of the Adventist's Office of Human Relations for the North American Division in 1970s (138).

17. Douglas illustrated the cover of the February 1958 issue of *Message,* under Reynolds's editorship.

18. Reynolds, *Little Journeys into Storyland,* 111. Subsequent citations of this book appear in the text.
19. I consulted James Smethurst, historian of black leftist movements, about my suspicion that Davis would be a household name and his face a household image (Facebook conversation).
20. "We Salute General Davis."
21. The description of Bunche's grandmother's advice must have been in circulation before 1947. See Bunche, *Selected Speeches and Writings.*
22. Mickenberg explains: "At least sixty juvenile books about Abraham Lincoln were published between 1945 and 1965. . . . Of those juvenile books on Lincoln published in the postwar period—arguably the 'zenith' of Lincoln's popularity (according to Merrill Peterson)—at least ten of those books, or nearly 20 percent, were by left-wing authors" (*Learning from the Left,* 241).
23. Ibid., 232.
24. Griffiths, "Ralph Ellison," 616.
25. Smethurst indicates that although Herndon would likely not have been recognizable to a young audience, the readers' parents—especially subscribers to the *Message,* where the image had appeared before—might have been able to identify Herndon (Facebook conversation).
26. See London, *Seventh-Day Adventists,* on white Adventist reluctance to attach theology to social progress. Reynolds's presentation of Jesus as social agent appears more daring when read through the traditional Adventist reluctance to follow the "social gospel" promoted by Martin Luther King Jr. or the ecumenicalism of the SCLC.
27. "We Can Tell Much."
28. Mitchell, *Righteous Propagation,* 113.
29. See K. C. Smith, "Childhood, the Body, and Race Performance."
30. Majors, *First Steps and Nursery Rhymes,* 7.
31. Floyd, *Floyd's Flowers,* 247–48.
32. One image is suggestive of black conduct-book iconography, and although it might not attach explicitly to the emphasis on childhood and racial progress, it does point back toward Reynolds's colonialist uses of religion. The image is of an SDA preacher from the Solomon Islands, who stands with the Bible in his right hand and elements of his culture of origin in his left. Wilson Gia Liligeto explains that Chief Kata Ragoso converted to Seventh-Day Adventism as a child and in 1936 attended the general conference meeting in San Francisco; during World War II, Ragoso "became the leader of the Seventh-day Adventist Church throughout the whole of the Western Solomon Islands" (*Babata,* 41). The Ragoso image is striking, given the long tradition of "before and after" imagery within black conduct material, an approach commonly employed in the late nineteenth and early twentieth centuries in depicting African American modernity and material success.
33. A further area of research would be the relationship of photography within religious publications to the shape of the black photographic tradition. The *Message* in the 1940s and 1950s contains many images of happy, vital, outgoing, confident children, all of whom have presumably benefited by knowledge of the love of God and by the health-reform efforts of the Seventh-Day Adventist Church.
34. hooks, *Art on my Mind,* 60.

35. Ibid.
36. Sontag, *On Photography*, 7.
37. Dawn Reynolds also remembers her father taking her as a child to hear King speak: "These folks would come to speak at Fisk in Nashville, Martin Luther King and Thurgood Marshall. My dad—we were in school at the time and even though we were not in high school or middle school—my dad said that something tremendous was going to happen because of their influence. He wanted us to meet them. He had the UPI [United Press International] and other credentials, he got in to special seats, and he visited Fisk's campus so Fisk people knew him. He was invited to receptions afterwards" (interview).
38. L. B. Reynolds, "March of Events," February 1952, 5–6.
39. L. B. Reynolds, "March of Events," April 1957, 5–6.
40. L. B. Reynolds, "March of Events," June 1957, 7.
41. Rampersad, *Life of Langston Hughes*, 309.
42. Blair, *Harlem Crossroads*, 200.
43. Hirsch, *Generation of Postmemory*, 33.
44. Ibid., 38.
45. Ibid.
46. Meltzer had originally approached Arna Bontemps with the project, and Bontemps suggested Hughes as a collaborator. Bontemps advised Meltzer and Hughes on the outline of the book and is thanked in the acknowledgments.
47. Barbara Chatton wrote in 2002, before Melzer's death, in 2009, "Five of his books have been nominated for the National Book Award, and his titles frequently appear on the 'best books of the year' lists of the American Library Association and the National Council for the Social Studies, and *School Library Journal*, *Horn Book*, and the *New York Times*" (Chatton, "Milton Meltzer," 438).
48. Meltzer, "Designing Narrator," 333. In the mid-1960s, Meltzer began working on a biography of Hughes for young people, which he published in 1968 after Hughes's death, in 1967.
49. Hughes wrote to Meltzer that he was finishing his autobiography and would soon start work on *Pictorial History*: "I'll start putting my shelf of Negro history books together in front of my desk. I've a pretty good collection. And fortunately, too, am only a few blocks from the Schomburg Collection" (Hughes, letter to Milton Meltzer, June 20, 1955). The book was largely written in the fall of 1955.
50. As Deborah Willis argues, "In reading African-American photographs in particular, the context of production, reception, and recollection needs to be specified and analyzed" ("Search for Self," 107).
51. Hughes's biographer describes the "triumphant reception" of *Pictorial History* and *The Sweet Flypaper of Life* (Rampersad, *Life of Langston Hughes*, 261).
52. Hughes, letter to Milton Meltzer, June 19, 1959.
53. "Ike gets Anderson, Hughes Books."
54. McNeil, interview.
55. Blair, *Harlem Crossroads*, 53.
56. A. Davis, "Integration and Race Literature," 145.
57. Buchman's narrative contains distasteful descriptions of enslavement and the civil war, such as this: "Northerners still looked upon themselves as the potential liberators of

some three million slaves. But in actuality, many of the slaves did not wish to be freed. There were numerous cases of slaves, caught in the no-man's land between advancing and retreating armies, choosing voluntarily to follow their owner-families rather than escape within the lines of the emancipated North" (*Pictorial History of the Confederacy*, 133).

58. Bardolph, "Negro Americans."
59. "Picture Books."
60. Bond, *Lincoln University Bulletin*.
61. P. L. P., "Week's Books."
62. Mickenberg, *Learning from the Left*, 276.
63. Platt, "Reviews of Related Literature." Platt wrote in September 1957 that *Pictorial History* was a model for other pictorial histories ("[u]ndoubtedly the best such book that has come to our attention"), warning, "The pictorial histories demonstrate again that the mass media are producing things which should carefully be incorporated into the normal fields of study. Our enthusiasm for newer types of teaching techniques, however, must be modified by careful and proper selection of material. To admit everything into the classroom that passes as 'modern' or 'a new way' could very conceivably bring about a frightening reaction to the very thing we are attempting to do: Use every means available for the proper instruction of our youth" (Platt, "Pictorial Histories," 59).
64. "Negro History Comes Alive in Pictures." Other reviews that mention the child audience for the book, whether at home or in classrooms, include *Kirkus* (October 1, 1956), *Library Journal* (December 1, 1956), *Black Dispatch* (November 28, 1956), and *Jet* magazine (November 29, 1956), among others.
65. Hughes, "Books as Christmas Gifts."
66. "About Books."
67. E. G., "Up From Slavery in Prose and Pictures."
68. Hogan, "Graphic Document."
69. H. A. W., "Negro."
70. "Negro in America."
71. Platt, "Reviews of Related Literature."
72. Byrnes, "Cameras over the World."
73. Hughes, "Press Reviews." Many reviews mention the need for the book in light of integration. A reviewer named E. S. is typical in the assertion, published in the *Lewiston (Maine) Independent*, that "[i]n view of the grave problems in the Deep South due to the U.S. Supreme Court's decision of May 17, 1954, outlawing racial segregation, these authors believed—and rightly—that a better knowledge of the Negro in America, his background, his struggle first for freedom, then equality, is badly needed at this time" (E. S., "Books and Authors").
74. J. B., "Negro in America Well Researched" (emphasis mine).
75. "Monumental Treasury."
76. Meltzer gave specific directions to the editor at Crown, Robert Simon, about marketing the book through civil rights venues. In a May 19, 1956, memo to Simon, Meltzer listed a number of approaches, including numbers ten and sixteen: "10. Journal American and New York Post are both very concerned with our era. JA ran series on Montgomery bus boycott and their writer should be given our book. Post should be

approached thru editor Wecshler and/or Ted Poston, Negro writer on staff. These and Scripps Howard chain trying hard to *sell* to Negroes. . . . 16. 1956 POLITICAL CAMPAIGN: I've learned that Dick Nixon is now in charge of 'integration' politicking for the Repubs. He calls in 50 business leaders at a time to special Washington sessions and urges them to abolish discrimination in their plants. He ought to get this book. So should Stevenson, Kefauver and Harriman. If any would mention it publicly, it'd be a big boost."

77. Rampersad, *Life of Langston Hughes*, 309.

78. See, for instance, De Santis's edited volume of Hughes's history of the NAACP, *Fight for Freedom and Other Writings on Civil Rights.* De Santis's introduction frames out the context for Hughes's history and explains that reviewers saw that book as a kind of manual for "ongoing battles for civil rights" (17).

79. Critics often speak, instead, of Hughes's stormy relationship with James Baldwin, for instance, or his envy of Ralph Ellison's successful novel *Invisible Man.* See Rampersad, *Life of Langston Hughes.*

80. Saunders Redding's review of *Pictorial History* emphasized American exceptionalism and brotherhood: "This is a kind of knowledge that is needed as background upon which to project the news of American race relations that lately fills the national and international press. But apart from telling us a great deal about the past and the present of the American Negro, the authors take a considered look at the future, and what they see should give encouragement to all those, white and Negro, who believe that the ancient idealism of the American creed still lives in the hearts of the American people."

81. Mays, "My View."

82. P. L. P., "Week's Books."

83. James Egert Allen, review. Allen was also the first president of the New York branch of the NAACP, a lifelong educator, and a historian. Allen's review was published in the *Atlanta World* on December 27, 1956, the *Waco (Tex.) Messenger* on December 28, 1956, and the *New York Amsterdam News* on December 29, 1956. These reviews are collected in Hughes's papers.

84. Hughes and Meltzer, *Pictorial History of the Negro*, 4. Subsequent citations of this book appear in the text.

85. Rogers, "History Shows."

86. Glassman, "About Books."

87. Parker, "Part, Not Thing Apart."

88. Cookman, "Two Books Tell Negroes' Story."

89. Review of *Pictorial History*, *Cleveland Plain Dealer*, December 9, 1956.

90. Hogan, "Graphic Document." Even the leftist journal the *Worker* commented on the lack of propaganda in *Pictorial History*, though with a tinge of regret: "The authors grind the axe for no particular political dogma in their book. Nevertheless it is marked by a definite identification with liberal thought and by a vigorous confirmation of that viewpoint which holds that the Negro people have fought—and properly so—during and since slavery times for full equality" ("Negro History Comes Alive in Pictures").

91. A review in the *New Leader* stated of the tone of *Pictorial History*, "Mr. Hughes never raises his voice, but writes dispassionately of the impact of America on the Negro, of

the Negro on America, and, most important, of his people's self-generated struggle to free themselves from bondage and oppression" (Bromley, "Negro Freedom-Fighters," 21).

92. Trachtenberg, *Reading American Photographs*, 6.

93. Meltzer, "Designing Narrator," 336.

94. In the only review I could locate from a pictorial magazine, *Picturescope* (April 1957), the anonymous writer described the effective relationship between text and image: "The selection of the pictures was controlled by the importance of the story to be told in image and word . . . an important example of the interdependence of pictures and words in order to tell an important story. . . . The design of the book and the arrangement of the pictures were done with the idea that one can browse at any point and still find a unified stretch of information in pictures and words" (review of *Pictorial History*, *Picturescope*).

95. Trachtenberg, *Reading American Photographs*, 203.

96. Trachtenberg explains Mead's faith in "internal dialogue," in which one "takes on the role or point of view of the other, imagines it provisionally as one's own in order to respond to it. To foster exactly this exchange between the subject and the viewer of his pictures, and between himself and them, Hine attempted to enter his pictures into the internal experience of his audience, to awaken in them an imaginative response which would issue in a revised identity, one which now acknowledges the imagined voices of his pictured workers as part of one's essential social world" (ibid., 204).

97. Ibid., 207.

98. The Ingram case was taken up by the NAACP and the Civil Rights Congress, an organization with a strong Communist membership, as well as by Mary Church Terrell. Black communities in Georgia envisioned the case through gender as much as through race, supporting Ingram as the mother of twelve children. See Martin, "Race, Gender, and Southern Injustice."

99. Abel, *Signs of the Times*, 105.

100. See K. C. Smith, *Children's Literature of the Harlem Renaissance*; and Farebrother, *The Collage Aesthetic in the Harlem Renaissance*.

101. Several reviews mentioned Lockerman with pleasure, including the *Black Dispatch*: "This book does not miss a thing worth while in American life. It carries pictures of Rev. Martin Luther King, Thurgood Marshall, and Autherine Lucy. This will be the best Christmas present any white or black man can contribute to his home. You'll even see the picture of Gloria Lockerman spelling 'chrysanthemum'" ("Langston Hughes's Best Effort").

102. The poem concludes, "Let a new earth rise. Let another world be born. Let a / bloody peace be written in the sky. Let a second / generation full of courage issue forth; let a people / loving freedom come to growth. Let a beauty full of / healing and a strength of final clenching be the pulsing / in our spirit and our blood. Let the martial songs / be written, let the dirges disappear. Let a race of men now / rise and take control."

103. Trachtenberg, *Reading American Photographs*, 88.

104. J. Berger, "Understanding a Photograph," 294.

105. Powell, *Cutting a Figure*, 16–17.

106. DeCarava's estate does not permit reproduction of his images, or else the study would have included the image of Allen Turner as well as others from *Sweet Flypaper*.

107. Cadava, *Words of Light*, 12–13.
108. Sontag, *On Photography*, 15.
109. Review of *Pictorial History*, Information Service.
110. "A&T Student Gets Award."
111. McNeil said of his high school experience with Hughes: "I had known of Hughes, and I can't exactly remember the location, in our racially segregated school. We had some pretty powerful teachers who didn't hold back in terms of being honest and truthful and forceful about the fact that we were all God's children and we should carry ourselves with dignity. His poems were so powerful: 'Mother to Son,' 'life for me has been no crystal stair.' That, coming with my background, was quite powerful, and so Hughes was always important to me" (McNeil, interview).

3. TODAY

1. Martin Berger, *Seeing through Race*, 6.
2. Raiford, *Imprisoned in a Luminous Glare*, 7.
3. Tom Levin, quoted in Friedman, "Tom Levin and Polly Greenberg's Reflections."
4. Matt Herron, e-mail correspondence, April 23, 2013.
5. See Dittmer, *Local People*; Payne, *I've Got the Light of Freedom*; A. Jordan, "Fighting"; and Marshall, *Student Activism* for a more comprehensive history of the CDGM.
6. Dittmer, *Local People*, 370.
7. According to Dittmer, "Of the fifteen workers in the top administrative positions, thirteen had civil rights credentials. Eight were women and six were black" (ibid.).
8. Payne, *I've Got the Light of Freedom*, 330. Ellen Tarry, author of *My Dog Rinty*, traveled to Mississippi in July 1965 to visit a less radical Head Start program. Tarry joined the interracial group Wednesdays in Mississippi, an organization founded by the National Council of Negro Women, to visit Head Start schools in Jackson, bringing her own books as well as other Viking titles to share with the children. The afterword to her autobiography describes "the little boys and girls who would be better prepared for the first grade in September because the Office of Economic Opportunity had launched HEADSTART" (*Third Door*, 309). Tarry did not visit the CDGM Head Start program, which created *Today*; her autobiography mentions Esther Sampson, the director of the Head Start program in Hines County, and Tarry's visiting schools in the city of Jackson. The press distinguished Jackson's program from the more radical CDGM. A May 26, 1965, article in the *Jackson Daily News* reassured readers about the politics of Sampson's program: "Officials say the project is 'completely independent' of other anti-poverty programs and in the words of one, 'is not affiliated with the Delta Ministry or the National Council of Churches.' At a press conference Tuesday afternoon, officials of the Jackson Head Start program emphasized they were not concerned with social revolution, but to help children from poverty-stricken families 'develop social skills and cultural experiences'" (Ezelle, "Beginning of Head Start in Jackson").
9. Lowen, "I Knew I Wasn't White," 550.
10. Dittmer, *Local People*, 373.
11. Greenberg suggests, "Tom Levin wanted to change, not just the image of school, as were other Head Starts with varying degrees of success, but the very nature of the

school. He knew that if, following the lead of Freud, Erikson, and others, psychoanalytic wisdom could be built into a social action project, the result would be a powerful organization. So he started there" (*Devil Has Slippery Shoes*, 98).

12. Ibid., 3.

13. Ibid., 114.

14. Ibid., 74.

15. For an interesting perspective on the lobbying efforts to save CDGM, see Sol Gordon's liner notes, "A Psychologist's Mississippi," on the album of CDGM children singing freedom songs. Titled *Head Start, with the Child Development Group of Mississippi*, the album was produced by Moses Asch, founder of Folkways Records, in 1967. It also includes beautiful images by movement photographer Bob Fletcher.

16. Payne, *I've Got the Light of Freedom*, 343.

17. Dittmer, *Local People*, 375, 382.

18. Roxy Meredith, in *Child Development Group of Mississippi: Histories*, 11.

19. Mantler, *Power to the Poor*, 94–95.

20. See A. Jordan, "Fighting," for an account of the long-term implications of CDGM.

21. In the material available about the comic, reviewers frequently cite the number 250,000. See T. Miller, "King Comic Book," for example.

22. A curriculum summary is available on the Internet. See Emery, Braselmann, and Gold, *Freedom School Curriculum*.

23. For instance, when I asked Polly Greenberg about the work of the Bank Street School in composing books, she replied, "I'm an early childhood educator, teacher, teacher of preschool and primary teachers, parents, etc., and have been since the early 1950s, so of course I knew about the Bank Street readers, but (1) they weren't made by children, (2) the children in the pictures weren't African American looking—they were white children painted brown, and (3) they were city children, not rural children like ours. They weren't relevant to our needs" (Greenberg, e-mail correspondence, March 6, 2013).

24. Kirksey would later become one of the first post-Reconstruction black state senators in Mississippi.

25. Greenberg, *Devil Has Slippery Shoes*, 157. The 1966 proposal for a full year's funding of CDGM explains the bookmaking strategy: "These stories may be only a sentence picked from his [a child's] conversation or play. Or they may be longer discussions written down. But whatever the length, quality, grammar, or dullness of the story may be, it will be treated with respect. These stories will be displayed in a special story corner, read to the children frequently, and used as a base for making the children's individual word cards to learn to read with. The best of these books (the most universally interesting to rural, Southern, Negro children, the most imaginative, those with the most colorful language) may be printed by our printing project" ("Proposal and Application").

26. These include *Today* (1965), *Pond* (1965), and *The Hike* (1966), as well as two books by Lucia Clapps, *The Bumble Bee Story* (1965) and *The Tougaloo Book* (1966); Henry J. Kirksey's *Haunted House* (1965); and Charlene Cooks and Hank Kirksey's *A Dog* (1965).

27. Greenberg wrote, "I established the Area Teacher Guide system—one for every eight centers, and showed the 16 Area Teacher Guides (ATGs) how to take dictation, make it

into extremely simple 'books,' add children's drawings, magazine cutouts, or whatever to illustrate them, and above all, how *to show the parent-teachers the ATGs worked with every week how to do this*" (Greenberg, e-mail correspondence, March 6, 2013).

28. Through e-mail correspondence with Matt Herron, the civil rights photographer listed along with John Wallace in *Today*'s credits, I learned that Derby likely authored the book and took most of its photographs. I am tremendously grateful to Derby for talking with me about the history and composition of the text.

29. In an interview with me, Derby spoke of her family's investment in photography: "I had my own background and experiences and teaching—educational—style, which was influenced by my background, my family background, my training, my interests. My father was a photographer. He gave my sister and I a camera when we were in elementary school. For any social occasion that we had with the family, and we had a lot of them, my father had his fancy camera, he took pictures and he made them into slides, and at the following social event, birthday, anniversary, Christmas, Thanksgiving, he would show the slides. So we were already in the mode of taking pictures."

30. Ibid.

31. Matt Herron, a prominent movement photographer and trainer in SNCC's photography unit, was not involved in the production of the book. However, he can identify particular images within *Today* as his (Herron, e-mail correspondence, April 24, 2013). Doris Derby identified her images for me; they appear to be the smaller, group photographs, whereas Herron's are larger and clearer. Derby said that Herron had a better-quality camera (Derby, interview).

32. Child Development Group of Mississippi, *Today*, 23. Subsequent citations of this book appear in the text.

33. Herron, e-mail correspondence, April 24, 2013.

34. Derby, interview.

35. I asked Derby to identify photographs that are hers; she sent me originals of some of the photos in the book, such as that of the ring game.

36. See Duganne, *Self in Black and White*, 196n54.

37. Neither the OEO papers nor the Smithsonian retains a list of this exhibition's photographers and images.

38. According to Duganne, "[W]hen *Profile of Poverty* opened in May 1965 at the Smithsonian Museum, the Moynihan Report, completed in March 1965, had only been distributed to a few persons within the Department of Labor and the White House. It was not until 4 June 1965, when President Johnson spoke at a Howard University commencement, that Moynihan's ideas about the pathological nature of African American poverty would first become public knowledge, and even then it was only between mid-July and early August that the first full summaries of the Report were made publicly available" (*Self in Black and White*, 80).

39. One might also recall divergences in depictions of the urban black family in the 1940s, when Viking Press issued both *12 Million Black Voices* and *My Happy Days*, as chapter 1 discusses.

40. Raiford describes the publicity effort at SNCC: "Under the general and expansive title 'Communications,' SNCC developed a formidable media structure of its own through which the organization published its own newspaper and promotional materials; printed its own posters and press releases; and conducted research and incident

investigations. In 1964–65, this structure would expand to produce political primers and teaching tools, and beginning in 1965, art exhibits, calendars, postcards, and more photoessay books in the vein of *The Movement*" (*Imprisoned in a Luminous Glare*, 72).

41. Lowen says of the links between CDGM and civil rights groups, "The leadership of CDGM was often identical to the leadership of the local movement and Mississippi Freedom Democratic Party infrastructure, spanning eighty communities in Mississippi from up north in the Delta down to the Gulf Coast" ("I Knew I Wasn't White," 550).

42. Both volumes of *Something of Our Own* also use the same printer, Henry J. Kirksey (Mississippi Action for Community Education and HJK Publishing appear to be names Kirksey used for his press), and the same style of font and layout as *Today* and other CDGM publications. In fact, *Part II* on its copyright page credits the CDGM and the Aaron E. Norman Fund (a philanthropy that supported civil rights efforts) for a grant to fund the publication. Varela describes her relationship with the publisher: "And there was this wonderful African American guy in Jackson who was a printer and who had been in the NAACP since God started the world. He was a veteran, one of those old-timey guys that supported the movement. But education was his bag. Anyway, to make a living he had a printing business, and he would print SNCC flyers. So SNCC people in Jackson said, 'Go see Mr. Kirksey.' And we developed a great friendship. I brought him business and he taught me how to do layout. He did all my stuff. He was a great mentor, and I *loved* printing books. I loved seeing a project go from beginning [to end]. In the chaos of the movement, the fact that you could [see something go] from beginning to end—create something, you know—kept you from going crazy" (quoted in Kelen, *This Light of Ours*, 221).

43. Matt Herron, quoted in Kelen, *This Light of Ours*, 238.

44. Raiford, *Imprisoned in a Luminous Glare*, 127.

45. Lester, e-mail correspondence.

46. Women's activist contributions to the movement have been charted by scholars. See Houck and Dixon, *Women and the Civil Rights Movement*, which collects speeches, for instance; and Collier-Thomas and Franklin, *Sisters in the Struggle*.

47. Lorraine Hansberry, *The Movement*, quoted in Blair, *Harlem Crossroads*, 118.

48. Blair, *Harlem Crossroads*, 219.

49. Greenberg explains in her history of the CDGM, "We thought that since the whole program was to be geared toward discovering (and helping the *children* discover) their qualities, characteristics, interests, and powers, it would be quite appropriate to begin building a reading program out of the resources, experiences, living techniques, friendships, interests, standards, thoughts, dreams, language, and wealth of 'material' inside a child. . . . [W]elcoming the child's world in our reading program would help each child unfold and dip inward and stretch out and reach around and continue becoming a person; for himself, for *his* sub-community. Using the material each child brought to the center with him, by making it into books for him to learn to read from, could help us work *with* him—not *on* him—toward evolving a strong sense of self that could cope and contribute in a manner that brought him satisfaction" (*Devil Has Slippery Shoes*, 157).

50. Varela, "Filmstrips."

51. Greenberg, *Devil Has Slippery Shoes*, 159.

52. Both Derby in an interview (May 6, 2013) and Greenberg in e-mail correspondence (April 23, 2013) confirmed that the process of bookmaking was the CDGM's priority.
53. Maria Varela, quoted in Kelen, *This Light of Ours*, 222.
54. I take this description from Crawford, "Textual Productions," 193.
55. Even Matt Herron, whose photos were added to Derby's at CDGM headquarters and included in *Today*, had never heard of or read the book until I shared it with him in 2013 (Herron, e-mail correspondence, April 23, 2013).
56. Derby told me about the men as guards in my interview; elsewhere, she talked about guns as being protective in the preschool depicted in *Today*: "At night the men kept watch with their rifles, because white people had shot into the house on several occasions. Rifles were also kept in the corner of the Head Start center in case of an attack, because white people hated the idea of there being a newly built center for black children and wanted to destroy it. Durant's white residents also hated the idea that the black community donated the land, labor, and materials to build the center" (Derby, "Sometimes in the Ground Troops," 443–44).
57. Gordon, "Psychologist's Mississippi."
58. As an example of the way Mississippians considered CDGM a means to resist white violence, Ben F. Faust, a "retired farmer and grandfather of three CDGM children," in a pamphlet on the history of the group, linked the 1961 murder of Herbert Lee and the 1964 murder of Freedom Rider Lewis Allen with the need for the CDGM. The text of the pamphlet concludes with Faust's description of Allen: "Later he was killed because he was going to testify against the sheriff [as a witness to Lee's murder]. He was shot with buckshots at his gate three times. His brain was piled up under the truck. So I think that CDGM should keep operating the Head Start for Negroes" (*Child Development Group of Mississippi: Histories*, 18).
59. Derby, "Sometimes in the Ground Troops," 443.
60. T. Davis, foreword, xiii.
61. "Little Sally Walker," in *Head Start with the Child Development Group of Mississippi*.
62. Jones and Hawes, *Step It Down*, 107.
63. Derby, interview.
64. Blair, *Harlem Crossroads*, 15–16. Blair is interested in the "logic of 'nervousness'" (16) of the Harlem-riot photographs.
65. King, interview.

4. THE BLACK ARTS MOVEMENT

1. As Lisa Gail Collins and Margo Natalie Crawford suggest, "black power" was a term applied to a variety of political positions: "[T]he brash phrase quickly became attached with numerous contradictory political strategies—from the development of black capitalism and the election of African American politicians to the ignition of a Marxist-inspired revolution and the creation of a new black nation" ("Power to the People!," 5).
2. According to James Smethurst, "One obvious problem that makes both 'Black Power' and 'Black Arts' such elastic terms is that there was no real center to the interlocked movements. That is to say, there was no predominant organization or ideology with which or against which various artists and activists defined themselves" (*Black Arts*

Movement, 15). Also see Amy Abugo Ongiri on the development of the black aesthetic and William L. Van Deburg on black power.

3. Critics recently have noted the complicated relationship of the BAM to the civil rights era, arguing that the two were not antagonistic. See Harper, "Nationalism and Social Division."

4. Neal, "Black Arts Movement," 29.

5. As Smethurst notes, "[T]he common thread between nearly all the groups was a belief that African Americans were a people, a nation, entitled to (needing, really) self-determination of its own destiny. While notions of what that self-determination might consist [of] (and of what forms it might take) varied, these groups shared the sense that without such power, African Americans as a people and as individuals would remain oppressed and exploited second-class (or non-) citizens in the United States.... [M]aking the actual seizing and exercise of self-determination the central feature of political and cultural activity differentiated Black Power from any major African American political movement since the heyday of Garveyism. And unlike the Garveyites, a major aspect of most tendencies of the Black Power and Black Arts movements was an emphasis on the need to develop, or expand upon, a distinctly African American or African culture that stood in opposition to white culture or cultures" (*Black Arts Movement,* 15).

6. See Crawford, "Must Revolution Be a Family Affair?," for an explanation of the naturalization of the black family within the BAM and this construction as a response to the defamations of the Moynihan Report.

7. See Smethurst, *Black Arts Movement;* and Clarke, *"After Mecca."*

8. Crawford, "Must Revolution Be a Family Affair?," 193.

9. Cade, "Pill," 205.

10. Lindsey, "Black Woman as Woman," 106.

11. Katz, "End Racism in Education."

12. Kelly, "Discipline and Craft," 684.

13. In *Muhammad Speaks,* Sanchez used her children's column to engage and, in some ways, to resist ideas coming from the Nation leadership. After Elijah Muhammad died, on February 25, 1975, his son Wallace took the reins of the organization. In many ways Wallace reformed the perspective of the Nation of Islam: his father had started to mitigate the organization's harsh antiwhite rhetoric, his "fire-and-brimstone approach to race relations" (E. Curtis, *Islam in Black America,* 63), and Wallace continued this trend, arguing in *Muhammad Speaks,* "I'm not calling those people [whites] 'devil.' I'm calling the mind that has ruled those people and you 'devil.' It ruled them for their glory and ruled you for your shame" (quoted in M. Lee, *Nation of Islam,* 63). Wallace prohibited use of the term "white devil" and invited whites, at least those who could cast off the white mind-set, into the Nation. Wallace was determined to eliminate some of the more fantastic elements of the religion, including a creation story that spoke of an evil scientist who fashioned white people, and to bring the Nation closer to Islam as a faith based in the Koran.

   Sanchez's children and women's page, entitled "New Frontiers," appeared tellingly at this moment of ideological change for the Nation. Wallace Muhammad wrote, "Sisters, I am here to do what 'women's liberation' can never do for you," arguing that "[t]he worst thing that could ever happen to hurt the growth of the child is for the father to take over the rearing of the child from its mother" (Muhammad, "Responsibility of Motherhood," 18). He concluded by excoriating women for faulty mothering and presumably for being influenced by the feminist movement: "You have become a curse to mind [men]. Your young men can't develop in your home like they should because you are a curse on their minds. It is time for you to wake up. . . . You are living in a world of lies and false mentality" (18). Sanchez began to interact with Wallace and Nation ideology a few weeks later, in an essay titled "Islam and the Rebirth of Women," where she emphasized the intellectual responsibilities of women's role as mothers: "The role of women is to be the repository of civilization; she is to raise a generation into a higher civilization; she is the link between generations; she determines progress or regression. Each generation of women gives rebirth to civilization. If she does not possess the knowledge of civilization then civilization is aborted" (Sanchez, "Islam and the Rebirth of Women," 19). Obviously the language of the feminist movement lies behind the passage, but given the Nation's opposition to birth control, the reference to abortion is cautionary; but even there Sanchez argued that another form of abortion happens when women are excluded from knowledge. In these columns we witness Sanchez revising the terms offered to her (and all other women) by Wallace and Elijah Muhammad, subtly evoking the women's rights movement and calling for male responsiveness in parenting.

14. Sanchez, "Black Family," 25.

15. Cherise A. Pollard explains that a position "that supports the black communal family" can also provide substantive critique of antifemale rhetoric ("Sexual Subversions, Political Inversions," 174).

16. See the web page "Forty-Eight Years of Service, Struggle, and Institution-Building, 1965–2014 C.E.––6205–6254 A.F.E." for Karenga's organization: http://www.us-organization.org/30th/30yrs.html.

17. See Huggins and LeBlanc-Ernest, "Revolutionary Women, Revolutionary Education," an essay on Oakland's Black Panther Party school.

18. Don L. Lee, quoted in Neal, "Black Arts Movement," 29.

19. Carmichael and Hamilton, *Black Power*, 36–37.

20. J. Jordan, "White English," 5.

21. Flynn, "'Kindergarten of New Consciousness.'"

22. Finley, "1969," 142. The connections between children's literature and the Black Arts Movement have yet to be explored substantially, although certainly the project is necessary to understanding the full involvement of children's literature in the black aesthetic.

23. D. Johnson, *Telling Tales*, 77.

24. Critically advancing a divide between artists typically recognized as Black Arts figures (like Giovanni and Sanchez) and those identified with a children's-literature tradition (like Hamilton and Mathis) is facile and unsubstantiated, for most, if not all, of the age's illustrators and authors embraced a black aesthetic. For instance, June Jordan's papers contain several letters from Mathis to Jordan.

25. Duganne, "Transcending the Fixity of Race," 199.

26. Bridget R. Cooks, in "Black Arts and Activism," explains, "At the time the art world at

large or Harlem's art and photography communities did not accept photographs as a form of art" (7).

27. Canaday, "Getting Harlem Off My Mind."

28. Lennon, "Question of Relevancy," 105. Lennon continues: "Holding signs reading, 'Visit the Metropolitan Museum of Photography' and 'That's White of Hoving!,' they handed out leaflets urging blacks to boycott the show. Titled 'Soul's been sold again!!!,' the leaflets expressed outrage at the absence of work by black painters and demanded that the museum 'seek a more viable relationship with the total black community'" (105).

29. Crawford, the leading scholar on Black Arts photography, argues for attention to be paid to the relationship of photography to black aesthetics: "Photography is one of the most neglected genres of the Black Arts Movement" ("Black Light," 24).

30. Parks worked for the Farm Security Association and the Office of War Information in the 1940s under Roy Stryker.

31. Lennon writes about the black New York art community: "Sharing a sense of urgency if not a fixed definition of the black aesthetic, creative artists during the Black Power era attempted to realize their relevance to the larger black community and its freedom through wide-ranging experimentation. Far from evidence of the movement's weakness, the diversity, complexity, and contradictions of 'black culture' as lived, interpreted, and practiced by black Americans was for many participants the source of its vitality and strength" ("Question of Relevancy," 97).

32. Crawford, "Black Light," 31.

33. See Morrison, "Rediscovering Black History" and "Site of Memory."

34. The Organization of Black American Culture (OBAC) was founded in 1967 by Hoyt Fuller, Jeff Donaldson, and Gerald McWorter.

35. Crawford, "Black Light," 33.

36. Smethurst explains: "As he later recalled, at least one of the mural's creators, William Walker, was fascinated by the aesthetic and political impact of combining visual images with text—a fascination he brought to other high-profile murals he helped create in Chicago and Detroit" (Black Arts Movement, 94). Crawford makes a similar point when she argues that "[t]he painting of the poem testifies to the concerted effort during the Black Arts Movement to make poetry concrete. . . . Christmas demonstrates that the written word itself must become visual art" (ibid., 29). A landmark of aesthetic experimentation, the *Wall of Respect* included a vital participatory element, as Crawford explains: "With the framed photography, paintings, painted poetry, poetry readings, dance performances, and political speeches, the *Wall of Respect* epitomized the breaking of boundaries between genres that defined the Black Arts Movement" (38).

37. Crawford sees Baraka's text as extending a photobook tradition: "Published by Bobbs-Merrill, *In Our Terribleness* continues the black narrative photography tradition that begins with *12 Million Black Voices* (1941), with Richard Wright's prose and photography edited by Edwin Rosskam, and *The Sweet Flypaper of Life* (1955), co-authored by Langston Hughes and the photographer Roy DeCarava" ("Black Light," 24).

38. Of course, Baraka is using the word *terrible* to suggest value, as he defines the term in the book: "*Terribleness*—Our beauty is BAD cause we bad. Bad things. Some bad bad bad ass niggers" (*In Our Terribleness*, 5).

39. See Crawford, "Textual Productions."
40. Baraka, *In Our Terribleness*, 4.
41. Ibid., 5.
42. Ibid., 49.
43. I am indebted to Cheryl Wall's discussion of Toni Morrison's *The Black Book* for her observations on the social implications of the size of photographic picture books (*Worrying the Line*, 95).
44. As Smethurst notes of published poetry's visual presentation on the page, "Rather than being a mere adjunct, the written/visual Black Arts text frequently existed in symbiotic relation to performance. That is to say, very often the written text draws on performative modes, including everyday speech, and is posed in dynamic relationship to those modes" (*Black Arts Movement*, 99).
45. Nielsen, *Black Chant*, 19.
46. See Smethurst, Black Arts Movement, 13 and 97 in particular. Smethurst comments on the rich visual component of the journals: "This visual impact was heightened by the frequent juxtaposition of nonverbal images (photographs, line drawings, block prints, lithographs, and so on) with written texts (poems, plays, essays, sketches, manifestos, and so on) in such Black Arts and Black Power journals as *Black Dialogue*, *Soulbook*, *Liberator*, *JBP*, *RAM's Black America*, and *Negro Digest/Black World*, as well as in many chapbooks, pamphlets, and broadsides produced by Black Art presses" (97).
47. Brooks, *Report from Part One*, 86.
48. Crawford, "Textual Productions," 199.
49. Garland, "Vibes from Verta Mae," 90.
50. See the *Ebony* feature on Kali and her sister, Garland, "Gifted Child," 96. See also Bowers, "Seven Thousand Volumes Sold."
51. See, for example, the *New York Amsterdam News* announcement of Kali's May 2, 1971, reading with Sanchez ("Poetry, Song Sessions Set").
52. Vertamae Smart-Grosvenor also toured with Sun Ra and created many of the costumes associated with his futuristic performance style. See Garland, "Vibes from Verta Mae." Grosvenor's contributor's note in *The Black Woman* calls her "[a]ctress, designer, cosmic force with the Sun Ra Solar Myth Science Orchestra" (Cade, *The Black Woman*, 325) and author of *Vibration Cooking*.
53. Fletcher's photographs of children appear on the jacket of the Child Development Group of Mississippi's album of freedom songs, for instance. Fletcher is the husband of CDGM worker Marilyn Lowen. Grosvenor suggested that she enjoyed working with Fletcher but that Halifax was added late in the production of the book by the publisher, against Grosvenor's wishes (Kali Grosvenor, interview).
54. Williams-Garcia and I talked at length in person about her admiration for *Poems by Kali*; in e-mail correspondence of November 26, 2012, Williams-Garcia describes Kali as her "childhood object of envy."
55. Grosvenor, *Poems by Kali*, 15. Subsequent citations of this book in this section appear in the text.
56. Kali Grosvenor, quoted in Campbell, " 'Poems by Kali,' " 41.
57. Grosvenor, interview.
58. Clarke, *"After Mecca,"* 70.

59. Giovanni, "Poem for Black Boys," in *Ego-Tripping*, 27.
60. The image also evokes Vietnam-era photography in Kali's pointing her gun-fingers at the face of her companion. There were several execution photographs circulating in the press in the late 1960s; the most famous, perhaps, is the February 1, 1968, Eddie Adams photo of General Nguyen Ngoc Loan executing a Vietcong prisoner. I do not know that Halifax, the photographer, was intending to evoke execution images.
61. Black ABC books relied on the conventions of the abecedary in order to claim a legibility and inevitability to a renewed African American identity. The familiar catchphrase in black ABC books is "A is for Africa," and as Clifton, Smith, and Bond invoked the phrase, they claimed a confident certainty for Africa in the reshaped, renewed sensibility of the black-child reader. Of course, one might also see "A is for Africa" as an ideological attack on the American apple (with its myriad associations: Puritan, Genesis, New England, American as apple pie, etc.), a phrase, then, that pleases both for its ease and naturalness appropriated from the alphabetic pattern and for its confident rebuttal to white American history and identity. Even the title of Clifton's book, *The Black BCs*, sets the stage for intervention by destabilizing the predictable linear narrative of the ABCs, claiming ownership and privileged positionality through the simple gesture of replacing *A* with *B* and "black."
62. Kelley, introduction, 9.
63. Kali's poem is reminiscent of the satirical photo text by Jewish poet Eve Merriam, with photographs by Lawrence Ratzkin, *The Inner City Mother Goose* (1969). Its version of the "Lady Bug" rhyme is titled "Taxi Man": "Taxi man, taxi man, / Quick drive me home! / My house is on fire / And my children all—! / Sorry, lady, / Even in an emergency / Cabs don't go to Harlem" (Merriam, 69). Merriam's text was published for adults and was made into a Broadway musical, *Inner City*, staged at the Ethel Barrymore Theatre beginning December 19, 1971.
64. Giovanni, "Poem for Black Boys," 28.
65. K. Grosvenor, interview.
66. An August 1974 *Ebony* article on Kali and her sister, Chandra, emphasized the creative agency of the sisters and their group of friends (Garland, "Gifted Child").
67. Sanchez, *It's a New Day*, 7–8.
68. Baraka, "Black Art," in *Black Magic*, 117.
69. K. Grosvenor, interview.
70. Kali's poetry also alludes to Hughes, particularly in her attention to beauty, and she includes a poem, "LETTER TO LANGSTON HUGHES," which describes Kali reading two poems by Hughes when performing in a play about the Birmingham church bombing.
71. K. Grosvenor, interview.
72. Ibid.
73. Flynn, "'Affirmative Acts,'" 166.
74. In speaking of the suburbs, Shearer explains, "People think of Westchester as a wonderfully affluent place. That's not all Westchester is" (interview). It should be noted that the other major photobook of the late 1960s that represented black childhood was set in the rural South: *Sweet Pea* (1969) was authored by the white photographer Jill Krementz and includes a foreword by Margaret Mead that places the text squarely in

the documentary/outsider position: "Her camera illuminates the particular circumstances of Sweet Pea's life—many of them strange to city and country children in other parts of the United States."

75. Ted Shearer is best known for his national comic strip *Quincy*, which ran in 1970–1986, but he had also published for the *New York Amsterdam News* columns "Next Door" and "Around Harlem," beginning in the early 1940s. Ted collaborated with John on the popular *Billy Jo Jive* mystery-book series in the 1970s, which were animated on the PBS program *Sesame Street*.

76. See Shearer, "Martin Luther King Funeral" and "Harlem Negro Riots—Aftermath."

77. Shearer, interview.

78. Parks himself is best known for images like "American Gothic, Washington, D.C." (1942), part of a series depicting the life of Mrs. Ella Watson, a janitor for the federal government; in more than eighty images, Parks explores the contrast between the workplace identity and personal life of an impoverished (but named and individuated) black subject.

79. Black Perspective, "Message to the Black Community," 22.

80. Ibid.

81. Parks, foreword.

82. Shearer's acknowledged inspiration for *I Wish*, aside from contact with Parks, was a children's photographic picture book about an urban boy in New York, *It's Wings That Make Birds Fly* (1968), authored by the Polish-born photographer Sandra Weiner. He explains: "I think I was really touched by that story, and thought, 'Gee, wouldn't it be interesting to do something like that?'" (interview). Weiner's book focuses on Otis, a ten-year-old black boy in Queens, New York, who shuttles between his grandparents and separated parents and who is frequently the target of violence from his grandmother and neighborhood children. The representation of urban childhood is quite bleak, leavened only by the boy's deep love for his brother. Parks also wrote the preface for this text, stating, "I hope a lot of things for Otis. . . . I hope that we, you and I, will come to know our responsibility toward helping Otis into a manhood of dignity." Despite Parks's words, the last page of the book belies any optimism about urban black childhood: "Shortly after this story was written, the young boy whose life it largely portrays was killed in an accident while playing in the street" (56). Although Shearer may have been affected emotionally by Weiner's text, in *I Wish* he unsettles the topos of urban blight invoked by books like Weiner's.

83. The texts' parallels go beyond narrative strategy and investment in the community's story; at one point, Rena describes herself in terms redolent of Morrison's text: "Sometimes I really wish I was white, with all the chances those people have! They can do so much for their kids. Lord knows what we'd do if John had money comin' in all year an' was white, too" (Shearer, *I Wish I Had an Afro*).

84. Also pertinent to the discussion of black power is Shearer's journalistic experience; at the time he was composing and revising *I Wish*, Shearer also covered for *Look* the Black Panthers in Chicago (Shearer, "Black Panthers"). He explained to me, "In terms of trying to define himself, Little John wanted to grow his hair, and that is a statement of 'I'm black and I'm proud!' That was his way of doing it. It's something that certainly touched me, because I know I went through the whole thing of growing my hair and having an Afro, and people used to tease me about that: 'Oh, you wrote a book

about how you want to have an Afro. Will you look at the size of your Afro!' If you've ever seen any pictures of me around that period, I had a large Afro. And it was funny, because when I was on the road doing Black Panther stories and civil rights stories, typically my hair was very long, and if I had to go to the White House I would have to cut it. And it would take a while for it to grow back. But I think he [Little John] was really trying to make a statement in his young voice: 'I am really proud to be black'" (interview).

85. See, for instance, the work of Horst Faas for the Associated Press, "Photographer Collection."

86. In reference to the Iraq and Afghanistan wars, Norman Beierle and Hester Keijser discover that in images accessible through the Department of Defense, the trope of the "sunset soldier" emerges as a dominant patriotic statement: "The army has a great love for the silhouetted image." Beierle and Keijser, "Sunset Soldiers."

87. Lachat, *Dimensions of Integration*, 6.

88. Berkvist, "Ages 9–12."

89. Hurst, "New Black Heroes."

90. West, "What's Happening in Westchester." West described the party: "When a hometown boy makes good—especially today—there is dancing in the streets. In Greenburgh, where John Shearer, son of BBDO art director Ted and Westchester Co-Op executive director Phyllis Shearer, was given a Book Party celebrating the publishing of his first book, over 1,000 people turned out to congratulate him. It was truly a community affair. Merchants contributed enough hotdogs to feed the crowd, Continental Baking Company donated rolls, and other local businesses delivered soft drinks."

91. "John McDuffy and John Shearer."

92. Clifton, "Writing for Black Children," 36.

93. Shearer, interview.

94. The list (Jordan, *Dry Victories*, 80) includes titles by John Hope Franklin, W.E.B. Du Bois, and Milton Meltzer, among others.

95. K. Grosvenor, *Poems by Kali*, 39.

96. Jordan, *Dry Victories*, viii. Subsequent citations of this book appear in the text.

97. Jordan submitted the script to Meltzer and Alvin Yudkoff at Niagara Films on May 2, 1969. Jordan offered revisions of the script, but Meltzer and Yudkoff eventually decided that they could not fund the film, and gave their enthusiastic blessing to Jordan's decision to publish her work as a photobook (J. Jordan, "Victories Neglected"). The structure and substance of the script resembles *Dry Victories* closely. The description of the film includes the following note: "Mechanical Organization: Two black kids have researched the Reconstruction Era, and the Civil Rights' decade, respectively. They have decided that the two periods are closely similar. It is their film: to present what they learned, what they think—about them, and about their own, immediate poverty. Each will narrate substantial portions of what they have to say. But a great part of the verbal film will happen in a situation of dialog between them."

98. Vertamae [Grosvenor], letter to June Jordan.

99. Whitehead, *Feminist Poetry Movement*, 85.

100. Smethurst, *Black Arts Movement*, 76.

101. Describing the mural genre during the Black Arts era, Smethurst explains, "[O]ne tends to find the representation of mythic or iconic historical figures but not much

rendering of historical events. Thus, redemption and salvation lie in the escape from history into a mythical counter-history and salvation" (ibid., 77).

102. Cheryl Clarke's important study of women poets of the Black Arts movement, "*After Mecca*," identifies the late 1960s as a period of mourning, when "black Americans gave up their reliance on various Euro-American discourses of freedom and rights: The Declaration of Independence, The Constitution of the United States, The Bill of Rights, *Brown vs. the Board of Education of Topeka, Kansas,* The 1964 Civil Rights Bill, The Voting Rights Act of 1965, to name a very few" (47).

103. The first photograph, commonly titled "Rebel Sharpshooter," is attributed to Alexander Gardner; the second, depicting supposedly Union bodies in the field, "Field Where General Reynolds Fell," was published in Gardner's *Photographic Sketch Book of the Civil War* (1866) and is attributed to Timothy O'Sullivan. William Frassanito explains that O'Sullivan used dead Confederate soldiers for this image (*Gettysburg*, 229). Although students of photography are familiar with the way in which the Gettysburg images were manipulated by Alexander Gardner, the photographer, in order to achieve the sense that men fell side by side on the field, for the purposes of Jordan's text such criticisms of Gardner's "staged" photography do not come to the surface; they did not become popularized until 1975, years after the publication of Jordan's book.

104. VISTA alludes to the federal program Volunteers in Service to America, which was founded in 1964 and, in the 1960s, was sponsored through the Office of Economic Opportunity. VISTA brought volunteers from a range of disciplines and interests into low-income communities.

105. Remembering that, as Steven Kasher suggests, not all civil rights–era images were created by sympathetic SNCC photographers, we can see that Jordan claims and reframes images created within hostile contexts: "Many of the pictures that turned out to be most important to the movement—pictures that inspired substantive support—were made by photojournalists who were hardly pro-movement and appeared in publications that were hardly liberal" (*Civil Rights Movement*, 12).

106. The strategy of using headlines recalls Hughes and Meltzer's *Pictorial History of the Negro in America.*

107. Jordan concludes by linking poverty among African Americans to poverty among whites, arguing that economic opportunity has been the failed promise of America. In some ways, this conclusion extends the text's emphasis on civil rights' legislative impotence and black activism.

108. Flynn, "Affirmative Acts,'" 163.

109. Mathis, review.

110. At least one reader thought the book too soft on the Kennedys. A friend of Jordan's was Ruby Sales, the civil rights worker who came to national attention when a white Episcopalian seminarian died after diving in front of a bullet meant for Sales. Sales praised the dialogue in *Dry Victories* but disagreed with Jordan about the treatment of the Kennedy-Johnson administrations: "NOW . . . the only difference we have is our understanding of certain historical parallels. Kennedy and Lincoln are both parallels in so far as they both exploited BLK. people. when BLK. people loved and trusted them. Both politicked with our lives. I feel that to present them as anything else is romantic and historically incorrect (see THE RACIAL ATTITUDES OF AMERICAN PRESIDENTS FROM LINCOLN TO THEODORE ROOSEVELT). Also peep speeches by

Kennedy. History is bringing 'truth out front.' Myths for any reason except pragmatic ones are bad. What is the parallel between L.B.J. and Andrew Johnson? Is it to imply that had Kennedy/Lincoln lived things would be different? Is it to say that both Johnsons had attitudes different from Kennedy/Lincoln? What about Beard's economic analysis of the Civil war? Please explain pictures #74, 22, and #23. Incidentally, Lincoln too was a Southerner. Where's the spill and photos on Rutherford Hayes? . . . Somehow lurks the sentiment that northerners were/are different. What about the riots (Civil war) in the North and Midwest? Immigrant attitudes? Big Business? Industrialism?" (Sales, letter to June Jordan). The book gave Sales much to consider in terms of framing history through images. Much as *Dry Victories* refuses to explain its juxtaposition of images, Jordan's papers do not include a response to Sales.

111. Madhubuti, "Black Writing," 37–38.
112. Wall, *Worrying the Line*, 88.
113. I do not know whether Morrison was familiar with *Dry Victories*; although the correspondences between the two are palpable, they may simply be a product of the era's experimentation with visual accounts of history.
114. Wall, *Worrying the Line*, 95.
115. Wall discusses this exchange in the prologue to ibid.

5. BLURRING THE CHILDHOOD IMAGE

Permission to reprint epigraph poetry "Afterimages," by Audre Lorde, granted by Charlotte Sheedy Literary Agency and W. W. Norton & Company, Inc., http://www.nortonpoets .com/. Copyright 1997 by Audre Lorde.

1. I frame the end of the early years of the civil rights movement with the passage of civil rights legislation, specifically the 1964 Civil Rights Act and the 1965 Voting Rights Act.
2. Marilyn Miller's *The Bridge at Selma* (1985) is one of few photographic children's texts on civil rights published before the 1990s.
3. Raiford and Romano, "The Struggle over Memory," introduction to *Civil Rights Movement in American Memory*, xiv.
4. Ibid.
5. Harding, "Re-visiting King's 'I Have a Dream' Speech."
6. I should note that recent children's illustrated picture books, like Nikki Giovanni's *Rosa* (2005), place their subjects within political networks and oppose an individualistic reading. See also Kohl, "Politics of Children's Literature."
7. Morgan explains that "[t]he iconic King is . . . claimed to support just about any cause justifiable within the boundaries of mainstream ideological assumptions" (146).
8. Raiford says it best: "Popular narratives of the civil rights movement offer us a Manichean tale in which the good guys, long-suffering pure-of-heart African Americans and their white supporters—including in some accounts the Kennedy administration and the FBI—vanquished the evil forces of fear, ignorance, and intransigence embodied by Klansmen, Bull Connor, and lone white gunmen. It is an all-American story in which nonviolence and love conquer violence and hate, resulting in tangible so-called race-blind legislation. And now all of us, black and white, Jew and Gentile, and not least of all American democracy, emerge as victor. We have all overcome. It

is a neat and straightforward story, effortlessly recounted to schoolchildren and other audiences who can experience sadness, indignation, and ultimately pride in how far we have come" (*Imprisoned in a Luminous Glare*, 236).

9. Fuller, "Debating the Present through the Past," 173.

10. See Margolick, *Elizabeth and Hazel* (2011).

11. Song, *Strange Future*, 206. See Song's discussion and endnote for sources on the policy of the 1990s.

12. As Lee argues, "Discussions of what to do about pervasive urban poverty turned into 'underclass' debates, and no matter how much liberal and progressive scholars bristled and tried to qualify the term, 'underclass' became shorthand for Black and Brown urban pathology, and cities became the crucible for cultures of poverty. The state's crisis and eventual transformation from a Keynesian broker into a militarized creative destroyer of communities could be smoothly displaced and recast as a problem of those it had once unevenly been called to protect" (*Urban Triage*, 22).

13. Song, *Strange Future*, 212.

14. Lee, *Urban Triage*, xix.

15. Bethany Bryson names other conservative articulations, like William Bennett's National Endowment for the Humanities 1983 report *To Reclaim a Legacy*, and books published in the 1990s by Dinesh D'Souza, Roger Kimball, John Miller, Pat Buchanan, and Arthur Schlesinger (Bryson, *Making Multiculturalism*, 7–8).

16. Ibid., 2.

17. It is not within the scope of this study to offer a comprehensive introduction to multiculturalism and education.

18. Lee attaches material consequence to the choices made by multiculturalists: "[M]ulticulturalism and the literary rubric in the 1980s laid the ground upon which one could rationally diagnose and then decide who would thrive, who would die, and who would remain the walking wounded in American cities" (*Urban Triage*, xvii).

19. Melamed, *Represent and Destroy*, 36.

20. Ibid., 37.

21. Melamed suggests that multiculturalism's acceptable texts adhered to the civil rights consensus narrative: "Literature was to testify to and teach about the race-differentiated history and present of the American experience, multiculturally developed. The story was to stay within the bounds of a master narrative about the civil rights movement that described the triumph of formerly oppressed minorities (symbolically African Americans) in defeating racism and gaining individual fulfillment and group dignity through full inclusion in American democracy" (ibid., 36–37).

22. Melamed suggests, "Liberal antiracisms have had to repeatedly institutionalize a notion of literary texts as practical and effective tools that Americans can use to get to know difference" (ibid., 15).

23. Alsultany, *Arabs and Muslims in the Media*, 21.

24. Mickenberg, *Learning from the Left*, 46.

25. Dudziak, *Cold War Civil Rights*, 51.

26. Fuller, "Debating the Present through the Past," 171.

27. This is Fuller's argument about 1990s racial melodrama (ibid.). She asserts that such narratives waned after 9/11; I believe that the instability and complication of racial dy-

namics have produced continued interest in stories that "solve" racial tensions through interracial collaboration.

28. Raiford, *Imprisoned in a Luminous Glare*, 211.

29. Raiford argues, "Even as these photographs mark movement participants' attempts to rewrite the meaning of black bodies in public space, the photographs also imprison —frame and 'iconize'—images of legitimate leadership, appropriate forms of political action, and the proper place of African Americans within the national imaginary" (ibid., 3).

30. See Raiford on the reinvention of the meaning of lynching images, especially her chapter "No Relation to the Facts about Lynching" (ibid., 29–66).

31. Laura Wexler on the image: "To be *seen*, photographs must be woven into other languages; otherwise, like the 'unexamined life,' the 'unlinguistic image' will float off in an anarchy of unincorporated data" (*Tender Violence*, 50).

32. Raiford, *Imprisoned in a Luminous Glare*, 17.

33. Hall, "Long Civil Rights Movement," 1235.

34. Sanders, "Chaperoning Words," 59.

35. Myers, *One More River to Cross*, 100, 103. Subsequent citations of this book appear in the text.

36. See Raiford's chapter on reframing lynching photographs, in *Imprisoned in a Luminous Glare*.

37. Wood, *Lynching and Spectacle*, 209–10.

38. Raiford, *Imprisoned in a Luminous Glare*, 60.

39. The next images are of black soldiers in Vietnam, a gesture that might signal King's resistance to the war, because Myers describes the conflict through biblical language (echoing Ps. 55:18) that insists on its antagonism to blacks: "He has delivered my soul in peace from the battle that was against me . . ." (Myers, *One More River to Cross*, 140).

40. Hirsch, *Family Frames*, 93.

41. For more on revaluing segregated communities, see Tim Libretti's discussions of John Sayles's films and Toni Morrison's *Sula* ("Integration as Disintegration").

42. Morrison, *Remember*, 5. Subsequent citations of this book in this section appear in the text.

43. Bernstein, *Racial Innocence*, 16.

44. Ibid., 241.

45. Ibid., 6.

46. See the Youtube video of that interview, titled "The Little Rock Nine on *Oprah*," http://www.youtube.com/watch?v=75dhe5Zsy8k.

47. Bridges, *Through My Eyes*, 59. Subsequent citations of this book appear in the text.

48. I am indebted to Marah Gubar for nudging me to think more about the anger submerged in Bridges's text.

49. Bernstein, *Racial Innocence*, 241.

50. John Steinbeck, *Travels with Charley*, quoted in Bridges, *Through My Eyes*, 25.

51. Robert Coles, *The Moral Life of Children*, quoted in Bridges, *Through My Eyes*, 47.

52. However much the book insists on the failure of the friendship orthodoxy, popular culture clung to that myth in imagining Ruby and her teacher; just as Oprah Win-

frey's television show reunited Elizabeth Eckford with the reformed racist girl from the iconic photo, it also brought together Bridges and Mrs. Henry, in 1996.

53. Belafonte, preface.

54. Morrison, *Remember*, 72.

55. Sorby, Thomas, and Flynn, "'from brain,'" 382.

56. Weatherford, *Birmingham, 1963*, 4. Poetry courtesy of Carole Boston Weatherford. Subsequent citations of this book appear in the text.

57. The shoes might allude to Dudley Randall's poem "Ballad of Birmingham."

58. Bernstein, *Racial Innocence*, 241.

59. Weatherford, e-mail correspondence.

CONCLUSION

1. The *Washington Post* reported that the date of the picture was August 2011, when Trayvon was sixteen, nearly seven months before his murder. Capeheart, "Five Myths about Trayvon Martin."

2. Bosman, "Trayvon Martin's Parents."

3. Perry, "Why Zimmerman Walked," 113.

BIBLIOGRAPHY

"A&T Student Gets Award for Sit-Ins." Clippings File, JWJ MSS 26, Box 567, Folder 13565A. Langston Hughes Papers, James Weldon Johnson Collection in the Yale Collection of American Literature. Beinecke Rare Book and Manuscript Library, Yale University.

Abel, Elizabeth. "Domestic Borders, Cultural Boundaries: Black Feminists Re-view the Family." In *The Familial Gaze*, edited by Marianne Hirsch, 124–52. Hanover, N.H.: University Press of New England, 1999.

———. *Signs of the Times: The Visual Politics of Jim Crow*. Berkeley: University of California Press, 2010.

"About Books." *Newark (N.J.) News*, January 7, 1957. Clippings File, JWJ MSS 26, Box 567, Folder 13565. Langston Hughes Papers, James Weldon Johnson Collection in the Yale Collection of American Literature. Beinecke Rare Book and Manuscript Library, Yale University.

Adorno, Theodor W. *The Authoritarian Personality*. New York: Harper, 1950.

Advertisement for *A Pictorial History of the Negro in America*, by Langston Hughes and Milton Meltzer. *New York Times Book Review*, November 1956, 29. Clippings File, JWJ MSS 26, Box 567, Folder 13565. Langston Hughes Papers, James Weldon Johnson Collection in the Yale Collection of American Literature. Beinecke Rare Book and Manuscript Library, Yale University.

Alland, Alexander. *American Counterpoint*. New York: Day, 1943.

———. Interview by Edward Applebome, June 3, 1986. Ellis Island Oral History Project, Series AKRF, no. 185. http://uconn.worldcat.org/search?q=no%3A822585935&fq=+&qt=advanced&dblist=283.

Allen, James. *Without Sanctuary: Lynching Photography in America*. Santa Fe, N.M.: Twin Palms, 2000.

Allen, James Egert. Review of *A Pictorial History of the Negro in America*, by Langston Hughes and Milton Meltzer. *New York Amsterdam News*, December 29, 1956. Clippings File, JWJ MSS 26, Box 567, Folder 13565. Langston Hughes Papers, James Weldon Johnson Collection in the Yale Collection of American Literature. Beinecke Rare Book and Manuscript Library, Yale University.

Alsultany, Evelyn. *Arabs and Muslims in the Media*. New York: New York University Press, 2012.

Andrew, Dudley. Introduction to *The Image in Dispute: Art and Cinema in the Age of Photography*, edited by Dudley Andrew, 3–7. Austin: University of Texas Press, 1997.

Apel, Dora. *Imagery of Lynching: Black Men, White Women, and the Mob*. New Brunswick, N.J.: Rutgers University Press, 2004.

Apel, Dora, and Shawn Michelle Smith. *Lynching Photographs*. Berkeley: University of California Press, 1997.

Avedon, Richard. *Nothing Personal*. New York: Atheneum, 1964.

Azoulay, Ariella. *The Civil Contract of Photography*. New York: Zone, 2008.

B., J. "Negro in America Well Researched." *Youngstown (Ohio) Vindicator*, February 17, 1957. Clippings File, JWJ MSS 26, Box 567, Folder 13565A. Langston Hughes Papers, James Weldon Johnson Collection in the Yale Collection of American Literature. Beinecke Rare Book and Manuscript Library, Yale University.

Baker, Benjamin J. *Crucial Moments*. Hagerstown, Md.: Review and Herald, 2005.

———. "The Precursor to the Sabbath in Africa Movement: Ethiopia in the Message Magazine (1935–1942)." Master's thesis, Howard University, 2006.

Bambara, Toni Cade, ed. *The Black Woman*. 1970. Reprint, New York: Washington Square, 2005.

Baraka, Immamu Amiri. *Black Magic: Sabotage, Target Study, Black Art; Collected Poetry, 1961–67*. Indianapolis, Ind.: Bobbs-Merrill, 1969.

———. *In Our Terribleness (Some Elements and Meaning in Black Style)*. Photographs by Fundi (Billy Abernathy). Indianapolis, Ind.: Bobbs-Merrill, 1970.

Bardolph, Richard. "Negro Americans." *Greensboro (N.C.) Daily News*, January 13, 1957. Clippings File, JWJ MSS 26, Box 567, Folder 13565. Langston Hughes Papers, James Weldon Johnson Collection in the Yale Collection of American Literature. Beinecke Rare Book and Manuscript Library, Yale University.

Barrett, Lindsay. "The Tide Inside, It Rages!" In Jones and Neal, *Black Fire*, 149–58.

Barthes, Roland. *Camera Lucida: Reflections on Photography*. 1980. Reprint, New York: Hill & Wang, 1982.

"Behind the Muslim Curtain." *New York Amsterdam News*, June 9, 1962. Clippings File, JWJ MSS 26, Box 567, Folder 13565A. Langston Hughes Papers, James Weldon Johnson Collection in the Yale Collection of American Literature. Beinecke Rare Book and Manuscript Library, Yale University.

Beierle, Norman, and Hester Keijser. "Sunset Soldiers." *Mrs. Deane*, February 24, 2011. http://www.beikey.net/mrs-deane/?p=4845.

Beim, Lorraine, and Jerrold Beim. *Two Is a Team*. New York: Harcourt, Brace, 1945.

Belafonte, Harry. Preface to Bridges, *Through My Eyes*, 3.

Bennett, William. *The De-valuing of America: The Fight for Our Culture and Our Children*. 1992. Reprint, New York: Touchstone, 1994.

Berger, John. "Understanding a Photograph." In *Classic Essays on Photography*, edited by Alan Trachtenberg, 291–94. New Haven, Conn.: Leete's Island Books, 1980.

Berger, Martin A. *Seeing through Race: A Reinterpretation of Civil Rights Photography*. Berkeley: University of California Press, 2011.

Berger, Maurice. *For All the World to See: Visual Culture and the Struggle for Civil Rights*. New Haven, Conn.: Yale University Press, 2010.

Berkvist, Margaret. "Ages 9–12: Facts and Speculation; Review of *I Wish I Had an Afro*." *New York Times*, May 24, 1970.

Bernstein, Robin. *Racial Innocence: Performing American Childhood and Race from Slavery to Civil Rights*. New York: New York University Press, 2011.

Bettelheim, Bruno, and Morris Janowitz. *Dynamics of Prejudice: A Psychological and Sociological Study of Veterans.* New York: Harper, 1950.

Black Perspective. "Message to the Black Community . . . from Black Journalists." *New York Amsterdam News*, February 21, 1970.

Blair, Sara. *Harlem Crossroads: Black Writers and the Photograph in the Twentieth Century.* Princeton, N.J.: Princeton University Press, 2007.

Bloom, Allan David. *The Closing of the American Mind: How Higher Education Has Failed Democracy and Impoverished the Souls of Today's Students.* New York: Simon & Schuster, 1987.

Bond, Horace Mann. *Lincoln University Bulletin*, Fall 1956. Clippings File, JWJ MSS 26, Box 567, Folder 13565. Langston Hughes Papers, James Weldon Johnson Collection in the Yale Collection of American Literature. Beinecke Rare Book and Manuscript Library, Yale University.

Bond, Jean Carey. *A is for Africa.* New York: Watts, 1969.

Bontemps, Arna. "For the Young Reader's Bookshelf." Review of *My Dog Rinty*, by Ellen Tarry and Marie Hall Ets. *New York Times*, June 16, 1946.

———. *Story of the Negro.* New York: Knopf, 1948.

Bontemps, Arna, and Langston Hughes. *Popo and Fifina: A Story of Haiti.* New York: Macmillan, 1932.

Bosman, Julie. "Trayvon Martin's Parents Are Planning a Book." *New York Times*, December 14, 2013. http://www.nytimes.com/2013/12/14/business/media/trayvon -martins-parents-are-planning-a-book.html?ref=juliebosman.

Bowers, Carolyn A. "Seven Thousand Volumes Sold of 9-Year-Old's Poetry." *Boston Globe*, September 14, 1970.

Bridges, Ruby. *Through My Eyes.* New York: Scholastic, 1999.

Bromley, Dorothy Dunbar. "The Negro Freedom-Fighters." *New Leader*, April 22, 1957: 21–22. Clippings File, JWJ MSS 26, Box 567, Folder 13565A. Langston Hughes Papers, James Weldon Johnson Collection in the Yale Collection of American Literature. Beinecke Rare Book and Manuscript Library, Yale University.

Brooks, Gwendolyn. *Report from Part One.* Detroit: Broadside, 1972.

Bryson, Bethany. *Making Multiculturalism: Boundaries and Meaning in U.S. English Departments.* Stanford, Calif.: Stanford University Press, 2005.

Buchman, Lamont. *A Pictorial History of the Confederacy.* New York: Crown, 1951.

Buck, Pearl S. Introduction to Alland, *American Counterpoint*, 9–16.

Bunche, Ralph J. *Selected Speeches and Writings.* Ann Arbor: University of Michigan Press, 1995.

Burrell, Natelkka E. "Our Parental Delinquency Problem." *Message*, April 1945, 3.

Butts, J. J. "New World A-Coming: African American Documentary Intertexts of the Federal Writers' Project." *African American Review* 44, no. 4 (Winter 2011): 649–66.

———. "Writing Projects: New Deal Guidebooks, Community, and Housing Reform in New York City." *Space Between* 2, no. 1 (2006): 113–38.

Byrnes, Garrett D. "Cameras over the World: Fine Photographs of '56." *Providence (R.I.) Sunday Journal*, December 16, 1956. Clippings File, JWJ MSS 26, Box 567, Folder 13565. Langston Hughes Papers, James Weldon Johnson Collection in the Yale Collection of American Literature. Beinecke Rare Book and Manuscript Library, Yale University.

Cadava, Eduardo. *Words of Light: Theses on the Photography of History*. Princeton, N.J.: Princeton University Press, 1998.

Cade, Toni. "The Pill: Genocide or Liberation?" In Bambara, *Black Woman*, 203–12.

Campbell, Barbara. "'Poems by Kali': A Little Black Girl Speaks Her Mind." *New York Times*, July 7, 1970.

Canaday, John. "Getting Harlem Off My Mind." *New York Times*, January 12, 1969.

Capeheart, Jonathan. "Five Myths about Trayvon Martin." *Washington Post*, July 3, 2013. http://articles.washingtonpost.com/2013–07–03/opinions/40348822_1_george -zimmerman-trayvon-martin-trial.

Carmichael, Stokely [Kwame Ture], and Charles V. Hamilton. *Black Power: The Politics of Liberation in America*. 1967. Reprint, New York: Vintage, 1992.

Carroll, Anne Elizabeth. *Word, Image, and the New Negro: Representation and Identity in the Harlem Renaissance*. Bloomington: Indiana University Press, 2005.

Carter, Michael. "Meet Ellen Tarry, Author of 'My Dog Rinty.'" *Baltimore Afro-American*, June 29, 1946, 10.

———. "244,000 Native Sons." *Look*, May 21, 1940, 8–13.

Chatton, Barbara. "Milton Meltzer: A Voice for Justice." *Language Arts* 79, no. 5 (2002): 438–41.

Child Development Group of Mississippi. *The Hike*. Jackson, Miss.: HJK Publishing, 1966.

———. *Pond*. Edwards, Miss.: Mississippi Action for Community Education, 1965.

———. *Today*. Edwards, Miss.: Mississippi Action for Community Education, 1965.

Child Development Group of Mississippi: Histories of Children, Employees, Centers, Community Support. Jackson, Miss.: HJK Publishing, 1966.

Cieciorka, Bobbi, and Frank Cieciorka. *Negroes in American History: A Freedom Primer*. Atlanta: Student Voice, 1965.

Clapps, Lucia. *The Bumble Bee Story*. Edwards, Miss.: Mississippi Action for Community Education, 1965.

———. *The Touglaoo Book*. Edwards, Miss.: Mississippi Action for Community Education, 1966.

Clarke, Cheryl. *"After Mecca": Women Poets and the Black Arts Movement*. New Brunswick, N.J.: Rutgers University Press, 2005.

Clifton, Lucille. *The Black BC's*. New York: Dutton, 1970.

———. "Writing for Black Children." *Advocate* 1, no. 1 (1981): 32–37.

Collier-Thomas, Bettye, and V. P. Franklin, eds. *Sisters in the Struggle: African-American Women in the Civil Rights–Black Power Movement*. New York: New York University Press, 2001.

Collins, Lisa Gail, and Margo Natalie Crawford, eds. *New Thoughts on the Black Arts Movement*. New Brunswick, N.J.: Rutgers University Press, 2006.

———. "Power to the People! The Art of Black Power." Introduction to Collins and Crawford, *New Thoughts on the Black Arts Movement*, 1–19.

Cookman, Arthur L. "Two Books Tell Negroes' Story." *Oregon Journal*, February 10, 1957. Clippings File, JWJ MSS 26, Box 567, Folder 13565A. Langston Hughes Papers, James Weldon Johnson Collection in the Yale Collection of American Literature. Beinecke Rare Book and Manuscript Library, Yale University.

Cooks, Bridget R. "Black Arts and Activism: Harlem on My Mind." *American Studies* 48, no. 1 (Spring 2007): 5–39.

Cooks, Charlene, and Hank Kirksey. *A Dog*. Edwards, Miss.: Mississippi Action for Community Education, 1965.

Cosby, Bill. Preface to Harris, *Black Book*.

Crawford, Margo Natalie. "Black Light on the *Wall of Respect*." In Collins and Crawford, *New Thoughts on the Black Arts Movement*, 23–42.

———. "Must Revolution Be a Family Affair?" In Gore, Theoharis, and Woodard, *Want to Start a Revolution?*, 185–204.

———. "Textual Productions of Black Aesthetics *Unbound*." In *Publishing Blackness: Textual Constructions of Race since 1850*, edited by George Hutchinson and John K. Young, 188–208. Ann Arbor: University of Michigan Press, 2013.

Credle, Ellis. *Flop-Eared Hound*. Photographs by Charles Townsend. New York: Oxford University Press, 1938.

Crown Publishing. Pamphlet on *A Pictorial History of the Negro in America* (Spring 1956). Clippings File, JWJ MSS 26, Box 567, Folder 13565. Langston Hughes Papers, James Weldon Johnson Collection in the Yale Collection of American Literature. Beinecke Rare Book and Manuscript Library, Yale University.

Curtis, Constance. "About Books and Authors." Review of *My Dog Rinty*, by Ellen Tarry and Marie Hall Ets. *New York Amsterdam News*, June 1, 1946, 11.

Curtis, Edward E. *Islam in Black America: Identity, Liberation, and Difference in African-American Islamic Thought*. Albany: State University of New York Press, 2002.

Davis, Arthur P. "Integration and Race Literature." *Phylon* 17, no. 2 (1956): 141–46.

Davis, Thulani. Foreword to Berger, *For All the World to See*, xi–xv.

DeMott, Benjamin. *The Trouble with Friendship: Why Americans Can't Think Straight about Race*. New Haven, Conn.: Yale University Press, 1998.

Denning, Michael. *The Cultural Front: The Laboring of American Culture in the Twentieth Century*. London: Verso, 1997.

Derby, Doris. Interview by Katharine Capshaw, May 6, 2013.

———. "Sometimes in the Ground Troops, Sometimes in the Leadership." In Holsaert et al., *Hands on the Freedom Plow*, 436–46.

De Santis, Christopher. Introduction to *Fight for Freedom and Other Writings on Civil Rights*, by Langston Hughes, 1–20. Columbia: University of Missouri Press, 2001.

De Schweinitz, Rebecca. *If We Could Change the World: Young People and America's Long Struggle for Racial Equality*. Chapel Hill: University of North Carolina Press, 2009.

Dittmer, John. *Local People: The Struggle for Civil Rights in Mississippi*. Urbana: University of Illinois Press, 1994.

Dollard, John, et al. *Frustration and Aggression*. London: Oxford University Press, 1939.

Dudziak, Mary L. *Cold War Civil Rights: Race and the Image of American Democracy*. Princeton, N.J.: Princeton University Press, 2000.

Duganne, Erina. *The Self in Black and White: Race and Subjectivity in Postwar American Photography*. Hanover, N.H.: Dartmouth College Press, 2010.

———. "Transcending the Fixity of Race: The Kamoinge Workshop and the Question of a 'Black Aesthetic' in Photography." In Collins and Crawford, *New Thoughts on the Black Arts Movement*, 187–209.

Dunbar, Paul Laurence. *Candle-Lightin' Time*. Photographs by Leigh Richmond Miner. New York: Dodd, Mead, 1901.

Dunlap, David W. "At Fifty, Harlem River Houses Is Still Special." *New York Times*, April

23, 1987. http://query.nytimes.com/gst/fullpage.html?res=9B0DEFDE133EF930A15757 C0A961948260.

"Editor's Note." *Youth's Instructor*, November 20, 1956, 2.

Emery, Kathy, Sylvia Braselmann, and Linda Gold, eds. *Freedom School Curriculum: Mississippi Freedom Summer 1964*. Accessed May 14, 2013. http://www.educationand democracy.org/ED_FSC.html.

Ezelle, Frank. "The Beginning of Head Start in Jackson." *Mississippi Civil Rights—One Man, One Story* (blog), November 6, 2007. http://robertezelle.blogspot.com/2007/11/ beginning-of-head-start-in-jackson.html.

Farebrother, Rachel. *The Collage Aesthetic in the Harlem Renaissance*. New York: Ashgate, 2009.

Farrell, Charles Anderson. "Comments on Photographs." Box 4, Charles Anderson Farrell Papers, 4452, Southern Historical Collection. Wilson Library, University of North Carolina at Chapel Hill.

———. "The Story Back of the Publication of *Tobe*." Box 6, Charles Anderson Farrell Papers, 4452, Southern Historical Collection. Wilson Library, University of North Carolina at Chapel Hill.

Federal Writers' Project. *New York Panorama: A Comprehensive View of the Metropolis*. 1938. Reprint, New York: Pantheon, 1984.

———. *The WPA Guide to New York City*. 1939. Reprint, New York: Pantheon, 1982.

Feelings, Muriel. *Jambo Means Hello: A Swahili Alphabet Book*. Pictures by Tom Feelings. New York: Dial, 1974.

Finley, Cheryl. "1969: Black Art and the Aesthetics of Memory." In *Incidences de l'événement: Enjeaux et résonances du mouvement des droits civiques* [The incidence of the event: The stakes and resonances of the civil rights movement], edited by Hélène Le Dantec-Lowry and Claudine Raynaud, 131–54. Tours, France: Presses Universitaires Francois-Rabelais, 2007.

Flowerman, Samuel H. "Portrait of the Authoritarian Man." *New York Times Magazine*, April 23, 1950, 9, 28–31.

Floyd, Silas X. *Floyd's Flowers: Duties and Beauties for Colored Children*. 1905. Reprinted as *Short Stories for Colored People Both Young and Old*. Washington, D.C.: Austin Jenkins, 1920.

Flynn, Richard. "'Affirmative Acts': Language, Childhood, and Power in June Jordan's Cross-Writing." *Children's Literature* 30 (2002): 159–85.

———. "'The Kindergarten of New Consciousness': Gwendolyn Brooks and the Social Construction of Childhood." *African American Review* 34, no. 3 (2000): 483–99.

"Forty-Eight Years of Service, Struggle, and Institution-Building, 1965–2014 C.E.— 6205–6254 A.F.E." *The Organization Us*. Accessed June 1, 2013. http://www.us -organization.org/30th/30yrs.html.

Frassanito, William. *Gettysburg: A Journey in Time*. New York: Scribner, 1975.

Freedom School Poetry. Foreword by Langston Hughes. Atlanta: Student Nonviolent Coordinating Committee, 1965.

Friedman, Ilana. "Tom Levin and Polly Greenberg's Reflections on the Rise and Demise of the Child Development Group of Mississippi." *Freedom Now! An Archival Project of Tougaloo College and Brown University*. Accessed May 13, 2013. http://www.stg.brown.edu/ projects/FreedomNow/ilana_friedman_thesis.html.

Fuller, Jennifer. "Debating the Present through the Past: Representations of the Civil Rights Movement in the 1990s." In Romano and Raiford, *Civil Rights Movement in American Memory*, 167–96.

G., E. "Up from Slavery in Prose and Pictures." *Milwaukee (Wisc.) Journal*, January 13, 1957. Clippings File, JWJ MSS 26, Box 567, Folder 13565. Langston Hughes Papers, James Weldon Johnson Collection in the Yale Collection of American Literature. Beinecke Rare Book and Manuscript Library, Yale University.

Galassi, Peter. *Roy DeCarava: A Retrospective*. New York: Museum of Modern Art, 1996.

Garland, Phyl. "The Gifted Child: For Kali and Chandra, for These Creative Girls, the Extraordinary Is Ordinary." *Ebony*, August 1974, 96–100.

———. "Vibes from Verta Mae: 'Double-O Soul' Chef Authors Fascinating Guide to Vibration Cooking." *Ebony*, March 1971, 86–88, 90, 92, 94.

Garrison, W. E. "Race Relations—Incidentally." *Christian Century*, January 3, 1945, 17.

Giffard, Adam. *Chance for Change*. New York: Scientific Film Services for Child Development Group of Mississippi, 1965.

Giovanni, Nikki. *Ego-Tripping and Other Poems for Young People*. 1973. Reprint, New York: Lawrence Hill, 1993.

———. *Rosa*. Illustrated by Bryan Collier. New York: Holt, 2005.

Glassman, Leo. "About Books." *American Examiner* (New York), May 16, 1957. Clippings File, JWJ MSS 26, Box 567, Folder 13565A. Langston Hughes Papers, James Weldon Johnson Collection in the Yale Collection of American Literature. Beinecke Rare Book and Manuscript Library, Yale University.

"Goodbye Mammy, Hello Mom." Photoeditorial. *Ebony*, March 1947, 36–37.

"Good for the Heart." Advertisement. *New York Times*, November 27, 1955.

Gordon, Sol. "A Psychologist's Misssissippi." Liner Notes. *Head Start with the Child Development Group of Mississippi*. Moses Asch, 1967. LP.

Gore, Dayo F., Jeanne Theoharis, and Komozi Woodard, eds. *Want to Start a Revolution? Radical Women in the Black Freedom Struggle*. New York: New York University Press, 2009.

Greenberg, Polly. *The Devil Has Slippery Shoes: A Biased Biography of the Child Development Group of Mississippi*. London: Macmillan, 1969.

———. E-mail correspondence with Katharine Capshaw Smith, March 6, 2013.

———. E-mail correspondence with Katharine Capshaw Smith, April 23, 2013.

Griffiths, Frederick T. "Ralph Ellison, Richard Wright, and the Case of Angelo Herndon." *African American Review* 35, no. 4 (2001): 615–36.

Grosvenor, Kali. E-mail interview by Katharine Capshaw, June 6, 2011.

———. *Poems by Kali*. Garden City, N.Y.: Doubleday, 1970.

Grosvenor, Vertamae. Letter to June Jordan, Oct. 24, 1972. Box 46, Folder 7. June Jordan Papers. Radcliffe Institute for Advanced Study, Harvard University.

Hall, Jacqueline Dowd. "The Long Civil Rights Movement and the Political Uses of the Past." *Journal of American History* 91, no. 4 (March 2005): 1233–63.

Hansberry, Lorraine. *The Movement: Documentary of a Struggle for Equality*. New York: Simon & Schuster, 1964.

Harding, Vincent. "Re-visiting King's 'I Have a Dream' Speech." *Veterans of Hope* (blog), September 5, 2010. http://www.veteransofhope.org/blog.php.

Harper, Phillip Brian. "Nationalism and Social Division in Black Arts Poetry of the 1960s."

In *Is It Nation Time? Contemporary Essays on Black Power and Black Nationalism*, edited by Eddie S. Glaude Jr., 165–88. Chicago: University of Chicago Press, 2002.

Harris, Middleton A. *The Black Book*. Edited by Toni Morrison. New York: Random House, 1974.

Head Start with the Child Development Group of Mississippi. Moses Asch, 1967. LP.

Herron, Matt. E-mail correspondence with Katharine Capshaw, April 23, 2013.

———. E-mail correspondence with Katharine Capshaw, April 24, 2013.

Higonnet, Anne. *Pictures of Innocence: The History and Crisis of Ideal Childhood*. New York: Thames & Hudson, 1998.

Hirsch, Marianne, ed. *The Familial Gaze*. Hanover, N.H.: University Press of New England, 1999.

———. "Familial Looking." Introduction to Hirsch, *Familial Gaze*, xi–xxv.

———. *Family Frames: Narrative, Photography, and Postmemory*. Cambridge, Mass.: Harvard University Press, 1997.

———. *The Generation of Postmemory: Writing and Visual Culture after the Holocaust*. New York: Columbia University Press, 2012.

Hogan, William. "A Graphic Document on the Negro in America." *San Francisco Chronicle*, November 29, 1956. Clippings File, JWJ MSS 26, Box 567, Folder 13565. Langston Hughes Papers, James Weldon Johnson Collection in the Yale Collection of American Literature. Beinecke Rare Book and Manuscript Library, Yale University.

Holsaert, Faith S., et al., eds. *Hands on the Freedom Plow: Personal Accounts by Women in SNCC*. 2010. Reprint, Urbana: University of Illinois Press, 2012.

hooks, bell. *Art on My Mind: Visual Politics*. New York: New Press, 1995.

Houck, Davis W., and David E. Dixon, eds. *Women and the Civil Rights Movement, 1954–1965*. Jackson: University Press of Mississippi, 2011.

Huggins, Ericka, and Angela D. LeBlanc-Ernest. "Revolutionary Women, Revolutionary Education: The Black Panther Party's Oakland Community School." In Gore, Theoharis, and Woodard, *Want to Start a Revolution?*, 161–84.

Hughes, Langston. "Books and the Negro Child." *Children's Library Yearbook* 4 (1932): 108–10.

———. "Books as Christmas Gifts of a Community Nature." *New York Age-Defender*, December 15, 1956. Clippings File, JWJ MSS 26, Box 567, Folder 13565. Langston Hughes Papers, James Weldon Johnson Collection in the Yale Collection of American Literature. Beinecke Rare Book and Manuscript Library, Yale University.

———. *The Dream Keeper*. New York: Knopf, 1932.

———. *First Book of Negroes*. New York: Franklin Watts, 1952.

———. Letter to Milton Melzer, June 20, 1955. JWJ MSS 26, Box 111A. Langston Hughes Papers, James Weldon Johnson Collection in the Yale Collection of American Literature. Beinecke Rare Book and Manuscript Library, Yale University.

———. Letter to Milton Meltzer, June 19, 1959. JWJ MSS 26, Box 111A. Langston Hughes Papers, James Weldon Johnson Collection in the Yale Collection of American Literature. Beinecke Rare Book and Manuscript Library, Yale University.

———. "Press Reviews." Clippings File, JWJ MSS 26, Box 567, Folder 13565. Langston Hughes Papers, James Weldon Johnson Collection in the Yale Collection of American Literature. Beinecke Rare Book and Manuscript Library, Yale University.

Hughes, Langston, and Roy DeCarava. *The Sweet Flypaper of Life.* New York: Simon & Schuster, 1955.

Hughes, Langston, and Milton Meltzer. *Black Magic: A Pictorial History of the Negro in American Entertainment.* Englewood Cliffs, N.J.: Prentice-Hall, 1967.

———. *A Pictorial History of the Negro in America.* New York: Crown, 1956.

Hurst, Charles G., Jr. "New Black Heroes." *Chicago Tribune*, November 8, 1970.

"Ike Gets Anderson, Hughes Books." *New York Age*, January 18, 1958. Clippings File, JWJ MSS 26, Box 567, Folder 13565A. Langston Hughes Papers, James Weldon Johnson Collection in the Yale Collection of American Literature. Beinecke Rare Book and Manuscript Library, Yale University.

Jenkins, Christine. "ALA Youth Services Librarians and the CARE-UNESCO Children's Book Fund: Selecting the 'Right Book' for Children in Cold War America, 1950–1958." *Libraries and Culture* 31, no. 1 (1996): 209–34.

"John McDuffy and John Shearer." *New York Amsterdam News*, September 12, 1970, 26.

Johnson, Dianne. *Telling Tales: The Pedagogy and Promise of African American Literature for Youth.* New York: Greenwood, 1990.

Johnson, Gerald W. Letter to Charles Anderson Farrell, May 20, 1943. Box 8, Charles Anderson Farrell Papers, 4452, Southern Historical Collection. Wilson Library, University of North Carolina at Chapel Hill.

Jones, Bessie, and Bess Lomax Hawes. *Step It Down: Games, Plays, Songs, and Stories from the Afro-American Heritage.* 1972. Reprint, Athens: University of Georgia Press, 1987.

Jones, Leroi, and Larry Neal, eds. *Black Fire.* New York: Morrow, 1968.

Jones, R. Clifford. *James K. Humphrey and the Sabbath-Day Adventists.* Jackson: University Press of Mississippi, 2006.

Jordan, Amy. "Fighting for the Child Development Group of Mississippi: Poor People, Local Politics, and the Complicated Legacy of Head Start." In *The War on Poverty: A New Grass-Roots History*, edited by Annelise Orleck and Lisa Gayle Hazirjian, 280–307. Athens: University of Georgia Press, 2011.

Jordan, June. *Dry Victories.* New York: Holt, Rinehart & Winston, 1972.

———. *His Own Where.* 1971. Reprint, New York: Feminist Press, 2010.

———. *Soulscript: Afro-American Poetry.* Garden City, N.Y.: Doubleday, 1970.

———. "The Victories Neglected." Box 74, Folder 10. June Jordan Papers. Radcliffe Institute for Advanced Study, Harvard University.

———. *The Voice of the Children.* New York: Holt, Rinehart & Winston, 1970.

———. "White English: The Politics of Language." *Black World*, August 1973, 4–10.

———. *Who Look at Me.* New York: Crowell, 1969.

Kasher, Steven. *The Civil Rights Movement: A Photographic History, 1954–68.* New York: Abbeville, 1996.

Katz, Maude White. "End Racism in Education: A Concerned Parent Speaks." In Bambara, *Black Woman*, 155–64.

Kelen, Leslie G., ed. *This Light of Ours: Activist Photographers of the Civil Rights Movement.* Jackson: University Press of Mississippi, 2011.

Kelley, William Melvin. Introduction to K. Grosvenor, *Poems by Kali*, 9–11.

Kelly, Susan. "Discipline and Craft: An Interview with Sonia Sanchez." *African American Review*, Winter 2000, 679–87.

King, Martin Luther, Jr. "Eulogy for the Martyred Children." September 18, 1963. Martin
 Luther King Jr. Online. http://www.mlkonline.net/eulogy.html.
———. "I Have a Dream." August 28, 1963. The King Center, http://www.thekingcenter.
 org/archive/document/i-have-dream-2.
———. Interview by Robert Penn Warren, March 18, 1964. *Robert Penn Warren's Who
 Speaks for the Negro? An Archival Collection.* http://whospeaks.library.vanderbilt.edu/
 interview/martin-luther-king-jr.
Kirksey, Henry J. *Haunted House.* Jackson, Miss.: HJK Publishing, 1965.
Kohl, Herbert. "The Politics of Children's Literature: What's Wrong with the Rosa
 Parks Myth." *Zinn Education Project.* Accessed May 22, 2013. http://zinnedproject.org/
 materials/the-politics-of-childrens-literature-whats-wrong-with-the-rosa-parks-myth/.
Kozol, Wendy. Life's *America: Family and Nation in Postwar Photojournalism.* Philadelphia:
 Temple University Press, 1994.
Krementz, Jill. *Sweet Pea: A Black Girl Growing Up in the Rural South.* New York: Harcourt
 & Brace, 1969.
Lachat, Mary Ann. *The Dimensions of Integration in Greenburgh Central, No. Seven, Green-
 burgh, New York.* Report for the U.S. Office of Education and Teacher's College,
 Columbia University. 1973.
"Langston Hughes's Best Effort." *Black Dispatch*, November 28, 1956. Clippings File,
 JWJ MSS 26, Box 567, Folder 13565. Langston Hughes Papers, James Weldon Johnson
 Collection in the Yale Collection of American Literature. Beinecke Rare Book and
 Manuscript Library, Yale University.
Lee, James Kyung-Jin. *Urban Triage: Race and the Fictions of Multiculturalism.* Minneapolis:
 University of Minnesota Press, 2004.
Lee, Martha F. *The Nation of Islam: An American Millenarian Movement.* Syracuse, N.Y.:
 Syracuse University Press, 1996.
Lennon, Mary Ellen. "A Question of Relevancy: New York Museums and the Black Arts
 Movement, 1968–1971." In Collins and Crawford, *New Thoughts on the Black Arts Move-
 ment*, 92–116.
Lester, Julius. E-mail correspondence with Katharine Capshaw Smith, February 15, 2013.
Levine, Ellen S. *Freedom's Children: Young Civil Rights Activists Tell Their Own Stories.* 1993.
 Reprint, New York: Puffin, 2000.
Levinson, Cynthia. *We've Got a Job: The 1963 Birmingham Children's March.* Atlanta:
 Peachtree, 2012.
Libretti, Tim. "Integration as Disintegration: Remembering the Civil Rights Movement
 as a Struggle for Self-Determination in John Sayles's *Sunshine State*." In Romano and
 Raiford, *Civil Rights Movement in American Memory*, 197–219.
Liligeto, Wilson Gia. *Babata: Our Land, Our Tribe, Our People.* Suva, Fiji: University of the
 South Pacific, 2006.
"Lincoln, the Emancipator." *Message*, January–February 1939, 8.
Lindsey, Kay. "The Black Woman as Woman." In Bambara, *Black Woman*, 103–8.
Liss, Andrea. "Black Bodies in Evidence: Maternal Visibility in Renee Cox's Family Por-
 traits." In Hirsch, *Familial Gaze*, 276–92.
"The Little Rock Nine on Oprah." *Oprah Winfrey Show*, 1996. Youtube. Accessed May 21,
 2013. http://www.youtube.com/watch?v=75dhe5Zsy8k.

London, Samuel G. *Seventh-Day Adventists and the Civil Rights Movement*. Jackson: University Press of Mississippi, 2009.

Lorde, Audre. "Afterimages." In *The Collected Poems of Audre Lorde*. New York: Norton, 2000.

Lowen, Marilyn. "I Knew I Wasn't White, but in America What Was I?" In Holsaert et al., *Hands on the Freedom Plow*, 540–52.

Mackenzie, Catherine. "Inquiry Group Seeks to Determine the Point at Which Children Begin to Show Prejudices." *New York Times*, May 28, 1946.

Madhubuti, Haki. "Black Writing." In *Jump Bad: A New Chicago Anthology*, edited by Gwendolyn Brooks, 37–39. Detroit: Broadside, 1971.

Majors, Monroe A[lpheus]. *First Steps and Nursery Rhymes*. Chicago: McElray & Clark, 1920.

Mantler, Gordon K. *Power to the Poor: Black–Brown Coalition and the Fight for Economic Justice, 1960–1974*. Chapel Hill: University of North Carolina Press, 2013.

Margolick, David. *Elizabeth and Hazel: Two Women of Little Rock*. New Haven, Conn.: Yale University Press, 2011.

Marshall, James P. *Student Activism and Civil Rights in Mississippi*. Baton Rouge: Louisiana State University Press, 2013.

Martin, Charles H. "Race, Gender, and Southern Injustice: The Rosa Lee Ingram Case." *American Journal of Legal History* 29, no. 3 (July 1985): 251–68.

Martin, Michelle H. *Brown Gold: Milestones of African American Picture Books, 1845–2002*. New York: Routledge, 2004.

Martin Luther King and the Montgomery Story. Nyack, N.Y.: Fellowship of Reconciliation, 1957.

Mathis, Sharon Bell. Review of *Dry Victories*, by June Jordan. *Latiko: The Drum and Spear Bookstore Newsletter*, October 1972. Box 46, Folder 7. June Jordan Papers. Radcliffe Institute for Advanced Study, Harvard University.

May, Elaine Tyler. *Homeward Bound: American Families in the Cold War Era*. New York: Basic Books, 1999.

Mays, Benjamin E. "My View." *Pittsburgh Courier*, January 26, 1957. Clippings File, JWJ MSS 26, Box 567, Folder 13565. Langston Hughes Papers, James Weldon Johnson Collection in the Yale Collection of American Literature. Beinecke Rare Book and Manuscript Library, Yale University.

McNeil, Joseph. Interview by Katharine Capshaw, April 11, 2011.

Mead, Margaret. Foreword to Krementz, *Sweet Pea*, 5.

Melamed, Jodi. *Represent and Destroy: Rationalizing Violence in the New Racial Capitalism*. Minneapolis: University of Minnesota Press, 2011.

Meltzer, Milton. "Comments on Hughes MS." May 24, 1956. JWJ MSS 26, Box 329, Folder 5355. Langston Hughes Papers, James Weldon Johnson Collection in the Yale Collection of American Literature. Beinecke Rare Book and Manuscript Library, Yale University.

———. "The Designing Narrator." In *The Voice of the Narrator in Children's Literature: Insights from Writers and Critics*, edited by Charlotte F. Otten and Gary D. Schmidt, 333–36. New York: Greenwood, 1989.

———. "Memo to Robert Simon at Crown, May 19, 1956, re: Publicity and Promotion on Negro Pictorial History." JWJ MSS 26, Box 111A. Langston Hughes Papers, James Weldon Johnson Collection in the Yale Collection of American Literature. Beinecke Rare Book and Manuscript Library, Yale University.

Merriam, Eve. *The Inner City Mother Goose*. Photographs by Lawrence Ratzkin. New York: Simon & Schuster, 1969.

Metress, Christopher, ed. *The Lynching of Emmett Till: A Documentary Narrative*. Charlottesville: University of Virginia Press, 2002.

Mickenberg, Julia. *Learning from the Left: Children's Literature, the Cold War, and Radical Politics in the United States*. Oxford: Oxford University Press, 2006.

Miller, Ivor. "'If It Hasn't Been One of Color': An Interview with Roy DeCarava." *Callaloo* 13, no. 4 (Autumn 1990): 847–57.

Miller, Marilyn. *The Bridge at Selma*. Englewood Cliffs, N.J.: Silver Burdett, 1985.

Miller, Thaddeus. "King Comic Book Inspires Fresh Calls to Fight Racism." *Los Baños Enterprise*, January 25, 2013. http://www.losbanosenterprise.com/2013/01/25/199656/king-comic-book-inspires-fresh.html.

Mitchell, Michele. *Righteous Propagation: African Americans and the Politics of Racial Destiny after Reconstruction*. Chapel Hill: University of North Carolina Press, 2004.

"A Monumental Treasury of the Negroes of America." Advertisement. *Crisis*, December 1956, 632. Clippings File, JWJ MSS 26, Box 567, Folder 13565. Langston Hughes Papers, James Weldon Johnson Collection in the Yale Collection of American Literature. Beinecke Rare Book and Manuscript Library, Yale University.

Morgan, Edward P. "The Good, the Bad, and the Forgotten: Media Culture and Public Memory of the Civil Rights Movement." In Romano and Raiford, *Civil Rights Movement in American Memory*, 137–66.

Morrison, Toni. Foreword to *Black Photographers Annual, 1973*.

———. "Rediscovering Black History." *New York Times Magazine*, August 11, 1974, 14–24.

———. *Remember: The Journey to School Integration*. Boston: Houghton Mifflin, 2004.

———. "The Site of Memory." In *Inventing the Truth: The Art and Craft of Memoir*, edited by William Zinsser, 123–24. Boston: Houghton Mifflin, 1987.

Muhammad, W[allace] D. "The Responsibility of Motherhood." *Muhammad Speaks*, August 1, 1975, 18.

Myers, Walter Dean. *One More River to Cross*. New York: Harcourt Brace, 1995.

Myrdal, Gunnar. *An American Dilemma: The Negro Problem and Modern Democracy*. New York: Harper, 1944.

Natanson, Nicholas. *The Black Image in the New Deal: The Politics of FSA Photography*. Knoxville: University of Tennessee Press, 1992.

Neal, Larry. "And Shine Swam On." In Jones and Neal, *Black Fire*, 638–56.

———. "The Black Arts Movement." *Drama Review* 12 (Summer 1968): 29–39.

"Negroes Are Americans: Jackie Robinson Proves It in Words and on the Ball Field." *Life*, August 1, 1949, 22–23.

"Negro History Comes Alive in Pictures." *Worker*, December 9, 1956. Clippings File, JWJ MSS 26, Box 567, Folder 13565. Langston Hughes Papers, James Weldon Johnson Collection in the Yale Collection of American Literature. Beinecke Rare Book and Manuscript Library, Yale University.

"Negro in America." *Variety*, December 19, 1956. Clippings File, JWJ MSS 26, Box 567,

Folder 13565. Langston Hughes Papers, James Weldon Johnson Collection in the Yale Collection of American Literature. Beinecke Rare Book and Manuscript Library, Yale University.

"A Negro Mother's Sacrifice." *Church Officers Gazette* 27, no. 5 (May 1940): 26.

The Negro Soldier. Directed by Frank Capra. 1944. VHS, Los Angeles: Spotlite Video, 1985.

Nielsen, Aldon. *Black Chant: Languages of African-American Postmodernism.* Cambridge: Cambridge University Press, 1997.

Nikolajeva, Maria, and Carole Scott. *How Picturebooks Work.* New York: Garland, 2000.

Nodelman, Perry. *The Hidden Adult.* Baltimore, Md.: Johns Hopkins University Press, 2008.

Oliver, Dexter, and Patricia Oliver. *I Want to Be.* Detroit: Third World Press, 1974.

Ongiri, Amy Abugo. *Spectacular Blackness: The Cultural Politics of the Black Power Movement and the Search for a Black Aesthetic.* Charlottesville: University of Virginia Press, 2009.

op de Beeck, Nathalie. *Suspended Animation: Children's Picture Books and the Fairy Tale of Modernity.* Minneapolis: University of Minnesota Press, 2010.

Ovington, Mary White. "Revisiting the South." *Crisis* 34 (April 1937): 42.

P., P. L. "The Week's Books." *Pittsburgh Courier,* November 24, 1956. Clippings File, JWJ MSS 26, Box 567, Folder 13565. Langston Hughes Papers, James Weldon Johnson Collection in the Yale Collection of American Literature. Beinecke Rare Book and Manuscript Library, Yale University.

Paddock, Charles Lee. *Gems from Storyland.* Oshawa, Ont.: Canadian Watchman Press, 1938.

Parker, John W. "A Part, Not Thing Apart." *Raleigh (N.C.) News and Observer,* February 17, 1957. Clippings File, JWJ MSS 26, Box 567, Folder 13565A. Langston Hughes Papers, James Weldon Johnson Collection in the Yale Collection of American Literature. Beinecke Rare Book and Manuscript Library, Yale University.

Parks, Gordon. Foreword to Shearer, *Little Man in the Family,* n.p.

———. Preface to Weiner, *It's Wings That Make Birds Fly,* 1.

Payne, Charles. *I've Got the Light of Freedom: The Organizing Tradition and the Mississippi Freedom Struggle.* Berkeley: University of California Press, 1995.

Perry, Imani. "Why Zimmerman Walked." *Ebony,* September 2013, 113.

Pescosolido, Bernice A., Elizabeth Grauerholz, and Melissa A. Milkie. "Culture and Conflict: The Portrayal of Blacks in U.S. Children's Picture Books through the Mid- and Late-Twentieth Century." *American Sociological Review* 62, no. 3 (June 1997): 443–64.

"Photographer Collection: Horst Faas in Vietnam." *Plog* (photo blog), Denver Post.com, May 15, 2012. http://blogs.denverpost.com/captured/2012/05/15/photographer-collection-horst-faas-vietnam/.

"Picture Books." *Saturday Review,* December 1, 1956. Clippings File, JWJ MSS 26, Box 567, Folder 13565. Langston Hughes Papers, James Weldon Johnson Collection in the Yale Collection of American Literature. Beinecke Rare Book and Manuscript Library, Yale University.

Platt, Myles M. "Pictorial Histories." *Clearing House* 32, no. 1 (September 1957): 58–59.

———. "Reviews of Related Literature." *Clearing House* 31, no. 6 (February 1957): 380.

"Poetry, Song Sessions Set." *New York Amsterdam News,* May 1, 1971, 16.

Pollack, Harriet, and Christopher Metress. "The Emmett Till Case and Narrative(s)." In Pollack and Metress, *Emmett Till in Literary Memory and Imagination,* 1–15.

————, eds. *Emmett Till in Literary Memory and Imagination*. Baton Rouge: Louisiana State University Press, 2008.

Pollard, Cherise A. "Sexual Subversions, Political Inversions: Women's Poetry and the Politics of the Black Arts Movement." In Collins and Crawford, *New Thoughts on the Black Arts Movement*, 173–86.

Powell, Richard J. *Cutting a Figure: Fashioning Black Portraiture*. Chicago: University of Chicago Press, 2008.

Preer, Bette Banner. "Guidance in Democratic Living through Juvenile Fiction." *Wilson Library Bulletin* 22, no. 9 (May 1948): 679–81, 708.

Priest, Myisha. "Flesh That Needs to Be Loved: Langston Hughes Writing the Body of Emmett Till." In Pollack and Metress, *Emmett Till in Literary Memory and Imagination*, 53–74.

"Proposal and Application for a Full-Year Program [for 1966] Child Development Group of Mississippi." SCM 8857 MG 265, Box 1, Folder 4. Child Development Group of Mississippi Papers. Schomburg Collection, New York Public Library.

"Proposal for Use of Visual Education Materials in CDGM Programs." May 16, 1966. Student Nonviolent Coordinating Committee Papers, 1959–1972. Microfilm, reel 37.

Rabinowitz, Paula. *They Must Be Represented: The Politics of Documentary*. London: Verso, 1994.

Raiford, Leigh. "The Consumption of Lynching Images." In *Only Skin Deep: Changing Visions of the American Self*, edited by Coco Fusco and Brian Wallis, 266–73. New York: International Center of Photography, 2003.

————. *Imprisoned in a Luminous Glare: Photography and the African American Freedom Struggle*. Chapel Hill: University of North Carolina Press, 2011.

Raiford, Leigh, and Renee C. Romano. "The Struggle over Memory." Introduction to Romano and Raiford, *Civil Rights Movement in American Memory*, xi–xxiv.

Rampersad, Arnold. *The Life of Langston Hughes*. Vol. 2, *1941–1967: I Dream a World*. New York: Oxford University Press, 1988.

Redding, Saunders. Review of *A Pictorial History of the Negro in America*, by Langston Hughes and Milton Meltzer. *New York Herald Tribune*, November 18, 1956. Clippings File, JWJ MSS 26, Box 567, Folder 13565. Langston Hughes Papers, James Weldon Johnson Collection in the Yale Collection of American Literature. Beinecke Rare Book and Manuscript Library, Yale University.

Review of *A Pictorial History of the Negro in America*, by Langston Hughes and Milton Meltzer. *Cleveland Plain Dealer*, December 9, 1956. Clippings File, JWJ MSS 26, Box 567, Folder 13565. Langston Hughes Papers, James Weldon Johnson Collection in the Yale Collection of American Literature. Beinecke Rare Book and Manuscript Library, Yale University.

Review of *A Pictorial History of the Negro in America*, by Langston Hughes and Milton Meltzer. Information Service, April 20, 1957. Clippings File, JWJ MSS 26, Box 567, Folder 13565A. Langston Hughes Papers, James Weldon Johnson Collection in the Yale Collection of American Literature. Beinecke Rare Book and Manuscript Library, Yale University.

Review of *A Pictorial History of the Negro in America*, by Langston Hughes and Milton Meltzer. *Picturescope* 5, no. 1 (April 1957): 4. Clippings File, JWJ MSS 26, Box 567, Folder 13565A. Langston Hughes Papers, James Weldon Johnson Collection in the Yale

Collection of American Literature. Beinecke Rare Book and Manuscript Library, Yale University.

Reynolds, Dawn. Interview by Katharine Capshaw, April 2, 2013.

Reynolds, Louis B. "A Brighter Horizon Beyond: Celestial Rays Light the Road Ahead." *Message*, June 1945, 6–7.

———. "Introducing in This Issue." *Message*, April 1947, 18.

———. "The March of Events: An Editorial." *Message*, February 1952, 4–7.

———. "The March of Events: An Editorial." *Message*, April 1957, 5–7.

———. "The March of Events: An Editorial." *Message*, June 1957, 5–7.

———. *We Have Tomorrow: The Story of American Seventh-Day Adventists with an African Heritage*. Washington, D.C.: Review and Herald Publications, 1984.

Reynolds, Louis B., and Charles L. Paddock. *Little Journeys into Storyland: Stories That Will Live and Lift*. 1947. Reprint, Nashville: Southern Publishing, 1948.

Richardson, Judy. "Black Children's Books: An Overview." *Journal of Negro Education* 43 (1974): 380–400.

Robeson, Mrs. Paul [Eslanda]. "American Family Portrait." *Hartford Courant*, February 4, 1945.

Rogers, J. A. "History Shows." *Pittsburgh Courier*, December 22, 1956. Clippings File, JWJ MSS 26, Box 567, Folder 13565. Langston Hughes Papers, James Weldon Johnson Collection in the Yale Collection of American Literature. Beinecke Rare Book and Manuscript Library, Yale University.

Romano, Renee C., and Leigh Raiford, eds. *The Civil Rights Movement in American Memory*. Athens: University of Georgia Press, 2006.

S., E. "Books and Authors." *Lewiston-Auburn (Maine) Independent*, January 5, 1957. Clippings File, JWJ MSS 26, Box 567, Folder 13565. Langston Hughes Papers, James Weldon Johnson Collection in the Yale Collection of American Literature. Beinecke Rare Book and Manuscript Library, Yale University.

Sales, Ruby. Letter to June Jordan, 1972. Box 46, Folder 7. June Jordan Papers. Radcliffe Institute for Advanced Study, Harvard University.

Sanchez, Sonia. "The Black Family." *Muhammad Speaks*, September 5, 1975, 25.

———. "Islam and the Rebirth of Women." *Muhammad Speaks*, August 22, 1975, 19.

———. *It's a New Day: Poems for Young Brothas and Sistuhs*. Detroit: Broadside, 1971.

Sanders, Joe Sutliff. "Chaperoning Words: Meaning-Making in Comics and Picture Books." *Children's Literature* 41 (2013): 57–90.

Schwebel, Sara L. *Child-Sized History: Fictions of the Past in U.S. Classrooms*. Nashville, Tenn.: Vanderbilt University Press, 2011.

Scott, Jonathan. "Advanced, Repressed, and Popular: Langston Hughes during the Cold War." *College Literature* 33, no. 2 (Spring 2006): 30–51.

Selig, Diana. *Americans All: The Cultural Gifts Movement*. Cambridge, Mass.: Harvard University Press, 2008.

Shackelford, Jane Dabney. "Book Signing." Accession number 800627, D.C. 1, folder 1. Ms. Jane Dabney Shackelford Collection, Community Archives. Vigo County Public Library, Terre Haute, Ind.

———. "Langston Hughes Statement." Accession number 800627, D.C. 2, folder 6. Ms. Jane Dabney Shackelford Collection, Community Archives. Vigo County Public Library, Terre Haute, Ind.

———. Letter to Carter G. Woodson, January 16, 1944. Accession Number 800627, D.C. 2, Folder 6. Ms. Jane Dabney Shackelford Collection, Community Archives. Vigo County Public Library, Terre Haute, Ind.

———. "A Message to Parents." Preface to Shackelford, *My Happy Days*, n.p.

———. "My Books and Why I Wrote Them." Accession Number 800627, D.C. 1, Folder 1. Ms. Jane Dabney Shackelford Collection, Community Archives. Vigo County Public Library, Terre Haute, Ind.

———. *My Happy Days*. Photographs by Cecil Vinson. Washington, D.C.: Associated Publishers, 1944.

———. "Rinty Comment." Accession Number 800627, D.C. 1, Folder 20. Ms. Jane Dabney Shackelford Collection, Community Archives. Vigo County Public Library, Terre Haute, Ind.

Sharpe, Stella Gentry. "Autobiographical Material on Mrs. Stella Gentry Sharpe, Author of *Tobe*." Box 6, Charles Anderson Farrell Papers, 4452. Southern Historical Collection. Wilson Library, University of North Carolina at Chapel Hill.

———. *Tobe*. Photographs by Charles Farrell. Chapel Hill: University of North Carolina Press, 1939.

Shaw, Esther Popel. Review of *My Happy Days*, by Jane Dabney Shackelford. *Journal of Negro History* 30, no. 2 (April 1945): 219–21.

Shearer, John. "Black Panthers." *Look*, June 22, 1970. *Look* Magazine Photograph Collection. http://www.loc.gov/pictures/item/lmc1999006725/PP/.

———. "Harlem Negro Riots—Aftermath." *Look*, April 11, 1968. *Look* Magazine Photograph Collection. http://www.loc.gov/pictures/item/lmc1998006102/PP/.

———. Interview by Katharine Capshaw, May 2, 2011.

———. *I Wish I Had an Afro*. New York: Cowles, 1970.

———. *Little Man in the Family*. New York: Delacorte, 1972.

———. "Martin Luther King Funeral." *Look*, April 11, 1968. *Look* Magazine Photograph Collection. http://www.loc.gov/pictures/item/lmc1998006101/PP/.

Sipe, Lawrence R., and Sylvia Pantaleo, eds. *Postmodern Picturebooks: Play, Parody, and Self-Referentiality*. New York: Routledge, 2008.

Smart-Grosvenor, Vertamae. *Vibration Cooking: or, The Travel Notes of a Geechee Girl*. Garden City, N.Y.: Doubleday, 1970.

Smethurst, James Edward. *The Black Arts Movement: Literary Nationalism in the 1960s and 1970s*. Chapel Hill: University of North Carolina Press, 2005.

———. Facebook conversation with Katharine Capshaw, April 5, 2013.

Smith, Jean Pajot. *Li'l Tuffy and His ABC's*. Chicago: Johnson, 1972.

Smith, Katharine Capshaw. "Childhood, the Body, and Race Performance: Early Twentieth-Century Etiquette Books for Black Children." *African American Review* 40, no. 4 (Winter 2006): 795–811.

———. *Children's Literature of the Harlem Renaissance*. Bloomington: Indiana University Press, 2004.

———. "From Bank Street to Harlem: A Conversation with Ellen Tarry." *Lion and the Unicorn* 23 (April 1999): 271–85.

Smith, Shawn Michelle. *American Archives: Gender, Race, and Class in Visual Culture*. Princeton, N.J.: Princeton University Press, 1999.

———. *Photography on the Color Line: W. E. B. Du Bois, Race, and Visual Culture*. Durham, N.C.: Duke University Press, 2004.

Something of Our Own, Part I. Jackson, Miss.: HJK Publishing, 1965.

Something of Our Own, Part II. Jackson, Miss.: HJK Publishing, 1965.

Song, Min Hyoung. *Strange Future: Pessimism and the 1992 Los Angeles Riots*. Durham, N.C.: Duke University Press, 2005.

Sontag, Susan. *On Photography*. New York: Farrar, Straus & Giroux, 1977.

Sorby, Angela, Joseph T. Thomas, and Richard Flynn. "'from brain all the way to heart': The 2008 *Lion and the Unicorn* Award for Excellence in North American Poetry." *Lion and the Unicorn* 32 (2008): 344–56.

Spitz, Ellen Handler. *Inside Picture Books*. New Haven, Conn.: Yale University Press, 1999.

Stange, Maren. "'Illusion Complete within Itself': Roy DeCarava's Photography." *Yale Journal of Criticism* 9, no. 1 (1996): 63–92.

Sterling, Dorothy, with Donald Gross. *Tender Warriors*. Photographs by Myron Ehrenberg. New York: Hill & Wang, 1958.

Stilgoe, John. Foreword to *Little Machinery*, by Mary Liddell, vii–xii. Detroit, Mich.: Wayne State University Press, 2009.

Stott, William. *Documentary Expression and Thirties America*. 1973. Reprint, Chicago: University of Chicago Press, 1986.

Tarry, Ellen. *Hezekiah Horton*. Illustrated by Oliver Harrington. New York: Viking, 1942.

———. *Janie Belle*. Illustrated by Myrtle Sheldon. New York: Garden City, 1940.

———. "Native Daughter: An Indictment of White America by a Colored Woman." *Commonweal*, April 12, 1940, 524–26.

———. *The Third Door: The Autobiography of an American Negro Woman*. 1955. Reprint, Tuscaloosa: University of Alabama Press, 1992.

Tarry, Ellen, and Marie Hall Ets. *My Dog Rinty*. Photographs by Alexander Alland and Alexandra Alland. New York: Viking, 1946.

Thomas, Alan. "Literary Snapshots of the Sho-Nuff Blues." *In These Times*, March 27–April 2, 1985, 20–21. Published as "Alan Thomas on Roy DeCarava," *The Sweet Flypaper of Life*, https://sites.google.com/site/roydecaravareview/.

Trachtenberg, Alan. *Reading American Photographs: Images as History, Mathew Brady to Walker Evans*. New York: Hill & Wang, 1989.

Van Deburg, William L. *New Day in Babylon: The Black Power Movement and American Culture, 1965–1975*. Chicago: University of Chicago Press, 1992.

Varela, Mary [Maria]. "Filmstrips." Memo to SNCC Staff, November 11, 1965. Student Nonviolent Coordinating Committee Papers, 1959–1972. Microfilm, reel 37.

W., H. A. "The Negro." December 2, 1956. Clippings File, JWJ MSS 26, Box 567, Folder 13565. Langston Hughes Papers, James Weldon Johnson Collection in the Yale Collection of American Literature. Beinecke Rare Book and Manuscript Library, Yale University.

Wagner, Mabel Garrett. *Billy Bates*. Photographs by Dodds B. Bunch. New York: Friendship Press, 1946.

Wall, Cheryl A. *Worrying the Line: Black Women Writers, Lineage, and Literary Tradition*. Chapel Hill: University of North Carolina Press, 2005.

Weatherford, Carole Boston. *Birmingham, 1963*. Honesdale, Pa.: Wordsong, 2007.

———. E-mail correspondence with Katharine Capshaw Smith, November 21, 2013.

"We Can Tell Much about Your Child's Future." *Message*, June 1947, 19.

Weiner, Sandra. *It's Wings That Make Birds Fly*. New York: Pantheon, 1968.

Weiner, Sonia. "Narrating Photography in *The Sweet Flypaper of Life*." *MELUS* 37, no. 1 (Spring 2012): 155–76.

"We Salute General Davis." *Message*, January–February 1941, 8.

West, Chester. "What's Happening in Westchester." *New York Amsterdam News*, June 13, 1970, 32.

Wexler, Laura. *Tender Violence: Domestic Visions in an Age of U.S. Imperialism*. Chapel Hill: University of North Carolina Press, 2000.

"What Next?" *CDGM Newsletter*, no. 4 (1966). SCM 8857 MG 265, Box 1, Folder 3. Child Development Group of Mississippi Papers. Schomburg Collection, New York Public Library.

White, Mus. *From the Mundane to the Magical: Photographically Illustrated Children's Books, 1854–1945 and Beyond*. Los Angeles: Dawson's Bookshop, 1999.

Whitehead, Kim. *The Feminist Poetry Movement*. Jackson: University Press of Mississippi, 1996.

Whitney, Phyllis A. "Children's Books." *Chicago Sun Book Week*, December 31, 1944. Accession Number 780222, Addendum 1, Folder 3. Jane Dabney Shackelford Collection, Community Archives. Vigo County Public Library, Terre Haute, Ind.

Wilkins, Roy. Advertisement for *Tender Warriors*, by Dorothy Sterling. *New York Times*, April 27, 1958.

Williams-Garcia, Rita. E-mail correspondence with Katharine Capshaw Smith, November 26, 2012.

Willis, Deborah. *Family History Memory: Recording African American Life*. New York: Hylas, 2005.

———. "Picturing Us." Introduction to *Picturing Us: African American Identity in Photography*, edited by Deborah Willis, 3–26. New York: New Press, 1994.

———. *Reflections in Black: A History of Black Photographers, 1840 to the Present*. New York: Norton, 2000.

———. "A Search for Self: The Photograph and Black Family Life." In Hirsch, *Familial Gaze*, 107–23.

Wise, James Waterman. *The Springfield Plan*. Photographs by Alexander Alland. New York: Viking, 1945.

Wood, Amy Louise. *Lynching and Spectacle: Witnessing Racial Violence in America, 1890–1940*. Chapel Hill: University of North Carolina Press, 2009.

Woodson, Carter G. "Books of United States History." *Journal of Negro History* 29, no. 4 (October 1944): 494–500.

———. Review of *Characteristics of the American Negro*, by Otto Klineberg. *Journal of Negro History* 29, no. 2 (April 1944): 233–36.

Wright, Richard. *12 Million Black Voices*. Photo direction by Edwin Rosskam. 1941. Reprint, New York: Basic Books, 2008.

Zinn, Howard. *SNCC: The New Abolitionists*. 1964. Reprint, New York: Greenwood, 1985.

INDEX

Katharine Capshaw is associate professor of English at the University of Connecticut. She is the author of *Children's Literature of the Harlem Renaissance.*